Jessica A

AA

Explorer Israel

Andrew Sanger

AA Publishing

Front cover
Top: *Tile detail, Dome of the Rock Jerusalem* (Pat Aithie); Centre (left to right): (a) *Dead Sea* (Julian Loader); (b) *Vase, Museum of Ancient Art, Haifa* (Pat Aithie); (c) *Pasties* (Pat Aithie); (d) *Sign, Tel Aviv* (Pat Aithie); (e) *Embroidery detail* (Pat Aithie)
Spine *Samaritan High Priest* (Julian Loader)
Back cover
Left: *Dome of the Rock, Jerusalem* (Julian Loader); Right: *Crops, Galilee* (Pat Aithie)

Page 3: *The Dome of the Rock, Jerusalem*
Page 4: *Olives*
Page 5 (a): *Jews praying at the Western Wall,*
(b): *Poppies, Galilee*
Page 5 (a): *Russian Orthodox Church, Jerusalem*
Page 6 (b): *Old City, Akko*
Page 7 (b): *Religious artist, Sefat*
Page 9: *Detail from the Dome of the Rock, a Greek Orthodox priest and the national flag with Star of David*
Page 29: *The Western Wall, Alexander the Great*
Page 46: *Tower of David*
Page 162: *Mosaic, Beit Alpha Synogogue, Galilee*

Written and revised by Andrew Sanger
Original photography by Jon Arnold and Pat Athie

Published by AA Publishing, a trading name of Automobile Association Developments Limited, whose registered office is Fanum House, Basing View, Basingstoke, Hampshire RG21 4EA. Registered number 1878835.

ISBN-10: 0-7495-4977-7
ISBN-13: 978-0-7495-4977-7

A CIP catalogue record for this book is available from the British Library.

Colour separation by M.R.M. Graphics Ltd, Bucks, UK
Printed and bound in Italy by Printer Trento Srl

Reprinted Feb 2007
Revised fourth edition 2006
First published 1996

Find out more about AA Publishing and the wide range of travel publications and services the AA provides by visiting our website at www.theAA.com/travel.

Titles in the Explorer series:
Australia • Boston & New England • Britain • Brittany
California • Canada • Caribbean • China • Costa Rica • Crete
Cuba • Cyprus • Egypt • Florence & Tuscany • Florida
France • Germany • Greek Islands • Hawaii • India • Ireland
Italy • Japan • London • Mallorca • Mexico • New York
New Zealand • Paris • Portugal • Provence • Rome
San Francisco • Scotland • South Africa • Spain • Thailand
Tunisia • Turkey • Venice • Vietnam

A03348

How to use this book

ORGANIZATION

Israel Is, Israel Was
Discusses aspects of life and culture in contemporary Israel and explores significant periods in its history.

A–Z
Breaks down the country into regional chapters, and covers places to visit, including walks and drives. Within this section fall the Focus On articles, which consider a variety of subjects in greater detail.

Travel Facts
Contains the strictly practical information vital for a successful trip.

Hotels and Restaurants
Lists recommended establishments throughout Israel, giving a brief summary of their attractions. Entries are graded budget, moderate or expensive.

ADMISSION CHARGES
An indication of an establishment's admission charge is given by categorising the standard, adult rate as:
Expensive (over 20 NIS),
Moderate (10–20 NIS), or
Inexpensive (under 10 NIS).

OPENING TIMES
Services and attractions in Israel close during Shabbat—Jewish Sabbath—which lasts from sunset on Friday to sunset on Saturday (see page 58).

ABOUT THE RATINGS
Most places described in this book have been given a separate rating. These are as follow:

▶▶▶ **Do not miss**

▶▶ **Highly recommended**

▶ **Worth seeing**

MAP REFERENCES
To make the location of a particular place easier to find, every main entry in this book has a map reference. This includes a number, followed by a letter, followed by another number, such as176B3. The first number (176) refers to the page on which the map can be found. The letter (B) and the second number (3) pinpoint the square in which the place is located. The maps on the inside front cover and inside back cover are referred to as IFC and IBC, respectively.

Contents

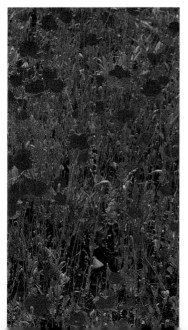

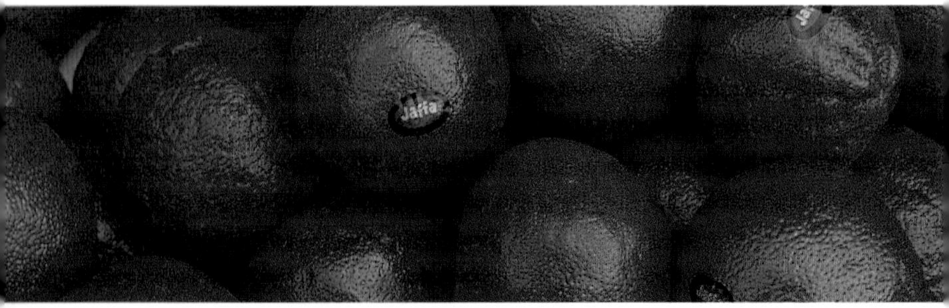

A–Z

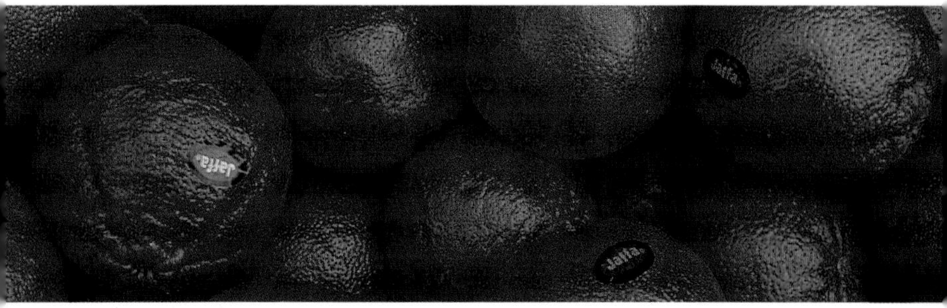

Andrew Sanger is a well-established and award-winning travel writer who has contributed to many British newspapers and magazines, including the *Guardian*, the *Daily Telegraph* and the *Jewish Chronicle*. From 1991 to 1999 he was the editor of French Railway's holiday magazine *Top Rail*. He is the author of 20 guidebooks to France, Ireland and other European countries. His long fascination with Israel and frequent visits have culminated in this book, his first about the country.

My Israel

Scratch the present and you'll find the past. Look at the past and you'll see the future. There's something about this place that thrills me. Places, like people, are all unique. But Israel is different. It just *isn't* like *anywhere* else.

Of course, certain comparisons are tempting, and inevitable. For example, I often see how Israel and Israelis fit into the warm, lively, noisy, out-of-doors Eastern Mediterranean culture that runs from, say, Italy to the Levant. And in its efforts to restore itself to nationhood after years of Ottoman domination, there's an obvious similarity to Greece.

But in Israel there's something else going on. There's a dizzying, exciting sensation, like being at the vortex of human experience, living in a vibrant, emphatic here-and-now that yet looks with passion to both the past and the future.

The land itself mirrors this. Everything converges here. Not only all human life, not only the old and the new are fused, but the climate and the topography—from sweet Galilee to searing Negev—are fantastically varied, and the flora and fauna of Europe, Asia, and Africa combine at this spot.

Once upon a time, we are told, this was a land of forests and fields, rich with milk and honey, or at least olives and grapes. Now as its people return and clear the dust from their heritage, they plant, irrigate, and rebuild. Every day in Israel, traveling from ancient site to beach resort, to hardworking town or kibbutz, I am astonished, impressed, and delighted by what is happening here.

This little patch of Mediterranean landscape, which already has taught so much to the rest of humanity, now offers another inspiration. Exploring the strange, tiny, kaleidoscopic country that is modern Israel is not just tourism or research: Here I catch a glimpse of the potential of human beings, if they are willing to cling to their dreams, to overcome even the most extraordinary obstacles, and make dreams come true at last.

Andrew Sanger

Israel

Old and new

The story of Israel has many beginnings. The creation of the modern state was just one step along a road that began in the first pages of the Bible. Since the nation's rebirth in 1948, there have been many more new beginnings. Israel today is marked by excitement and a strange sensation of moving both ways in time: retrieving the past, and creating the future.

UNDER THE SPOTLIGHT The gaze of the world often focuses on Israel. It is a place that exists deep in the psyche of the Western world but that, for many, is more myth than reality. For anyone with Sunday school notions about "the Holy Land," the dynamic, restless, abrasively energetic modern nation of Israel will come as a big surprise. Many Israelis just wish theirs could be a "normal" country. But normal countries do not encourage waves of large-scale immigration when they already have an unemployment problem. In normal countries, vibrant capitalism would not thrive within a monolithic socialist infrastructure where the state owns nearly all the land. But then, normal countries do not have Israel's problems. And somehow, the world does not expect Israel to find normal solutions.

❑ The official emblem of the State of Israel is the Golden Menorah, the seven-branched ritual candelabrum once used in the Temple in Jerusalem. ❑

MATTERS OF OPINION People hold strong views about Israel. It is hard to grasp that a place only the size of Wales or Massachusetts can be so crucial to world politics and world religion. The problems have an old-new look about them too. Those ancient Assyrians, Egyptians and Babylonians who vied for control over the land of the Hebrews have modern inheritors. Those Canaanite tribes who made life difficult for Israelites might almost have been the prototype for today's West Bank militants.

As always, different people lay claim to the same patch of earth. Can such deep and intractable conflicts ever be resolved? The world's press certainly has plenty of easy answers, as do governments around the globe. Politicians and pundits, concerned more about their own national interest, are all too ready to instruct Israel in the error of its ways. Visitors often come up with quick solutions. Israelis know it is not so simple, and that their whole survival is at stake. They, more than anyone, want to be free to enjoy life in peace. But how is peace to be obtained? Was it right to

Above right: Roman-era menorah
Below: Timeless architecture—Jerusalem's Islamic Museum

hand Gaza over to a Palestinian Authority which cannot govern it? Should Israel also pull out of the West Bank? All of it? But parts of the West Bank are almost in the Tel Aviv suburbs. Was it right to put up the barrier that keeps suicide bombers out of Israel? Is the barrier in the right place? Should it be torn down? When there is peace, Israelis say. Only then. The country is alive with debate, a kaleidoscope of opinions, ideas, choice, diversity.

THE LAND That diversity of opinions is just one other facet of Israel's extraordinary spectrum of peoples and landscapes. For sheer physical variety, the country is phenomenal, with four climate zones and four types of terrain, ranging from handsome and verdant Mediterranean hills in the north to parched desert in the south; from majestic snow-capped Mount Hermon to the salty Dead Sea, the lowest point on the earth. Journeying between the two, you will pass vineyards and olive groves mentioned in the Bible, apple orchards, fields of corn and banana plantations, tomatoes and strawberries—truly a bewildering range of crops. Today, after just a century of labor and reclamation, Israel looks again like a land of milk and honey. This is the ancient-modern "Eretz Israel"—literally Land of Israel. Some call it the Promised Land, some the Holy Land, some the Zionist Entity. Most Israelis call it simply HaAretz: the Land.

HISTORY AND HERITAGE Past, present and future seem to converge here. Uninspired apartment complexes in well-ordered planned towns give an impression of modernity, but builders digging the foundations usually have to call in the archeologists. Every walk or drive involves an encounter with Israel's long and dramatic history. Almost every Israeli family has its own story of events that span the globe—but that started here.

Unchanging desert landscapes, which the Children of Israel crossed thousands of years ago

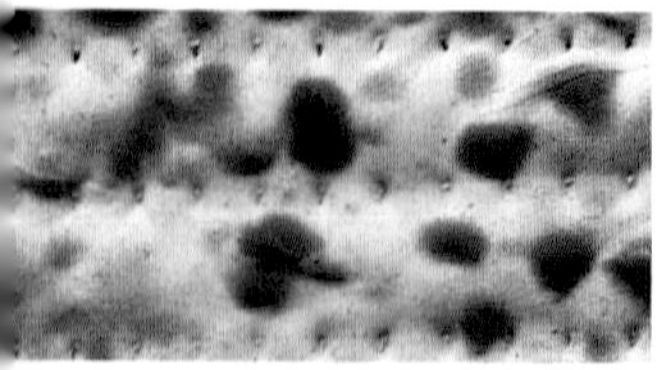

The state of Israel came into being in 1948 as a result of half of a century of struggle by the Zionist movement to re-create the ancient homeland of the Jewish people. From all over the world, Jewish people are still arriving to make a home in the Land of Israel.

Many migrants are motivated by religious or cultural zeal, many by the simple promise of food, a roof and a regular job, and many by the longing to escape persecution. The service that Jewish families read together over the annual Passover meal, celebrating the Exodus from Egypt, concludes "Next year in Jerusalem." Daily, that wish is made a reality.

NO ORDINARY HOMELAND The cornerstone of Israel's existence is the Zionist dream of gathering in all the Jews who have been exiled across the globe and bringing them back to their true home. The idea was even set down in the Book of Genesis. Yet any country that willingly promotes a policy of mass immigration must seem at best foolishly philanthropic, at worst, suicidal. The economic logistics alone appear formidable. To an Israeli, however, the case looks different. Israel is a nation born of new immigrants: They are its life force.

Since 1948 millions of Jews have "made *aliyah*"—literally, gone up—to Israel. These *olim* (new arrivals) not only must adjust to a new language and culture, but also to the fact that their new country is itself at risk. Despite the pressure new immigrants sometimes impose on the employment sector, their decision to make a life in Israel is greeted by Israelis as evidence that the creation of a Jewish homeland really is working as its founders had planned.

WHO CAN COME? In 1950, the Israeli parliament passed the Law of Return. This enshrined as a right what had, until then, been an unwritten tenet: namely, that any person of Jewish descent would be welcomed to the country. Even as Orthodox authorities restricted the definition of Jewishness, immigrants have arrived in waves from Eastern Europe, North Africa, the Gulf states, the former Soviet Union and Ethiopia.

MAKING IT HAPPEN Often these "exiles" were in such difficult circumstances that they could not afford to make their own way to Israel. Some were not even in a position to let anyone know of their plight.

So the job of finding and retrieving the exiles goes on. The task of bringing to Israel any Jewish person who wishes to come is planned, if need be, with military precision—often capturing the attention of the world in the process. One such operation was its daring airlift to safety of 30,000 Ethiopian Jews, rescued in two phases in the mid-1980s and early 1990s, called Operation Moses. Contrast this with the arrival of a

Matzoh (top), unleavened bread eaten during Passover
A Hasidic Jew (below) wearing traditional dress

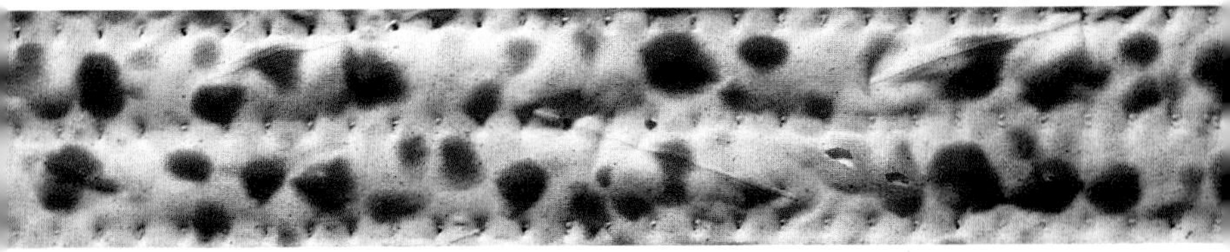

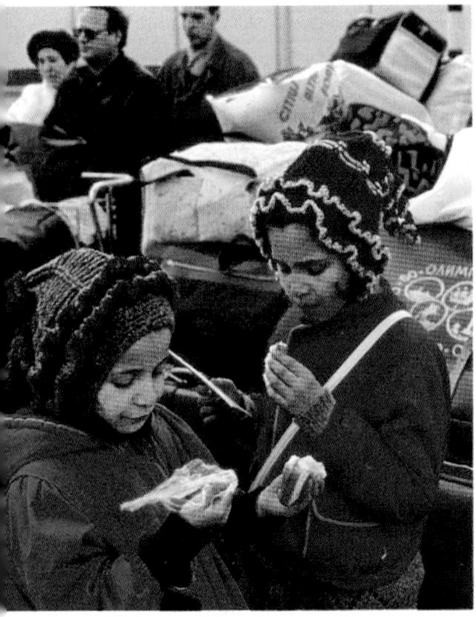

Refugees from the former Soviet Union in Tel Aviv

> ❑ All new immigrants attend *ulpan*, an intensive Hebrew language school with daily lessons for every standard, from total beginners to advanced students. Since an *ulpan* may comprise as many as 45 different nationalities, all lessons are in Hebrew. By the end of the five-month course, most immigrants can read, write and converse in the language of the Bible. ❑

well-to-do family of South Americans who simply want to be closer to their heritage. Either way, each new arrival is channeled through a welter of absorption processes: language school, location and housing choices, educational options, career guidance, health service registration. Those who arrive with few possessions, such as refugees from the former Soviet Union, receive welfare benefits to help ease the first months. All immigrants receive start-up assistance, such as tax rebates on the essentials of a new home.

The induction process takes six months, but full integration may take longer. It may not be until the next generation that people feel thoroughly Israeli. Among the immigrant generation, some groups, like the Yemenites, see no reason to abandon all their old ways. Some, like the Ethiopians, find it almost too hard to adapt to the Israeli lifestyle. Others, like the new Russians, are sometimes criticized for their lack of Jewishness and their perceived unwillingness to pull their weight for the country. Yet, as Jewish people, all are entitled to make their escape to Israel, and the belief is that all will eventually play their part in Israel's destiny.

A jeweler in the Jewish Quarter, Jerusalem

For centuries Israel was no more than a dream. Not for nothing is its national anthem called The Hope (HaTikvah). *The greatest hope is still the old one: to be accepted as a country like any other, yet without losing its biblical imperative to be "a Light unto the Nations." Underlying that is a simpler hope: that the Jewish homeland will survive.*

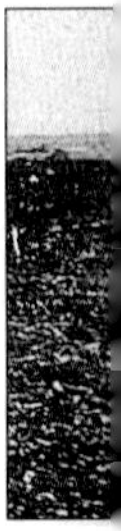

ALL FOR ONE If you listen to Israelis discussing the most innocent topic, it is easy to get the impression that divisions burn deep. Everyone has individual goals, but all that is forgotten when the country is under threat. War has been Israel's jailer since 1948, and you would not need to be religious to say a morning prayer for peace sometimes. What most Israelis crave is the ordinariness of daily life enjoyed by other nations. Yet the demanding and tense pattern of existence in Israel—begun by early settlers who fought adversity with undaunted optimism —has created a unique national character. In Israelis, you will find a rare pride and a sense of achievement that relishes the differences and feeds off stresses.

REDEMPTION OF THE LAND No matter what their politics or attitude to religion, Israelis all have a bond with the earth of Israel—the land of their origin, of their identity, faith and history. Since the Jews fled the Romans in AD70, religious belief has fueled the hope of all Jews that they will be able to return to their homeland. In the 19th century, when Diaspora Jews (those living outside Palestine) were the target of persecution, that ambition took on a political dimension and became known as Zionism. In Israel, Jews of whatever affiliation believe that reclaiming the land is a fundamental responsibility, metaphorically and literally. It is their dream to see the Promised Land bloom with the life of returned Jews and, for the secular, to see it flourish again with the fruits of their labors.

VOLUNTEERS More than a nation, Israel is a movement. Hundreds of Zionist charities around the world exist solely to provide funds or volunteers for Israel. Some, like

Pioneers (top)
Jews from Ethiopia (below)

❑ *HaTikvah* (*The Hope*), Israel's poignant national anthem, was composed by Naftali Herz 'Imber more than 60 years before the founding of the state. It includes the words: "As long as...the soul of a Jew yearns, our hope is not yet lost, the hope of two thousand years, to be a free people in our land, the land of Zion and Jerusalem." ❑

Keren Kayemet L'Israel (Jewish National Fund, founded 1901), benefit the land by tree-planting or creating reservoirs. Others pay for hospitals, sports facilities, or help disadvantaged immigrant groups. The New Israel Fund works to ensure equal treatment for all Israeli citizens, religious or secular, Jewish or non-Jewish.

Each year thousands of foreign volunteers give their time to Israel's medical services, schools and the army. In the past, countless young people worked as volunteers on kibbutzim, Israel's settlements that in those days epitomized the communal ideal. Today, kibbutzim have changed beyond recognition, yet their legacy of volunteering and hard work cannot be overestimated.

Sentiment motivates many Israelis to achieve near-impossible dreams

THE PRICE OF PEACE Becoming 18 in most parts of the world means entering adulthood, with unrestricted access to all its risks and rewards. In Israel, however, it is also the time when girls and boys begin their compulsory army service.

Israel's greatest dream is to live in peace but it may be a while before the world gives the country its blessing. Paradoxically, were peace ever fully to envelop the Middle East and end the necessity to have a fit, young army on standby all the time, Israel might lose a vital part of its character.

Diversity

One nation, a hundred nationalities—people from all over the world have poured their influence into this tiny state. Then there are the country's non-Jews, a significant minority. Israel manages to accommodate—and celebrate—all their diversity under a single unifying flag.

THE TYPICAL ISRAELI The average Israeli is hard to define. He or she may be dark-eyed and olive-skinned. Then again, you can find pale-skinned blondes, brunettes and redheads and black skin too. The Jewish majority may (or may not) share a common faith, but each person is colored by his or her background and maintains traditions from the "old country," be it in food, music or family structure.

Israelis of Eastern European origin are called Ashkenazim. Those from the Mediterranean, many of whose ancestors were expelled from Spain in 1492, are Sephardim. Jews from the other Islamic states are Oriental, or Mizrahim.

Israel's non-Jews, totaling more than one in five of the population, are found mainly in Jerusalem, Akko, Haifa and the smaller northern towns. They are mainly Muslim and Christian Arabs as well as Druze and other religious groups, Bedouin in the south, and a plethora of other cultures that have a home here.

❑ About half of the population of Israel are Sabras—Israeli-born Jews. It is interesting that they do have, already, a distinct character. Like the fruit from which they take their name (also known as prickly pear), Sabras are said to be spiky on the outside, but sweet inside. Israelis do sometimes appear rude, unpolished and peremptory. The direct, forthright speech and abrasive manner really come from a dislike of pretense, combined perhaps with the effects of living a knife-edge existence. After all, Sabras are also noted for their astonishing informality, irreverence, spontaneous warmth and unexpected generosity. ❑

Native Israelis are called Sabras (prickly pears): spiky on the outside but sweet (top)
Every generation contributes to the Israeli identity (below)

Israeli legislation aspires to full equality of all citizens regardless of race or creed, and each group has had a distinctive cultural impact on Israel. As these backgrounds mix and matchmake (about a quarter of Jewish marriages are between Ashkenazim and Sephardim), exciting combinations emerge. With each new wave of immigration, the picture of the typical Israeli is constantly being reinvented.

POWER PLAY Chaim Weizmann, David Gruen (better known as David Ben-Gurion), Isaac Shimshelevitz (Moshe Sharett), Zakam Rubashov (Zalman Shazar), Levi Shkolnik (Levi

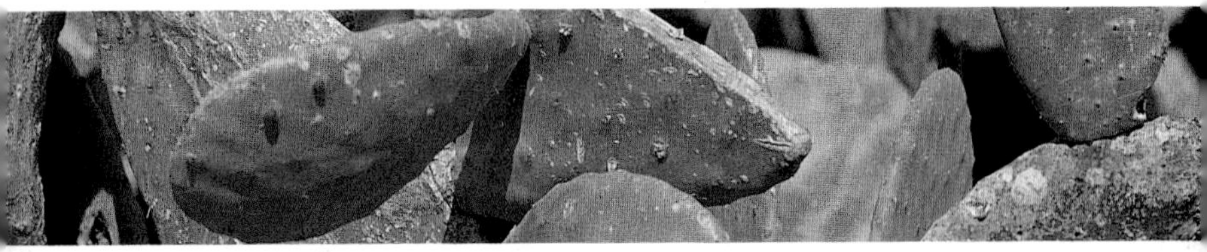

Sephardi Jews came to Israel from Mediterranean countries

Eshkol), Golda Meir—the names of the first prime ministers and presidents of Israel reveal that they were all of East European origin. For decades, this sector of society, for whom Hebrew was a second language, dominated all important areas of life, from commerce and politics to education and defense. The Sephardic and Oriental communities, which now constitute over 40 percent of society, came from lands where democracy was unheard of and education optional. Only recently have they made strides into the power zones of life in Israel, taking government positions, wielding industrial clout and spicing up public debate. Eventually, Israelis say, every group and community will be equally involved.

LANGUAGE AND CULTURE If speaking Hebrew and English does not work with your interlocutor, try French, Arabic, Portuguese, Romanian, Russian or a mix of tongues. Not only did most older Israelis master Hebrew only after settling here, many already spoke more than one language when they arrived. Every facet of Israeli culture—music, theater, literature, politics—has become textured with the threads of other lands. Ethnic variations mean diverse cuisines, and there are restaurants to reflect each one: Moroccan, Indian, Italian, American, Argentinian, French, Russian and native Israeli, to name a few. Most towns have a "Chinese" restaurant—often in fact Vietnamese, since Israel gave haven to a number of boat people.

THE DIVERSE LANDSCAPE Israel also packs a great deal into its borders. A short drive can begin in a mountain range and end at lush, fertile plains. It's a quick trip from the urban metropolis to the stillness of the desert. Tel Aviv is humid, but Jerusalem, an hour away, is dry. You can ski in the north, then fly south for an hour to scuba dive in the tropics.

Israeli soldiers in training. All single women undergo two years of service

Israel teems with the passion of its believers. In few other places is devotion so concentrated as in the country that gave monotheism to the world. For Jews, Christians, Muslims and their many offshoots, the land is filled with holy sites—a great source of inspiration for living faiths.

THREE PARALLEL ROADS Israel's population of nearly 7 million is roughly 80 percent Jewish and 18 percent Sunni Muslim Arabs. There are about 100,000 Christians too—Maronite, Greek Orthodox, Roman and Greek Catholic. The land has been the spiritual home of the Jewish religion since about the 12th century BC. King David founded Jerusalem as the Jewish capital in 1004BC. The "Common Era" (as Israelis call it) starts with Christianity's presence in the Holy Land. Since Byzantine times (the 4th century AD), Bethlehem and Nazareth have ranked close behind Rome as spiritual centers for Christians. Though Mecca is holiest for Islam, with Medina a runner-up, the legend was born in the 8th century AD that Muhammad ascended to heaven from the rock now enclosed within Jerusalem's Dome of the Rock. Thus, Israel brings together three monotheistic religions, all with unbreakable links: Yet those who practise these faiths live remarkably separate and antagonistic lives.

Jerusalem's Muslim Dome of the Rock

CITY OF FAITH The skyline of Jerusalem's Old City reveals the hold it has on the hearts of millions. At sunset, the rosy light throws into relief the cross atop the Church of the Holy Sepulchre and the golden Dome of the Rock glistens as muezzins call the Muslim quarter to prayer. Below stand the immense, immutable stones of the Western Wall—remains of the Jews' Second Temple. In the noisy, confused maze of Old City streets that divide it into four sectors—Jewish, Muslim, Christian and Armenian—nuns, priests, rabbis and imams hurry past each other to fulfill God's work.

Israel allows freedom of worship to all. Each religious community runs its own affairs, exercises its faith as it wishes, observes its own holidays and weekly rest days, and administers its religious sites. That's why, after regaining Temple Mount in 1967, Israel nevertheless allowed Muslim authorities to run that holy place. Most of the piety focuses on Jerusalem, and at religious festival times the city's population swells with thousands of devoted pilgrims.

SECTS AND SECRECY The biblical Good Samaritan has descendants. Six hundred altogether, they live in Holon, south of Tel Aviv, and in

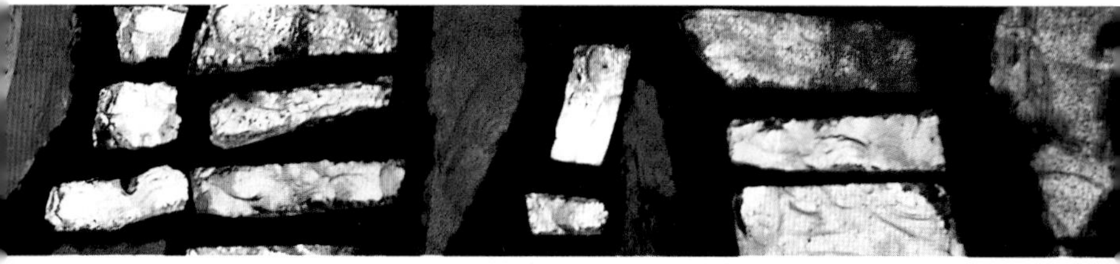

Nablus, in Samaria, and treat the Torah (the first five books of the Old Testament) and the Book of Joshua as their scripture. Their first language is Arabic. The Karaites, a separate group that believes in the Torah but rejects all later writings, number 15,000. Up in the Galilee are 3,000 Sunni Muslim Circassians. Neither Arab nor Islamic in origin, they maintain an independent identity, even speaking the Circassian language. Elsewhere, over 70,000 Druze populate 22 villages in the north. Little is known about their religion except that they have a small caste of learned initiates, though the concept of loyalty to the ruling power is one precept. Israel is also the center of the Baha'i faith, an independent religion promoting universal love and equality, whose holy city is Haifa.

Christian pilgrims pray at Solomon's Pools, near Bethlehem

NON-JEWS Many non-Jews see Israel as a place of divinity, and seek to live there. One group is known as the Black Hebrews, African-Americans with a communal creed, who regard themselves as Jewish. They came to Israel during the 1970s, but since they are not descended from Jewish families and do not practise Judaism their status as Jews is not recognized by the State. Many other groups around the world say they are Jews—but are not always accepted by the Israeli authorities. Ethiopia's Falash Mura, who claim to have been converted from Judaism; Bene Israel, an ancient Indian community; and the descendents of all non-Orthodox converts, are examples. The Israeli media periodically reports the finding of communities who claim a religious or cultural connection to the Holy Land.

THE MANY FORMS OF JUDAISM
Judaism comes in many forms, with differences based on attitudes to the Jewish books of law (the Torah), subsequent prophetic writings, the codified oral law and the Talmud (rabbinic commentary). The Orthodox purport to believe that the scriptures were all physically handed down by the Divine, already written. Hasids (with side locks, long black coats and wide black hats) are the most observant of the Orthodox. Conservative (or Masorti) Jews believe that the scriptures are divinely inspired, but written by human beings. Reform and Liberal Jews prefer to emphasize Judaism's ethical tenets, seeing the scriptures as inspired, but not binding. Some secular Jews adopt a humanist version of Judaism that rejects the authority of the scriptures completely.

Israel works hard and plays hard. The country nearly bursts with joie de vivre, *the epitome of an energetic, creative upbeat nation. Eager for income and rewards, Israelis put in long hours and struggle for promotion. But the real point of life is not money but what it can buy: leisure, pleasure, fun and freedom.*

WANTING IT ALL Almost anything you care to name is available in Israel. A combination of enterprise and acquisitiveness has made it the consumer country *par excellence.* Since the early days, the price of imported goods has been sky-high, so Israelis are used to supporting their lifestyle by working ferociously hard. With salaries roughly one-third lower than in most Western countries, and with the constant tension of war, the population has learned to extract the maximum intensity from every experience. Israelis will not miss an opportunity to enjoy themselves, yet they still manage to be up and at it early next morning.

The Israeli working day starts at 7 or 8am and can last until 8pm or later. All the while, the bars and restaurants quench the Israeli thirst for social interaction, virtually 24 hours a day. Many Israelis work a six-day week, as set down in biblical law, resting only on the Sabbath (Saturday). Sunday is a normal weekday in Israel, though working on Friday, when the Sabbath (Shabbat) starts, is increasingly on the way to becoming optional.

WORKERS' RIGHTS Despite the long hours many Israelis put in, most workers are members of Histadrut, which is powerful and active—indeed, it is part of the bedrock of Israeli society. Histadrut takes a cradle-to-grave approach to its role, running a vast health-insurance plan, with its own hospitals, as well as offering social and welfare services to its members.

Some question Histadrut's position, and many workers feel obliged to

Israelis are great readers of newspapers—in several languages

stay within its health plan when they might prefer an alternative. This monolithic organization, in an apparent possible clash of interests, is also the nation's largest non-governmental employer. Yet Histadrut has been the strongest ally of both Jewish and Arabic workers since it was established in the 1920s, with formidable leverage. Strikes are not uncommon in Israel, but Histadrut has, on the whole, been a positive force in ensuring that wages and conditions reach a consistently high standard.

LOVE OF LIFE With their free time, Israelis head for the beach, the streets, sports grounds, pools, national parks and picnic places in the country, or open-air cafés in the cities. On the beaches, they swim and

play interminable games of beachball and *matkot*—a simple bat-and-ball game. Israel has a vibrant cultural life, in which opera, theater and classical concerts are not viewed as elitist or remote, but are tremendously popular. Tel Aviv and Haifa are the main cultural centers. Tel Aviv is also the focal point for late-night entertainment, discos and nightclubs. But even people who are not going out anywhere special will spend the evening hours strolling in the open air, meeting and talking.

SPEAK UP! Conversation is easy to strike up in Israel: All you need is split-second eye contact and you're connected. People are friendly and outgoing, even though sometimes desperately short on politeness and pleasantries. The ease with which people get together is a lesson in human relations. Explanations for this, perhaps, lie in the crowded apartment complexes, the group ethos of schools and institutions, and the universal army experience—a great leveler as well as a dumping ground for prejudices and vanities. The downside is that it is hard to find privacy or peace and quiet.

Surprisingly, Israel is a country of romantic encounters, too. Though immodest behavior is frowned on for people above a certain age, youngsters—who seem to radiate health and energy—have an unashamed physical confidence. Coyness is certainly not an Israeli characteristic.

WHY STAY INDOORS? The sun is usually shining somewhere in Israel. Even in the brief winter, the temperature in the southern city of Eilat is likely to be around 70°F (21°C). And when the sun is out in Israel, so are the people. At the end of the day, in the balmy sweet-scented evenings, the balconies of the ubiquitous Israeli apartment houses are used as informal dining rooms and lounges. Entertainment of every kind is available under the Mediterranean sky—from spontaneous beach parties to classical concerts at ancient amphitheaters, from craft markets to weddings. In this respect, Israelis enjoy a superb quality of life.

The varied climate even allows for winter sports

Having an opinion is not optional for Israelis—it is inevitable. Passions run high on every issue. To say that Israel is the only democracy in the Middle East understates the case. While the rest of the region consists largely of one-party dictatorships, Israel's proportional representation allows almost every faction, group or viewpoint a place in parliament.

THE SYSTEM The Knesset (literally "Meeting" or "Assembly"), the Israeli parliament, takes its name from an ancient Jewish assembly that functioned in Jerusalem in the 5th century BC. Now, as then, there are 120 seats. Proportional representation ensures that any party with at least 2 percent of the vote gains a seat. The result is a bewildering number of political parties. The advantage is that it accurately reflects the diversity of viewpoints in Israeli society. The clear disadvantage is that the need to build coalitions gives undue power to small parties. Elections are held every four years both for a government and (in a separate vote) for a prime minister. Israel also has a president, elected by Knesset members, whose term lasts seven years.

PARTY PLAYERS Nothing is as it seems in Israeli politics. Since the formation of the Likud ("Cohesion") party by Menachem Begin and Ariel Sharon in 1973, foreign journalists have branded Labor as left wing and Likud as right. Yet both support private enterprise and both wish to protect Israel's egalitarian infrastructure. Labor—which emerged from the mainstream collectivist pre-State Zionist movement—has been the party of the educated, affluent Ashkenazim. Likud—its ideological roots lie in the pre-State Revisionist breakaway that demanded a tougher response to the Arabs and British—represented the poor, especially the Sephardim. In 2005, after implementing his Gaza withdrawal, premier Ariel Sharon—one of Israel's popular politicians—left Likud to form a new party, Kadima ("Forward").

Smaller parties cover every religious and philosophical hue. No Israeli party has ever won a full majority. To form a government, a succession of coalition deals has historically been struck between unlikely bedfellows.

First step to peace: Begin, Carter and Sadat at Camp David, 1978

❑ The 2006 Knesset elections typified Israel's vibrant democracy. Thirty-one political parties put up candidates, most representing special interests such as Russian-speakers, Israeli Arabs and pensioners. Any winning at least 2 percent of the votes has seats in the Knesset. Twelve parties won Knesset seats. Centrist Kadima ("Forward"), headed by Ehud Olmert gained 23 percent (28 seats). The leftist Labour alliance garnered 17 percent (20 seats), while ultra-religious Shas came third with 11 percent (13 seats). Eight of the members of the Knesset are Muslims and two are Druze. ❑

❑ Almost all political parties in Israel, including the far left and the peace lobby, are Zionist (that is, they believe Israel should be maintained as a homeland for the Jews). There are also non-Zionist parties and organizations in Israel, some Arab, some Jewish. They oppose Israel's existence as a Jewish state. ❑

POLITICS AND PEACE Since the birth of modern Israel in 1948, politics has been dominated by the Arab/Israeli conflict. Huge amounts of energy, and vast sums of money, have been spent on defense, reducing the budget for everything else. Peaceful periods allow political choices and government freedom to invest in health, education and industry. Difficult times like the second Intifada, from 2000 to 2005 , bring austerity and sacrifices in the interest of security.

It was so-called right-wing Menachem Begin and Likud who shook hands with President Sadat of Egypt in 1979 and made the first lasting peace treaty. Similarly in 2005, it was Ariel Sharon, another rightist premier, who gave Gaza (formerly part of Egypt) to the Palestinian Authority, so creating the first self-governing Palestinian territory in history. The bloody fatigue of war has made peace more desirable than ever, and trading land for that vision seems to offer a tentative way forwards. No one in Israel expects such cordial arrangements with their Arab neighbors as exist between some European countries. But even if peace simply means no war, it would be priceless to almost all Israelis.

A UNIQUE POSITION As the only democracy in an undemocratic and anti-Western region, Israel has long been seen by the US as its firm ally (the UK and Europe have tended to see their best interests being served through support for the Arab states). America's "special relationship" provided Israel with billions of dollars as a buffer against economic sanctions in the form of boycotts, embargos and cold shoulders. The rise of Al-Quaida and the global jihad (holy war), and the US response of a "War on Terror"—including regime change—has dramatically changed Israel's situation. Despite continuing Palestinian militancy, the willingness of some Arab states to support America's fight against Islamic extremism has brought real hope of a Middle East *entente.*

First meeting of the new Kadima party in the Knesset in November 2005

It was a tough battle to bring the nation of Israel into being, and it is a tough battle to prevent it from being destroyed. That is why security is tight at all entry points into the country, and soldiers, both men and women, are a distinct part of everyday life. Of course, soldiers are inseparable from the very existence of this constantly threatened country.

ON PERMANENT STANDBY On and off duty, conscripts or professionals, members of the armed forces—the Israel Defence Forces (IDF)—carry their weapons at all times. This can be startling for unsuspecting tourists who have never seen anything like it before. Out of uniform, most of the conscripts wear jeans, T-shirts and sneakers, with an Uzi submachine gun hanging from one shoulder. In uniform, it has been normal for gun-carrying soldiers to travel the country by hitchhiking (now, though, they enjoy free bus travel).

Soldiers are treated with enormous respect and affection by the public. For one thing, and unlike the situation in many other countries, Israelis feel that the army is on their side. In fact, Israel is in one sense just one big army. All boys and all girls join the IDF at the age of 18, complete their term (three years for men, two for women), and in effect remain in the army as reservists until the age of 51 (men) or 24 (women). Reservists have to serve around 30 days a year minimum. Certain occupations are entitled to exemption, and women do not serve if they have children.

The IDF is one of the most highly trained and battle-experienced armies in the world, having endured five wars since 1948. As a spinoff, Israel has become a major weapons manufacturer, a process started when the US arms embargo on Israel took effect. As a result, Israel started its own arms manufacture—now it even sells weapons to the United States.

THE TERROR THREAT Since Israel's birth, determined foes in the Arab world—nations like Syria and Iran and the militias like Hezbullah, Islamic Jihad, Hamas and the PLO's Fatah—have attacked its civilians and soldiers alike in an effort to eliminate the Jewish state. That's why vigilance is high and security tight throughout the country. All

Israeli armed forces maintain a watchful but unobtrusive role

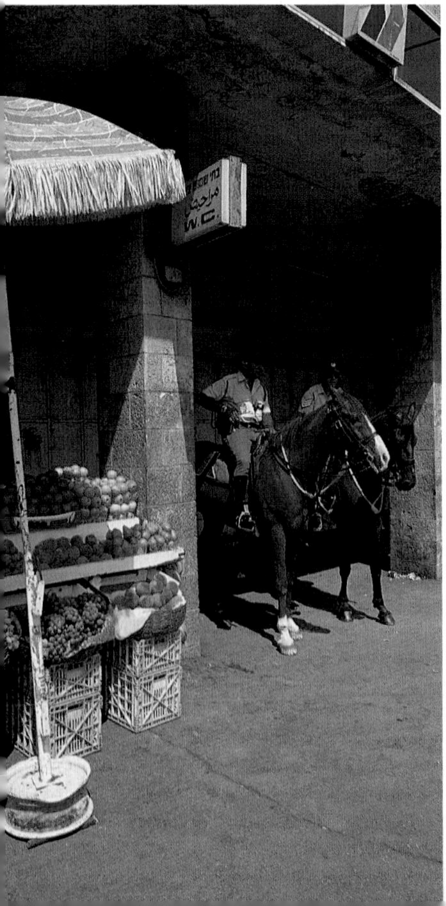

public places employ security staff. School groups are always accompanied by an armed guard, as children were frequently a target. From 2000 to 2004 (the Second Intifada) scores of suicide bombers entered Israel, causing huge physical and mental injury. With few options—suicide bombers obviously have to be prevented rather than arrested after the event—Israel launched strikes against the leaders of terrorist organizations. Efforts to stop bombers entering Israel led to the building of a security barrier. Such measures, together with a changed political scene after Palestinian leader Yasir Arafat's death, brought the Intifada to an end. Although vigilance and security are still essential, the danger from terrorism in Israel is now no worse than in most other countries.

A JEWISH ARMY Israeli soldiers are sworn in at Masada (see page 35), where they vow that "Masada shall not fall again." Back in 1973, Golda Meir was asked by a reporter whether Israelis did not have some sort of Masada complex. "Yes," she said, "we do. And a pogrom complex, and a Hitler complex." The point was that Israelis see themselves as having a duty to protect the Jewish people and ensure their survival. The name Israel Defence Force is intended to be taken literally. The military grew out of brigades that stood guard at agricultural settlements, and continues to see itself in that defensive light. Memories of the Holocaust, of the powerlessness of Jews before the creation of the state of Israel, add extra force to the idea of Jews being armed and capable of self-defense. Even so, there remains, for Israelis and other Jews, something remarkable about the idea of an army of Jews. Despite the ferocity of the biblical Israelites, Jews came to be regarded, and to regard themselves, as vulnerable to attack. Israel, by changing that, has had a profound effect on Jewish psychology.

Jerusalem's Damascus Gate, the main entrance to the Old City

Israel has always held an uneasy place in the world. Many countries were slow to recognize the state and quick to condemn its handling of the Intifada. But changing global realities since 9/11 have undermined many of the anti-Israel prejudices and misconceptions, and old adversaries have made peace approaches.

THE WEST BANK Ever since the start of the Intifada in 1987, Israel has been portrayed in Europe as a militarist power harassing innocent Palestinian civilians. Sensationalist, often untrue reports of Israeli violence against the West Bank Arabs were based on a reality—Israel's struggle to contain an armed popular resistance. Under Arafat's leadership, the West Bank descended into a chaotic and menacing state of unrest in which the activists, ranging from rock-throwing teenagers to Islamists who organize suicide bombers, were terrorizing fellow Palestinians as well as Israelis.

For taking successful measures to deal with the situation, former Prime Minister Ariel Sharon was vilified by the world's media. News stories—and some politicians—typically portray suicide bombers as innocents, are apparently unconcerned by the Israeli victims and seem unaware of the complex background to events. On the other hand, it is not just outsiders who find the situation disturbing—most Israelis do too. The latest, some say risky, approach is to support and strengthen the Palestinian Authority which officially runs Palestinian affairs and let it deal with the unrest, whose root cause is not the occupation of the West Bank, but, as the militant organizations put it, "the occupation of Akko, Haifa and Jaffa."

ISRAEL AND ISLAM Israel came into being in a region that did not want it. The Arab states fought hard to prevent the establishment of the state of Israel and pledged to destroy the "Zionist entity", which they have seen as an outpost of Western imperialism and an offence to the principle that Islam will supplant Judaism. Israel's successes in repulsing the attacks of 1967 and 1973, and its ruthless approach to terrorist organizations, intensified the hatred for Israel and the Jews who are demonized in Arabic and Islamic media.

Israel was not only threatened with military action, but faced economic war too. The Arab Boycott office in Damascus spent decades working on a worldwide campaign to pressure all companies into ceasing trade with any other company that dealt with Israel. Such boycotts failed to prevent

War relics—abandoned Egyptian tanks in the Negev desert

Israel from becoming the most economically active country in the Middle East. Despite these realities, the changing political climate world-wide has tempted Arab states away from their traditional party line, to look instead at ways of making peace with their unstoppable neighbor.

ISRAEL AND THE WEST In the United States, there is a certain amount of warmth toward Israel, and the United States has greatly assisted Israel in holding its ground for tactical reasons—among them Israel's presence as a pro-Western state in a hostile region. Without American support, Israel might well have been destroyed by now.

By contrast, the European Union has over the years shown favor to the Arab cause—both Britain and France have long-standing links in the Arab world, which they think it is in their interest to preserve. The EU has been the principal financial supporter of the Palestinian cause, and European media appears unsympathetic to

The famous handshake: Israeli Prime Minister Rabin and PLO Chairman Arafat make peace in 1993, watched by President Clinton

Israel. On the other hand, Israel does a huge proportion of its trade with Europe.

ISRAEL AND THE THIRD WORLD
Not all Third World and non-aligned states joined the anti-Israel bloc. With the changing political scene, dozens of countries have struck up ties with the Jewish state. For some, there is a chance of tangible benefits. The states in the Organization of African Unity has maintained amicable relations and close contacts with Israel, while openly admitting that Russian and Arab pressure had forced them to cut off diplomatic relations in the past. As a result, Israel has given a lot of commercial, cultural and technical assistance to these countries, including aid in the form of freshwater wells, technical expertize, hospitals and medical staff.

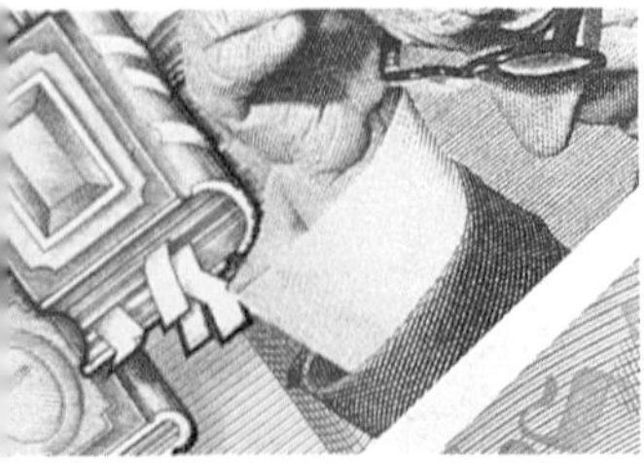

Israel seems to be on the verge of another new beginning. With peace accords in place, the hostilities of past decades might at last be swept aside. Freed from preoccupation with defense, Israel has boundless plans and potential that could make it an influence for good in the world out of all proportion to its size.

WHAT WILL PEACE BE LIKE? A hundred years of Zionism, from the 1890s to the 1990s, created a Jewish nation state on the verge of international acceptance. The next step is normalization. After peace treaties, perhaps trade treaties could come. But peace raises more questions. Army service has played an essential part in forging the national identity. Can anything else fulfill that role? And without external enemies, Israel faces two explosive internal divides: between Sephardim and Ashkenazim, and between Orthodox and secular. Three other groups—Ethiopian *olim*, Israeli Arabs and non-Orthodox religious Jews—all urgently demand full and genuine equality. When peace eventually comes all these social issues will have be be squarely faced and dealt with.

THE AGE OF ECONOMIC MIRACLES Even taking into account the 10 percent unemployment rate (the labor force grows by 3 percent per year) and even after the slowdown and austerity caused by the Intifada, growth is around 3 to 4 percent and still rising. In high-tech industries, medical and scientific research, fashion design, diamonds and jewelry making, Israel ranks among world leaders. The country's stock market is becoming a focal point for the Middle East sector, and foreign investment is pouring into the country. Each treaty-signing brings about a jump in share prices. And as centers of entertainment and leisure, the tourist resort of Eilat and the city of Tel Aviv are destined to become world-class travel destinations.

GOOD NEIGHBORS Peace and co-operation have the power to bring ambitious regional projects to fruition. Problems such as water shortages can be tackled together. Israel's medical expertise now helps previously hostile states. Israelis believe that their neighbors will abandon their opposition and join with them in a better future when they see the benefits Israel can bring to the region.

Eilat (below) and Tel Aviv are developing into major leisure resorts

Israel Was

The world's best-selling book is essentially the history, cosmology and ethics of the land and people of Israel. Whether you think God, Adam and Eve, Abraham, Moses and Jesus are real, symbolic or imaginary, the Bible's basic story line is broadly accurate. Archeologists are constantly digging up new supporting evidence.

The countryside of this tiny nation is sprinkled with the scenes and sites of great events that have made their mark on humanity. And as you travel from place to place, the Bible deserves to be ranked as one of Israel's best guidebooks.

IN THE BEGINNING The Torah (the Jewish name for the Pentateuch, or the first five books of the Bible) tells the story of the world from Creation up to the Israelite conquest of Canaan. Its human history roughly spans the 20th to the 12th centuries BC. Each part of the narrative is full of information about the peoples of this country, then called Canaan, their beliefs, customs, conflicts and ambitions. As a record of early habitation in the Middle East, it is an incomparably valuable document, the like of which hardly any other nation possesses. The pre-Israelite tribes that lived here in the late Stone Age and Bronze Age—before and during Abraham's time—are named, and their territories delineated.

The lifestyle and relationships, world view and codes of behavior of nomadic herdsmen of this period, as well as the origins of urbanization, are described in detail. The places where Abraham and the patriarchs and their families pitched their tents are named (and still called by the same names today). The places where they built shrines to the unseen God that Abraham believed in, and the cave that he purchased to bury his wife, are named, their locations described and their significance known ever since.

Pharaoh's army drowns chasing the Israelites through the Red Sea

THE PROMISED LAND Around 1700BC, many of the Israelites (more correctly called Hebrews in this pre-Judaic era) made their way to Egypt. The Sinai and Negev are thoroughly described, and their landmarks identified, in the biblical account of the Exodus, the return from Egypt that took place in about 1250C. That adventure is celebrated in the festival of Pesach (Passover). On the way, the Israelites paused at Mount Sinai, where Jewish Law was born,

Moses receiving the Ten Commandments (top)
Moses descending from Mount Sinai with the Ten Commandments (above)

an event remembered at the festival of Shavuot.

In 1200BC, Joshua led the Israelites across the Jordan to defeat one local king after another. In places, the Israelites failed to secure a victory, but by and large the land of Canaan was won. These Children of Israel had only a weak grasp of their forefathers' religion, and frequently took up the local cults of Ba'al and Astarte, which required human sacrifice. Much of the Torah deals with the consolidation of power among the Israelite tribes, and the growing hold of the Jewish ethical code.

DEFENDING THE LAND In the time of the Book of Judges (the 10th and 11th centuries BC), the Israelites were often at war, notably with the Philistines, who established "the five cities" on the Israelite shore (later six). These subsequently became known as Philistia: Gaza, Ashkelon, Ashdod, Ekron, Gath and Jaffa. From here, they extended their territory across Judah and Galilee, the Israelites unable to defeat them until the era of the Book of Kings (from 1025BC).

In the reign of King Saul, the shepherd boy, David of Bethlehem, considerably weakened the Philistines by killing their "giant," Goliath. In 1006BC, King Saul was killed fighting the Philistines. He had already chosen David to be his successor.

THE FIRST TEMPLE David's outstanding achievement was to complete the Israelite conquest and bind together the Jewish people. Under him, the Land of Israel stretched from Damascus to the Red Sea. Conquering Jerusalem, the city of the Jebusites, he built a shrine there for the Ark of the Covenant. The ark was a gold-encrusted wooden chest containing Moses' tablets of stone, inscribed with the Law, which the Israelites had been carrying with them for several centuries. Deeming himself, or being deemed by God, unfit for the task of constructing the Holy Temple as a permanent sanctuary for the Ark, he left this to his son Solomon. In 953BC, King Solomon built the awesome, magnificent temple on what was to be called Temple Mount. Much subsequent political and religious history was to emanate from here.

A new era started under Solomon. The temple became the focal point of the nation and Jerusalem extended its political authority throughout the country. But it was a land caught between empires, crossed by trade routes and coveted by others. Its strength, in forming the wealth and character of the nation, was its weakness too, as one regional power after another laid claim to the Land of Israel.

FIGHTING FOR SURVIVAL Solomon's unified nation did not survive long after his death in 928BC. A split resulted in two Jewish kingdoms: Israel in the north, and Judah in the south. Jerusalem remained the spiritual center for both until, in the 8th century BC, the northern kingdom came more and more under the influence of Phoenicians, Assyrians and others. The 7th century BC saw a similar trend in Judah, but, in 727BC, King Hezekiah purified the temple and vigorously revived Jewish practise. Despite today's Orthodox belief that the Torah (the first five books of the Bible) was given to Moses at Sinai, the text makes plain that it was written in Jerusalem at this time.

Meanwhile, Assyrians conquered the northern kingdom; the mixing of the local Jews (many of whom were taken into slavery) with their colonists created the Samaritan people. Assyria moved on to re-create Philistia, virtually surrounding Judah. However, the Babylonians were also at war with the Assyrians. When they crushed the Assyrians in 630BC, King Josiah of Judah quickly retook the north. He closed down all places of worship, except for the Temple at Jerusalem, which he purified.

A NEW TEMPLE The whole of Israel was then conquered by the Babylonians under Nebuchadnezzar II. In 597BC, the Jews rebeled against Babylonian rule, but soon lost ground. The Jewish élite and priesthood were exiled to Babylon and, in 587BC, the Temple was demolished. However, though significant in religious terms, the Babylonian Exile only lasted 46 years. In 539BC, the Persians conquered the Babylonian Empire and permitted the exiles to return to Jerusalem. They marched back in two stages, one of them under Ezra, who revitalized Judaism and inspired the building of the Second Temple, dedicated in 519BC. It is likely that the last part of the Torah was written at this time.

Jerusalem then enjoyed a renaissance and was enclosed by new ramparts. However, a new influence was being felt throughout the land: Greek culture.

HELLENIZATION During the 5th and 4th centuries BC, Hellenistic Greek culture, ideas, gastronomy, religion, architecture and art swept through the Mediterranean and the Middle East. In 333BC, Alexander the Great, the King of Macedonia (northern Greece), set out to conquer the world. He began by defeating the Persians and setting up the Seleucid dynasty in Damascus, to rule the whole region. The Seleucids often had to go to war to defend their territory, and from 312BC to 198BC, much of Judaea, including Jerusalem, fell to the rival Egyptian Ptolomaic dynasty.

As soon as the Seleucids had regained their losses in 198BC, they started to come under pressure from the growing might of a new rival empire—that of Rome. In 175BC the new Seleucid king, Antiochus IV, set out to replace Temple Judaism with worship of the Greek gods. He sold off the Temple treasures to pay the debts of his army. An altar to the

Babylon conquers Israel (top)
Mattathias slays an idolator (above)

wine god Dionysus (also known as Bacchus) was erected in the temple in their place.

THE MACCABEES This was too much of a sacrilege for the Hasmoneans, one family of the priestly line, to bear. In 166BC, the father (Mattathias) and his five sons (including Judah, known as the Maccabee, probably meaning "the Hammer") killed a Seleucid official and a pagan priest. The killing sparked a war between the Jews and the Seleucids. Mattathias was killed, but Judah continued with the rebellion, which resulted in complete independence for Judaea under Hasmonean rule. The Maccabees purified and rededicated the Temple (an act commemorated by the festival of Hanukka). Judah's brother Jonathan became high priest, later replaced by his brother Simeon. Yet the power-hungry Hasmonean dynasty proved a disaster for Israel. From 103 to 63BC, religious traditionalists and their Hellenised neighbors were in open conflict with their Hasmonean rulers. Taking advantage of the chaos, the Romans simply moved in and conquered Judaea.

Five centuries of Roman rule brought dramatic, disastrous changes. It was a messianic age, marked by turmoil, violence and despair. The Jews were in conflict with their imperial masters, whose repression proved inadequate to break the will of this proud people. Among the several messiahs who attracted a following, the influence of one was to stand far above the rest: Jesus of Nazareth. By the end, Israel was no longer a Jewish land.

HEROD In 37BC, an ambitious, tough-minded half-Jewish friend of Rome, the notorious governor of Galilee, took control of the country. This was Herod, who arrived in Jerusalem heading a Roman force sent to execute the Hasmonean king, Antigonus. Accepting no opposition to his egomaniacal rule, Herod murdered anyone who might stand in his way, including his wife, two of his younger sons, his brother-in-law (Aristobulus III, the last Hasmonean high priest) and, finally, his faithful oldest son, Antipater.

Herod's grandiose building schemes took in palaces and forts, such as Masada and Herodion. It also included entire towns, such as Caesarea, and the reconstruction of the Temple along more Hellenistic lines. There was widespread discontent, murmurings of political rebellion and mass longing for the coming of a "messiah" (the Jewish name for a great liberator or leader). Towards the end of his reign (perhaps in 5BC, though the exact year is not known), Jesus was born.

Romans at war (top)
Roman Jerusalem's main street, the Cardo (below)

JESUS Herod's death, in 4BC, brought the disintegration of his kingdom, which was divided among his three remaining sons: Herod Antipas, Archelaus and Philip. All faced a popular mood of seething insurrection. According to Matthew's gospel, the family of Jesus fled to Egypt to escape the unrest, later settling in relatively safe Galilee. A messianic teacher, John the Baptist, attracted a big following. Herod Antipas had him executed. Jesus emerged as another possible messiah, urging Jews to remain faithful to Jewish law. Also, Jesus stressed its ethical content and new egalitarian ideas. After three years, he too was executed, but his following continued. Meanwhile the Zealots, an underground rebel movement whose members combined religious with

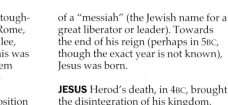

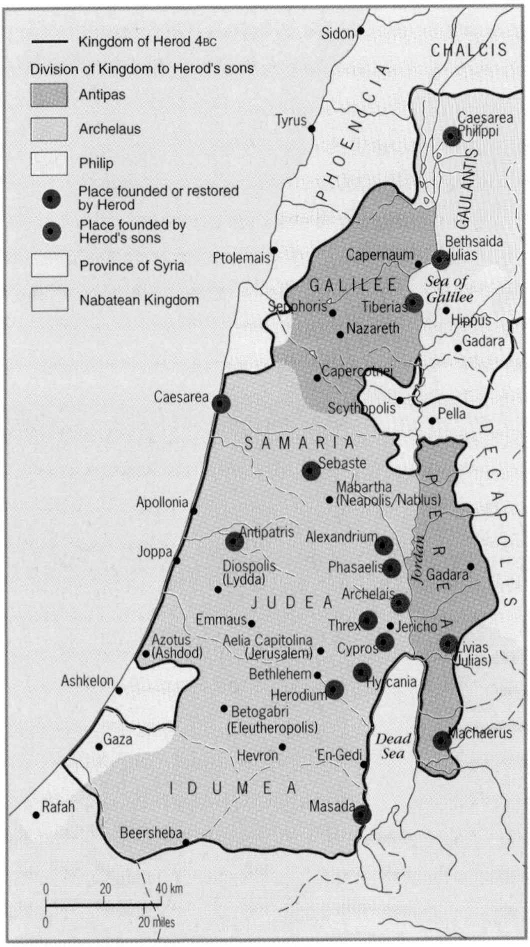

political fervor, were preparing for all-out war.

THE FIRST REVOLT From AD44, a succession of brutal Roman procurators were sent to administer the province, which they named Palaestina, or Palestine. In AD66, the Zealots made their first attack on a Roman garrison: The soldiers surrendered, but were killed anyway.

This was the trigger for a nationwide uprising. In one incident, Roman reinforcements numbering 6,000 soldiers, trapped by Jewish insurgents at Beit Horon, were slaughtered. A number of cities came into the hands of the rebels. Eventually, Rome began to master the situation. Town after town was destroyed, including major centers such as Gamla and Jericho. Eventually, in AD70, Roman troops retook Jerusalem and destroyed the Temple itself. Only the Western Wall survived. Diehard Zealots gathered at Masada, but, facing defeat, they committed mass suicide in AD73.

THE SECOND REVOLT Roman troops were poured into Palestine, with large new military colonies created on the sites of destroyed towns such as Nablus, Caesaria and Jerusalem. Yet Jewish life and law continued, even thrived, away from Jerusalem, with Galilee the principal center. Christianity too was on the rise. St Paul's new universal vision of Christ's message gained ever more converts among the Gentiles, including the Romans.

Hadrian became emperor in 117. He prohibited Torah study, circumcision and other Jewish practises. In 132, the Second Revolt erupted. Its leader, known as Bar Kochba (Son of the Star), was acclaimed as a messiah and scored "miraculous" victories. The Roman response was ferocious. Almost a thousand Jewish towns and villages were wiped out. The revolt was smashed by 135. Jerusalem was totally reconstructed, and a statue of Hadrian placed on Temple Mount. Entry to the city was forbidden to Jews, except on just one day a year. The Diaspora began—and would not end until the 20th century.

The decline of Jewish Israel was soon offset by the rise of Christian Israel. The new religion grew beyond its Jewish roots and spread fast through the Roman Empire, its ideas and credo evolving in the Near East. After Emperor Constantine granted tolerance to Christianity, huge numbers embraced the faith. The land of Jesus became the Holy Land. The Byzantine period brought three centuries of piety and pilgrimage, church-building and colonization.

FROM ROME TO BYZANTIUM
Following the two revolts, the Romans allowed the decimated Jews freedom to practise their religion and live by their own laws. However, they were only allowed to enter Jerusalem on one day a year—Tisha b'Av, the supposed anniversary of the Temple's destruction. The Jews marked this day by chanting mournful lamentations at the Western Wall (hence the name Wailing Wall). Palestine became increasingly Romanized and Christianized, and when Emperor Constantine decreed official tolerance for Christianity in AD313, tens of thousands joined the new creed. In 323, Constantine became sole ruler of the Eastern and Western Empires and made Christianity, in effect, the state religion. Later the Roman Empire split again into eastern and western spheres. In 379, Byzantium, or Constantinopolis (today's Istanbul), became the capital from which Palestine was ruled.

TO BE A PILGRIM Constantine's own mother, Empress Helena, came to the Holy Land in 326 to search out relics of Jesus. She found them, with surprising ease. As soon as she arrived in the Holy City, the Bishop of Jerusalem showed her the exact spot where, he claimed, Jesus had been crucified. The burial tomb was immediately at hand. Nearby were some old crucifixes, one of which she clearly identified as the True Cross. Over the site, Helena ordered the vast, splendid Church of the Holy

Top: Constantine carries the Cross in battle. Above: Constantine's baptism

Sepulchre to be built, still the focal point of Christian devotion in the city. On the Mount of Olives, she made more discoveries, such as the Garden of Gethsemane and the place

from which Jesus had ascended into heaven. Here, another fine church was erected.

Moving on to Bethlehem, Helena at once identified the place where Jesus had been born, and enclosed it within the Church of the Nativity. Traveling through the Holy Land, she located scores of other sites which she believed were associated with Jesus. Most were of doubtful authenticity, but this did not deter her from ordering churches to be built or stop Christians from flocking to see them. Relics of saints' bodies were eagerly sought out and found everywhere. Numerous non-biblical legends date from this time: Mary drew water from this well, for example, or the Archangel Gabriel appeared in that cave.

Constantine made Christianity the Roman state religion

THE BEGINNINGS OF SCHISM In this early stage, churches became a feature of the land. Christian communities flourished around holy places. Jerusalem again grew to be as large as in Herodian times. By the year 450, most people in Palestine were Christian. But the division of the empire into east and west mirrored a cultural gulf. Arguments about doctrine and practise shattered the unity of the church.

In 451, the Roman and Eastern churches agreed to differ, and the Patriarchate of Jerusalem became part of the Eastern, or Orthodox, Church. In 456, the Monophysite doctrine, that Jesus had a single nature, part human, part divine, was condemned as heresy. The Orthodox view was that Christ had two natures. But large numbers of Christians in Palestine were Monophysite. This rather academic matter threatened the unity of the Byzantine Empire. The Copts and other Eastern churches remained Monophysite.

THE END OF THE DREAM Along with growing discord in the Church, there was sporadic unrest among the Jewish population from 484 onwards. When the Persians invaded Palestine in 614, they were aided and advised by disaffected Jews, whose complaints had been ignored by the Byzantines. The empire proved too weak to defend Palestine's holy places, and even the True Cross was carried off as booty. Fourteen years later, the Byzantines took on the Persians, this time defeating them and restoring the Cross to the Church of the Holy Sepulchre. But already the end was in sight for the Byzantine Christians. Islam was on the march from Arabia.

Islam rose like a whirlwind from the Arabian desert, taking the whole of the Middle East by storm. Islam (literally meaning "submission") prescribed forcible conversion of pagans. To the Christians and the Jews—"Peoples of the Book"—Muhammad promised mercy, while replacing their spent, outdated religions with the teachings of the Koran.

MUHAMMAD'S VISION Muhammad, born in Mecca in AD570, married a wealthy widow and became an influential figure. He took other wives, one of them Jewish, and became interested in religion and ethics. The defeat of the Jews was seen as a lesson. He felt the time was right for a creed that could not be conquered. In 610 he had the first of the revelations that were to be recorded in the Koran. He argued that Arabs, like Jews, were descendants of Abraham. He went on to claim that his new religion had been revealed to supersede both Judaism and Christianity. Arming his supporters, he compelled the inhabitants of Mecca to adopt his faith in 630. When Muhammad died in 632, his followers set about fulfilling his dreams.

ISLAM'S TRIUMPH Islamic forces reached Palestine just two years after the Prophet's death, and they defeated the Byzantines in 638.

Exquisite tilework (top), Dome of the Rock. Remains of Nimrod (below), a 12th-century Crusader castle

The region was then ruled from Damascus by the Omayyad dynasty, whose leaders bore the title Caliph (literally, successor—i.e. successor to Muhammad). In Jerusalem (which the Arabs called Aelia, the Roman name) Caliph Omar went to Temple Mount to pray at the rock where tradition has it that Abraham placed his son for sacrifice. He toured the Holy Land, his followers claiming for Islam each place where he prayed. He refused to pray at the Church of the Holy Sepulchre, so that it would remain a Christian shrine. The next caliph, Abd el-Malik, wanted to establish a place of pilgrimage within his own domain. He declared Temple Mount was "the far distant place of worship" to which Muhammad flew in a dream, according to the Koran. He built the Dome of the Rock on top of the Mount about AD700. Aelia was then renamed Beit al-Makds (from Beit HaMikdash, the Hebrew name of the Temple), later abbreviated to Al-Kds. Abd el-Malik's son, Al-Walid, converted another church on the Temple Mount site into the Al-Aqsa (El-Aksa) mosque.

VIOLENCE AND CHAOS In 750 the Abbasids succeeded the Omayyads and gradually lost control of Palestine, which they had ruled from distant Baghdad. For a century, Turkish warlords vied for mastery of the region. Christians were attacked, and the Holy Sepulchre set on fire, but later repaired. Around AD977, the brutal Fatimid dynasty, based in Egypt, took over. Between 1004 and 1021, their caliph Al-Hakim (the Mad) destroyed almost all Palestine's churches. In 1055, the Fatimids were overrun by the equally savage Seljuk Turks. Christian pilgrims were often murdered when visiting holy sites.

THE CRUSADES Full of naïve zeal, thousands of Christian soldiers (mainly young noblemen) set off in waves from Western Europe to "save" Palestine's holy places. The First Crusade of 20,000 men entered Jerusalem on July 15, 1099, and massacred the entire population. On Christmas Day, 1100, Baldwin I was crowned King of Jerusalem. Meeting no resistance, they conquered more of Palestine, built fortified churches and castles, and discovered countless dubious saintly relics and holy places. Military monastic orders came into being, notably the Knights Hospitallers and the Templars.

The Second Crusade arrived in 1147. Now a powerful Muslim opponent emerged: Salah ed-Din (Saladin), the Egyptian sultan. In 1187, at the Horns of Hittim, he and his army encountered a vast force of Crusaders and slaughtered them. Almost at once, the Crusader kingdom collapsed, though Soldiers of the Cross continued to arrive. With

Christian captives suffer the vengeance of the mighty sultan Salah ed-Din

the Third Crusade of 1189, the Fourth of 1202, the Fifth of 1228 and the Sixth of 1248, the Crusaders established a new capital at Akko, or Acre. In 1261, the Mamelukes, under Sultan Baibars, rode in. These terrifying master horsemen and swordsmen, bloodthirsty former slaves, were to rule for two centuries. They made brisk work of the Europeans. In 1270, the final Crusade arrived and was massacred.

The Mamelukes ruled Palestine for two centuries, and the Ottomans ruled for four. The Mamelukes were noted for anarchy and turbulence; the Ottomans imposed a regime of suffocating stability. Progress in science and mathematics languished. An obscure Ottoman province, Palestine went into steady decline.

MAMELUKES The Mamelukes were freed slaves of the Egyptians, mostly of Circassian origin. They failed to establish any cohesive government in Palestine. Nevertheless, they constructed fine buildings, some of which still stand to this day. At the end of their period of rule, an Islamic defeat on the other side of the Mediterranean began to send out ripples that would last for centuries: tens of thousands of Jews, expelled from Spain by the Christian conquerors in 1492, began making their way back to Palestine.

Top: Akko, the once mighty fortress town revived under Ottoman rule
Above: Suleiman the Magnificent

TURKISH RULE The Crusader period was a disaster for the Holy Land, and for Christendom. The Crusader attack on Constantinople so weakened it that Sultan Osman would soon be able to add this remnant of the Byzantine Empire to his own massive Ottoman (Turkish) Empire. The Ottoman Sultan Selim next defeated the Mamelukes in 1517 to gain the Holy Land. So Palestine was once again ruled from Constantinople (now called Istanbul). The famous flowering of the Ottoman period took place at the start under Selim's son, Suleiman (the Magnificent). He did much to improve Jerusalem, in particular repairing and restoring its ramparts. The majestic city walls that stand today are principally his work.

Thereafter, Ottoman rule was characterized by neglect. The population divided into small local clans and fiefdoms, often involved in insoluble feuds. Exceptions to the general decline were the rebuilding of Galilean towns (notably Akko) by the Druze Emir ed-Din in the mid-17th century. In the late 18th century came the rise to power in Galilee of Ahmed el-Jazzar (known as the Butcher), and the brief early 19th-century takeover of Palestine by Egyptian pashas. Then, in the 1870s, to the surprise of all, large numbers of East European Jews began arriving.

In the 1880s, the destiny of Palestine was being decided by events in Poland and Russia. Tsar Alexander III (1881–94) and his son Tsar Nicholas II (1894–1917) oversaw repressive anti-Jewish legislation and vicious pogroms. These added fuel to the new Zionist movement, which was calling for a return to the Jewish homeland.

THE FIRST ALIYAH Aliyah means "ascent" and that is how Jews speak of going to live in Israel. From 1850 to 1880, some 20,000 came to live in Palestine. This was followed in 1882 to 1903, by the first organized mass immigration driven by religious and political ideals. It brought 25,000 settlers, almost all fleeing Russian pogroms. The settlers' enthusiastic desire to farm and "redeem" the land often petered out as they ran into serious difficulties, many reaching starvation point or dying of disease. Several settlements were bailed out by well-to-do Western Jews, who also contributed large sums for the purchase of land.

THE SECOND ALIYAH In Europe, Theodor Herzl's influential book *The Jewish State* was published in 1896, and the First Zionist Conference, held the following year, announced plans to create a Jewish home in Palestine. The Jewish National Fund was founded to buy land for settlements.

A new type of immigrant also began to appear. Many Russian Jews had been involved in the attempted revolution of 1905; with its failure, and the subsequent pogroms, these tough socialists embraced the dream of creating a Jewish nation in the ancient homeland. From 1904 to 1914, some 40,000 of them settled in Palestine, founding farm collectives and small towns. Arab opposition numbered among the problems they faced, but these Halutzim (pioneers), as they are still known, seemed undeterred by any obstacle. To rousing songs in Hebrew, they took on the Hula swamp, Judaean desert and coastal dunes. They founded the city of Tel Aviv and set up a network of armed groups for self-protection.

Zionist pioneers (above and below)

As the Second Aliyah ended, the Turks were drawn into World War I—on the losing side. It was to cost them Palestine. The arrival of thousands of Jewish refugees seemed, perhaps, the least important of anyone's concerns. From the end of World War I to the end of World War II, Palestine was in the hands of the British. They were to discover that the Jewish return to Israel was unstoppable.

DIPLOMACY AND DECEPTION In 1914, the Turks joined the war on Germany's side. It was a decision that was later to give the Allies, in victory, an opportunity to exert greater influence in the Near East. Britain was eager for a role in the Arab world. Behind the scenes, a leading Zionist, Chaim Weizmann, a persuasive diplomat as well as a distinguished scientist, was visiting people of influence in the Western world to win international support for a Jewish homeland in Palestine. Due to his efforts, the British Foreign Secretary, A. J. Balfour, wrote a letter, the famous Balfour Declaration of 1917. It guaranteed British support—against the wishes of many other British politicians. In the same year, British forces moved into Palestine, seizing it with ease from the Turks. A dignified and emotional General Allenby entered the Old City of Jerusalem on foot and announced the start of British rule.

General Allenby, head of the British forces

ZIONISM ON THE MARCH 1920 was a busy year. In the aftermath of the war, Palestine (on both sides of the Jordan) came under British Mandate on behalf of the League of Nations. At the same moment, the Third Aliyah (1919–23) began, bringing 40,000 youthful Zionist activists from Eastern Europe. This Aliyah, the first to be given advance training, had a dramatic effect on farming. Within weeks, the Hashomer defence volunteers regrouped to form Haganah, an underground army whose aim was to protect the Jews of Palestine. In the same year, the first collectives of the new kibbutz and *moshav* movements (see page 174) were established, and the

Arab opposition

labor union, Histadrut, was founded. It remains part of the bedrock of Israeli society. Hebrew was declared the official language of the Yishuv (Jews living in Palestine). Suddenly, the area's 700,000 resident Arabs realized the possible consequences of Zionism.

ATTACK AND DEFENCE 1920 was also the year of the first big anti-Jewish riots by Arabs in several towns. Worse followed in 1921, in two outbreaks that left 79 Jews and 48 Arabs dead. In 1924 came the Fourth Aliyah (1924–26), and another 80,000 Jews arrived, mainly Polish artisans and small businessmen, accelerating urban development. The ports grew, Tel Aviv expanded, Haifa's Technion research institute opened in 1924 and the Hebrew University at Jerusalem in 1925. Arab fury erupted again in 1929 and left 133 Jews dead, with the destruction of the ancient Jewish community in the city of Hebron.

The decade of the Fifth Aliyah (1931–40)—the flight from Nazism—brought 180,000 newcomers. The 1929 massacres had led to a split in Haganah, which had failed in its aim of protecting the Jews. The more hard-line Irgun was born, with guerrilla warfare, attacks on hostile strongholds and retaliation its tactics. The year 1936 saw a change in the Arab side too, with the start of the Arab Revolt against both the Jews and the British. Within two years, 415 Jews had been murdered. To appease the Arabs, who were leaning towards the Nazis, the British agreed to curtail Jewish immigration. At the same time, they were attempting to appease Hitler. Both proved to be blind alleys.

Yad Vashem Holocaust memorial (top)
British law enforcement (below)

HOLOCAUST The Fifth Aliyah ended with two years of "restricted immigration" (1939–40). As many as 15,000 arrived clandestinely, aided by the secret Aliyah Bet group. In Europe, the Nazi conquest had begun and the Jewish extermination plan was ready to start. Some Jews could see what was coming. The Sixth Aliyah (1941–47) brought those frantic to escape the Holocaust and the few who survived.

Throughout the war, the British held the doors of Palestine firmly closed to "unauthorized immigrants." They came anyway and 20,000 were detained as soon as they set foot in Palestine. Most were returned to Europe, via detention centers. In a notorious incident in 1947, the ship *Exodus*, with 4,554 camp survivors crammed on board, reached the coast of Israel. British ships took them all back to Europe, forcibly disembarking them at Hamburg. This was the last year of British rule in Palestine.

Zionist emotion ran high before World War II, due to the trauma of Nazism. The movement split on whether or not to help the British war effort against the Germans. Both viewpoints had their day. When World War II was won, the Zionists reunited for a last push against the British, who finally left Palestine in 1948. After 50 years of determination, Israel was reborn.

FRIENDS AND ENEMIES Palestine's Jews were incensed by the British White Paper of May 1939, proposing that the Balfour Declaration be ditched and Jewish immigration halted. The Irgun decided to use guerrilla tactics against the British. But the outbreak of war with Germany changed all that. The Arabs supported the Nazis. David Ben-Gurion spoke for both Haganah and Irgun when he said: "We shall fight the War as if there were no White Paper , and we shall fight the White Paper as if there were no War." Not all agreed, however. The Irgun breakaway group Lehi (the Stern Gang) vowed to fight the British even during the war.

FIGHTING THE BRITISH With Germany's defeat in 1945, Irgun rejoined Lehi in its battle. The British headquarters, at the King David Hotel, was blown up. Irgun prisoners were daringly freed from Akko's fortress prison. The British took the Jewish homeland issue to the United Nations, and on November 29, 1947, the UN voted to partition Palestine (west of the Jordan) into Jewish and Arab areas. Jews would have small, unconnected zones in Galilee, on the coast and in the Negev. It looked unworkable even on paper, but the Zionists agreed. The Arabs rejected it.

David Ben-Gurion declares the founding of Israel

PROCLAIMING A STATE The day after the UN vote, the Arabs began a campaign of violence which flared into full-scale civil war. By April 1948, Haganah held territory that included the coast, western Jerusalem, the Negev and Galilee. On May 14 ,1948, at Tel Aviv, David Ben-Gurion, the first prime minister, proclaimed the founding of the State of Israel with the words: "In the Land of Israel the Jewish people came into being."

WAR AND PEACE At once Jordan, Egypt, Syria, Lebanon and Iraq invaded to crush the new "Zionist entity." Israel emerged the vistor, as it did in 1956. In 1967, Israel took just six days to decisively repulse another attack, winning Sinai and Gaza from Egypt, the Golan from Syria, and from Jordan the West Bank and East Jerusalem, which the Jews had prayed for centuries to regain. In 1973, with Russian help, Syria and Egypt again attacked, but were defeated. In 1978, Egypt's President Sadat decided to look to a better future and signed a peace treaty with Israel.

More problematic was terrorism. The PLO (Palestine Liberation Organization), founded by the Arab League in 1964 and led by Yasir Arafat, unleashed attacks of savagery on Israel's schools, buses, planes, and murdered Israel's team at the 1972 Olympic Games. During the 1980s, especially the 1987 Intifada, militias

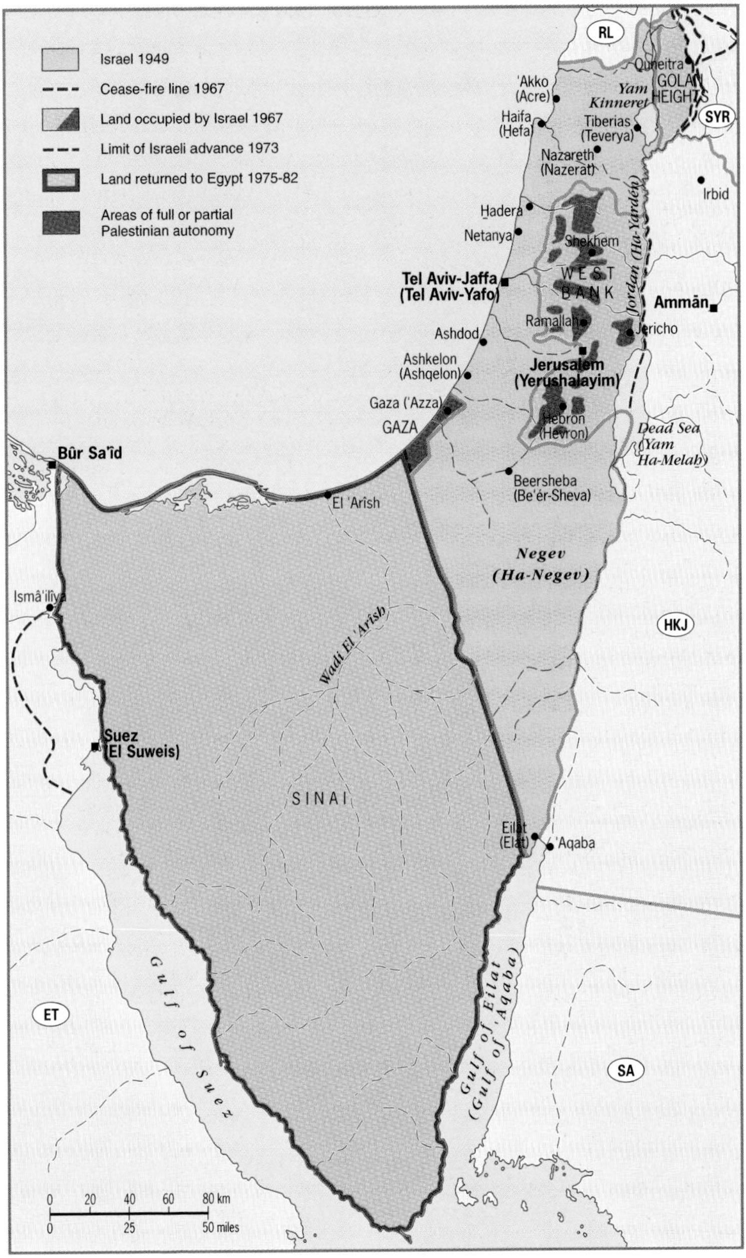

funded by Islamic states emerged to rival the secular PLO.

IN 1993, with a handshake, Arafat and Israel's premier Yitzhak Rabin agreed to create a Palestinian state alongside Israel. Jordan also made peace with Israel. A year later Rabin was assassinated, while in 2000 Arafat launched a Second Intifada with hundreds of suicide bombers. Arafat's death in 2004 ended his Intifada, but the election of a Hamas-run government in 2006 emphasized Palestinians enduring hostility towards Israel.

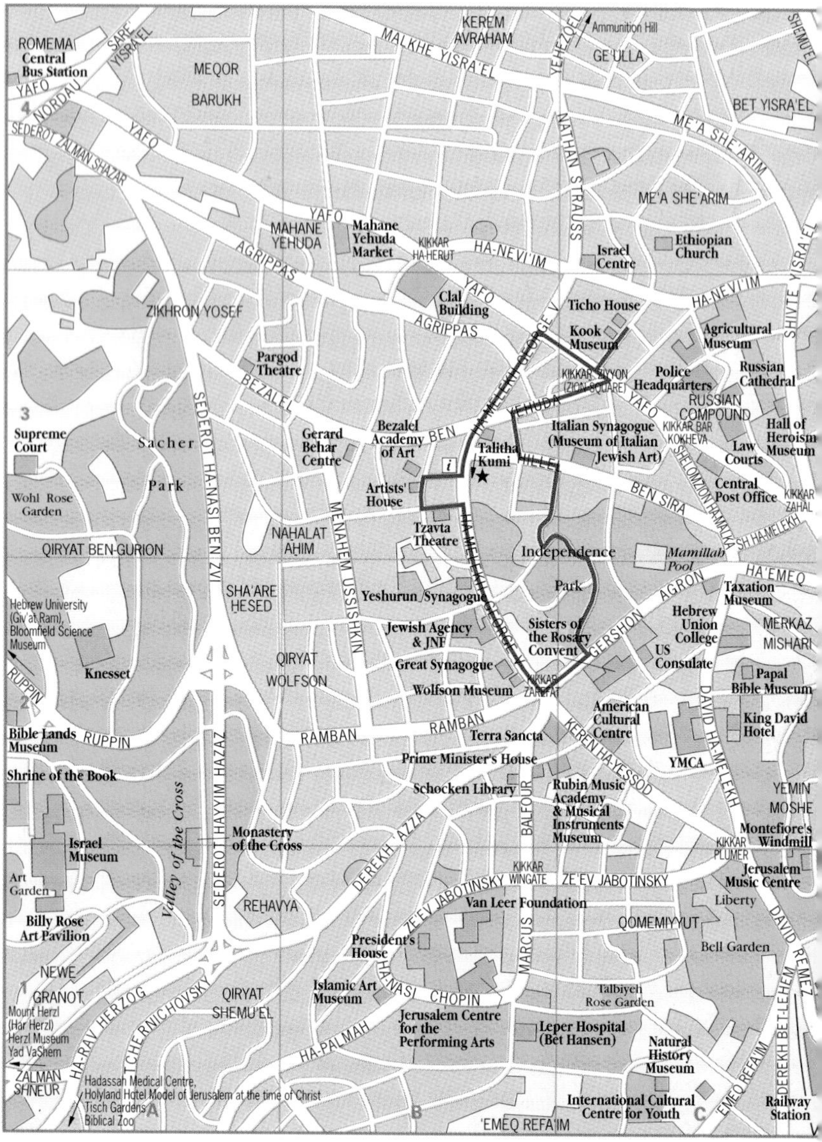
KEREM AVRAHAM
MALKHE YISRA'EL
Ammunition Hill
YEHEZQEL
SHEMU'EL
GE'ULLA
ROMEMA
Central Bus Station
SARE YISRA'EL
YAFO
NORDAU
MEQOR BARUKH
BET YISRA'EL
SEDEROT ZALMAN SHAZAR
NATHAN STRAUSS
ME'A SHE'ARIM
YAFO
MAHANE YEHUDA
Mahane Yehuda Market
KIKKAR HA-HERUT
HA-NEVI'IM
Israel Centre
Ethiopian Church
AGRIPPAS
Clal Building
ZIKHRON YOSEF
Ticho House
HA-NEVI'IM
SHIVTE YISRA'EL
Kook Museum
Agricultural Museum
Pargod Theatre
BEZALEL
KIKKAR ZIYYON (ZION SQUARE)
Police Headquarters
Russian Cathedral
YEHUDA
RUSSIAN COMPOUND
Supreme Court
Sacher Park
SEDEROT HA-NASI BEN ZVI
Gerard Behar Centre
Bezalel Academy of Art
BEN YEHUDA
Talitha Kumi
Italian Synagogue (Museum of Italian Jewish Art)
KIKKAR BAR KOKHEVA
Hall of Heroism Museum
Law Courts
HILLEL
SHELOMZION HA-MALKA
Central Post Office
KIKKAR ZAHAL
Wohl Rose Garden
Artists' House
BEN SIRA
SH HA-MELEKH
NAHALAT AHIM
MENAHEM USSISHKIN
Tzavta Theatre
HA-MELEKH GEORGE V
Independence Park
Mamillah Pool
HA-'EMEQ
QIRYAT BEN-GURION
SHA'ARE HESED
Yeshurun Synagogue
AGRON
Taxation Museum
Hebrew University (Giv'at Ram), Bloomfield Science Museum
Jewish Agency & JNF
Sisters of the Rosary Convent
GERSHON
Hebrew Union College
MERKAZ MISHARI
QIRYAT WOLFSON
US Consulate
Knesset
Great Synagogue
Papal Bible Museum
RUPPIN
Wolfson Museum
KIKKAR ZARFAT
DAVID HA-MELEKH
American Cultural Centre
King David Hotel
Bible Lands Museum
RUPPIN
RAMBAN
Terra Sancta
KEREN HA-YESSOD
YMCA
Prime Minister's House
Shrine of the Book
SEDEROT HAYYIM HAZAZ
Schocken Library
BALFOUR
Rubin Music Academy & Musical Instruments Museum
YEMIN MOSHE
Valley of the Cross
Monastery of the Cross
Israel Museum
Montefiore's Windmill
KIKKAR PLUMER
DEREKH AZZA
KIKKAR WINGATE
ZE'EV JABOTINSKY
Jerusalem Music Centre
Art Garden
REHAVYA
Van Leer Foundation
Liberty Bell Garden
Billy Rose Art Pavilion
MARCUS
QOMEMIYYUT
DAVID REMEZ
President's House
NEWE GRANOT
TCHERNICHOVSKY
QIRYAT SHEMU'EL
Islamic Art Museum
HA-NASI
CHOPIN
Talbiyeh Rose Garden
Mount Herzl (Har Herzl) Herzl Museum Yad VaShem
HA-RAV HERZOG
HA-PALMAH
Jerusalem Centre for the Performing Arts
Leper Hospital (Bet Hansen)
Natural History Museum
DEREKH BET-LEHEM
ZALMAN SHNEUR
Hadassah Medical Centre, Holyland Hotel Model of Jerusalem at the time of Christ, Tisch Gardens, Biblical Zoo
'EMEQ REFA'IM
International Cultural Centre for Youth
Railway Station
'EMEQ REFA'IM
A
B
C
1
2
3
4

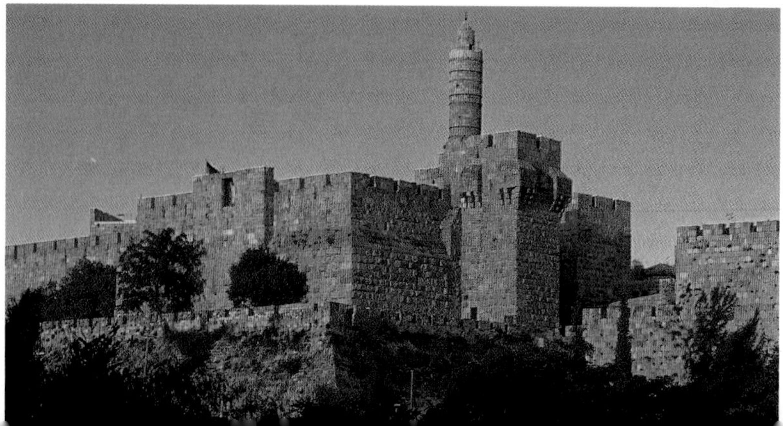

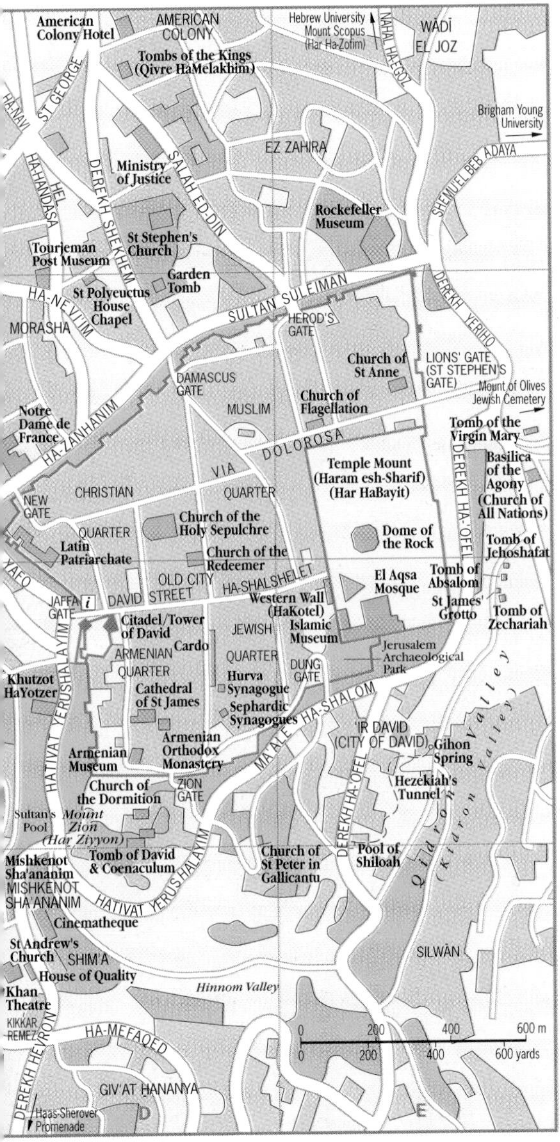

JERUSALEM (Hebrew: Yerushalayim; Arabic: Al-Quds) Highway 1 climbs gradually into the hills of Judaea and up to the city of Jerusalem. This is the way that most people arrive, in a taxi or a rental car. When, at last, the city entrance sign is reached, it makes the town look just like any other. No brilliant light radiates from the earth at this point. The sign is not encrusted with gold or jewels. Yet there is, without doubt, something magical about the name of Jerusalem. The fact that so many people, through the centuries, have yearned for this city—the fact that it became a metaphor for heaven, for the kingdom of God on earth, for a return to the Promised Land—cannot fail to affect anyone who arrives here today.

▶▶ CITY HIGHLIGHTS

David's Tower (page 46)
The Old City from the Mount of Olives (below)

CULTURE COLLISION In Jerusalem, Israel meets Arabia and West meets East. Behind the scenes, battles rage on diplomatic, economic and political fronts for full legal title to the city. However, the conflict of interests is barely apparent to outsiders, and visitors are warmly welcomed nearly everywhere. The intensely Arab character of parts of the city creates an exotic air, one that adds another dimension to Israel's otherwise overwhelmingly Jewish capital. In the Muslim and Christian quarters of the walled Old City, and in East Jerusalem just outside the walls, Arab culture powerfully predominates. To wander through the souks (markets) assailed by spicy aromas and numerous invitations to buy—or at least to look at the merchandise—is to plunge straight into the midst of the Orient. It's a reminder, perhaps, that Abraham himself, father of both the Jews and the Arabs, arrived here from the East.

ANCIENT CAPITAL Archeology and the Bible concur in saying that Jerusalem, as capital of the Jews, was built by King David about 1004BC. His original city covered a ridge of land encircled to the south by the valleys of the Kidron and Hinnom rivers. The area is now outside the city walls. This was not virgin land, however, and a Jebusite city-state already existed here, on a site that had been inhabited since 3500BC. Egyptian texts of 1900BC call

it Urushamem. In the Book of Genesis, Chapter 14, it is called Salem, the place where, in about 1800BC, Abraham visited Melchizedek. Centuries later the Jews returned to the city, led by David (II Samuel 5). David purchased a threshing floor (II Samuel 24), the site on which his son, King Solomon, was to erect the Temple.

A TIME OF WAR Although the Israelites were to become divided, Jerusalem, with its Temple, was to remain their capital ever afterwards. Over the millennia, the city walls were built, knocked down and then rebuilt, sometimes along a different course. The city suffered conquest, destruction and oppression (with episodes of Jewish independence in between) at the hands of half a dozen imperial powers. This period of history stretched from the Babylonians to the British (see side panel). Most of these conquering civilizations have waxed and waned; their day is over. Despite their efforts to take and hold Jerusalem, despite competing claims upon the city's holy sites, despite being divided in two (from 1948 to 1967), the city's identity as an "Eternal City," and capital of the people of Israel has survived.

CITY OF FAITH Yet Jerusalem is a city of other peoples too. The city witnessed events that lie near the heart of millions of believers worldwide—Jewish, Christian and Muslim. The finest landmark in the Old City is an Islamic shrine, the glorious Dome of the Rock. The Dome covers the Holy Rock, which in turn marks the site of the Jewish Temple's Holy of Holies. The latter sanctuary contained the Ark of the Covenant. It is from here, some Muslims believe, that Muhammad flew to meet God on a winged horse. The spires and domes of scores of churches pierce the skyline, chief among them being the Holy Sepulchre. This sepulcher, atop Golgotha or Calvary, enshrines the place where, Christians believe, Jesus died on the cross and then rose again.

NEW AND OLD There is more to Jerusalem than the Old City at its center. The East and West Jerusalem neighborhoods have, for the most part, sprung up in the last 100 years. West Jerusalem is dynamic and teeming with energy. For most residents and for many visitors, this is the "real" Jerusalem, the Jerusalem of today. The Old City, within its magnificent cordon of ramparts, serves as an evocative reminder of the city's origins in the unfathomable past.

ORIENTATION The walled Old City, focal point for most visitors, lies close to Jerusalem's eastern edge. The Old City is informally divided into four quarters—Muslim, Christian, Armenian and Jewish. To the east rises the Mount of Olives. Just north of the Old City walls lies the mainly Arab neighborhood known as East Jerusalem. Farther north are extensive Jewish residential areas, which technically are also part of the eastern section. The majority of the city, extending westward, is known as West Jerusalem or New Jerusalem. Consisting of dozens of more or less modern neighborhoods, this part is almost entirely Jewish. Jerusalem's "downtown" area is around Zion Square, a short distance west of the Old City.

OCCUPIED TERRITORY
Though the people of Israel have regarded Jerusalem as their capital since 1004BC, the city has been under foreign occupation for much of history. Despite the ferocious attacks made upon it, the city has shown remarkable powers of survival.
The foreign conquerors of Jerusalem were the Babylonians (587BC), the Egyptians (320–198BC), the Seleucids (198–167BC), the Romans and Byzantines (37BC–AD638), the Arabs (638–1099), the Crusaders (1099–1187), the Mamelukes (1260–1517), the Ottoman Turks (1517–1917), the British (1917–48) and the Jordanians (1948–67).

LITTERED HIGHWAY
Alongside Highway 1, on both sides of the road, are the burned-out wrecks of cars and trucks that once plied between Tel Aviv and Jerusalem, keeping the route open and bringing supplies to the besieged Jews of Jerusalem during the 1948 War of Independence. To reach the city, they had to cross Arab-held territory, and were bombarded all the way. Vehicles that didn't make it were never cleared away—just pushed to the side of the road as a memorial.

Jerusalem's walls are the legacy of Suleiman the Magnificent

Walk

On the City Walls

Turreted ramparts of golden stone enclose the Old City. Built by Suleiman the Magnificent in the 16th century, they stand on top of 2,000-year-old ruins. Part of the walkway, around Temple Mount is closed for security reasons. The rest is reached in two sections, both starting at the Jaffa Gate (*Open* Mon–Thu 9–4. *Admission charge*). *Allow 3 hours.*

The towers of the Citadel dominate the west of the city

Jaffa Gate to Damascus Gate A wide stone walkway, skirting the Christian quarter, at first passes by the battlements that peep onto busy West Jerusalem. It then turns a series of corners into the Arab side of town. Below, on the city side, gardens, a school and the dome of a mosque are passed. The tall spire of the **Franciscan Church of St. Savior** stays in view. Steps take the path up and down, and over the 19th-century

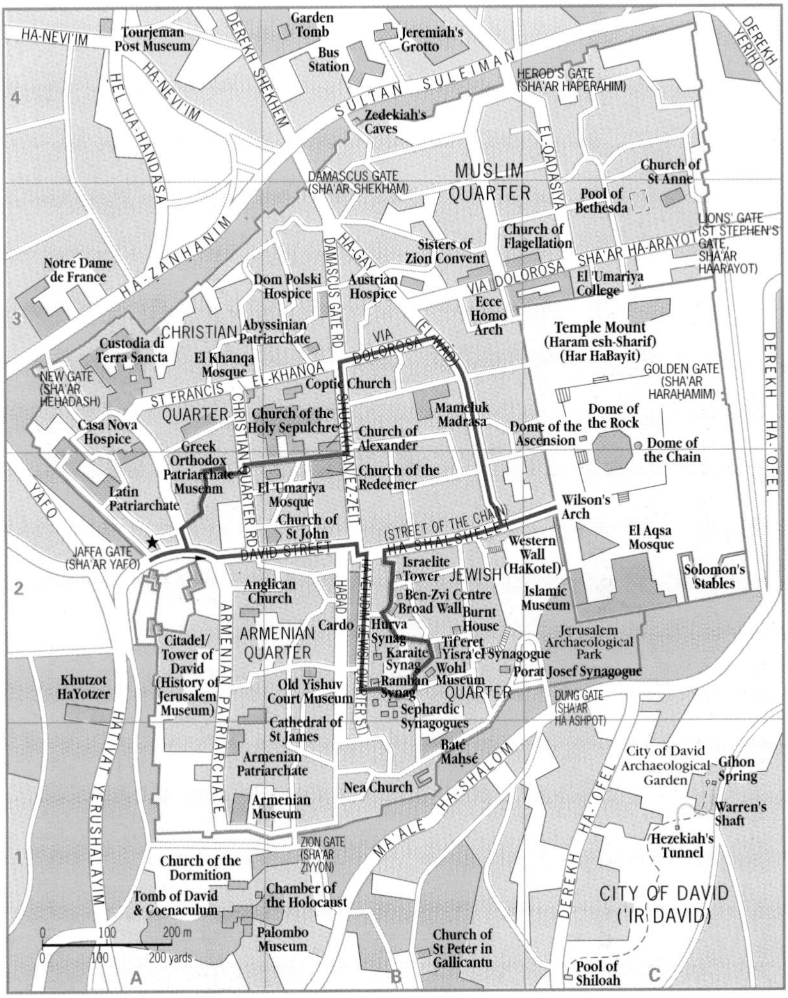

New Gate (possible exit here). The path then narrows. Suddenly, ahead, the golden **Dome of the Rock** (see page 72–73) rises spectacularly above the gray roofs. The path then enters the chambers over the fortified **Damascus Gate**, built in the 16th century. Below, the streets throng with Arab crowds and a wonderful view sweeps over the Old City. Descend from this section of the walkway at Lion's Gate.

Jaffa Gate to Dung Gate The footway, reached by metal steps beside the Citadel, goes between high walls. There are views into the **Armenian quarter**, where no housing abuts the wall. At the **southwest tower**, the view extends over stony Judaean hills to the south. Turning here, the wall passes a few dwellings and lush gardens belonging to the Armenian Patriarchate. The Dome of the Rock comes into view. The walk now crosses the splendid 16th-century **Zion Gate** and reaches the **Jewish quarter**. Narrow steps go down to a wider path looking onto a little Old City **archeological park**. Here, the ramparts run along the side of a hill looking over a poor Arab district to barren hills beyond. There is a good view of Temple Mount and the Mount of Olives. The path now descends to the road.

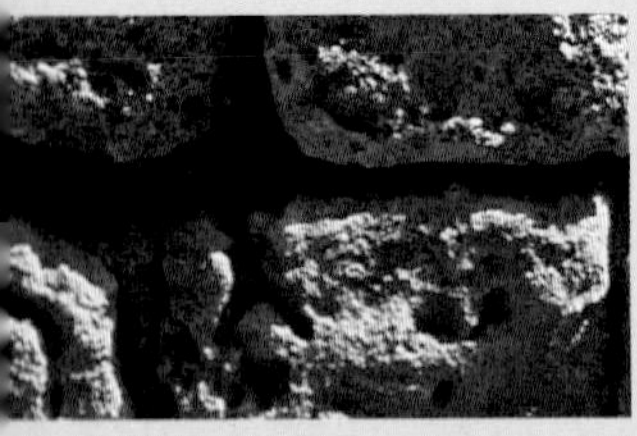

The gateways that enter the Old City tell as much of Jerusalem's story as the walls themselves. From the simple New Gate to the imposing fortifications of Zion Gate, from the sealed and silent Golden Gate to the thronging Jaffa or Damascus Gate, the city's complex character is reflected in its handsome, historic entrances.

HOLE IN THE WALL
The hole that was knocked through the fortifications beside the Jaffa Gate was made by the Ottomans in 1898 to allow Kaiser Wilhelm II to drive through without having to leave his carriage. Contrast the Kaiser with the more respectful General Allenby, who, when taking the city for the British, dismounted from his horse and came through on foot, pausing at the gate to say, "We return to you."

Jaffa Gate Forming the main entrance to the Old City from West Jerusalem, this magnificently fortified gateway (built in 1588) is the best known to visitors, and the most used by residents. Unfortunately, the Ottomans knocked a road through the fortifications beside the gate (see side panel). The original pedestrian entrance turns a couple of sharp corners within the gateway to deter attackers. Jaffa is one of the oldest of the city gates, protected by the might of Herod's Citadel (or David's Tower), rising beside it. The gate opens directly onto David Street, which leads to the Street of the Chain—the Old City's colorful main thoroughfare—marking the boundary between the Armenian and Christian quarters.

Zion Gate This superb fortification of 1540 marks the line between the Armenian and Jewish quarters. The road passing through it forms the main access to West Jerusalem on the south side of the city walls, and is much used by residents of the Jewish quarter. It was through this gate that the quarter's residents were driven out of the city by the Jordanians in 1948. The gateway was then sealed, and remained so until 1967, when the Jews returned.

Dung Gate This historic gateway, built in 1540 on the site of an older gateway mentioned in the Bible, is the closest to the Western Wall. It originally gave access to the Temple. It stands between the Jewish quarter and an Arab district outside the walls, and is therefore subject to security measures, though it is much used by buses, whose terminal is just inside the gate.

Golden Gate Blocked up by the Muslims in 1530 to protect their holy sites, this gateway gives access to the Temple Mount from the Mount of Olives and the Kidron Valley. Christians say that this is the gateway through which Jesus rode on a donkey on Palm Sunday. Some Jews assert that a messiah will one day enter the city through this gate, or that it will be reopened on Judgement Day. Both groups attach much significance to an enigmatic passage in Ezekiel, Chapter 44, which says that the gate will be shut because God has passed through it, and will, in the future, only be used by the prince.

The Jaffa Gate, most splendid of the entrances into the Old City

Lions' or **St. Stephen's, Gate** The only gateway on the eastern wall (apart from the Golden Gate), this guards the main route from the Old City to the Mount of Olives and forms the principal connection between the Muslim quarter and the Arab neighborhoods to the east and southeast. The gate was built in 1538 on the site of a Roman gateway, and various Christian legends attach to it. One of these says that St. Stephen was led through this gate to be stoned to death; however, this story, and the name St. Stephen's Gate, were originally attached to the Damascus Gate. Another story claims that the Virgin Mary was both born and buried beside it. The stone lions on the walls to either side of the entrance have given the gate its other name.

DIVINE WRITING
Pious Orthodox Jews claim to believe that a *mezuzah* (doorpost scroll) hidden within the Jaffa Gate masonry was written by God himself.

Herod's Gate or **Gate of Flowers** Nothing at all to do with either Herod or flowers, this 16th-century gate opens from the Muslim quarter into the heart of East Jerusalem.

Damascus or **Shechem, Gate** Superbly fortified, this turreted main entrance to the Old City from East Jerusalem, is exotic and fascinating. On the plaza in front, vendors hawk their wares to a bustling Arab crowd. Constructed by Suleiman the Magnificent in 1538, the gateway separates the Muslim and Christian quarters. The Crusader-period and Roman remains upon which it stands are still visible and inside the gateway are impressive remains of the **Roman plaza**. The entrance to **Zedekiah's Cave**, biblical quarries, is beneath the wall east of Damascus Gate.

New Gate Correctly named, this simple opening into the Christian quarter at the northwestern corner of the ramparts was constructed in 1887, closed during the Jordanian occupation and reopened in 1967.

Herod's Gate

The Lions' Gate

The small plot of land that makes up the Old City of Jerusalem is packed with 20,000 residents of varied faiths and backgrounds. As is normal in the Middle and Near East, different commuities live in different areas. Although there are no physical barriers between the Old City's four quarters (and at times their borders do change), in atmosphere and culture the dividing lines between them could hardly be plainer.

ARMENIAN MEMORIES
The Armenian Museum, on Armenian Patriarchate Street (*Open* Mon–Sat, 10–5. *Admission: inexpensive*) contains displays of Armenian art and artifacts, and documents relating to the destruction of the Armenian people. April 24 is the Armenians' Remembrance Day, in honor of the 1.5 million Armenians killed by the Turks during their campaign of genocide, which was carried out between 1894 and 1920.

The Christian quarter The calm, quiet streets and lanes of the northwestern sector are home to thousands of Arab and European Christians. The area contains many hospices and the large, grandiose buildings of the offices, churches and patriarchates of several sects, clustered around the Holy Sepulchre.

The Armenian quarter Although Armenians are Christians, they have their own separate quarter in the southwestern corner of the Old City. The atmosphere is extremely tranquil, with an almost secretive air, the area's institutions and dwellings concealed behind high walls. Although the place seems virtually uninhabited, thousands of Armenians live here, over 1,000 of them in a single, converted hostel. Apart from the Zion Gate, which it shares with the Jewish quarter, the Armenian district has no city gate of its own. On the city walls as they pass around the Armenian quarter, maps and notices recall massacres of the Armenians at the hands of the Turks in the 25 years leading up to 1920, giving details of locations, dates and the number of dead. Armenians feel bitter that the world has taken little interest in these events.

The Jewish quarter The Jewish quarter, lying south of the Street of the Chain, is the smallest and most attractive of the city's districts, and it has a distinctive bustling yet quiet atmosphere. There are even signs requesting

An intimate moment in the Jewish quarter

visitors not to make too much noise. It is clean and new-looking, partly because the entire district had to be rebuilt from scratch after 1967. During their occupation of the Old City (1948–67), the Jordanians destroyed this neighborhood and attempted to erase all traces of Jewishness. Most of the quarter's ancient buildings were reduced to rubble, though often the ground floors escaped. Some of the ruins have since been beautifully restored. Behavior in these streets is decorous and peaceful. Although densely populated, the narrow winding lanes often seem deserted. The quarter's center is the pleasant Hurva Square plaza.

The Muslim quarter By far the largest and the most colorful district of the Old City, the Muslim area embraces the north and center of the walled city. It is a confusing and densely populated warren of squalid lanes and bustling souks (markets), where Westerners encounter a vibrant culture very different from their own. Arab crowds, in flowing traditional dress throng the narrow streets and Oriental music fills the air.

WHAT'S IN A NAME?
The name Jerusalem comes from the Hebrew biblical name of the city, Yerushalayim. It is sometimes mistakenly said that the name means City of Peace (*shalayim* resembling *shalom*, peace). It probably derives from Salem, the name of the settlement that was here before the Israelites arrived. David called his fortress Zion, and this became an alternative poetic name for the city. The Romans called it Aelia Capitolina. Islamic conquerors turned this into Ilya. Muslim Jerusalem became Al-Quds or El Kuds (the Holy). Jews continued to call the city Yerushalayim (the name is used in the Torah over 700 times), and this again became the official name of the city in 1948.

Muslim-quarter souk/ market (left). Quiet lanes thread the Jewish quarter (below)

Walk

Within the walls, Jerusalem assails the mind with a dizzying blend of sights, sounds and historic sites. Along busy lanes, stores hawk anything from souvenirs to spices, sandals to silver. East and West mingle freely, natives and tourists together, imams, rabbis and priests, until you are no longer sure which is which. *Allow a full day.*

Start at the **Jaffa Gate▶▶▶** (see page 52), the superb fortified entrance to the Old City (tourist office here). Beside it is Herod's vast Citadel, or the **Tower of David▶▶▶** (see page 66). Go straight ahead on David Street, a narrow hectic Arab and Jewish souk (market). At the junction, turn right (Jewish Quarter Street) for the **Cardo▶▶** (see page 58), the Byzantine city's main street. At the end, turn left (Beit El Street) to enter the Jewish quarter's quiet lanes. Pass the **Four Sephardic Synagogues▶▶** (see page 63) and come to **Hurva Square▶** (see page 68). Around it are many things worth seeing – the **Ramban▶**, **Hurva** (see page 68) and **Karaite▶** synagogues and the **Wohl Archeological Museum▶▶** (see page 80).

Across the square, take Tifret Yisrael Street and Plugat HaKotel Street, following the city limits of 2,000 years ago. Pass the **Broad Wall▶** (see page 57), remnant of former ramparts. Turn right along the bustling, covered Street of the Chain. At the end, walk to the entrance of **Temple Mount▶▶▶** (see page 72). If it is before 3pm, go in and visit the **Dome of the Rock▶▶▶** and **Al-Aqsa Mosque▶▶▶** (for both see page 72). A few paces back along the Street of the Chain, steps on the left twist down to the tunnel, which leads to the **Western Wall▶▶▶** (see page 78).

Return via the tunnel to El-Wad Street. At a turning on the left, join the **Via Dolorosa▶▶▶** (see page 76), which climbs in steps back into the souk district, passing the Stations of the Cross emblazoned on the walls in Roman numerals. These lead to the **Holy Sepulchre▶▶▶** (see page 60). From here, continue up Souk ed-Dabbagha, cross into St George Street, and return to the Jaffa Gate.

The Old City

(for map see page 51)

Through the Jaffa Gate, the main entrance to the Old City

Strolling in the souk (market)

The Old City

▶ Batei Mahaseh (Shelter Houses) Square *51B1*

Entered through a gate, this attractive little plaza was a main square of the Jewish quarter in the 19th century. It is enclosed on one side by the Rothschilds' almshouse-like dwellings, known as Batei Mahaseh, which provided shelter and temporary accommodations for newly arrived Jews from Europe. A memorial reminds visitors that it was in this square that the Jews of Jerusalem were gathered with their possessions in 1948, when the Jordanians captured the city. The square was largely destroyed. Beside the Rothschild building, steps lead down, through a door, to the ruined subterranean apse of the Nea Church, built in AD543. Once this was one of the most splendid and best-known churches in Christendom.

▶ Broad Wall *51B2*

Plugat HaKotel Street

Just off the Cardo, this is a length of massive, ancient stonework exposed to view. It was constructed in about 800BC to protect Jerusalem from a Syrian attack (referred to in Isaiah 22:10–11, Nehemiah 3:8 and 12:38) thus becoming part of the city walls. In total the Broad Wall was 72 yards (66m) long (50 yards/46m are now visible) and a full 23ft (7m) thick. The biblical account describes dwellings having to be demolished to make way for the wall, which does run across the ruins of ancient houses.

▶ Burnt House (or Kathros' House) *51B2*

2 Tiferet Israel Street (tel: 02-6287211)

Open: daily 9–5 excluding Shabbat. Admission: inexpensive

This is the basement of a grand private dwelling of the 1st century AD, burned down during the Roman destruction of Jerusalem. Inscriptions inside suggest it was the home of Kathros, a high priest mentioned in the Talmud. An audiovisual on the house and its historical background is shown in the midst of the excavations every 30 minutes.

EXILE'S LAMENT

"By the waters of Babylon
we sat down and wept
When we remembered
thee, O Zion...
If I forget thee,
O Jerusalem, let my right
hand forget her cunning!
If I do not remember thee,
let my tongue cleave to the
roof of my mouth;
yea if I prefer not
Jerusalem in my mouth."
—from "The Babylonian
Exile" (Psalm 137)

Discover Roman Jerusalem in the Burnt House

Souvenirs galore in the Cardo district

OPENING TIMES
Israel shuts down for Shabbat—the Jewish Sabbath, which lasts from Friday sunset to Saturday sunset. Most of the city's sights, museums, shops and attractions are open at the following times:
Sunday to Thursday: 8.30 or 9am to 5.30 or 6pm.
Friday: early closing, usually 1pm.
Saturday: closed all day.
Exceptions are shown in the text for each entry.

JORDANIAN OCCUPATION
On the Cardo, the One Last Day Museum records details of the events and consequences of May 28, 1948, the day when the Jewish quarter fell into the hands of the Jordanians.

►► The Cardo *51B2*

Off the Street of the Chain, and beside Jewish Quarter Street, can be seen one of the most remarkable archeological accomplishments in Jerusalem, the uncovered 218-yard (200m) length of the city's Roman and Byzantine main street. Much of it lies about 19.5ft (6m) below present-day ground level. Steps lead down to the Byzantine paving, with information panels. Take a look at the 6th-century mosaic **Madaba Map**, taken from a church in Jordan, which shows the street plan of Jerusalem at that time. From it, much can be learned about the Cardo. A fine arcaded avenue lined with 16.5ft (5m) high columns (supporting the roof), the original thoroughfare was more than 22 yards (20m) wide and handsomely paved. The Crusaders tried to revive the Cardo, restored part of it and lined it with vaulted **traders' and craftsmen's shops**. Almost as impressive is the modern attempt, partially successful, to revive the Crusader section of the street by turning it into an arty, stylish shopping area.

A new city After the crushing of the First Jewish Revolt in AD70, most of Jerusalem was destroyed by the Romans, the population driven out and their houses demolished. With the defeat of the Second Jewish Revolt, in AD135, old Jerusalem was razed and the Romans began constructing a completely new city on the site—Aelia Capitolina. The street plan of today originates from that new Roman city.

The main street The main street of Aelia Capitolina was Cardo Maximus. It ran due south from today's Damascus Gate, along the course of what is now Souk Khan ez-Zeit, as far as David Street. After Emperor Constantine legalized Christianity in AD313, churches sprang up and Christians flocked into the town. It was the start of the Byzantine period. The Holy Sepulchre was built and the town grew and flourished. In the 6th century, the Cardo, its lively central promenade, was extended southwards along what is now Jewish Quarter Street. It is that section of the Cardo that can be seen today.

► Cathedral of St. James *51A2*

St James Street
Open: for services only (around 3pm daily)
Part of a complex of ecclesiastical and theological buildings at the heart of the Armenian quarter, this 12th-century Crusader-era cathedral has an elaborate interior, heavy with ornament. Note especially the carvings and

painted tiles. It honors both the disciple James, stoned to death, whose body is beneath the altar, and the beheaded James the Apostle, whose head is in a side chapel.

▶ Church of the Holy Sepulchre

See pages 60–62.

▶ Church of the Redeemer *51B2*

Muristan Road
Closed Sun, Mon pm
This handsome Lutheran church, just outside the Church of the Holy Sepulchre, is all in bare pale stone and almost entirely without adornment, inside or out. There is an excellent view from the top of the tall tower. The ground on which it stands was presented as a gift to Charlemagne by Caliph Haroun el-Rashid. It remained in the hands of Western religious orders until 1868, when Crown Prince Frederic Wilhelm of Prussia made an official visit to Jerusalem. The Ottomans, with debatable legality, gave him this land and he ordered the building of this church, which was consecrated in 1898.

▶ Church of St. Anne *51C3*

Via Dolorosa
Near Lions' Gate, inside a courtyard, this Crusader-era church, with its shallow dome and triangular apse, is striking for its stark dignity. It is said to stand on the site of the home of the Virgin Mary's parents, St. Anne and St. Joachim. A chapel beneath purports to be Mary's birthplace. The adjacent **Pool of Bethesda** is described in the Gospels (see side panel).

▶ Church of St. John *51B2*

Muristan Road
An 11th-century Greek Orthodox church standing on 5th-century Byzantine ruins (which now form the crypt), this intriguing old building incorporates some Roman masonry in the facade.

CURING ON THE SABBATH
In Roman times the Pool of Bethesda was believed to have restorative powers. Here, according to the Gospels (John 5:1–18), Jesus healed a man on the Sabbath simply by saying "Take up thy bed and walk." For this, he incurred the wrath of "the Jews," as the Gospel writer puts it (John often uses this term, creating an impression that only the villains of his tale were Jews, yet Jesus and the sick man were also Jews). The Gospel appears to suggest that "the Jews" objected to Jesus healing on the Sabbath. In fact, Jewish law permits medical treatment on the Sabbath. It does not, however, permit carrying, considered a serious breach in those days. The objection was that Jesus had told the man to carry his bed.

Sphinx-shaped handle (above) and palm-shaded cloister (left) in the Church of the Redeemer

DIFFERENCES OF OPINION
The Church of the Holy Sepulchre and its relics are officially recognized by the Catholic and Orthodox churches. The Protestant churches do not all acknowledge the veracity of the sites, some preferring the Garden Tomb, north of the city walls in East Jerusalem. Nonconformist churches take the same view as the early Christians, that revering such sites is a departure from Christ's teaching and tantamount to paganism.

ONE MAN'S VIEW
"When one stands where the Savior was crucified, he finds it all he can do to keep it strictly before his mind that Christ was not crucified in a Catholic Church. He must remind himself that the great event transpired in the open air, and not in a gloomy candle-lighted cell, upstairs, all bejewelled and bespangled with flashy ornamentation, in execrable taste."
—Mark Twain, on the Church of the Holy Sepulchre, in *The Innocents Abroad* (1869)

Focus of Christian devotion, the Holy Sepulchre Church is believed to contain Christ's tomb (right and below)

►►► Church of the Holy Sepulchre 51B3

Souk ed-Dabagha and Christian Quarter Road
Open: summer, daily 5am–8pm; winter, daily 4am–7pm
This striking edifice, an Old City landmark, the larger of its two domes topped by a gilded cross, is physically and spiritually the heart of the Christian quarter. It has been revered and fought over for centuries. The church is approached across a paved courtyard, and entry is through a large arched doorway trimmed by a narrow façade of pale Jerusalem stone. This complex of shrines, tombs, relics and churches is all contained under a single roof, and there is even an Ethiopian monastery on the roof. According to the mother of Constantine, the 4th-century Empress Helena, Christ was crucified, laid in his tomb, and resurrected here.

Within the building—main sights To follow the last of the Stations of the Cross marking Jesus's route to his Crucifixion (see pages 76–7), you can, immediately upon entering the dark, labyrinthine interior, turn right onto a short staircase. This leads up 16.5ft (5m) to the top of a rock reputed to be the summit of Golgotha (Calvary). Here you will find the highly ornate chapels, decorated with mosaics, dedicated to the **Nailing to the Cross** (Station X, at the door—*Jesus Stripped;* Station XI, at the altar—*Jesus Nailed to the Cross*) and the **Crucifixion** (Station XII—*The Cross Is Raised and Jesus Dies*). In the latter is a lifesize model of Christ and (behind glass) a slab of rock that is claimed to be the very one on which the cross stood. Between the two chapels is a statue of the Virgin Mary (Station XIII—*Jesus Removed from the Cross*).

Descend the stairs from the second chapel to the **Stone of Unction**, a red slab said to mark the spot where Jesus's body was anointed prior to entombment. Behind this stone (under Golgotha) is the atmospheric **Chapel of Adam**. This chapel houses a skull found during 12th-century excavations and, rather unscientifically, immediately declared to be the skull of Adam. Tombs of two Crusader kings that used to lie here were subsequently destroyed by Greek monks.

To the left of the Stone of Unction, you enter the extravagantly ornate **Rotunda**, probably the only part of the present church resembling Empress Helena's original. At the center is the **Holy Sepulchre** (Station XIV—*Jesus Is Entombed and Returns to Life*). Enter the low doorway into the narrow marble-clad burial chamber, along the side of a marble slab, the place where the body of Jesus is claimed to have lain. Also within the Rotunda, the **Jacobite Chapel** has its own bare and unclad rock-cut tomb. This tomb is said to be that of Joseph of Arimathaea. North and east of the Rotunda are chapels dedicated to events—some biblical, others entirely legendary—associated with the death and resurrection of Christ, including the **Prison of Christ**.

Pull of emotions Reactions to this astonishing church vary across the entire spectrum of human emotion. Awe and reverence it certainly does inspire in the most pious. You may even see pilgrims entering on their knees or weeping in their fervor. For others, there is disappointment and disbelief, even despair. Some have come with unreasonable expectations. This is, after all, just a building, standing on ordinary ground. Sometimes, though, the expectation that has been dashed is simply that this would be a splendid edifice, worthy of its sanctity, and that the sites within it would at least seem credible. Instead visitors find a chaotic, confusing structure containing a jumble of implausible holy places and relics. People may be shocked by the uncouth, unseemly behavior of the custodian monks, of a variety of sects, permanently in dispute with one another. To some visitors, and to the dismay of others, the church inspires overt ridicule and disrespect. In addition, there are plenty of tourists who wander in aimlessly without respecting its deserved sanctity.

History Empress Helena, mother of Emperor Constantine, ordered the building of the original church in AD326. It was completed in 335, but destroyed by the Persians in 614. When Emperor Heraclius took Jerusalem again for the

BUILDING REPAIRS
The ownership of the Church of the Holy Sepulchre is divided among six Christian denominations, each with responsibility for its own shrines and areas of the building. They are the Roman Catholics, the Greek Orthodox, and the Armenian, Syrian, Coptic and Abyssinian churches. Over the years disputes between the factions were so fierce that maintenance of the building could not be carried out. After discussions that lasted from 1927 to 1959, the factions finally agreed to have some building work done at the church. This remains incomplete owing to further disagreements.

Sacristy lamp, lit as a sign of the presence of the living Christ

Faithful pilgrim

A VISITOR WITH FAITH
"Tradition could not err in the identity of so famous a spot, and the smallest scepticism would deprive it of all its powerful charm."—John Carne, on the Church of the Holy Sepulchre, in *Letters from the East* (1830)

Detail of two Crusader doorways at the entrance to the Church of the Holy Sepulchre

Byzantines about 15 years later, the church was rebuilt. The Persians returned Christ's Crucifix, which they had removed. However, in 1009, Caliph el-Hakim demolished the whole church and the Crucifix. In 1048, another smaller church was built on the site by the Byzantine emperor Constantine IX. The Crusaders enlarged the church in 1149. After an earthquake in 1927, discussions began between the part-owners of the church about renovations. These didn't start until 1959 and have continued intermittently ever since.

Authenticity Most of the sites associated with Christ's early years and ministry are legendary and mythical. But the hill on which he was executed was, and remained, visible for all to see. In AD70 Jerusalem was destroyed, but, in AD135, when Hadrian built Aelia Capitolina upon its ruins the place of the Crucifixion was so well known that the emperor erected a temple to Venus on the site, to discourage Christian worship.

Constantine the Great legalized Christianity in 313, at the instigation of his convert mother, Helena. In 326 she was taken by Jerusalem's Bishop Macarius to Golgotha. Hadrian's shrine to Venus still stood here, outside the city walls and on the site of a former quarry, exactly as described in the Gospels. In the base of the hill were caverns dug out of rock, one of which Helena declared was the sepulchre of Jesus. In fact, we know from the Gospels that the tomb in which Jesus lay was that of Joseph, "a rich man of Arimathaea" (Matthew 27:57) and that it was a new one, set in a garden (John 19:41). As a rich and pious man, Joseph is not likely to have made his tomb beside a place of public execution. The preferred burial places were on the Mount of Olives, or a little north of the city. However, his tomb was also described as "hewn out of the rock" (Matthew 27:60 and Mark 15:46) and "nigh at hand" (John 19:42).

Nearby, Helena was shown some old wooden crucifixes in an abandoned cistern. Having selected one of these as the cross upon which Christ had died, she ordered it erected on the top of Golgotha and a church built over the whole site. In the construction, much of the hill was removed. Other holy sites in the church, such as the Stone of Unction and the place where Adam's skull is buried, have no biblical or historical foundation.

Four beautiful little synagogues, the city's center of Sephardi worship since the 16th century

▶▶▶ Citadel 51A2

See Tower of David, pages 66–67.

▶▶▶ Dome of the Rock and Al-Aqsa Mosque 51C3

See Temple Mount, pages 72–73.

▶▶ Four Sephardic Synagogues 51B2

Off Beit El Street
Open: Sun–Mon and Wed–Thu 9.30–4, Tue and Fri 9.30–12.30. Admission: inexpensive

At the end of a little alley in the heart of the Jewish quarter, these four small connecting synagogues are gems. They are delightfully set together within a courtyard enclosed behind a beautifully carved door and decorated archway. With the closing of the Ramban Synagogue in 1588, the Sephardim made their center here for 300 years.

The oldest of the four synagogues is the Kahal Kadosh Talmud Torah, which became the Eliahu HaNavi Synagogue in 1588—supposedly, according to an appealing legend, because Elijah (Eliahu) appeared during a High Holy Days service to make up a *minyan* (10 men, the minimum worshipers required for a service). Ever since, a chair has been reserved for his next appearance in a room at the back!

The age of the Kahal Kadosh Gadol, or Rabbi Yohanan ben Zakkai Synagogue, is undetermined but it certainly dates to before 1615, and could be much earlier. Indeed, this may be the oldest of the four. The Middle Synagogue, opened about 1750, was previously the site of a women's courtyard attached to the Yohanan ben Zakkai. The Istambuli Synagogue, of 1764, was erected by refugees from Turkey.

During the 1948 War of Independence, 800 Jewish residents of the Old City hid here for 14 days. Taken by the Jordanians, the synagogues were partially destroyed and looted and remained derelict until the Six Day War of 1967. After the recapture of the area by Israel, these four historic buildings were painstakingly reconstructed and were rededicated in 1972. Since then, the synagogues have been in regular use by residents of the Old City, though no longer just by Sephardi Jews.

CITY OF SYNAGOGUES

During and after the Jordanian capture of the Jewish quarter in May 1948, a total of 58 synagogues were destroyed or badly damaged – almost the whole number of synagogues in the city at the time. Although many of the ruins have been preserved or partly restored since 1967, few have been as completely reconstructed as the four Sephardic synagogues. However, there are now 450 synagogues in Jerusalem, most of them outside the Old City walls.

The Jews of modern Israel have come from 80 countries. But the population is mainly divided into two major groups: the Ashkenazim, whose background is in Christian Northern Europe, and the Sephardim, whose culture evolved in the Islamic Mediterranean. Other Israelis include the Mizrahim of Eastern origin, the Ethiopians, the Cochin Jews of India and others.

THE LANGUAGE OF THE JEWS
A century ago almost no one spoke Hebrew. Yiddish, based on medieval German mixed with Hebrew, was the everyday language of Ashkenazi Jews. Hitler's "Final Solution" decimated the Yiddish-speaking world —its culture, its people and their language. Those who fled to America and the British Commonwealth became fluent in English, which now stands alongside Hebrew as a new language for the Jews. Many Sephardi Jews, especially the elderly, speak Ladino, a mix of old Spanish, Arabic and Hebrew created in the Middle Ages.

Skull caps (top)
Hasidic sidelocks (below)
Young Crusaders (right)

The cross and the swastika Modern Israel's Ashkenazim did not all come here from Eastern Europe—though their parents or grandparents probably did. They probably were born in Israel, England or America. Their culture absorbed violent antisemitism, as well as the Enlightenment, the French Revolution, the rise of secularism and socialism—and Zionism.

Ashkenaz is a biblical place name that came to mean Germany. As far back as Roman times, Jews settled along the Rhine Valley and from there spread across Germany. The Crusades forced them east into Poland and Russia. For centuries, Eastern Europe was the focal point of Jewish culture and religion. In Russia, there were thousands of *shtetls*—Jewish towns and villages—within the Pale of Settlement (the permitted area of Jewish settlement under the Tsars). Millions of people lived in the Jewish ghettos of the larger cities. Russian pogroms in the 1880s caused an exodus to Palestine, the United States and the British Commonwealth. The rise of the Nazis in the 1930s caused another rush to escape. Six million or more of the Ashkenazim who remained behind died in the Holocaust. A culture and a language died with them, and Eastern Europe was almost entirely emptied of Jews.

Under the crescent Some visitors assume that Sephardim are Arabs, something to which the Sephardim would not take kindly. Most are refugees from Arab countries. The Sephardim, after a long medieval Golden Age

during the Arab occupation of Spain, remained only slightly affected by Europe's intellectual developments, until they arrived in Israel in the late 15th century. A more cohesive, traditional society, the Sephardim brought to Israel a resistance to secularism, allied to a more easy-going and accepting approach to Jewish traditions. They have also given Israel its best food. They remain largely on the lower rungs of society, but that is changing.

Sefarad means Spain, a place where Jews lived since biblical times, and where the Sephardi culture evolved during 680 years of Muslim domination (711–1391). When Christians completed the conquest of Spain, in 1492, all Jews were forced to renounce their religion or face expulsion. Most Jews followed the Muslims to North Africa and to other areas of the Mediterranean, such as Turkey, Greece, the Balkans and Palestine. Under Islam, Jews suffered discrimination but rarely outright persecution. They lived in their own districts, with the official status of *dhimmis* (second-class citizens). Persecution increased in the 20th century, however, and when the State of Israel was created, most were forced from their homes.

Jews with other backgrounds Most other Israelis fall into one of two conspicuous groups, both of which arrived *en masse* in big rescue operations. Mizrahim (though they are also called Sephardim) come from Muslim countries, further to the east, often from the Yemen. They have brought ancient tradition, ethnic color and superb oriental cuisine. The black Jews of Ethiopia (no longer called "Falashas," or strangers, a hated name in Ethiopia) add yet another dimension to Israel's extraordinary cultural and ethnic diversity.

Children of Israel Half the population of Israel was born in the country, and one-third of its children now have mixed Ashkenazi/Sephardi parentage. The effect has been dramatic in creating a new culture. It is also remarkable how alike Ashkenazi and Sephardi children have become in appearance, mannerisms and outlook after growing up in the sunshine of Israel. Without the pressures of being a minority population, and after going through school in Hebrew and doing army service together, they emerge as young adults, neither Ashkenazi nor Sephardi, but truly Israeli.

ASHKENAZIM DOMINANT
Modern Israel was created by Ashkenazim. They dominate government and institutions in Israel, and have been credited with giving the country its idealism, secularism, democracy and know-how, but also its red tape and bureaucracy. However, their role has given way to the increasing influence and numbers of the Sephardim—Jews of the Mediterranean, whose cultural roots pass through the Islamic world.

WORLD POPULATIONS
In 1933, there were 16.5 million Jews in the world, 90 percent of them in Eastern Europe. Of today's 15 million Jews, only 2 million now live in Europe, over 5 million live in Israel and 6 million in the US.

Happier here than in Ethiopia

BRITISH RULE IN PALESTINE
In December 1917, an emotional General Allenby entered Jaffa Gate on foot and walked to the eastern steps of the Citadel (today's main entrance). Standing on the steps he read his Proclamation to the People of Jerusalem formally announcing the start of British rule in Palestine.

The Tower of David bears the name of Jerusalem's founder

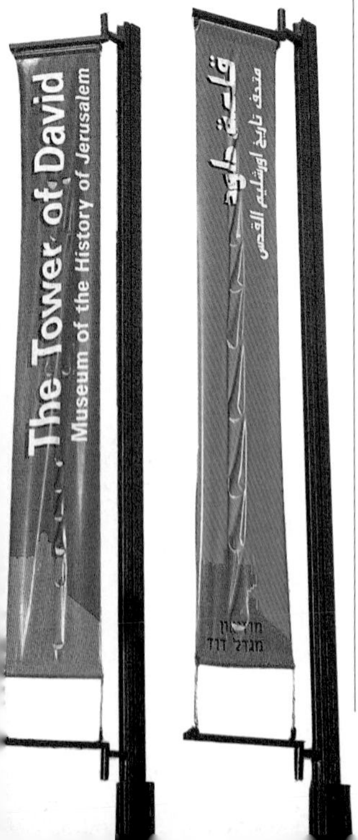

▶▶▶ History of Jerusalem Museum – Tower of David *51A2*

Beside Jaffa Gate (tel: 02-626 5310; www.towerofdavid.org.il)
Open: see panel opposite. Admission: expensive
The History of Jerusalem Museum is housed in the city's ancient Citadel. Four possible quick itineraries through the museum are indicated at the entrance: the Exhibit Route (2 hours), the Excavation Route (1.5 hours), the Observation Route (1 hour) and the Short Route (40 minutes). The entrance charge for the museum includes a 1.5-hour guided tour (in English) each morning at 11am. The museum and tour provide a uniquely informative, entertaining and accessible overview of Jerusalem and its history.

Herod's Citadel One of the most imposing and evocative landmarks of the Old City is the high, slender Tower of David, rising from within the massive defenses of the superb medieval fortress known as the Citadel. This stands alongside the powerful stonework of Jaffa Gate. Despite the name, nothing but myth connects this magnificent structure with King David, the city's founder. The Citadel, standing on the Old City's highest point, was in fact constructed much later, by King Herod in the 1st century BC. Archeological exploration points to the presence of major fortified structures here as early as the First Temple period (950–538BC). Herod's fortress was even more imposing than today's mainly medieval building. His fortress had three monumental square towers, one more than 131ft (40m) high, named after his brother, his close friend and his wife—Phasael, Hippicus and Miriam.

Through the centuries After crushing the Second Jewish Revolt (AD132–135), the Romans ordered Jerusalem be razed to the ground. Only the Citadel and its tallest tower, Phasael's (the bulky square tower, beside Jaffa Gate), were left standing. Roman troops were stationed inside the fort. In later centuries it served as a garrison for Arabs (who built a smaller—now ruined—fortress within the Citadel), Crusaders, Mamelukes and Ottomans. It was the ferocious Mamelukes who, in 1310, restored the Citadel and rebuilt the walls that stand today. Under the Ottomans it was similarly reconstructed in 1610, and it was they who erected a mosque within the fortress. This slender stone minaret became known romantically to many a 19th-century visitor as the Tower of David.

In 1917, under British rule, the fortress retained a nominal military function. For the most part, it has been transformed into a cultural and historical site, with performances and exhibitions. It has maintained this meaningful use.

On the roof From the flat roof of the Phasael Tower, restored in 1987, there is an impressive panorama over the Old City. The dominant position of Temple Mount, a huge lofty plateau elevated above the town's warren of crowded alleys and streets, gives a powerful impression of its importance in Temple times. Today, the beautiful blue-walled and gold-crowned Dome of the Rock occupies the site. From the elevated point, the building can be appreciated in all its glory. The Mount of Olives rises magnificently behind. Within the city, a surprising number of buildings have black and white stripes, a Mameluke style. The astonishing number of fine churches testifies to centuries of Christian devotion in Jerusalem.

Inside the museum The Citadel's ancient halls, rooms, cellars and outdoor terraces today house a superb and extensive museum of Jerusalem's history. The structure forms a five-sided enclosure around a large central open-air archeological site. Using films, maps, attention-grabbing pictures, dioramas, holograms, life-size fiberglass statuary, superbly detailed models and numerous other types of displays, as well as thousands of the historic objects found here, the museum leads room by room, age by age, through the long and intricate Jerusalem story, allowing even the most casual visitor to grasp something of its scale and scope. The final stages are presented with genuine film footage and modern artifacts.

TOWER OF DAVID/ HISTORY OF JERUSALEM MUSEUM OPENING HOURS AND EVENTS:
Open: summer, Sun–Thu 9–4, Sat and day before public holidays 9–4; winter, Sun–Thu 10–4, Sat and day before public holidays 10–4. *Closed:* Fridays, Yom Kippur (late Sep or early Oct).
On summer evenings an entertaining *son et lumière* is put on in the Citadel courtyard. Under the stars in the dramatic setting of the fortress, it tells the story of the city and its citadel. Shows in English take place at 9.30pm on Monday and Wednesday, and on Saturday at 10.30pm.

As it was: Stefan Illes's 1872 model of the Old City

MUSEUM OF THE SEAM
This very unusual museum is a record of relations between Jews and Arabs at the "Seam"—the meeting point of East and West Jerusalem—when the city's eastern part was under Arab occupation. The story continues to the present, with Israeli and Palestinian administrations having to co-operate over day-to-day issues. *Beside Mandelbaum Gate.*

▶ Hurva Square *51B2*

This pleasant peaceful plaza lies at the heart of the Old City's Jewish Quarter. At one side is a modern high arch reaching over the attractive Rambian Synagogue, founded 1267 by Raban (Rabbi Nachmanides) himself, and over the ruins of the Hurva Synagogue (under restoration). On the other side stands the attractive **Wohl**

Near them stands a mosque, looking out of place in this quarter. Just off Hurva Square are handsome remnants of other historic synagogues damaged and looted during the occupation. Several streets lead off, including HaKaraim Street, named for the Karaites.

▶ Islamic Art Museum *46B1*

2 Hapalmach Street (tel: 02-661291)
Open: Sun–Thu 10–5, Sat 10–1. Closed Fri.
Admission: moderate
Correctly called the L. A. Mayer Memorial Institute for Islamic Art, this collection of art from the Islamic world includes beautiful metalwork, ceramics, jewelry and carpets, as well as archives and a library.

Relics of Hurva Synagogue's former glory

▶ Israelite Tower 51B2

Plugat HaKotel Street (tel: 02-283448)
Admission: inexpensive
Some 33ft (10m) below street level, this remnant of a tower of the First Temple period was once part of the city walls. Inside is a small museum. Beside it stand remains of another tower, dating from the 2nd century BC.

▶ Jerusalem Archeological Park (and Davidson Center) 47E2

Dung Gate (tel: 02-6277550; www.archpark.org.il)
Open: Sun–Thu 8–5, Fri 8–2. Closed Shabbat and public hols
Admission: moderate. Guided tours in English (must be booked well ahead in peak season. Free audioguide in English. Davidson Center Virtual Reality Reconstruction is only open to tour groups.
Arriving at the Old City via the hectic Dung Gate entrance, a large parklike archeological site on the south side of Temple Mount effectively extends the Western Wall Plaza around to the Southern Wall. Excavations at this site over a period of many years have yielded an extraordinary and impressive array of discoveries.

Entrance to the park lies on the left, inside the Dung Gate. Ask for a map of the site. Immediately upon entering, the **Davidson Center▶▶▶** uses the archeological discoveries as the basis for an imaginative high-tech showcase of life in the Second Temple times and other periods. A film of a pilgrim visiting the Temple is among the effective attractions. The high-tech Virtual Reality Reconstruction (you may be able to join a group for a fee) is similar, but enables a guide to give you a tour around the Temple exterior, though not inside, as no excavation of the Temple itself has been possible.

Continuing farther into the park, you may visit the fascinating underground of a **Byzantine House▶▶** (note that there are narrow passages and steep stairs) before passing through the pressent day city walls to the south side of the Temple Mount. Along the south wall of the Temple platform is the immense **Hulda Stairway▶▶** (now partly reconstructed) that gave direct access to the Temple via the Hulda Gates. Tens of thousands of Jews coming here in Temple times, including Jesus, would have climbed these steps. The steps are uneven widths to ensure, according to the Mishnah, that visitors to the Temple had to approach slowly.

Among other sights are *mikvaot* (ritual paths) used for purification before entering the Temple, and ruins of structures built here both before and after the destruction of the Temple, for instance a palace of the Islamic period.

▶ Old Yishuv Court Museum 51B2

6 Or HaHaim Street
Open: Sun–Thu 9–2. Admission: moderate
Yishuv refers to the Jewish community living in Palestine before the creation of the modern State of Israel. It effectively came to an end with the Jordanian capture and occupation of the city in 1948.

This intimate and eclectic private collection of artifacts, housed in what survives of two former historic synagogues, illustrates Yishuv life just before the Jordanian occupation.

CITY CENTER
In Jewish prayer, the name "Jerusalem" is still synonymous with the Temple, the vast gilded palace of sacrifice and worship that dominated the life of the city for more than 1,000 years (950BC to 70AD). Even though the Temple has been destroyed, it remains the theoretical center of Judaism; at morning sevices in synagogues through the world, sacrifice instructions used in the Temple are read aloud as part of the prayers.

HOLY ROCK AND WAILING WALL
"Until 688AD Jews met yearly, to mourn over and anoint the 'Stone of Foundation,' on which the Holy of Holies once was raised, and which is now covered by the old Arab Dome of the Rock which was erected in 688AD. In later times they were only able to wail at the outer wall of Herod's great temple enclosure, and they have continued to do so down to our own times."
—*Palestine Exploration Fund Lectures*, 1892

"And it came to pass in the four hundred and eightieth year after the children of Israel were come out of the land of Egypt, in the fourth year of Solomon's reign over Israel, in the month Zif ...that he began to build the house of the Lord" (I Kings 6:1). Though the Temple has gone, it remains at the very heart of Judaism.

GOD AS A CLOUD
According to II Chronicles 6:13–14, when Solomon's Temple was complete it was dedicated by placing the Ark in the Holy of Holies. During the ceremony, hundreds of men in white linen played trumpets, cymbals and other instruments. As they did this a cloud filled the building "so that the priests could not stand to minister by reason of the cloud: For the glory of God had filled the house of God."

Holyland Hotel's model of the Second Temple (above)
The building of the Temple (below)

The center of a nation The First Temple was completed in 950BC, the 11th year of his reign, by King Solomon, son of King David, the Israelite ruler who took Jerusalem from the Jebusites and proclaimed it the capital of Israel. In Solomon's Temple was placed the Ark of the Covenant—the gold-encrusted chest containing Moses' Tablets of the Law—and other sacred objects that the Jews had carried with them in their exile. The Temple became the focal point for the Jewish people, and, wherever they lived, adult males were obliged to come to it for three annual festivals: Pesach (Passover), Sukkot (Tabernacles), and Shavuot (Weeks or Pentecost). Destroyed in 586BC by Nebuchadnezzar, it was rebuilt as the Second Temple between 538 and 515BC, being enlarged and aggrandized on several occasions afterwards, especially under King Herod in the decades before his death in 4BC. After the First Jewish Revolt, this Second Temple was reduced to rubble by the Romans in AD70. Jerusalem's most spectacular landmark, the Dome of the Rock, a Muslim holy place, now occupies the site. Part of the Temple Mount outer wall survives as the Western Wall, the holiest place of prayer for Jews.

History and myth Tradition has it that Mount Moriah was the place where Abraham bound Isaac and prepared to sacrifice him (Genesis 22:2–14; Sura 37, Koran), though there is no mention of this event in II Samuel 24:16–25, describing David's purchase of the threshing floor on which the Temple would stand, nor in II Chronicles 3:1, describing the Temple's construction. In 167BC, the Maccabees drove the Syrians out of Israel and had to rededicate the Temple: The festival of Hanukkah commemorates their victory and the miracle of a single day's lamp oil being sufficient to light the Temple menorah (candelabrum) for eight days, as required for the rededication. The Temple is featured several times in the life of Jesus: When he remained for three days in learned discussion with the elders at the age of 12 (Luke 2:46); when he overturned the money changers' tables (Matthew 21:12) and when he predicted the Temple's total destruction (Matthew 24:2). Finally, it was mentioned when the Temple veil was torn in two at the moment of Christ's death (Matthew 27:51).

Lamentation and longing The destruction of both the First and the Second Temple is commemorated on the ninth day of the Hebrew month of Av. By coincidence, the

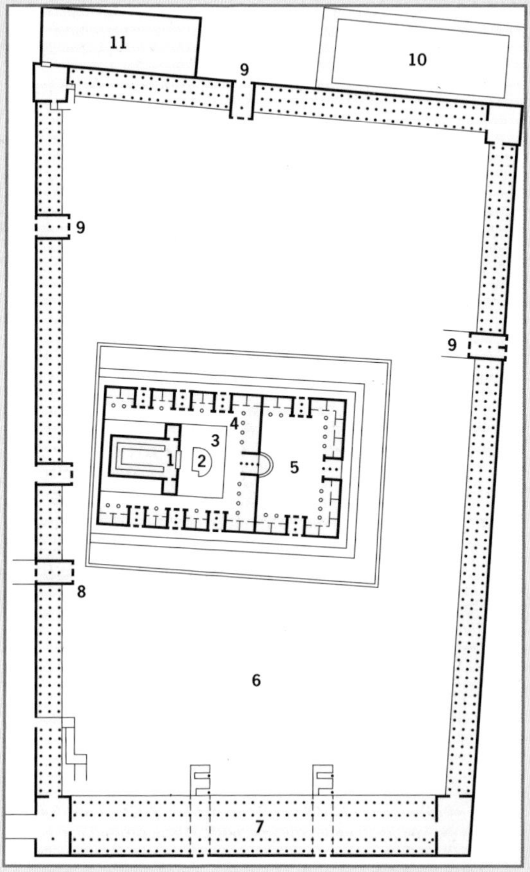

THE SECOND TEMPLE – KEY TO PLAN

1 Temple
2 Altar
3 Court of Priests
4 Court of Israel
5 Court of Women
6 Court of the Gentiles
7 Royal Portico
8 Bridge and gate
9 Gate
10 Pool of Isra' il
11 Antonia

Jews were expelled from Spain on the same day. When the Arabs conquered Jerusalem, they allowed Jews to visit Temple Mount for just one day in the year, to mourn their lost Temple. That day, also, was the ninth of Av (Tisha b'Av in Hebrew). Today it is also a day of fasting, of not wearing leather and for reciting, in a wailing tone, the Book of Lamentations. In later centuries, the Jews were permitted only to come as far as the Western Wall, and only on that day. Thus, the Western Wall became known as the Wailing Wall because of the Jewish practise on that day. This ceremony can still be seen every year, on Tisha b'Av (mid- to late July).

The Third Temple Much of today's synagogue service takes the form of a temporary substitute for Temple practice. At every Orthodox service, prayers are said for the rebuilding of the Temple. But many Jews have doubts about the wisdom of this; if it were rebuilt, Temple practises such as animal sacrifice would have to be resumed. Some say it can only be rebuilt when the Messiah comes. There are those who wish to begin at once. For others, it will be rebuilt when the time is politically right, which is not just yet. Some Israeli parliamentarians have referred to the State of Israel itself as the Third Temple.

All that now remains: the Western Wall below the Al-Aqsa mosque

MUSLIM GATES
Non-Muslims may only enter Temple Mount through Bab el-Maghrebeh (the Moors' Gate) and Bab el-Silsileh (the Chain Gate). Both pass into the enclosure on either side of the Western Wall. Muslims may enter or leave by any of the other gateways. The other Temple Mount gates are (on the western side) Bab el-Masatarak, Bab el-Qatanin, Bab el-Hadid, Bab el-Nazir, Bab el-Ghawanima and (on the northern side) Bab el-Atim, Bab Hitta and Bab el-Asbat.

▶▶▶ Temple Mount (Arabic: Haram esh-Sharif; Hebrew: Har HaBayit) *51C3*

Open: Sat–Thu 8–noon and 1.30–3
Admission: Temple Mount is free, but mosques and museum require a ticket (expensive) from Temple Mount entrance
The star of the Old City is the glorious Dome of the Rock, on Temple Mount. It is just one of several fine Muslim Islamic constructions within the ancient Temple Mount enclosure, which is entered at the end of Street of the Chain (through the Chain Gate; Bab el-Silsileh in Arabic) or on the ramp from Western Wall Plaza (through the Moors' Gate; Bab el-Maghrebeh in Arabic). Inside, the grand enclosure is partially shaded by trees. Ahead rises the exquisite blue-tiled façade and golden dome of the Dome of the Rock. To either side stand arches and minarets and two fountains where Muslims wash before prayers.

Claims to holiness Sura 17 of the Koran states: "Glorified be He Who carried His servant by night from the Inviolable Place of Worship to the Far Distant Place of Worship, the neighborhood whereof We have blessed, that We might show him of Our tokens!" Although Muhammad never visited Jerusalem, Muslims came to believe that Temple Mount was "the far distant Place of Worship" referred to. The legend developed that Muhammad traveled on a winged horse with the Angel Gabriel to the Temple Mount. He then ascended through the seven heavens and met God, before awaking back in Mecca.

Principal sights Mosques and museums are closed to non-Muslims during prayer times (five times daily). Before entering, remove your shoes and leave all bags and cameras with the attendant. The **Al-Aqsa Mosque▶▶▶**, considered by most Muslims to be their third holiest shrine (after Mecca and Medina) was extensively restored in 1948. Jerusalem's main place of Islamic prayer is sumptuous with marble columns, fine carpets, stained-glass windows, and an impressive gilded wooden ceiling. Adjacent is the **Islamic Museum▶** containing a collection of artifacts from several mosques.

The Dome of the Rock▶▶▶ (Arabic: Qubbet el-Sakhra) is an awesomely beautiful, symmetrical, octagonal structure of blue tiles topped by a gleaming dome of gold. The building is reached by broad flights of steps on each side over which are triple arches built by the Crusaders.

Inside, the combination of elegantly simple design, finely carved wood and marble, and intricate decoration is thrilling. The air is evocatively filled with echoing prayer and music and soothing light filtered through stained-glass windows. Exquisite mosaic covers the interior of the dome. The huge black stone beneath the dome,

Gilded magnificence: inside the Dome of the Rock

Burnished bronze and azure blue

the impressive rock for which it is named, has an indentation that Muslims believe was made by Muhammad's flying horse as it leapt to the sky.

Smaller, attractive structures within the enclosure include the **Dome of the Chain▶**, the **Dome of the Ascension▶** and the **Islamic schools▶**. Also inside are the sealed **Golden Gate▶** and the other **gates▶** that lead into the Muslim quarter (see panel opposite).

History and politics Having destroyed the Temple, the Romans erected their own temple on the site. In the 6th century this was replaced by a church. After the Arab conquest in 638, Caliph Omar visited Temple Mount to pray at the black rock. It is said that here Abraham laid his son Isaac for sacrifice. The present Dome of the Rock was built under Omayyad rule in 691. The church was converted into the Al-Aqsa mosque in 715.

Crusaders took Jerusalem in 1000 and made Al-Aqsa into a residence that became the headquarters of the Knights Templar (who took their name from the site). The Templars renamed Al-Aqsa the Temple of Solomon. The Dome of the Rock became known as the Temple of the Lord. The sites were taken by Islam in 1187, and the Mamelukes built new structures there.

Following the 1948 war, Arab states took great interest in Temple Mount, and the Dome of the Rock was restored jointly by Jordan, Egypt and Saudi Arabia. After reconquering Jerusalem in 1967, the Israelis allowed Temple Mount to remain under Islamic administration. Since that time, the legend of Muhammad's night journey has led the Arab world to lay claim not just to Temple Mount, but to the whole city of Jerusalem. This creates yet more friction between the Jewish and Arab communities.

NIGHT RIDE
In real life, Muhammad did not visit Haram esh-Sharif (Temple Mount), and the Koran's reference to his "being carried by night" makes no mention of angels, or flying horses, or of leaping to heaven. The importance of the legend lies in its metaphorical meaning: That Muhammad, as the last of the prophets, with a mission to take the word and laws of God (or Allah) to the entire world, had taken over Judaism and replaced it. Judaism at the time had suffered dispersion and defeat. It was almost logical for Muslims to view the sanctity of the Jewish holy site as subsumed into the newer, conquering sanctity of the Prophet.

Contemplation

Israel's population of 7 million includes more than one million Arabs. Arabic is one of Israel's two official languages. Arabs have full citizenship, send their children to Arabic-speaking state schools and elect Arab members of parliament (who address the Knesset in Arabic).

THE POPULATION OF ISRAEL:
76.55 percent Jewish
16.00 percent Muslim
2.00 percent Christian
1.64 percent Druze
3.81 percent others
(Central Bureau of Statistics: Statistical Abstract of Israel 2005)

Gentile populations The Israelite conquest of Canaan was never total and—despite a biblical injunction—the non-Jews (Gentiles) were not wiped out. Numerous biblical references show that the land of the Jews always had its minority of Gentiles. Big population changes followed each subsequent conquest. It was Roman policy to dilute difficult peoples. After the Jewish Revolts of AD70 and 135, non-Jewish settlers were brought into the area around Jerusalem and the coastal towns. Subsequently, the legalization of Christianity encouraged its followers in the Near East to move to the Holy Land.

New religion, new empire In 630 Muhammad and his followers forcibly converted Mecca to the new Islamic religion. Forced conversion (except of Christians and Jews) was part of Islam's creed, and just six years later Muslim forces swept up the Arabian Peninsula and into Palestine. Some settled, and the non-Jews of Israel were converted by the sword. By the middle of the 8th century a vast region—extending from Spain, across North Africa and the entire Middle East to the Indus valley—had been brought under Islam's influence. The whole empire was ruled from Mecca by the Umayyad dynasty. The administration of Palestine was centered on Damascus, in Syria. People then moved freely over the border, and Israel's Arabs still speak the Syrian dialect.

A Muslim Israel The defeat of the Umayyads by the Abbasids meant a transfer of power from Damascus to distant Baghdad. Apart from the brief Crusader kingdom, Israel was to remain under Muslim rule for many centuries—under the Egyptians, Persians, Mamelukes, and, for 400 years, as part of the Ottoman Empire. Each ruler brought changes, to the cost of Palestine. When the British took over in 1917, the land was largely uncultivated, with inadequate water and extensive areas of desert, rock, dunes and swamp. The population stood well under one million.

Face of Palestine, citizen of Israel

The fight against Zionism British rule was benign, created work and improved the country. Arab workers drifted in from surrounding lands to take advantage. From the 1880s onwards Jews also flocked to Palestine, but for a different reason. By 1936, the population of Palestine had risen to 1,367,000—of whom 384,000 were Jews. The Arabs were uneasy. Jews traditionally held low status in

Muslim society. Muhammad had said that their time was over, their religion supplanted. Yet the Jews were purchasing land, displacing Arab tenants, forming settlements and draining swamps, all in pursuit of their avowed aim of creating a Jewish state. During the 1920s and 1930s, riots and attacks against the newcomers were frequent. When the State of Israel was declared in 1948, the Arab nations joined with the Arabs of Israel to crush the new country. To their surprise, they failed; many then fled across Israel's borders into Gaza and the West Bank, joining those who had left in advance of the war. Jews call this the War of Independence. Arabs call it the Catastrophe. Some 700,000 Arabs fled, leaving about 200,000 who stayed and became Israeli citizens.

Israeli Arabs Not all Arabs opposed Israel, and in particular not the Christians or the Druze. Many who fought against Israel also stayed. Israel's largest Arab town is Nazareth. Other main centers of Arab population are Jerusalem, Haifa and Akko, with communities in Ramla, Jaffa and several small towns in Galilee. At first sight, they appear to have come out on the winning side. Under no Arab regime do citizens have anything like the rights and freedoms of Israelis: All religions and sects enjoy full freedom of worship and Arabs are exempt from military service (though some, the Druze in particular, have chosen to accept conscription). Yet there is discontent, as Israeli Arabs compare themselves not with the Arabs who fled, but with their Jewish fellow citizens. Undoubtedly there is discrimination against Israeli Arabs—as against non-Jews generally (though most Israelis deplore this). And of course, they will forever be seen as a minority: Gentile citizens in a Jewish land.

IN THE EYE OF THE BEHOLDER

"Palestine, a country scarcely superior to Wales either in fertility or extent."
—Edward Gibbon, *Decline and Fall of the Roman Empire* (1776)

"A bare limestone country of little natural beauty."
—Charles Doughty, *Travels in Arabia Deserta* (1888)

"A good land and a large, flowing with milk and honey."
—Exodus 3:8

Arab schoolchildren in the souk

TO BE A PILGRIM
Pilgrimage was rare during the first 200 years of Christianity. Early Christians did not worship the physical Christ or revere the ground where he had walked. As Christianity moved westwards into pagan Europe, it met an increasing tendency to worship places, objects and relics. Pilgrimages to the Holy Land began in the 4th century, when persecution ceased. Later, Christians began to venerate Christ's mother and an increasing number of saints. The church taught that sinners could be absolved by visiting a holy site, that contact with parts of the bodies of saints and martyrs resulted in miracles. These were eagerly sought when the great era of pilgrimage began in the 10th century.

Jesus Meets His Mother, Station IV (top right)
The Via Dolorosa, the Sorrowful Road (below)

▶▶▶ Via Dolorosa *51B3*

The "Sorrowful Road" passes through the Muslim quarter to the Church of the Holy Sepulchre. It is honored as the route taken by Christ as he carried his cross to Golgotha, where he was crucified. Along the way, the Stations of the Cross—the different stages on his journey to death—are marked.

History The idea of the Stations of the Cross arose in the Middle Ages. Popular notions of what had happened to Jesus on the way to Calvary, additional to the Gospel accounts, passed into folklore and church tradition. In response to the demands of pilgrims, sites for the Stations of the Cross were first chosen in the mid-18th century by the Franciscans. In the 19th century, the route of the Via Dolorosa was altered to its present course.

Spiritual journey Most Christian communities take the view that Christ's suffering was spiritual and symbolic as well as physical, and that it is not essential to know the actual route Jesus followed. However, tens of thousands of pilgrims of all denominations walk the Via Dolorosa each year. They believe that, in spirit if not in fact, they are stepping in Christ's footsteps.

The route *I—Condemnation:* the first part of the way is relatively wide and quiet. The First Station is the courtyard of the **Omariye Islamic College (El U'mariya College)▶**, which some claim as the site of the Praetorium, where Jesus was sentenced. A minaret has been fancifully named Antonia Tower, after Herod's Antonia Fortress, which once stood here. Historically, it is more likely that Jesus was sentenced at the Citadel. It would have been most unusual for the Temple priests to be involved, as recounted in the Gospels, since the day of his trial was the first day of Passover.

II—Taking up the cross: across the street the ancient paving or **Lithostratos▶** in the Franciscan Churches of the Condemnation and the Flagellation is said to be where

Jesus was mocked, crowned with thorns and given his cross to carry. A stone archway, or buttress, spanning the street here is called **Ecce Homo Arch▶**. Traditionally, it is thought to mark the spot where Pilate said of Jesus: "Behold the man" (*Ecce homo*). In fact, the arch was erected in AD135, as a support for Herod's fortress.

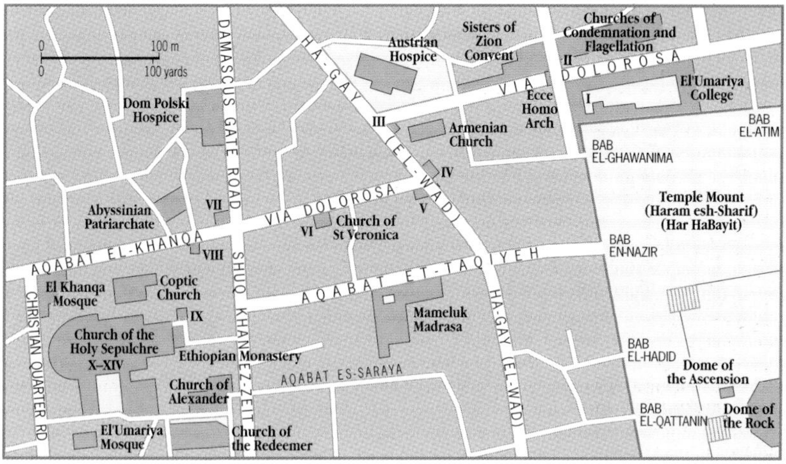

III—Jesus falls: continue to the Austrian Hospice and turn left onto busier El-Wad Street. Here a plaque shows where Jesus fell under the weight of the cross. The route passes Arab shops and tea shops.

IV – Meeting Mary: on the left (opposite a right turn), a shrine marks the place where tradition claims that Jesus saw his mother. Turning right, the street is again called Via Dolorosa.

V – Simon helps Jesus: take the turning, and straight away on the corner is where Simon the Cyrenian is said to have taken the cross from Jesus to help him (see panel right). Narrower and climbing, frequently in steps, the route passes souvenir shops.

VI – Veronica wipes the face of Jesus: a door leads down to **St. Veronica's Church▶▶** in Crusader vaults. The story that a woman named Veronica (the name simply means "true image") wiped the face of Jesus arose in the 7th century. A cloth, said to have belonged to Veronica and marked with the image of a man's face, is kept in Rome.

VII – Jesus falls again: the route reaches a junction in the midst of the crowded shopping streets of the Arab souk (market). Here, believers say, Jesus fell again.

VIII – Speaking to the women: the site (marked by a Latin cross on the wall of a Greek monastery) lies a few paces ahead. Here Jesus urged the women of Jerusalem to weep not for him but for themselves and their children.

IX – Jesus falls again: return to the junction, turn right along the covered Souk Khan ez-Zeit. A right turn leads off the souk to a Roman column at the back of the Holy Sepulchre. Here, the faithful say, Jesus fell for a third time.

X – XIV – Golgotha: return to the souk. Via Dolorosa turns right, passes the Lutheran Church of the Redeemer, and reaches the Holy Sepulchre. The remainder of the Stations are inside the church (see pages 60–61).

VIA DOLOROSA – KEY TO PLAN

- I Condemnation
- II Taking up the cross
- III Jesus falls
- IV Meeting Mary
- V Simon helps Jesus
- VI Veronica wipes the face of Jesus
- VII Jesus falls again
- VIII Speaking to the women
- IX Jesus falls again
- X Jesus is stripped
- XI Nailed to the cross
- XII Jesus dies on the cross
- XIII Taken down from the cross
- XIV Laid in the tomb

THE WAY OF THE CROSS

"They took the robe off from him, and put his own raiment on him, and led him away to crucify him. And as they came out, they found a man of Cyrene, Simon by name: and him they compelled to bear his cross. And when they had come unto a place called Golgotha, that is to say, a place of a skull, they gave him vinegar to drink mingled with gall: and when he had tasted thereof, he would not drink. And they crucified him."
—Matthew 27:31–35

Temple remnant: the Western Wall

WESTERN WALL (OR HASMONEAN) TUNNELS
"The Western Wall epitomizes recollections of the Jewish past and the hopes and aspirations of the Jewish future" (sign in Western Wall Tunnels). The tunnel tour starts in the medieval basement from which archeologist Charles Warren set out in 1867 to make the first exploration of the underground remains of the Temple Mount. Additional excavations since 1967 have exposed a 490-yard (450m) stretch of the Wall (one stone alone weighs 40 tonnes). You enter the area through a secret passage, come to stairs that date from the time of the Second Temple and enter a large hall behind Wilson's Arch. A long stroll through a tunnel beside the Wall reveals part of a Herodian street, a quarry, an ancient aqueduct and a pool. There's also an impressive model of Jerusalem in Second Temple times. The final section emerges onto the Via Dolorosa.

▶▶▶ The Western Wall (also known as the Kotel, HaKotel, Kotel Ma'aravi or the Wailing Wall) *51C2*

The Western Wall is revered by Jews because it is the last remnant of the only sacred place in the world, the Temple. Two millennia of prayer and tradition have sanctified this link with Temple times, making it the holiest place of prayer in the Jewish world. In addition, its relative proximity to the Holy of Holies (which was at the western end of the Temple) confers an additional claim to reverence. Today, as always, every Jew in prayer, anywhere in the world, faces the Holy of Holies inside the Temple on Temple Mount in Jerusalem—even though it physically no longer exists.

The stonework The Western Wall is the western section of the outer retaining wall of the Temple compound that, until 1900 years ago, entirely covered Mount Moriah, or the Temple Mount. The Wall was not part of the Temple building itself. The Second Temple, completed in 513BC, was reconstructed by Herod in about 30BC. The Wall's massive blocks of limestone were put in place. The visible part of the Wall reaches 59 feet (18m) in height, while a further 18m extends below the present-day ground level.

Visiting the Wall A visit to the Western Wall can be one of the most thought-provoking, interesting and satisfying experiences in the schedule of Old City sightseeing. After Israel recaptured the Wall in 1967, a vast plaza was created, enabling thousands of people to gather for festivals or special occasions. The exposed length of the Wall has been cordoned into two sections, one for men and the other for women, in keeping with Orthodox practice.

A low barrier a few paces from the Wall keeps sightseers apart from the area reserved for prayer and religious ritual, which is carried out in the open under the gaze of tourists. Any man, Jew or non-Jew, may enter the men's enclosure so long as he is wearing a head covering (even a baseball cap will do), just as any woman may enter the women's section. Most who do, come to recite prayers or simply to take a closer look at the Wall whose gaps are filled with tiny scraps of paper. Inscribed with people's simple wishes, prayers and blessings, these have been crammed into every cranny by devout souls who believe the Wall is directly scrutinized by God. Good times to visit the Western Wall are Monday and Thursday mornings, when the Torah is read by barmitzvah boys in family ceremonies; Shabbat mornings and all Jewish holidays; and at night, when the Wall is floodlit and the plaza empty.

Beside the Wall Off the men's section (so there is no access for women), the Wall continues into the structures abutting it. These consist of **two rooms▶** beneath the arches that support the Street of the Chain. These are synagogues, with shelves of prayer books and, attached to the Wall, arks containing Torah scrolls that are constantly being taken out and read by groups of men, while crowds of visitors file in to have a look around. The first narrow chamber has a glass-covered opening in the floor providing a view to the lower levels of the Wall. Beyond, in a larger room, thought to date from 100BC, is **Wilson's Arch▶**, the ancient vaulted structure which used to support the original access road to the Second Temple. At the foot of the arch, illuminated openings give a view to the Wall's lower levels.

Off the plaza On the north side of the plaza an entrance leads into the **Western Wall Tunnels▶▶** (Kotel HaIdra). To view these you must sign up for the guided tour (*Book three days ahead; some tours in English. Admission: moderate*) which passes through the underground passages that run along the excavated Wall for several hundred metres. At the western side of the plaza, the **northern passage▶** runs beneath the Street of the Chain, linking the plaza with El Wad (or Hagai) Street. Its roof is composed of an arch of massive stones, dating from the 8th to the 11th centuries. On one side of the floor, openings reveal Roman paving, now below ground level. South of the plaza are Dung Gate and the **Jerusalem Archeological Park▶▶▶** (see page 69).

WALL ETIQUETTE
Be prepared for hassle at the Wall. The enclosure is technically a synagogue, so modest dress and behavior are required and on Shabbat it is forbidden to eat or smoke there, or take photographs. Begging is also forbidden, but religious beggars harass visitors constantly (sometimes while they are praying), asking for "donations."

Jewish visitors can seek assistance at one of the stands within the men's section, where volunteers will help you to put on the *tefillin* and say the blessings (there is no charge).

Praying at the holiest place in the Jewish world

The uniform of the ultra-Orthodox Hasidic Jews

JEWISH BATHS
Mikvehs, or, more correctly, *mikvaot*, are ritual baths, that are filled with rainwater. Religious law requires immersion in the *mikveh* for men before a number of Temple rituals, but since the destruction of the Temple, these are no longer required. Women have to immerse themselves at the end of each menstrual period. Before marriage, both bride and groom enter (separately!). Converts to Judaism immerse themselves to complete the conversion process. Some *mikvaot* in the Herodian Houses have separate entrances and exits (unusual today), allowing the person to enter impure on one side and leave purified on the other. Immersion is total with the body upright, entirely clean and naked and without any jewelry.

►► Wohl Archeological Museum (Herodian Houses) 51B2

HaKaraim Street off Hurva Square (tel: 02-6283448)
Admission: inexpensive (joint ticket with Israelite Tower and Burnt House)

The Wohl Archeological Museum preserves *in situ* the extraordinary discoveries made when this handsome religious institution, built in pale Jerusalem stone, was being constructed. From the small, unassuming museum entrance, steps lead down to the preserved area, which lies 10ft (3m) below the street level and 2,000 years back in time. Here the floor-level rooms of ruined houses of the period are displayed in a remarkable state of preservation.

History The Jewish quarter of today covers the remains of the Upper City of 37BC–AD70. In AD70, during the crushing of the First Jewish Revolt, the Romans totally destroyed the Temple and buildings surrounding it. Then they drove the population, including the priestly class, out of the city. The whole area was set alight in a vast fire, which was described by the 1st-century historian Josephus Flavius. Seventy years later the city was transformed and given new buildings, new ramparts and a new, non-Jewish name—Aelia Capitolina. On the site of ruined Jewish homes new houses were erected.

The museum The Wohl Museum stands on an archeological site where part of a prosperous residential district of the Herodian period has been exposed. Here wealthy families of the Jerusalem aristocracy and priesthood used to live in fine homes overlooking Temple Mount. A wide low-ceilinged room has been built around the ruins of six of these 1st-century houses, including the largest ever found in the Upper City, the 600sq m (717 square yards) "Mansion." Their state of preservation varies; what can be seen are ground floors and basements, with sections of the ground floor walls standing as much as 8ft (2.5m) high in parts. In some cases, original mosaic floors and wall decorations survive in good condition. In one house, a mosaic of the Herodian period was discovered when drains were installed for later Byzantine dwellings.

Steps lead down to the next level following the ancient walls as they descend the hill. Walkways enclose the house ruins, giving an excellent view into the rooms, and descriptive diagrams indicate the significance of everything that can be seen. A great many artifacts were discovered among the ruins, and it has been possible to give some idea of the furnishing and decor of the houses. In the museum there are displays of the numerous luxury and household items found, as well as a detailed model of the Mansion.

The houses Built close together on the hillside facing Temple Mount, the houses are constructed of large pale blocks of the local Jerusalem stone still used today. The interiors of the homes bear a startling resemblance to modern well-to-do interiors in today's eastern Mediterranean countries. In fact, the similarity to Greek houses gives an insight into the Hellenism that influenced life before and during Herod's reign. The impression is of uncluttered elegance and plenty of cool stone and plasterwork. Houses are divided into large and small rooms, some with attractive mosaic floors. Patterned mosaic often features in the middle of the room, with an undecorated area around the edges. Walls are decorated with paintings and stucco.

The occupants The wealth of the inhabitants is shown by the spaciousness of their homes, the fine quality of the stucco, and the excellence of the mosaic work. Inside, they have private bathrooms and their own *mikveh* (ritual bath), an indication that they were quite religious Jews. It is clear that rooms were often redecorated, old frescoes being painted over with new.

Step down 10ft (3m) and back 2,000 years at the Wohl Archeological Museum

The New City

Despite Jerusalem's 3,000-year-old history, nearly all of the city outside the walls is less than 100 years old—and most is under 50. This New Jerusalem spreads in every direction except east, a fact that is critically confusing since Jerusalem has a large Arab district known as East Jerusalem. In fact, East Jerusalem lies north of the Old City walls, while to the geographical east of Jerusalem rises the Mount of Olives. There is another Arab district just to the south of the City Walls, but the rest of the city, including the modern city center, consists of Jewish districts.

All buildings in New Jerusalem must be constructed of the attractive traditional golden sandstone, called Jerusalem stone.

Byzantine chancel screen from Gaza, dating from around 579AD

► Ammunition Hill 46C4

Eshkol Boulevard (northeastern edge of the city)
Admission: moderate

On the site of a Jordanian army position captured after a long battle, this is the city's principal memorial to the liberation of Jerusalem in 1967. Now an important symbolic site in Jerusalem, with an excellent museum and video presentation, the preserved battleground is dedicated to the 183 Israelis who died. Beneath it, the underground Jordanian command post has also been preserved as a museum.

►► Bible Lands Museum 46A2

Museum Row (between Knesset and Shrine of the Book)
(tel: 02-5611066; www.blmj.org)
Open: Sun–Tue, Thu 9.30–5.30, Wed 9.30–9.30 (1.30–9.30 in winter), Fri 9.30–2, Sat 11–3. Admission: expensive

With remarkable displays of thousands of superb archeological finds, this bright, attractive museum explores Near East ritual and religion throughout the 6,600-year period from Abraham to the Byzantines.

Roman mosaic (right) in the Bible Lands Museum

► Bloomfield Science Museum 46A2

Museum Boulevard, Hebrew University, Givat Ram campus
Open: Mon–Sat. Admission: expensive

This is an imaginative and highly entertaining hands-on science museum with fascinating displays, talks, exhibitions and workshops geared for different age groups.

►► City of David (Hebrew: 'Ir David) 47E2

Open: see panel, this page

This Jebusite settlement, once conquered by King David, lies along the Ofel (or Ophel) Ridge. Here he constructed the first Jewish capital in 1004BC, later acquiring a threshing floor on Mount Moriah as a site for the Temple. Under Solomon the city grew north to encompass the Temple area. In 1978 a project was established to bring together all the finds from the area and to create a single Ancient Jerusalem Archeological Park. So far, 25 layers of civilization have been discovered, dating back to 4000BC. Work is still in progress.

What to see Outside Dung Gate, cross Ofel (or Ophel Boulevard to look across the fascinating Ophel Archeological Gardens to the broad **Hulda Steps►►►** climbing to the south wall of Temple Mount, below Al Aqsa mosque. The Ophel site (part of the Jerusalem Archeological Park, see page 69) reveals what was once a busy access to the Temple for people coming from the City of David. You can see remains of Roman and Byzantine houses, 2,000-year-old *mikvaot* (Jewish ritual baths) and a paved street of the same period. Turn right down Observation Point Path to reach the **City of David Archeological Garden►►**. Here too are impressive ruins, including Israelite houses destroyed by Babylonians in 586BC and the foundations of David's fortress. Some 328ft (100m) downhill is **Warren's Shaft►►**, the ancient city's underground water system. This tunnel and well shaft were used to pull water up from the sporadic gushing **Gihon Spring►**, inside a cave. David's men managed to invade the Jebusite town by climbing up the inside of the shaft (British soldiers did the same thing in 1910).

Continue on to **Hezekiah's Tunnel►**, built 700BC. Dug from both ends at once, it stretches for 600 yards (550m) and was used to channel water from the Gihon Spring to the **Siloam Pool►**. The pool acted as a reservoir within the city walls. Jesus healed a blind man here by rinsing his eyes. The water still flows, and visitors can wade from one end of the tunnel to the other. It's quite an adventure, takes half an hour and requires suitable clothing and footwear. And bring a torch!

CITY OF DAVID OPENING TIMES

Note that a visit involves a lot of steep walking outside in the sun.
Open: all parts of site Sun–Thu 9–4, Fri 9–2.
Admission: inexpensive.

David's City in ruins

OUTDATED DEFINITIONS

In 1967, after Israel had recaptured East Jerusalem from the Jordanians, the total population of the city was about 267,000. Some 70,000 Arabs lived east of the former border, and 197,000 Jews to its west. Today, those sharp divisions have been blurred. Owing to the influx of population from both sides, new housing developments, people moving around within the city and a redefinition of the city limits, Jerusalem's total population exceeds 700,000, of whom 70 percent are Jewish. The districts east of the 1948 border now have just as many Jewish residents as Arab.

►► East Jerusalem *47D4*

Lying to the north, rather than east, of the Old City walls, this mainly 19th-century area is Jerusalem's principal Arab district. The neighborhood is bounded by Hatzanhanim and Suleiman boulevards, beside the Old City wall, Shivtei Israel and St. George boulevards, curving northeastward to the American Colony, and the slopes of Mount Scopus to the east. The busiest thoroughfares are Sultan Suleiman and Salah ed-Din, both just outside the Old City's Herod's Gate. The whole densely populated area has a fascinating Oriental atmosphere.

Archeology and caves In the eastern part of the district is the **Rockefeller Museum►►►** (*Open* Sun–Thu 11–3, Sat 10–2. *Closed* Fri. *Admission: moderate*), a substantial building beneath a large tower at the end of Suleiman Street. It houses one of Jerusalem's leading archeological collections. In a sequence of well laid-out rooms set around a central courtyard, its displays cover the full range of human history, from man's origins almost to the present day. Among the most interesting and impressive items are the Galilee skull (dated 200,000BC) and other very early human remains found in Israel. Also on display is ancient jewelry (some over 4,000 years old), a board game (of about 1600BC) and ancient Egyptian and Mesopotamian items found in Israel. There are especially interesting reconstructions of a 7th-century Islamic palace and baths. The free guided tours by qualified volunteers are an additional attraction for visitors.

The Old City wall leads to **Zedekiah's Caves►**, a group of subterranean tunnels, probably former quarries, that run for some 218 yards (200m) beneath the streets. Among various stories about the caves, it is said that Zedekiah, together with hundreds of other Jerusalemites, hid here at the time of the Babylonian conquest.

If you continue along the wall, you will reach the lively area in front of **Damascus Gate►►►** (see page 53). Cross the road and head up the busy Nablus (or Shehem) Road, turning right for the **Garden Tomb►►** (see page 86), the calm and attractive spot that many Protestants believe to be the true place of Christ's crucifixion and resurrection.

Heading to the western edge of the district, a left turn along Nablus Road leads to the interesting **Tourjeman Post Museum►**, located at the junction of narrow Hayil Handassa Street and wider Antara ben Shadad and HaNevi'im streets. The museum building stands beside the old Mandelbaum Gate (named after the Mandelbaum family whose house once stood alongside). This was the only crossing point between the eastern and western sectors of Jerusalem during the Jordanian occupation of 1948 to 1967. Further down HaNevi'im Street, the **St Polyeuctus House Chapel►** is an Armenian establishment with an exceptionally beautiful 5th-century mosaic floor.

On the north side of the Arab district, the **Tombs of the Kings►**, at the top of Salah ed-Din Street (close to the junction with Nablus Road), form a majestic complex of

Ancient art, the Rockefeller Museum

AMERICAN COLONY
This district, part of East Jerusalem, was founded by American Christians in the 1880s. It still has a strong Western and Christian presence and its buildings include the US Consulate, a YMCA, the American Colony Hotel, and St George's Anglican Cathedral of 1898.

Falafel stall near the Damascus Gate

catacombs, now known to be the 1st-century AD burial place of two unlikely converts to Judaism—Helena, Queen of Adiabene (present-day Kirkuk, in Iraq), and her son Izates. The queen took the name Sarah and became a distinguished benefactor of the Jewish people. She actually died in her homeland, but wished her remains to lie in Jerusalem. The sarcophagi from the tombs are in the Louvre, in Paris.

Just behind the tombs is the **American Colony** district, built in the 1880s. The **American Colony Hotel**►► is one of Jerusalem's best-known hotels. Formerly the grand, opulent palace of a Turkish pasha, handsomely restored, it is now the favorite haunt of the many foreign correspondents based in the city.

Trade flourishes before the Damascus Gate

CHAGALL MASTERPIECES
The Russian artist Marc Chagall (who was Jewish) created a great deal of work for Israeli institutions. Particularly fine are his 12 stained-glass windows in the synagogue of the Hadassah University Hospital, just south of En Kerem. They show, in his typically vivid, other-worldly style, Jacob blessing his sons, the founders of the 12 tribes of Israel.

En Kerem (above), birthplace of John the Baptist
The Garden Tomb (below)

► En Kerem 206B2

This pretty village on the city's western edge is believed to be the birthplace of John the Baptist where the Virgin Mary visited John's mother, Elizabeth. The reverence for the village dates mainly from the Crusader period. Barluzzi's modern **Sanctuary and Church of the Visitation►►** and the 17th-century **Church of John the Baptist►►** are attractive buildings honoring these events.

►► Garden Tomb 47D3

Access from Nablus (Shehem) Road
The supposed site of the burial and resurrection of Jesus was chosen by British General Charles Gordon in 1883, and has been acknowledged by several Protestant denominations. Gordon was concerned that the accepted site, inside the Church of the Holy Sepulchre (see page 60), stood within the city walls, in contradiction to the Gospels. In fact, the city walls at the time of Christ took a different course, and the Holy Sepulchre does lie outside those walls. For all that, this hill looks like a skull (the Gospel description of Golgotha), has a fine rock-hewn burial tomb adjacent and is in a garden location. Other high-quality rock-cut tombs found nearby, for example the Tombs of the Kings (see pages 84–85), suggest that this was a burial area preferred by the wealthy. Christ was laid in the tomb of Joseph, a rich man of Arimathaea.

► Holyland Hotel Model 46A1

Off David Nezer Street, Ramat Sharett
This superb miniature model of Jerusalem at the time of Christ, built on a scale of 1:50 and covering 2.47 acres (1ha), has been laid out on the grounds of this hotel for some years but is due to move to the Israel Museum.

►►► Israel Museum 46A1

Ruppin Road (near the Knesset)
(tel: 02-6708811; www.imj.org.il)
Open: Mon, Wed, Sat (including Jewsh holidays) 10–4, Tue 4–9, Thu 10–9, Fri and day before Jewish holidays 10–2. Closed Sun. Admission: expensive
This large modern museum is the nation's leading showcase for history, anthropology, art and cultural heritage, and places Israel within its regional and global context. A full appreciation of its exhibits would take several days; in a short visit, it is better to concentrate on highlights.

The museum provides free **guided tours in English** of the most important and interesting exhibits. The famous Dead Sea Scrolls are housed in the **Shrine of the Book▶▶▶** (see page 98). It is a striking structure, separate from the rest, and takes some time to visit.

Highlights Outside the main complex there are 55 modern sculptures set in the **Art Garden▶**, including works by Henry Moore. The main part of the museum is a huge arrangement of rooms and halls. Of special interest are the **Ethnography and Judaica Wing▶▶▶**; the **20th-century Art Pavilion▶▶▶**, with works by Picasso, Chagall, Van Gogh and other seminal modern artists with important Impressionist works and a remarkable donation of over 750 works of Dada and Surrealism; the **Israel Art Pavilion▶▶**, where artists such as Reuven Rubin are displayed; and the **Archeological Galleries▶▶**, where the main discoveries made in Israel are exhibited.

Exhibitions, concerts and talks The Israel Museum is exceptionally good for its many "extracurricular" activities. There are always special exhibitions on a wide variety of themes, such as design, photography, or the art of America, Asia or Africa, often on loan from leading museums. The **Youth Wing** has activities and exhibitions for children. Concerts, mostly classical music but also jazz and Jewish genres, take place by day and evening. Lectures and talks include academic, Jewish or general interest.

JUDAICA

The Israel Museum's Judaica section has the world's most complete collection of Jewish ceremonial art and ritual objects, gathered together from every part of the world in which there have ever been Jewish communities. The Ethnography section includes, among the varied displays, the costumes of Jewish brides in Yemen, Bukhara, Morocco, and other Islamic countries.

The Art Garden, Israel Museum

An Israeli meal is served from a melting pot of cultures, with cooking styles from around the world. The robust, filling Ashkenazi (East European) and more delicate, tastier Sephardi (Mediterranean and Middle Eastern) cuisines are both well represented, together with American and international dishes, and more exotic options like the exquisite spicy food of the Yemenite Jews.

HOW TO EAT FALAFEL IN PITA
The easiest way to spot a tourist is by the amount of mess they make when trying to eat this awkward, overflowing hand-held snack. The trick is to nibble from the top, not the sides. Use the wrap-around paper to hold the whole snack together as you gradually eat downwards. Israelis can eat this without dropping even a shred of lettuce. After a couple of weeks' practice you will be almost as good as the locals.

Falafel, commonly served with salad in pita bread

Salad days Israelis may be the only people in the world who start the day with a salad. Not just as a little accompaniment to something else, and not just a slice of tomato and a leaf of lettuce, but a huge pile of chopped green peppers, radishes and grated carrot, topped by a generous helping of yogurt-like cheese. In fact, a salad appears at every meal, and in huge quantities. It can vary from something roughly cut and thrown together, to a superb mix of finely cut vegetables, all at the peak of freshness, ripeness and color, in a delicious olive oil dressing. Then there is hummus (chickpea purée), served in vast amounts with a big splash of olive oil and a delicious condiment called *za'atar* (hyssop and sesame). Similar dishes include avocado purée and *salat khatzilim* (eggplant purée with tomatoes, lemon juice and onion). They are mostly eaten with pita bread.

Milk and honey Milk, it seems, can be made into more variations on the theme of cottage cheese, cream cheese, sour cream and yogurt than most of us ever dreamed of. A breakfast or lunch buffet can include half a dozen soft or semi-liquid white cheeses, some bland, some flavored with herbs and spices, some mouthwatering, some more of an acquired taste! Generically, they are known just as *leben*, literally "white." One particular plain white cheese, moist with a cuttable consistency, could be regarded as one of the country's staple foods; it is called simply *gvina lavana*, white cheese. Of course, because of Jewish dietary laws, milk products are never eaten at the same meal as meat in kosher restaurants.

One falafel or six The basic snack meal is falafel in pita with salad. Flexible enough to be either a quick bite or a full sit-down meal, it is also utterly delicious. The falafel itself is a deep-fried ball of seasoned chickpea paste (plus wheatflour, onions and garlic). Usually four or five of them are crammed into the bottom of a cut-open pita with as much diced salad and chopped vegetables as will fit. All this is then smothered with hummus and tahini (sauces made of chickpeas and of sesame seeds with olive oil respectively) and, optionally, either sweet mango sauce or

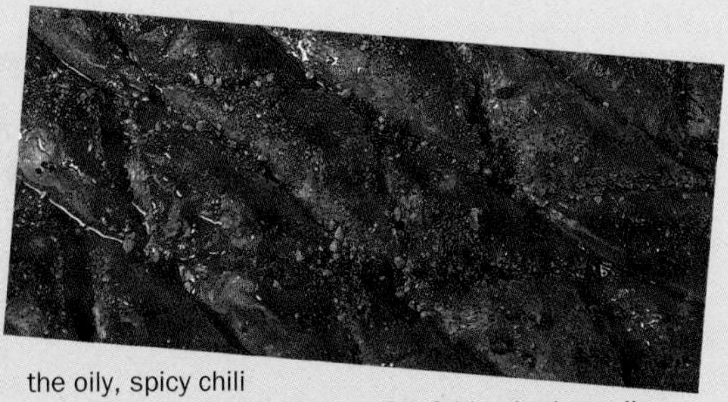

Lebanese delicacy: a honey-soaked dessert

the oily, spicy chili pepper sauce called *zehoug*. Falafel in pita is available everywhere. In the cheaper places where you serve yourself, you can refill as often as you like.

Meat and fish Plain grilled meats and delicious fresh fish, served with French fries, *hamutzim* (pickles), and (of course) fresh salads make a good, typical meal. Succulent stews with plenty of beans and pulses, especially *ful* beans, are widely seen. *Shwarma* (slices cut from pressed mutton roasted on a vertical spit) is ubiquitous, popular, and (when stuffed into a pita with salad) provides a mobile carnivorous alternative to falafel. Menus often feature *schnitzel*, but in Israel it is usually made of turkey or chicken, not veal. Blintzes (stuffed rolled pancakes) can be filled with meat or cheese, sweet or savory, and can make a good snack, a filling meal, or (especially a cheese blintz sprinkled with sugar) a gorgeous dessert. Chunky little wedges of *baklava*, the super-sweet honey-and-nut filo pastry, also make a good finish to any meal. Israeli ice-cream and yogurt desserts are great too.

So eat! Wherever you eat, the portions served are huge. Cooking reaches a decent level almost everywhere, though rarely exceeding it. Most Israeli restaurants lack finesse and imagination, though some now truly merit the ubiquitous "gourmet" label. The bread served is beautifully fresh and the fruit, vegetables and fish can be wonderful. Many resaturants in Israel serve seafood, although seafood is not kosher, and much of it is imported or is imitation seafood, made from fish. The widespread admiration in Israel for the rough-and-ready, and the down-to-earth, works against refinement. Diners are not especially discerning, and they generally care little about the finer points of cuisine, but they expect properly prepared, good quality food, and plenty of it. That is what they get.

VEGETARIAN TREATS
Salads and delicious vegetable dishes are the norm everywhere and the numerous meat-free "dairy" restaurants (which also serve fish) supply a wealth of interesting choice. However, despite the excellent salads, you might get tired of the factory-made vegetarian *schnitzel*—the automatic response to a request for a vegetarian hot dish in a meat restaurant.
Mealtimes are flexible. Many Israelis eat early, with breakfast at 6–8am, lunch around noon, and an evening meal at 7pm. Some restaurants are open from 11am to 11pm.

A barrow of bagels

Waiting for Judgement Day: tombs in the Kidron Valley

HEROD'S FAMILY TOMB
Behind the King David Hotel is a tomb of the Second Temple period, now known to contain the graves of members of Herod's family—many of whom he murdered. The opening still possesses its rolling stone "door."

YMCA
The wonderfully grand building, opposite the King David, seeming even to outclass the famous hotel, is a YMCA. It was designed in 1933 by Arthur Louis Harmon, architect of the Empire State Building in New York.

► Jerusalem Time Elevator *46B3*

Beit Agron, 37 Hillel Street (tel: 02-6248381; www.time-elevator.co.il)
Open: Sat–Thu 9am–10pm, Fri 9–3.30. Admission: moderate
Three screens, moving seats, and multi-sensory sets offer a rip-roaring 30-minute trip through the highlights of Israel's 3,000-year story. You'll have virtual encounters with kings, prophets and conquerors, enter the Temple and flee from a Jerusalem in flames.

► Kidron Valley *47E2*

The dry valley of Nahal Kidron forms the eastern limit of the original City of David. Pious Jews and Muslims both believe that the Last Judgment will take place below the Mount of Olives (see page 94). For that reason, this part of the valley is also known as Jehoshaphat Valley (literally, "valley of God's judgment"), a name used metaphorically in the scriptures for the place of judgment.

Elaborate **Kidron Valley tombs►**, on the lower slopes of the Mount of Olives, are popularly thought to be those of early biblical characters. These are, in fact, the tombs of wealthy Jews of the 1st century BC and are constructed in typical style of that period. One with a curious conical roof is referred to as the **Tomb of Absalom►**, a son of King David. Another is said to be the **Tomb of Zacharia►** and a third is called **St. James's Grotto►**, supposedly the place where James the Less hid when Jesus was arrested.

► King David Hotel *46C2*

King David Street
This dignified 1930s hotel, equipped with every modern amenity, is the venue for state banquets and receptions. It is the flagship of the Dan chain, Israel's most prestigious hotel group. The King David entered the pages of Israel's history when the front of its right wing, used as the military headquarters of the British in Palestine, was blown

Historic hotel: the King David, former headquarters of the British in Palestine

apart by the Irgun guerrilla group in July 1946. Ninety-one people were killed. Other explosions at that time aimed to persuade the British to withdraw from Palestine.

KNESSET ROSES
The beautiful Knesset Rose Garden, open to the public, contains hundreds of different varieties of roses. People come here from time to time with placards to voice their concerns.

▶▶ The Knesset *46A2*

Eliezer Kaplan Street (HaKyria district) (tel: 02-6753420 or 02-6753416; www.knesset.gov.il
Open: guided tours (in English and 8 other languages) Sun, Thu 8.30–2.30 (pre-booking essential). Knesset sessions may be watched from the public gallery Mon, Tue, Wed, usually at 4pm (11am Wed). ID card or passport essential

The Israeli parliament building of 1966 is a bleak fortress, on a hill west of the center of Jerusalem. This is the focal point of modern Israel. It was built with defense very much in mind: A good deal of the structure lies below ground level. Here, in debates, the nation's divisions are starkly revealed, as is its essential unity. Religious and secular forces, left- and right-wing ideologues, meet, clash and form pragmatic alliances. Few countries are as wholeheartedly democratic: Proportional representation permits almost any and every voice to be heard here. Its name (*knesset* means assembly) reflects this role too, and the name has an echo of Beit Knesset, the Hebrew for synagogue.

Debate in the chamber (in Hebrew or Arabic) is lively, with displays of real temper. The 16.5ft (5m) tall bronze menorah outside, a gift from Britain, symbolizes the central place of the Knesset in the Jewish homeland. Tapestries in the entrance hall, with scenes from Genesis and Exodus, are by Marc Chagall.

Heart of Israeli democracy: the Knesset in its hilltop setting

In this neighborhood, strict rules are observed: Hasidic Jews uphold the Orthodox view

HASIDISM

The Hasidic movement was founded by Israel ben Eliezer (known as Baal Shem Tov, meaning "Master of the Good Name") during the mid-17th century in the Ukraine. At the time, following savage persecution by the Church, Jewish life in Eastern Europe was at a low ebb. He taught that communication with God could only be attained through real fervor, whether in study or observance. The dress of the Hasidim, varied according to sub-sects to which an individual belongs, reflects devotion to their 17th-century roots, as does their elaborate observance.

►► Me'a She'arim *46C4*

This downtown district north of Zion Square is a strictly Orthodox Jewish area where Hasidim (see panel) can be seen at leisure. Here they are on home ground, and children play in the streets (boys making sure never to lose their *kippot*, or skullcaps) watched by the men in their *tsitsit* (fringed garments), while the demurely clad women go about their business. Understandably, the residents object to being a tourist attraction, and many streets have been closed off with barriers and signs erected bearing this message: "Entrance for women immodestly dressed, tourists and groups, STRICTLY FORBIDDEN!!! This is a residence area, not a tourist site; please do not irritate our feelings. Neighborhood Council." It is wise to heed this warning, as Hasidim have a reputation for acting violently against those they regard as transgressors. Men or women in shorts will be spat upon, maybe even stoned.

Certain other streets have no such barriers, and it is even possible to go on an organized synagogue tour (ask at the tourist office). Descriptions of this neighborhood as like an East European *shtetl* (Jewish township) are quite misleading—there is almost no resemblance at all. Me'a She'arim's housing, narrow lanes and overhanging balconies seem as much Middle Eastern as East European. The European *shtetls* were simple and rustic, and long predated the Hasidic movement. Many residents were not especially religious. Nor were there any cars, paved streets, electricity...or signs warning visitors to keep away.

► Monastery of the Cross *46A2*

Hayim Hazar Boulevard
Open: daily 10–1.30

Built in the 11th century on 5th-century ruins, this fortified Greek Orthodox monastery looks incongruous among the modern offices and museums. Hundreds of monks used to live in the monastery, and its library of precious manuscripts (now kept elsewhere) had a good reputation. Today it is a college for Orthodox priests. Tradition has it that it was from among the olive groves in front of the building that Christ's cross was made.

►► Mount Herzl 46A1

Herzl Boulevard winds through western Jerusalem to this hill, which has been turned into a magnificent shrine to the creation of the State of Israel. At its summit rests a massive plain black stone sarcophagus inscribed with no sentiments of praise or pathos, but one simple word: Herzl. Around the tomb, a lovely, serene garden honors the memory of the founder of the Zionist movement, Theodor Herzl.

Without this cosmopolitan, secular Jew from Hungary, who was born in 1860, it is unlikely that the State of Israel would exist. Herzl was suddenly fired into activity when he witnessed the public parade-ground humiliation of the Jewish officer Alfred Dreyfus in France. He decided to devote himself to the creation of a worldwide Zionist movement. He wished to work on all fronts—especially through politics and diplomacy—to win a homeland for the Jews. He convened the First Zionist Congress in 1897, and by the time of his death in 1904, his dream had almost become a reality. When the State was proclaimed by David Ben-Gurion in 1948, a picture of Theodor Herzl hung on the wall behind him. In 1949, Herzl's remains were brought to Israel and laid to rest here.

The tombs of Herzl's parents and many prominent Israeli figures also lie here, including Zeev Jabotinsky (1880–1940: head of the Irgun guerrilla organization), Levi Eshkol (1895–1969: Israel's third prime minister), and Golda Meir (1898–1978: Israel's fourth prime minister). The principal military cemetery is also on this hill, lower down. The **Herzl Museum►►►** (tel: 02-6433266. *Open* summer, Sun–Thu 9–6.30, Sat 9–1; winter, Sun–Thu 9–4, Sat 9–1. *Admission: moderate*), is the first building reached at the site. Using a high-tech story method in which an actor is taught to play the part of Herzl, it vividly explores Herzl's life experience, achievement and the utopian dreams, and touches on the ways his vision parts company with today's realities. The museum preserves original documents, artifacts such as Herzl's desk, and includes a research center.

BUS 99
The easy way to see the sights of Jerusalem beyond the walls is to catch a number 99 bus. Running on a circuit right around the city, it calls at 36 stops, all of them places of interest. You can get off wherever you like, take a look round, and catch the next 99 bus to continue with your tour.

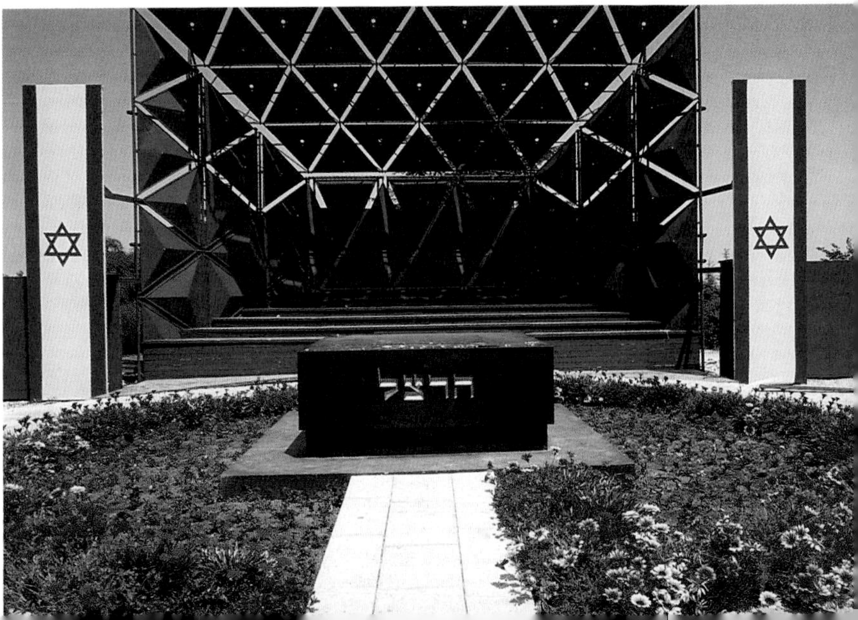

The tomb of Theodor Herzl, founder of Zionism, on the summit of the hill which bears his name

Ancient tombs on the Mount of Olives

THE END OF DAYS
"And the Mount of Olives shall cleave in the midst thereof towards the east and towards the west, and there shall be a very great valley; and half of the mountain shall remove toward the north, and half of it toward the south."
—Zechariah 14:4

"The sun shall be turned into darkness, and the moon into blood, before the great and the terrible day of the Lord come. And it shall come to pass, that whosoever shall call upon the name of the Lord shall be delivered; for in Mount Zion and in Jerusalem shall be deliverance."
—Joel 2:31–32 (3:4–5)

"Beat your plowshares into swords, and your pruning hooks into spears: let the weak say, I am strong. Assemble yourselves, and come, all ye heathen...Let the heathen be wakened, and come up to the valley of Jehoshaphat: For there will I sit to judge all the heathen round about."
—Joel 3(4):10–12

The Russian Church of Mary Magdalene, built by Tsar Alexander III

►►► Mount of Olives *47E3*

White tombs, not olives, cover the steep hillside rising beyond the city wall east of Temple Mount. This slope has long been wreathed in myth and legend.

Fact, fiction and faith Almost the only time the hill is mentioned by name in Jewish scripture comes after the revolt of Absalom, when his father, King David, is described as weeping while he walks barefoot up the Mount of Olives to pray (II Samuel 15:30). However, the apocalyptic predictions of Joel 3, that the nations shall be judged in the valley of Jehoshaphat (meaning "God's Judgement") has been taken by some to refer to the nearby Kidron Valley. Zechariah's hallucinatory vision (14:4) of the Mount of Olives being torn into two, and the whole world coming to Jerusalem for the festival of Sukkot has also led pious Jews to believe that the Last Judgement will take place here. The notion that the dead will physically rise on the Day of Judgement caused some pious Jews to attach special value to being buried on this slope, above the Kidron.

Christians know this as the place to which Jesus and the disciples came on the night before his arrest and trial. The "place called Gethsemane" (Matthew 26:36) is assumed to be on the slope. Fine buildings on the Mount of Olives commemorate these events, although, almost without exception, they are based on Byzantine fervor rather than biblical or historical evidence.

Down the mountain There is direct access to the mount from the Old City via Lions' Gate. An easier way to visit the shrines and churches is from the top of the hill. Take a bus or taxi to **Et-Tur►**, the Arab village at its summit, and walk past the Church of the Ascension (no entry) to the **Chapel of the Ascension►**, a simple domed structure within the grounds of a mosque converted from a Crusader church. This is claimed to be the place from which Christ ascended into heaven (although Luke 24:50, sets this event in Bethany, present-day Eizaria). Inside, a mark in the floor is said to be the footprint of Christ. **Pater Noster Church▶**, belonging to Carmelite nuns, recalls Christ's teaching of the Lord's Prayer at a grotto which now forms part of a lovely cloister. Beyond the church, on the left, rises the unsightly Hotel InterContinental. Just below, an **observation point▶▶▶** gives one of Jerusalem's best views.

Another road from the Carmelite church leads down past the so-called **Tombs of the Prophets▶** (Haggai, Zacharia and Malachi), in reality a much later complex of catacombs, to the entrance of the **Jewish cemetery▶▶**, the oldest, as well as the largest, continuously used Jewish cemetery in the world. Tragically, it was badly damaged during the Jordanian occupation, when graves were smashed or removed for use as building stone.

The curious **Dominus Flevit Church▶▶** (meaning "the Lord wept"), was built in 1953 and incorporates 5th-century ruins. It has a glass wall and is shaped as a teardrop in memory of Jesus weeping for Jerusalem. The 19th-century Russian **Church of Mary Magdalene▶▶**, with its elaborate colored façade and cluster of onion domes topped with prominent Orthodox crosses, is one of the city's more distinctive landmarks. Ironically, it was built by Tsar Alexander III, whose savage pogroms in the 1880s inspired the first great influx of Zionists into Palestine.

At the bottom of the hill, a putative **Garden of Gethsemane▶**, pretty with flowers and a few olive trees, recalls Christ's last hours. Some believe the trees date back to those days. The **Cave of Gethsemane▶** is said to be where the disciples slept while Jesus prayed. The **Basilica of the Agony▶**, an attractive modern building on a Byzantine and Crusader site, is decorated inside and out with mosaics and murals.

The **Tomb of the Virgin Mary▶▶**, a mainly Byzantine and Crusader structure, is reached through a fine doorway. It leads to an underground shrine, where various tombs (in reality medieval) are said to be those of Mary's parents, Joachim and Anne, her husband Joseph, and, at the end of a long chamber, Mary herself. This is one of many places, in Israel and in other countries, where the Virgin Mary is said to have been entombed.

THE BIBLICAL MOUNT OF OLIVES

"And David went up by the ascent of the Mount of Olives, and wept as he went up, and he had his head covered, and went barefoot."
—II Samuel 15:30

"Then returned they unto Jerusalem from the mount called Olivet, which is from Jerusalem a Sabbath day's journey."
—Acts 1:12

A BEACON TO THE JEWS

In Second Temple times, the Mount of Olives had, on its summit, the first in a chain of beacons that extended all over Israel and into Babylon, used to inform Jews of the timing of new moons and festivals.

Beneath here lies the Virgin's tomb

THE VALLEY OF THE SHADOW OF DEATH
Encircling the foot of Mount Zion is the Hinnom Valley, called Gehenna (meaning Hell), in the Bible. Its evil associations can be traced back to Canaanite times when the valley was sacred to the cult of Moloch, whose followers sacrificed children by burning them alive. Fires were kept aflame here specifically for that purpose. Incredibly, such a religion had a strong appeal and was widely practiced throughout the region. Even the Israelites sometimes succumbed to it. The Haceldama Monastery along here, in another link with evil, is believed to stand on the Field of Blood purchased with the 30 pieces of silver given to Judas for betraying Jesus.

► Mount Scopus (Hebrew: Har HaTsofim) *47E4*

The Hebrew name for Mount Scopus means "Looking Over," as does the Greek translation, Scopus. As a viewpoint over the Old City and the hills beyond, it is hard to beat. Roman legions camped here in AD70 before moving to crush the Jewish rebels. The Crusaders, too, camped at the summit on the eve of their attack on Jerusalem. In 1917, British forces rallied on Mount Scopus before their descent to the city. In 1948, however, when the Arab Legion assembled here for the advance on west Jerusalem, they were defeated and driven off the peak. The Israelis then held it as a besieged island of Jewish territory east of the ceasefire line until 1967, when normal life resumed.

Much of Mount Scopus was purchased in the 1920s by Jewish organisations. High on the hill, the impressive **Hebrew University►►**, opened in 1925, was rebuilt on dramatic lines (tours daily at 9 and 11am). Nearby stands the **Hadassah Hospital►**, also opened in 1925. Just below is the **Commonwealth Cemetery►**, containing the graves of British soldiers who fell fighting in Palestine during World War I.

►► Mount Zion (Hebrew: Har Tsion) *47D2*

The name Zion, as a synonym for Jerusalem and even for Israel, conjures much passion. The hill called Zion today is the westerly of two small peaks lying south of the Old City. Apart from the Armenian quarter, which climbs the northern slope, Mount Zion lies outside the city wall. It is dominated by churches built over revered religious sites, yet these, more than most, are without biblical or historical provenance.

A place of history In earlier times, Zion was the name given to the easterly of the two hills—the one on which stood the Jerusalem of King David and King Solomon. Nowadays that is called Mount Ofel (Ophel). Under Hezekiah, the city grew to cover Ofel, Zion, and Mount Moriah (Temple Mount): His city limits remained right up to the time of Herod. Then Jerusalem expanded into the area of today's Old City, except for the northeastern and northwestern corners. By Byzantine times, it filled the whole of the present Old City, plus the Zion and Ofel peaks, and so it stayed until Crusader times. The Soldiers of the Cross erected new defences, roughly following the city walls as we see them now—this time leaving the Ofel and Zion hills outside their defensive circle.

Mount Scopus is now dominated by the Hebrew University

A place of piety Half the hill is taken up by Christian cemeteries. The pretty **Church of St. Peter in Galicantu►**, meaning "at the cock-crow," was built in 1931 by Barluzzi on 1st-century ruins, and recalls St Peter's three denials of Christ before daybreak. It is also claimed as the site of the **House of Caiaphas►**, the high priest before whom Jesus was brought after his arrest. The 19th-century pale stone **Church of**

SCHINDLER'S GRAVE
Jews and Catholics alike make their way through the Catholic cemetery on Mount Zion to pay their respects to this notorious womanizer, drinker and wheeler-dealer. He joined the Nazi party and played the Nazi era for all he could make out of it. Oskar Schindler, immortalized in Spielberg's 1994 block-buster, *Schindler's List*, lies buried here. Like many other German business-men, Schindler used Jewish slave labor in his Polish factory but, while other manufacturers worked their slaves to death, Schindler found ways of helping them escape to Palestine. Some 1,200 owed their lives to him. Schindler died in Germany in 1974 and, at his own request, was buried on Mount Zion.

Lavish gold mosaic work adorns the interior of the Church of the Dormition

the Dormition▶, with its conical roof, stands where, according to Byzantine tradition, Mary fell asleep, instead of dying, before being assumed bodily into heaven.

Just beyond is a building that contains **David's Tomb▶**, revered by Orthodox Jews as well as Christians even though its location is incorrect. David was buried in the City of David (I Kings 2:10). This present "tomb" is a 4th-century invention within the remnant of a synagogue later incorporated into a Crusader church. It is richly adorned, with an embroidered cloth cover. The room itself contains Torah scrolls and is used as a synagogue. Many Jews pray here on Shavuot, traditionally the day of King David's death. Upstairs is the vaulted **Cenacle▶**, the so-called Room of the Last Supper, a location chosen in the 12th century. Inside, a slab of stone shows where Jesus sat during the meal! Facing it is a Muslim prayer niche. This room is also revered as the place where the Holy Spirit descended upon the disciples as they gathered for Shavuot (Pentecost in the Christian church), seven weeks later.

Opposite David's Tomb, the **Chamber of the Holocaust▶▶▶** (*Open* Sun–Thu 9–5, Fri 8–2. *Admission: donation*) may lack Yad VaShem's awesome memorial (see page 102), but this small museum is just as heart-wrenching. A particularly horrifying feature is the display of anti-Jewish material published since the Holocaust.

Sun symbol carved on the façade of the Room of the Last Supper

The lid-shaped Shrine of the Book

▶▶▶ Shrine of the Book *46A2*

Ruppin Street (tel: 02-670 8811; www.imj.org.il/eng/shrine)
Open: Sun–Mon, Wed–Thu 10–5, Tue 10–10, Fri 10–2, Sat 10–4. Admission: expensive

The the permanent home of the Dead Sea Scrolls (see pages 222–23) and other ancient manuscripts, including original biblical texts is part of the Israel Museum, and stands beside the main museum complex. The strange white shape of the Shrine of the Book represents the lids of the earthenware jars in which the scrolls were found.

Inside, the unusual roof covers a vast circular room, around which is displayed an unrolled scroll containing a large part of the Book of Isaiah, written in 100BC. Almost identical in every detail to the Book of Isaiah contained in later and modern Bibles, it is used as evidence that the Jewish scriptures remained unchanged as they were copied faithfully by generations of scribes.

Other rooms downstairs display a range of letters and scripts from the Second Temple period. Also displayed are documents from Masada (AD70) and others written during the Second Revolt (AD135), all of which have been of vital importance in enabling scholars to reconstruct the events of this troubled period. The low lighting of the room has a perfectly scientific rationale, yet it inspires a fitting sense of awe and an almost reverential atmosphere. The official guides seem infected, too, speaking with quiet urgency and passion about the writings.

BEDOUIN SCROLL HUNTERS

The first of the Dead Sea Scrolls was found in 1947 by a young Bedouin shepherd. He sold it a few months later to Arab traders who divided the scroll up and offered the parts for sale separately to academics and institutions. In 1949, archeologists and researchers moved in to look for more scrolls. Even while they were conducting their research unsuccessfully, new finds were being made by Bedouins. Of the 10 new caves containing scrolls, most were discovered by Bedouin shepherds, including the two caves that contained the most important of the documents.

▶ Supreme Court *46A3*

(tel: 02-6759612; www.court.gov.il)
Open: Sun–Thu; guided tours in English at noon

Israeli architecture has won few accolades. From 1948 to the 1990s, it can be characterized as bland and functional. A breakthrough came with the opening in 1992 of the new Supreme Court building on a hilltop near the Knesset, to which it is linked by a walkway. Since then several often inspired, imaginative and satisfying designs have been brought to fruition. Brother and sister architects Ram and Ada Karmi were responsible for the Supreme Court. It is a triumph of elegant, traditional simplicity in pale Jerusalem stone which proves that the modern, functional and unpretentious can be beautiful as well. The building was entirely paid for by the Rothschild family and estate.

Misconceptions about the Jewish faith and religion are rife among outsiders, and that has led to wild accusations, prejudice and murderous hatred in the past. Some visitors to Israel may not find Jewish people very forthcoming about their beliefs, and even on an extended visit it is possible to spend time among observant Jews and yet come away with no real idea what they believe or how they practise their religion.

An open book "People of the Book" is an apt description for the Jews. Jewish prayer is formalized and traditional, with set words being read in a set order from an authorized prayer book. Synagogue services are relaxed, amiable and not especially formal. At morning prayers many men wear a *tallit* (prayer shawl), *tefillin* (two small leather boxes containing scriptural texts, worn every day except Sabbath), and *kippah* as a head covering. At least 10 men (or women, in non-Orthodox congregations) must be present for key prayers to be said. At Monday, Thursday and Saturday (Sabbath) services, the week's "portion" of the Torah (the first five biblical books) is read aloud by selected congregants from a handwritten scroll while other members of the congregation follow the text in a book (the *Humash*). Much daily ritual, blessing and prayer, again from the prayer book, takes place at home.

Time and ritual The weeks, months and years are marked by their own prayers and rituals. High point of the week is Sabbath, welcomed on Friday night with blessings, candle-lighting, wine and *hallah* (Sabbath bread), and followed by a family meal. Annual festivals recall historical events, in accord with biblical precepts and seasonal customs. Pesach (Passover), for example, is a spring festival, decreed in the Torah as a memorial to the Jewish exodus from their enslavement in Egypt.

Getting it right The essence of Judaism is not belief, but behavior. The important thing is to observe the *mitzvot* (commandments) laid down in the scriptures. Numbering 613 altogether, these encompass every area of life from business to bedroom, childbirth to charity.

Traditions For most Israelis, though, the *mitzvot* are not really rules at all, but traditions. Some are considered part of "being Jewish"—like having sons circumcised, keeping the festivals and not eating pork. Many Israeli Jews consider others are unnecessary—like going in the *mikveh* (ritual bath) after menstruation, saying a blessing over bread before every meal or having the hairstyle described in Leviticus. Even some observant Jews don't obey all the rules, and those who do are in the minority.

FOR NON-JEWS VISITING A SYNAGOGUE...

- Any room containing a Torah scroll may be a synagogue.
- Men should cover their heads whether or not a service is in progress. Paper *yarmulkes* (skullcaps) are usually provided for visitors.
- Formal dress is not required but modesty is. Legs should be covered to the knee; women should not wear trousers.
- Do not walk about while the congregation is standing or while the Torah is being read, and do not speak or distract anyone while the silent prayers are being read.
- In an Orthodox or Conservative synagogue, ensure that you remain in the men's or women's section as appropriate.
- Do take a *Humash* (Torah text) and *siddur* (prayer book) from the shelves, but do not touch *tefillin* (leather scroll boxes), as these are sanctified ritual objects.

Torah scrolls (top) Reading the Torah (below), from right to left

AFTER DARK
After you have seen the Nahalat Shiv'a pedestrianized area during the day, come again in the evening. These traffic-free lanes, between Jaffa Street and King George V, are the city's favorite after-dark hangout. There's a café every few yards, scores of crowded tables in the open air, bookshops, jewelry shops, and snack take-outs open late into the night.

▶ University Library Albert Einstein Exhibition *46A2*

Hebrew University, Givat Ram campus
Open: Sun–Thu 9–7, Fri morning. Admission free.
The Hebrew University Library displays its archives on Einstein's life and work in a series of 20 panels. Einstein's personal papers illustrate his multifaceted interests.

▶▶▶ West Jerusalem *46B1 and 2, C1 and 2*

Sir Moses Montefiore built the first new district outside the Old City in 1860. Mishkenot Sha'ananim, as it is called, stands at the southern end of what is now the **Yemin Moshe** district (see page 104). Nowadays, most of Jerusalem's residents (including the Arab minority) live, work and play outside the walled tourist heartland. The area west of the Old City has become the bustling downtown of today. The second new district was Nahalat Shiv'a. Part of it, a tangle of renovated pedestrianized lanes around **Ben Yehuda Street▶▶▶**, is now the favorite area of Jerusalemites for strolling, browsing and whiling away the hours at outdoor cafés. In 1886 the city's busy food market was started at **Mahaneh Yehuda▶▶**, a few minutes' walk northwest from Ben Yehuda. Later, broad avenues were laid out linking the new neighborhoods. They have since become the city's traffic-filled main streets. **King George V▶▶** (and its continuation, Keren Ha-Yessod) and **King David▶** are lined with civic and religious buildings, offices and hotels. The two streets form the arms of a triangle whose third side is **Yafo (Jaffa) Street▶▶**, a hectic, crowded, fascinating thoroughfare.

Passing the time in the streets of Jerusalem (above and right)

Walk

West Jerusalem

Allow 3–4 hours for this quick tour of Jerusalem's modern center (for map see page 46B2/C2). From the **Tourist Office** at 24 King George V Street, head along King George and right onto Shatz Street, which reaches HaNagid Street. At No 12, see the **Jerusalem Artists' House▶**, with galleries and a café, next to the **Bezalel Academy of Art▶** founded about 100 years ago. Turn back to King George and turn right, passing the **Tzavta Theater**. At the **Jewish National Fund** office, you can arrange to plant a tree in one of the forests on the city's perimeter.

The Orthodox **Great Synagogue▶** is well worth a look inside. Beside it, the **Wolfson Museum of Art▶**, specialising in Judaica, shares a building with the Chief Rabbi's office. Then comes **Kikkar Tsarfat (Zarefat)▶** (or France Square, also called Place de France). This is Jerusalem's central square, at the meeting of King George V, Keren HaYesod, Ramban, Aza (or Gaza) and Gershon Agron streets. On one corner stands the main Conservative Synagogue.

A few paces along Ramban Street, an old windmill has become the basis for a shopping center full of fashion boutiques and eating places. Turn left along Gershon Agron and left again into pleasant **Independence Park▶**. Stroll across to Hillel Street. At No 27 is the interesting **Museum of Italian Jewish Art▶** and a restored 18th-century **Italian synagogue▶**, brought stone by stone from Italy.

Take Angelo Blanchini Street to reach the pedestrianized area. Walk along **Ben Yehuda Street▶▶▶** to another focal point, **Kikkar Tsion▶** (or Zion Square). Head up Harav Kook Street to **Ticho House▶▶**, now part of the Israel Museum. It was once the home of artist Anna Ticho and is full of her artwork. Walk along Jaffa Road and turn left on King George V. This busy section has many stores selling clothing, books, food and much else.

The Great Synagogue

Independence Park

YAD VASHEM
The name Yad v'Shem means "A Memorial and a Name"—that is, for every victim of the Holocaust.

The symbolic Pillar of Heroism

The Silent Cry, *one of the sculptures making up Yad VaShem's Art Museum*

THE HOLOCAUST
Holocaust (*shoah* in Hebrew) literally means 'burn whole'. Until the Nazi era, the word usually referred to religious sacrifices. The Nazi Holocaust burned deep scars in the contemporary Jewish psyche, and the creation of the State of Israel received much of its impetus from the heightened desperation of Jews to find a safe haven, just as much of its international support is due to the moral legitimacy conferred by the tragedy.

►►► Yad VaShem *46A1*

(tel: 02-6443400; www.yadvashem.org)
Open: Sun–Wed 9–5, Thu 9–8, Fri and eve of holidays 9–1. Closed Shabbat. No entry in last hour before closing. Admission free

The world's leading Holocaust memorial, museum and documentation center covers a ridge of high ground named Har HaZikaron—literally, the Hill of Memory—rising west of the Mount Herzl summit.

For anyone who has come to Israel for enjoyment and relaxation, a visit to Yad VaShem may seem a daunting prospect. Difficult though the experience can be, it will only heighten an appreciation of the country and its people. Once you have absorbed the awful facts of recent Jewish history, you will view with new eyes the energy and determination of Israelis to enjoy life to the full. For those who have come to Israel to gain greater understanding of the Jews and their land, a morning at Yad VaShem is essential. The sprawling site, wooded in part, offers broad views westward toward central Jerusalem.

Visiting the site Start by walking the length of the **Avenue of the Righteous Among the Nations►**, along the south side of the memorial area. This commemorates non-Jews who risked their own lives in order to save Jews during the Holocaust. They are named individually. This leads to the **Holocaust History Museum►►►**, a prismlike structure of bare concrete below ground—only the top is visible—arranged as chambers entered in sequence, where the Holocaust story is vivily told from the rise of Hitler

The Hall of Names records all known victims of the Holocaust

onward. Multimedia presentations bring together the broad historical picture with 90 intimate stories. There is also harrowing film footage shot by the Nazis: a Warsaw ghetto scene, and cattletrucks transporting people to the death camps. Many dry German government publications and posters are displayed, matter-of-fact material which contrasts with the disturbing photographs of dead women piled in heaps like rag dolls, camp inmates pushing corpses into furnaces, and of laughing German soldiers humiliating or arresting Jewish children. The last chamber is the **Hall of Names▶▶**, where the names of Holocaust victims are inscribed after all the evidence has been verified. So far, over 3 million names are recorded. The museum's exit opens up dramatically onto a plaza with a panoramic view of modern Jerusalem, an astounding and uplifting vision of Jewish rebirth and hope.

Among the other buildings, the huge, undecorated **Hall of Remembrance▶** is a large, grim chamber containing little but a memorial flame before a vault of victims' ashes. The names of the Nazi death camps are set into the floor.

The **Art Museum▶▶** is a remarkable collection of drawings and paintings made by concentration camp inmates. Farther on is the **Partisan's Memorial▶▶** and, farther still, the wooded, walled **Valley of the Communities▶▶**, the former memorial recording the names of the communities entirely destroyed during the Holocaust.

In the grounds, **sculptures▶▶▶** form an integral part of the memorial. Across the plaza stands the powerful *Silent Cry*. From here, walk toward the Children's Memorial, pausing at the heart-rending *Korczak and the Children of the Ghetto*. Korczak was a teacher who voluntarily accompanied his pupils to death at Treblinka because he could not bear to see them taken away with no one to care for them.

The underground **Children's Memorial▶▶▶** is in memory of the 1.5 million young children and babies killed in the death camps. Inside, it is dark except for myriad pinpoints of light like stars, each representing the life of a child taken away. A ceaseless, droning tape reads the list of their names, places of birth and ages.

TIPS FOR A VISIT TO YAD VASHEM

- Come in the morning, giving time to see the whole museum and memorial without haste.
- Avoid coming with a group if possible. Yad VaShem should be seen at your own speed, with time and privacy to reflect on the exhibits.
- However long or short a time you spend here, do not miss the Children's Memorial on any account.
- Don't take children to see Yad VaShem. Although groups of older Israeli schoolchildren are taken around the site, most clearly either do not understand its importance or, in a few cases, are very deeply shocked by what they see. Noisy, laughing youngsters also diminish the impact of the memorial for others, dishonoring the Holocaust victims. Under 12s are not allowed at Yad VaShem.

Residences in the Yemin Moshe district

▶ Yemin Moshe 46C2

This charming, picturesque neighborhood, constructed by the philanthropist Sir Moses Montefiore in the 1860s, rises from close to the southwestern tower of the Old City walls. This was the first settlement to be built outside the walls, and it has since attracted a number of artists whose work is sold in the area's galleries. The whole district has a quiet sense of well-being. Its pale stone paving and buildings climb in stepped alleys and lanes, giving glorious views, up to **Bloomfield Gardens▶** and the famous Jerusalem landmark, **Montefiore's Windmill▶**. Intended to provide a means of income for the area's first residents, the windmill has since been turned into a museum dedicated to the life and times of Sir Moses Montefiore (1784–1885), a remarkable, early pioneer of Jewish rights. Born in Livorno, Italy, he made a fortune as a stockbroker in London, became sheriff of the city in 1824, then retired to devote the rest of his life to founding schools and hospitals in Britain and Jerusalem.

▶ Zoo 46A1

Open: summer, Sun–Thu 9–7, Fri 9–3, Sat 10–6.30; winter, daily 9–5. Admission: expensive

At Manahat (also known as Malka), on the southwestern outskirts of the city, is the modern **Tisch Gardens Biblical Zoo** consisting of 64 acres (26ha) of landscaped parkland with lakes, waterfalls and lawns set against a backdrop of desert hills. Animals wander freely, separated from humans by moats or natural earth banks. Here you can see the now-rare animals of the Old Testament, all once native to the region, including lions and tigers.

HAAS AND SHEROVER PROMENADES

The most spectacular view of Jerusalem, Old and New, is from the Walter and Elise Haas Promenade, a handsome walkway some 654 yards (600m) long, set on a ridge of high ground in the new southern neighborhood of East Talpiot. The more recent Gabriel Sherover Promenade (more usually called by the Hebrew name Tayelet Sherover), again with superb Old City views, descends through fine landscaped gardens.

Israel adores its children. Even more than in other countries they are indulged and forgiven by everyone. Somehow, their exuberance and enthusiasm, their noisy boisterousness, their energy, and their robust good health, all seem to symbolize the state itself. Israel, too, is young and new and vulnerable. But above all, the children of today are alive. Even now, when Israelis look at their children, they are reminded of a dark past, and an uncertain future.

A precious generation Children seem to be everywhere. School groups, sometimes in neat lines, but more usually like a horde of Tartars, are taken to see every monument and memorial to Israel's creation, every museum of importance. They are always accompanied by an armed guard, sometimes a soldier but more often a parent who is an army reservist with full weapons training (the guns are not loaded—bullets are carried separately).

Those who died Before the policy of providing guards began in the 1970s, Palestinian attacks on children were common. School parties, school buses and children's houses in kibbutzim were considered legitimate targets by the PLO. Scores of children were murdered. But overshadowing even these tragedies looms the Holocaust. Common images of Holocaust victims are of adults. In reality, a quarter of all Jews killed in the gas chambers were children. For Israelis today, it is a joy to see Jewish children alive and enjoying their liberty.

A new type The *sabra* is a prickly pear cactus, spiny outside, sweet within. That is how the new generation of Israelis looks to outsiders. A third of all Israeli children now have mixed Ashkenazi/Sephardi families. Chattering (or rather, shouting) in fluent secular Hebrew, a language that did not exist a century ago, taller, stronger, healthier than their mothers and fathers, bold and forthright, and with a country to call their own, they are being nurtured as a new type of Jew.

Israeli children enjoy a freedom their parents did not know

Innocent play

BED AND BREAKFAST
"Good Morning Jerusalem" is the organization that co-ordinates over 100 bed and breakfast guesthouses in the city and environs. Prices are relatively modest, guesthouses are graded by size and comfort, and all the host families speak English. For bookings or information, contact the reservations office in Jaffa Road, opposite Jerusalem's central bus station, tel: 02 651 1270.

King David Hotel is the grandest in Israel, full of historic importance
Opposite: The grand but inexpensive YMCA

Inbal Hotel, with innovative architecture and luxurious accommodation, is the modern style of Israeli hotel

Accommodation

The key to enjoying this sprawling city is to be in the right part of it. Top choice would be to stay near the attractions of the Old City, though not too near, as it can be noisy and crowded. The vivacious downtown (west Jerusalem) has most of the best hotels in every price range and is an easy walk from the Old City. The smallish Arab district (East Jerusalem) just north of the Old City walls is atmospheric but less modern. A few of the farther-flung districts are also convenient and enjoyable. Of some 8,000 hotel rooms in the city, over 3,000 are graded de luxe, but there is a good range of budget-priced accommodation as well.

Central Jerusalem On the top rung, the King David Hotel (King David Street, or Rehov David HaMelek), built in 1931 (see page 90), is legendary. Due to continuous reno-

vation and modernization, it has left behind much of its prewar grandeur. It is supremely comfortable, well located, with excellent food, facilities and service, and set on considerable grounds which face the Old City. The King David is part of the top-level Dan chain, which also owns the atrium-style Dan Pearl, facing Mount Zion and not far from Jaffa Gate.

Several big names are on, or near, King David, Keren HaYesod and King George V streets. Here you will find the Sheraton, Dan Panorama, David Citadel and King Solomon. Plenty of good places fill the middle and lower price ranges, such as the Caesar (Jaffa Road), the Montefiore (off King George V Street), the three Prima hotels, and less expensive, the simple but attractive Jerusalem Inn (Horkanos Street, near Ben Yehuda pedestrian mall). Lower down the scale, the inexpensive YMCA (opposite the King David) is almost absurdly grand looking, and the facilities (especially for sports) are very good. The excellent Yitzhak Rabin Youth Hostel (1 Nahman Avigad Street), near the Israel Museum, is for Youth Hostel members.

The Old City and East Jerusalem There is a plethora of budget hotels, dorms, religious hospices and hostels in the Arab districts around Damascus and Jaffa gates and in the Old City Christian and Muslim quarters. Most are rather shabby. The best are in HaNeviim Street. Note that late-night music and noise, as well as early morning muezzins calling the faithful to prayer, can be a nuisance. Up Salah ed-Din (Saladin) Street there is a string of low-priced hotels. At the end of Saladin, the Arab quarter reaches the smarter American Colony district, where East meets West. Here are some high quality hotels, such as the Jerusalem Novotel and Olive Tree Royal Plaza (both in St George Street). In the American Colony you will find arguably the most interesting and atmospheric hotel in the whole city, the Oriental-style American Colony Hotel. A luxurious former pasha's palace, it is now a favorite venue for foreign correspondents and Palestinian leaders.

On a limb Park Plaza (formerly Sonesta) and the huge Renaissance hotel, both well equipped and comfortable, stand out west on or just off Herzl Boulevard. They are not far from the Knesset and the major museums, and close to the bus station with its regular departures to points all over the country. Farther out, to the southwest, is the Holyland Hotel and in the other direction is the vast and luxurious Hyatt Regency (32 Lehi Street) on the slope of Mount Scopus with a magnificent city view.

Kibbutz near the city One of the best choices on many counts is the hotel at Kibbutz Ramat Rahel (or Rachel). This is quiet and civilized, has good food, extensive grounds and a pleasant atmosphere, offers full use of the kibbutz leisure facilities, and enjoys fine views towards the Judaean hills. The kibbutz passed into Jewish and Arab lore in the 1948 war, when it was on the front line and focus of ferocious battles. A kibbutz museum (*Open* daily 8–noon) tells the story. The kibbutz is between Jerusalem and Bethlehem, 3 miles (5km) from each.

Jerusalem's annual festivals and events

Events using lunar dates or the Hebrew calendar are "moveable" in the international calendar.

Tu b'Shvat (celebration of nature): about Feb (1 day)
Jerusalem half-marathon: Mar
Purim: early Mar (1 day)
Pesach (Passover): about Apr
Yom HaShoah, Holocaust memorial day: about May
Israel Independence Day: about May
Israel Festival: May–Jun
Yom Yerushalayim (Jerusalem Day): Jun
Shavuot (Pentecost): Jun/Jul (2 days)
Abu Gosh Music Festival: Jul
Jerusalem Film Festival: Jul
Tisha b'Av: about Aug
Rosh Hashanah (Jewish New Year): about Sep/Oct
Ramadan (Arab areas): moveable (1 month)
Yom Kippur (Day of Atonement): 10 days after Rosh Hashanah
Sukkot (Tabernacles) : 4 days after Yom Kippur (1 week)
Abu Gosh Music Festival: at Sukkot
Sigd (Ethiopian Jewish Festival): Dec
Hannukah: Dec (1 week)
Christmas: 24–25 Dec

KOSHER
The majority of eating places in Jerusalem are kosher (although most in Arab districts are not). Most big hotels offer something special and traditional for the Friday night Sabbath dinner. On Sabbaths and festivals, many Jerusalem restaurants are closed, but nearly all hotel restaurants remain open.

ONE CENTURY AGO
"In 1873 it was calculated that the Jerusalem Jews, who then numbered only a few hundred in all, were increasing at the rate of 1,200 or 1,500 souls per annum. The Russian persecution gave a great impetus to the movement. I suppose that the present Jewish population of the Holy City cannot be reckoned at less than 40,000 souls. And they are no longer a timorous, oppressed minority, but something more resembling the masters of the city."
—*The Future of Palestine*, Major C R Conder, 1892

Israeli restaurants are refreshingly informal

Eating out

Bed and board Almost all hotels offer a magnificent self-service buffet breakfast of hot and cold dishes, salads, fresh breads and fruit juices. It makes a great start to the day and can take the edge off lunchtime appetite. Bed and breakfast is a good option when booking your trip, giving the freedom to eat dinner in or out of the hotel.

On the hoof In the Old City, there are many small, unpretentious café-restaurants. The format is generally the same: frontage open to the street and, within, a display of salads, pastries, sweets and savories, falafels cooking, shwarma on the spit, and some wipe-clean tables. Downtown (West Jerusalem) has scores of small restaurants offering hummus, falafels, latkes (potato fritters), omelets, grilled meats, shwarma or shishlik (lamb or turkey kabob), salads, pizzas, ice-cream, cakes, juices and coffee.

Some wonderful little bakeries can be found on Jaffa and King George V streets near Ben Yehuda Street and on the other pedestrian lanes—Lunz, Rishonim, Ben Hillel, and Nahalat Shiv'a—which are packed with open-air café tables. Most of these are adequate rather than good, though some have more style and reach a higher standard. Well-established favorites include the Rimon and Alno cafés around Ben Yehuda.

Dinner time Most hotels in town have at least one restaurant, usually "dairy" as well as "meat"-eating places. Try the King David and the American Colony. Away from the hotels, for better restaurants aim for either a French-Italian or an Austro-Hungarian style, though Yemenite and Arabic restaurants provide a more exotic experience as well as excellent food. Well established are Little Italy (38 Keren HaYesod Street) for home-made pasta, the cultural center Mishkenot Sha'ananim (Yemin Moshe, below the windmill) for Moroccan and French dishes and El Gaucho (22 Rivlin Street) for grills. For more ideas, pick up *Jerusalem Menus* from the tourist office.

Shopping

Where to shop Wandering along David Street and Street of the Chain, in the Old City, is sheer delight, with a cornucopia of products ranging from cheap souvenirs to antique silver. Outside the walls, away from the central shopping district along and between Jaffa Street and King George V Street, almost every other neighborhood has its well-stocked shopping malls and centers. Some are huge. Talpiot (in the southwest) has the big Canyon Israel Shopping Center, and Manahat or Malka (in the west) has the Malka Mall, the largest shopping center in Israel.

What to buy The Druze weavings, olive-wood carvings and other craft goods make excellent souvenirs. Jewelry and silverware are great specialties. Silver ornaments and modern Judaica are seen in numerous stores throughout downtown and in the souks of the Old City. Necklaces and other jewelry of silver, gold and precious stones are also widely available at specialist shops, including along the Cardo, in the Jewish quarter of the Old City.

Diamonds are a major Israeli product, and a tour of the National Diamond Center (143 Bethlehem Road) is worthwhile. All sorts of creative jewelry, imaginative and of a high standard, is for sale. Take a look, for example, at galleries along the main downtown streets. The King David Hotel has shopping arcades selling some of the best. Also look for fine fashions, especially swimwear, in which Israel excels (swimwear giant Gottex is based here). Leather goods are another local strong point, including sandals, which are reasonably priced. And don't miss the unique—and effective—skin-care products (by Ahava, for example) made of mud from the Dead Sea.

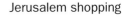

Bargain-price tapes and worry beads

HAGGLING

Haggling is almost unknown in Israel today, though it's possible to try your luck asking for a "discount." Even in the Arab parts of Jerusalem, haggling has all but died out in the last few decades as traders accustom themselves to the more straightforward, take-it-or-leave-it style of Israelis. Certain goods are never haggled over—food, for example—but in Arab areas, at stalls selling souvenirs, clothing or trinkets, you may (occasionally) find that goods have no fixed price. Then you should respond to the initial asking price with a shrug, a laugh...and a much lower offer. After a few counter offers, and some dramatic declarations about not making any profit, family to feed, selling below cost price, and so on (designed to weaken your resolve), you and the trader will agree a price, traditionally about 55 percent of what was first asked.

SHOPPING HOURS

Most businesses, including shops, are open Sunday to Thursday 8.30–1 and 4–7. Bigger shopping malls and centers do not close during the day. On Friday, shops open in the morning only; on Saturday some open after dusk.

DRESS CODE
Whatever the event or venue, informal or casual dress is the norm in Israel. It often startles foreign visitors at official events to see Israeli dignitaries without jackets or ties. Televised Knesset proceedings likewise show members of Israel's parliament—including the prime minister—wearing open-neck, short-sleeve shirts. For his important treaty-signing ceremony with King Hussein of Jordan, the late premier Yitzhak Rabin wore a baseball cap. However, sloppy, scruffy clothing is not favored, and immodest or provocative dress is definitely considered unacceptable.

WHAT'S ON
For more details of what's on during your stay, ask the tourist office for copies of the current *This Week in Israel*, *Events in Jerusalem* and *The Jerusalem Tourist Guide*.

Nightlife

Good clean fun It might be thought that this capital city of religion and faith would go to sleep at an early hour. That is far from being the case. There is an infinite choice to entertain you around the clock, however, nightlife does tend to be of a clean and wholesome variety. Raunchy nightclubs are few, and risqué acts frowned upon. Drama, ballet, concerts and cheerful folklore shows are constantly available. The only exception is the Sabbath (Saturday), when Jerusalem is quieter than many other Israeli towns. The city's leading venue is the Jerusalem Center for the Performing Arts, at 20 Marcus Street (tel: 02-617167).

Evening air The heart of after-dark Jerusalem is the Nahalat Shiv'a area around Ben Yehuda Street and Zion Square. Along the pedestrian streets, crowds stroll in the open air and outdoor cafés are packed far into the night. From certain doorways comes the throb of popular music —late-night discos appealing mainly to the young.

Top notch Some evening entertainments are unashamedly touristic, but still top quality. The outdoor *Son et Lumière* at the Citadel (Tower of David) is superb (nightly except Fridays). It tells the history of the city in a magnificently appropriate setting. Take a sweater; tickets from hotels or the Citadel entrance at Jaffa Gate.

Song and dance Slick Israeli/Jewish folklore shows are put on in the big hotels. Often there are specials, such as a dramatized performance of a Yemenite wedding. Folk shows are put on at the YMCA, on King David Street, and at the Khan Theater, in an old Turkish inn south of Yemin Moshe. Open-air summer performances are staged at the Sultan's Pool amphitheater below Yemin Moshe.

Arabian nights If you have seen the Israeli shows before, or want a change, take a trip into East Jerusalem for clubs and restaurants that put on the Arab version. They feature lilting Oriental music and exotic (not erotic) dance shows.

Nightlife is clean and wholesome

Practical points

Information The Jerusalem tourist office is at Jaffa Gate (tel: 02-6271422; *closed* Fri and Sat). It has masses of leaflets, ideas for guided tours, and copies of the latest editions of *This Week in Israel*, *Events in Jerusalem* and *The Jerusalem Tourist Guide*. Staff speak English and are very helpful.

Getting around The Old City of Jerusalem is compact, with major sights close to each other. Outside the walls, by far the best way to get from one sight to another is on bus No 99. The bus follows a round-town circular route every two hours (Sun–Thu 10–4; Fri and the evening before public holidays 10am and noon). You can get off at any point of interest, take a look around and board the next No 99 bus to continue.

City buses in general are frequent and inexpensive. Bus drivers speak English, and stops have brief route details in English. For bus information tel: 03-6948888, English spoken). Services run from 5.30am to midnight, except on Friday (when services stop for the Sabbath an hour before sunset) and on Saturday (no service until after Sabbath ends, an hour after sunset). Services on Jewish holidays are the same as for the Sabbath. From the city's main Jaffa Road bus station, buses leave every few minutes to towns and cities all over Israel.

Regular taxis (called "special taxis"), which generally wait outside hotels, are expensive. Agree upon the fare in advance, or insist that the meter be used (Jerusalem cab drivers are notorious for overcharging). Cheaper *sherutim* (singular: *sherut*), shared taxis which stick to a particular route, depart from set locations.

Business hours Banks are open Sunday to Friday 8.30–12.30, and on Sunday, Tuesday and Thursday 4–6. In tourist areas, some open Sunday to Thursday 8.30–5.30, and Friday 8.30–12.30. Main post offices open Sunday to Thursday 8–6. Post office local branches open daily 8–12.30 and 3.30–6, but mornings only on Monday, Wednesday and Friday.

Emergencies Police 100; Ambulance 101; Fire 102; Tourist Police 391250.

GUIDED WALKS
Numerous firms offer guided walking tours. Their leaflets are displayed at the tourist office and big hotels. The tourist office itself runs guided walks, free of charge. Ask for dates and times.

RETURN TO SENDER
"How much better informed the public now is than twenty years ago, when my letters were shelved in an English country post office, because they were directed to me at Jerusalem, and the postmistress said in explanation that she thought 'all that was done away with'."
—Major C R Conder, 1892

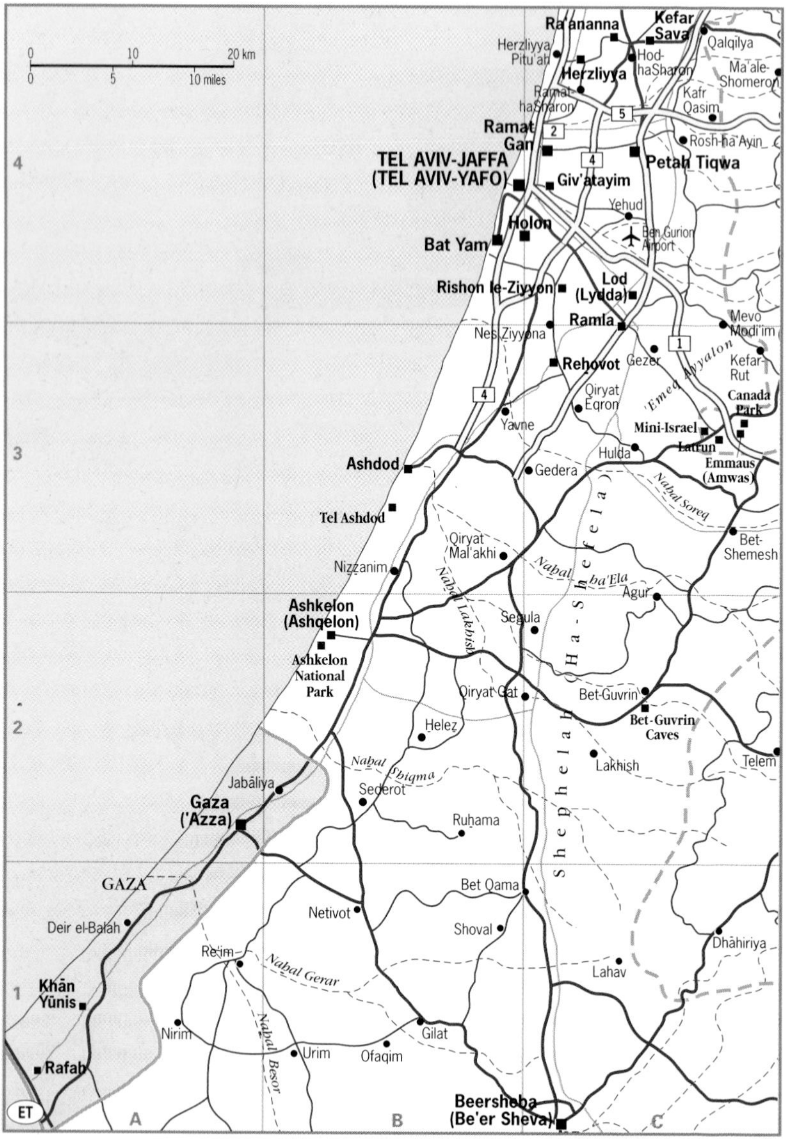

▶▶▶ REGION HIGHLIGHTS

Akko *pages 138–40*
Beit Jabotinsky *page 119*
Caesarea *pages 146–7*
Carmel Market *page 117*
Carmelite Monastery, Haifa *page 152*
Jaffa *pages 124–5*
Mount Carmel *page 154*
Museum of the Jewish Diaspora *pages 126–7*
Tel Qasile *pages 118–19*

TEL AVIV AND THE COAST The Mediterranean has dominated Israel's life and civilization throughout the ages. Psychologically as well as physically, Israel faces west, for commerce, culture and communication. Almost the entire population lives on a narrow strip along the coast. Most of Israel's wealth comes from this busy, densely populated strip and from the farms of the well-watered Plain of Sharon, running north to south just inland from the sea. For the visitor wanting to combine beach life with exploration of the country's unrivaled array of ancient sites, it is convenient that (apart from the Negev desert) few places in Israel are farther than about 12.5 miles (20km) from a Mediterranean beach.

Tel Aviv and the Coast

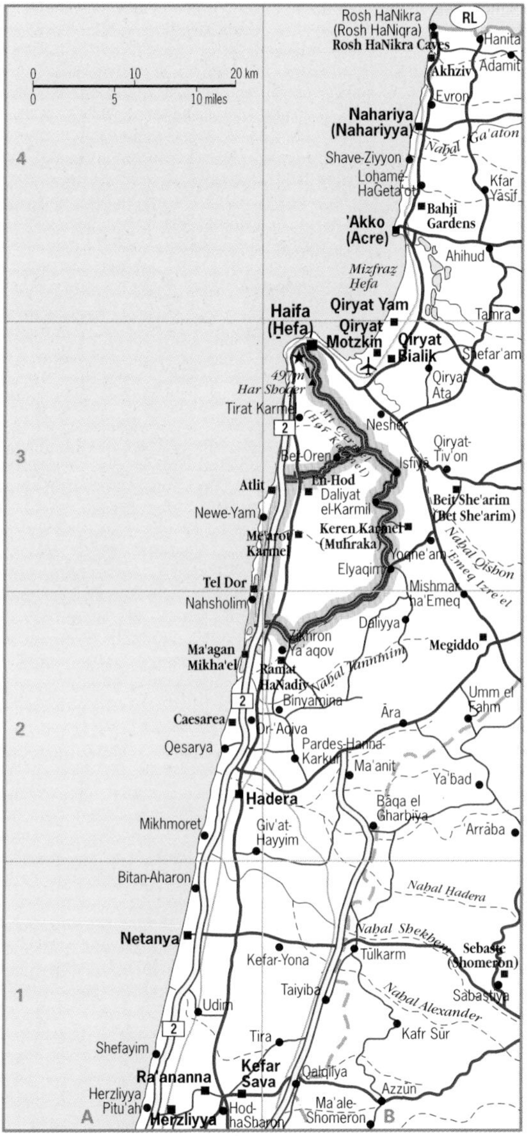

NEW AND OLD RESORTS While Tel Aviv is a big city, bursting with energy, there is a string of quieter resorts, such as Netanya and Herzliya, up and down the coast. Here leisure facilities and accommodations tend to reach a far higher standard than anywhere else in the eastern Mediterranean. It is also possible to stay by the sea without being in town at all—for example, at a kibbutz hotel. Few resorts, whether in the town or the country, date back more than a few decades, and most were designed as resorts in the first place. Yet nearly all have a historical site nearby, remnants of some earlier town—Phoenician, Jewish or Roman—which stood there thousands of years before, including the star attractions of Caesarea and Akko.

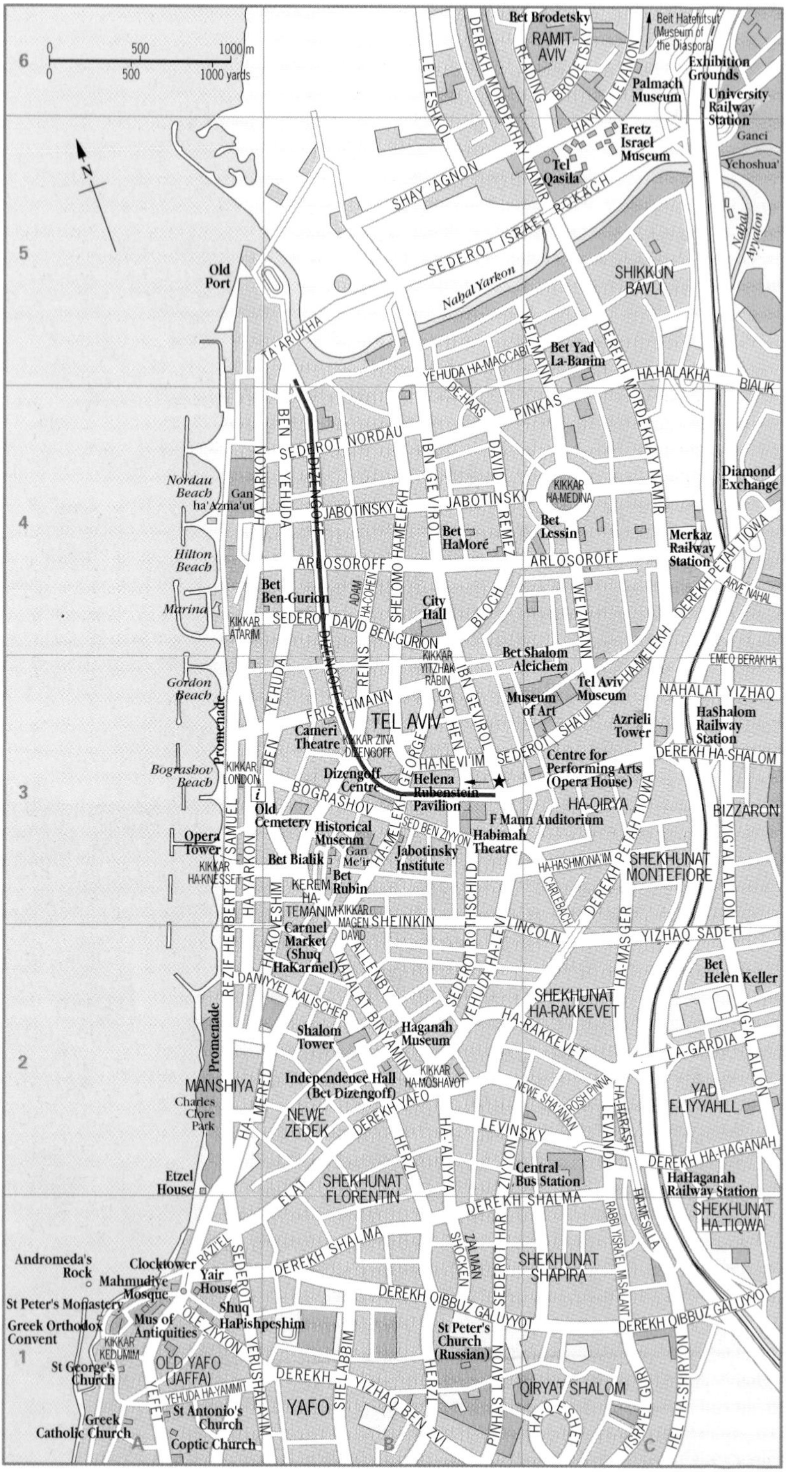

0
500
1000 m
0
500
1000 yards
N
6
5
4
3
2
1
A
B
C
Bet Brodetsky
RAMIT-AVIV
Beit Hatefutsut (Museum of the Diaspora)
Exhibition Grounds
University Railway Station
Ganei
Yehoshua'
Palmach Museum
Eretz Israel Museum
Tel Qasila
LEVI ESHKOL
DEREKH MORDEKHAY NAMIR
READING
BRODETSKY
HAYYIM LEVANON
SHAY 'AGNON
SEDEROT ISRAEL ROKACH
Nahal Ayyalon
Old Port
Nahal Yarkon
SHIKKUN BAVLI
TA'ARUKHA
YEHUDA HA-MACCABI
Bet Yad La-Banim
WEIZMANN
DEREKH MORDEKHAY NAMIR
HA-HALAKHA
BIALIK
DE-HAAS
PINKAS
SEDEROT NORDAU
BEN YEHUDA
DIZENGOFF
HA-YARKON
IBN GEVIROL
DAVID REMEZ
KIKKAR HA-MEDINA
Diamond Exchange
Nordau Beach
Gan ha'Azma'ut
JABOTINSKY
Bet Lessin
Bet HaMoré
Merkaz Railway Station
DEREKH PETAH TIQWA
Hilton Beach
ARLOSOROFF
ADAM HA-COHEN
SHLOMO HA-MELEKH
Bet Ben-Gurion
City Hall
BLOCH
ARVE NAHAL
Marina
KIKKAR ATARIM
SEDEROT DAVID BEN-GURION
KIKKAR YITZHAK RABIN
REINS
Bet Shalom Aleichem
EMEQ BERAKHA
Gordon Beach
FRISHMANN
Tel Aviv Museum
Museum of Art
NAHALAT YIZHAQ
HaShalom Railway Station
Azrieli Tower
TEL AVIV
Promenade
YEHUDA
Cameri Theatre
KIKKAR ZINA DIZENGOFF
SHA'UL
SEDEROT
DEREKH HA-SHALOM
HA-NEVI'IM
Centre for Performing Arts (Opera House)
Bograshov Beach
KIKKAR LONDON
BEN
Dizengoff Centre
Helena Rubenstein Pavilion
HA-QIRYA
BOGRASHOV
Old Cemetery
F Mann Auditorium
BIZZARON
Opera Tower
Historical Museum
SED BEN ZIYYON
Habimah Theatre
YIG'AL ALLON
KIKKAR HA-KNESSET
HA-YARKON
Bet Bialik
Gan Me'ir
Jabotinsky Institute
HA-HASHMONA'IM
SHEKHUNAT MONTEFIORE
Bet Rubin
KEREM HA-TEMANIM
CARLEBACH
KIKKAR MAGEN DAVID
SHEINKIN
REZIF HERBERT SAMUEL
HA-KOVESHIM
Carmel Market (Shuq HaKarmel)
LINCOLN
YIZHAQ SADEH
ROTHSCHILD
YEHUDA HA-LEVI
HA-MASGER
Bet Helen Keller
DANIYYEL
KALISCHER
ALLENBY
NAHALAT BINYAMIN
SEDEROT
SHEKHUNAT HA-RAKKEVET
HA-RAKKEVET
Shalom Tower
Haganah Museum
LA-GARDIA
Promenade
MANSHIYA
Independence Hall (Bet Dizengoff)
KIKKAR HA-MOSHAVOT
YAD ELIYYAHU
Charles Clore Park
HA-MERED
NEWE ZEDEK
DEREKH YAFO
NEWE SHA'ANAN
ROSH PINNA
HA-HARASH
LEVANDA
LEVINSKY
HA-'ALIYYA
ZIYYON
HERZL
DEREKH HA-HAGANAH
Etzel House
SHEKHUNAT FLORENTIN
ELAT
Central Bus Station
HaHaganah Railway Station
DEREKH SHALMA
SHEKHUNAT HA-TIQWA
HA-MESILLA
RABBI YISRA'EL MI-SALANT
Andromeda's Rock
Clocktower
RAZI'EL
Yair House
ZALMAN SHOCKEN
SEDEROT HAR
SHEKHUNAT SHAPIRA
Mahmudiye Mosque
DEREKH QIBBUZ GALUYYOT
St Peter's Monastery
Shuq HaPishpeshim
Greek Orthodox Convent
Mus of Antiquities
OLE ZIYYON
St Peter's Church (Russian)
KIKKAR KEDUMIM
St George's Church
OLD YAFO (JAFFA)
YERUSHALAYIM
SHELABBIM
DEREKH YIZHAQ BEN ZVI
QIRYAT SHALOM
YEHUDA HA-YAMMIT
PINHAS LAVON
HA-QESHET
YISRA'EL GURI
HEL HA-SHIRYON
Greek Catholic Church
St Antonio's Church
YAFO
EFET
Coptic Church

Tel Aviv

A century ago it wasn't here. The largest Jewish city ever to have existed has sprung up beside the Mediterranean with dizzying speed. The sense of liberation and excitement in the air is almost palpable. Tel Aviv has pulled fragments of a nation from the world's ghettos and Jewish quarters and, like a crucible, fused them together once again. A fifth of Israel's population lives in the city and its suburbs, which together form a hectic, dynamic metropolis dominating the country's cultural life.

Tel Aviv plays, Haifa works, Jerusalem prays. That is the popular summary of Israel's three cities. It is true that, in Tel Aviv, very few pray: Signs of Jewish observance, or of any other religion, are scarce. This is a breezily materialistic, pleasure-loving city. For round-the-clock entertainment and sheer *joie de vivre*, this is the place.

On the other hand, Tel Aviv at leisure will not appeal to everyone. It is a touch civilized. The city has dozens of first-class galleries and museums. People going out for the evening head to symphony concerts or stage plays, though there are jazz and rock spots too. Performers in the street, almost without exception, play the violin: Their repertoire is mainly classical or East European folk music. You probably won't, in any part of town, see anyone drunk. Nightclub acts tend toward satire, not strippers. Day and night, it is the vast beach and its waterside promenade which pull the biggest crowds of all.

An East Mediterranean city
Tel Avivians compare their home town grandly to New York or Paris. True, there are chic shops and good restaurants, but the lively avenues and big squares, the generous sidewalks shaded from the sun, the outdoor tables and exuberant (but crime-free) street life, and the little backstreet shops with a pre-war feel, add up to an inescapably East Mediterranean feel. A more accurate comparison might be with Athens (but without the level of pollution), for Tel Aviv, like the Greek capital, is newly built, yet echoes with history. And, again like that city, it represents the joyful rebirth of a Mediterranean land swallowed up for centuries by the Ottoman Empire.

TEL AVIV'S BAUHAUS STYLE
UNESCO's listing in 2003 of central tel Aviv as a World Heritage Site under the name The White City was a wake-up call to Israelis. Almost every downtown building, apart from modern high-rises, dates from the 1930s and is in a style derived from Germany's Bauhaus movement, which favored simple, functional, unadorned, geometric structures. World War II destroyed most of Europe's Bauhas heritage, while Tel Aviv's builders adapted the style to their own needs. Since those days, many Tel Aviv Bauhaus buidings have been ineptly modernized or become dilapidated. The World Heritage label has brought planning laws and an ambitions restoration program, with thousands of facades earmarked to be returned to the original Tel Aviv style.

Mounts of olives

FOLLOW THE FLAG
All down Israel's Mediterranean coast, swimming conditions are indicated by colored flags on the beach. White shows that swimming is safe where a lifeguard is on duty. Red shows that swimming could be dangerous, but is permitted at the discretion of the lifeguard on duty. Black means no swimming at all.

ON THE BEACH
Opposite the Dan Hotel, where now sunbathers laze, a ship carrying 850 clandestine Jewish immigrants finally came to rest on August 22, 1939. The overcrowded *Parita* had spent 42 days wandering at sea, avoiding British craft intent on preventing Jews from reaching Palestine.

Space to enjoy a swim or a stroll

►►► Beaches 114A2–4

A glorious 5 miles (8km) of wide, soft white sand runs beside the heart of the city. It is only a 10-minute walk from deckchair to Dizengoff, the main central avenue. More spectacular is the broad beachside **promenade►►►**, paved in swirling patterns, stretching from North Tel Aviv nearly into Jaffa. In Hebrew it is simply called the Tayelet, the word for a walkway. For most of the distance, busy Herbert Samuel Boulevard runs parallel. From 6am to 2am, you will see swimmers in the water and joggers on the promenade. And, facing west, the beach and promenade are perfect for sunsets. In the evening, street musicians play the violin, sometimes even joining to form string quartets. Well past midnight, thousands of people still stroll or sit here in the tender night air.

Frequent lifeguard stations are a reminder to be prudent when swimming—the undercurrents are powerful. Join the Israelis, who happily swim and surf under the watchful eye of the lifeguards.

North of the main beach Extensive development is underway north of the marina, improving the promenade and the small bays of the sandy Hilton and Nordau (or Sheraton) beaches. Farther north, Tel Aviv's former port is becoming a lively and popular entertainment area.

Marina and public pool This popular pay-to-enter swimming and sunbathing area, below the Carlton Hotel, has lawns, shade, showers and snack bar.

Main beach and promenade This starts at **Kikkar Atarim** (or Namir), an ugly plaza with unenticing cafés. About 110 yards (100m) beyond, a more agreeable traffic-free

section lies below the Sheraton Hotel. Then the boulevard sweeps down to the promenade and a string of smart sea-view hotels. The low-rise **Dan Hotel**, despite a garish exterior, is considered the city's best. Below it, the terraces of **Kikkar London▶** face the sea, and **Yotvata Dairy Restaurant** attracts big crowds. The **Opera Tower** apartment block is a landmark at busy Allenby intersection. Beach and promenade, less opulent south of this point, fade away just before litter-strewn **Charles Clore Park**.

South of the main beach From here on, the waterfront has a more local, les touristy character. The boulevard turns away from the sea by a mosque, but the promenade continues. Finally there is a pleasant sand beach with a bar, but swimming is discouraged. Here the part-old, part-new **Etzel Museums▶▶** tell the story of the Irgun Tzvai Leumi (see page 119). Where the beach ends, an attractive narrower walkway follows a rocky waterfront all the way.

▶ Ben-Gurion House *114B4*

17 Ben-Gurion Boulevard (tel: 02-5221010; www.ben-gurion-house.org.il)
Open: Sun, Tue–Thu 8–3, Mon 8–5, Fri 8–1. Closed Sat. Admission free

This was the home of Israel's charismatic and powerful first prime minister, David Ben-Gurion (1886–1973) and his wife Paula. The small and surprisingly modest house has been preserved as it was during their lifetime. It is full of personal memorabilia, items of political and historical interest, and a library of 20,000 volumes.

▶ Bialik House (Beit Bialik) *114B3*

22 Bialik Street (tel: 02-5252530
Open: Sat–Thu. Admission: moderate

Haim Nachman Bialik (1873–1934), revered as the greatest modern Hebrew poet, designed this house, with its Moorish echoes, as his home (1926–33). Kept unchanged since his death, it contains pictures, letters and memorabilia that tell the story of his life and work.

▶▶▶ Carmel Market (Shuk HaCarmel) *114B2*

This big market (every day except Shabbat) extends along narrow HaCarmel Street (off Allenby Street) and several adjoining lanes. Despite the lack of traffic, it is noisy with stallholders' cries and the crush of people walking, talking and haggling as they look over CDs, shoes, clothes, garlic, fruit, herbs and spices, vegetables and bagels. Some stalls have only nectarines or olives, others are buried in tomatoes. In parallel Yomtov and Gedera streets, some are loaded with meat. Here the robust younger generation mingles with graybeards and their headscarfed wives, and Eastern Europe meets Jewish Arabia. In the adjacent attractive **Yemenite quarter▶▶** (or Kerem HaTemanim), many of the simple houses have kept their overhanging balconies and small courtyards.

OPERA TOWER

This beachside apartment tower, with its shopping complex, cinemas and restaurants, stands on the the site of Israel's first Knesset (parliament building) at 1 Allenby Street. The War of Independence made occupation of the Jerusalem Knesset impossible until December 1949. Later, the Tel Aviv Knesset building was used as the city's opera house, until a magnificent new opera house was opened in October 1994.

YITZHAK RABIN (1922–95)

As Sabbath ended on November 4, 1995, gunshots rang out at the Rally for Peace in Tel Aviv's Kings of Israel Square, killing Prime Minister Yitzhak Rabin. The general who in 1967 led the Six-Day War victory, Rabin was already a national hero when he pledged to create peace treaties between Israel and her Arab enemies. Many opposed his "land for peace" policies, and the fatal gunshots were fired by an Orthodox student.

Yitzhak Rabin Memorial Day is on 12 Heshvan, the Hebrew date of his death, and Kings of Israel Square has been renamed Yitzhak Rabin Square.

Who could resist Carmel Market's inviting stalls?

EARLY TOWN PLANNING
When Tel Aviv's avenues were first laid out, they say, the plan was to make them in the shape of a menorah, the seven-branched candelabrum that once stood in the Temple and that is now the symbol of the state. Instead, the builders were persuaded to divert what is now Ben-Gurion Boulevard towards a smart beachside bar, called the Casino.

Traditional crafts at the Eretz Israel Museum

118

THE FIRST STREETS
The first streets in Tel Aviv were laid on sand just north of Jaffa, in the area called Neve Tzedek. It's a neighborhood of quiet, narrow streets lined by small two-story houses. Many are scruffy and run down, but others have been tidied up as the merits of the neighborhood are gradually being redis-covered.

▶▶ **Eretz Israel Museum** *114C5*
2 University (or Haim Levanon) Street, Ramat Aviv
(tel: 03-6415244; www.eretzmuseum.org.il)
Open: Sun–Thu 9–3, Fri–Sat 10–2. Admission: expensive.
Guided tour in English on Sat at 11

Take a No. 25 bus out of central Tel Aviv to travel north of the Nahal (river) Yarkon to this immense and imaginative national museum, on the site of an excavated *tel* (settle-ment mound). Eretz Israel means "Land of Israel," and the museum covers various themes spanning 3,000 years in the history of Israel's material culture and ethnography.

An inexpensive site map makes it easy to find your way around, and museum literature recommends two possible routes through the grounds; one short (half a day) and the other long (a full day). Many exhibits were actually discov-ered here and are displayed *in situ*. Between the pavilions and the open-air exhibits there are pleasant lawns and trees, plus a good restaurant and snack bar.

Among the best exhibits are **Roman winepresses**▶, **Byzantine mosaic paving**▶▶, and two **ancient roads**▶ discovered one on top of the other. There is a superb **Planetarium**▶▶, but the commentary is in Hebrew. The **Numismatics Pavilion**▶▶ displays coinage across the millennia from shells to shekels, including biblical weights (the shekel is one). The **Nehushtan Pavilion**▶▶ explains ancient mining, with information about Timna (see page 251). The **Folklore and Ethnology Pavilion**▶▶ shows the unchanging traditions of Jewish ritual objects and apparel from ancient times to today. At the **Man and His Works Pavilion**▶▶, devoted to traditional crafts, you can see a glassblower and the work-shops of a blacksmith and a potter.

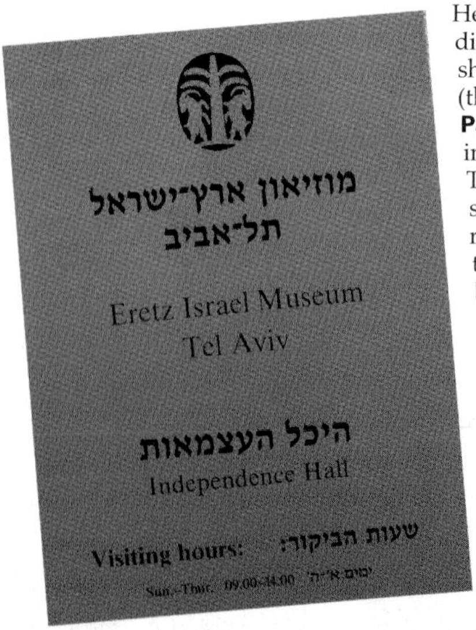

The grounds also include an entire archeological site, **Tel Qasile**▶▶▶, one of several *tels* on Tel Aviv's northern boundary. This was the first archeolog-ical site to be excavated by Israel (in 1949): Twelve settlement phases date back to 1150BC, with remnants of a

מוזיאון ארץ-ישראל
תל-אביב

Eretz Israel Museum
Tel Aviv

היכל העצמאות
Independence Hall

Visiting hours: שעות הביקור:
Sun.–Thur. 09.00–14.00 ימים א'–ה'

temple and houses with domestic objects.

▶▶ Etzel Museums 114B3

These three museums, known collectively as the Etzel Museums, tell the fascinating story of the Irgun Tzvai Leumi guerrilla organization (1937–48), also known as Etzel, which took on the British Army (except during World War II) and helped to bring about the creation of the State of Israel, by using tactics condemned by the Haganah and official Zionist movement (see page 43). From 1943 to 1948, its leader was Menachem Begin, later Israel's prime minister.

The plain white **Beit Jabotinsky (Jabotinsky Institute)▶▶▶** building, opposite the Dizengoff Center, at 38 Rehov HaMelech George (*Open* Sun–Thu 8–4. *Admission: moderate*), covers the pre-1948 history of the organization. Secret operations which attracted worldwide headlines are explained with chilling clarity. Included is the blowing up of the British headquarters in Jerusalem's King David Hotel (July 1946) when 91 people died, the destruction of the British Officers' Club (March 1947) when 17 people died, and the breaching of Akko Fortress (May 1947), when 30 Irgun and Lehi prisoners escaped.

A second museum, by the beach, close to Jaffa, can be found in **Etzel House▶** (*Open* Sun–Thu. *Admission: moderate*), restored "in memory of the liberators of Jaffa." It reveals Irgun's activities during the 1948 War of Independence. A third museum in **Beit Yair (Yair House)▶**, 8 Avraham Stern Street (*Open* Sun–Thu 8.30–4. *Admission: moderate*), covers the history of the Lehi movement (also known as "the Stern Gang"), the hardline splinter group that refused wartime co-operation with the British.

LITTLE TEL AVIV
The beginnings of Tel Aviv lie in small Jewish neighborhoods that were technically still part of Jaffa. The city really took off in 1921 when it was granted a charter as a separate town. A whole new district was immediately constructed a little farther north, around Bialik Street, the nucleus of the first new Jewish city to be built in modern Israel. Its town hall in Bialik Square later became the Historical Museum. Full of socialist theory, the city's founders declared there would be no commerce or private business at all in Tel Aviv: everything would be run by the municipality. This dream bit the dust as entrepreneurial immigrants flocked in and opened the corner kiosks which are still such a feature of the city. As the town expanded, this original center became known as Little Tel Aviv.

▶ Haganah Museum (Beit Haganah) 114B2

23 Rothschild Boulevard (tel: 03-5608064)
Closed Shabbat. Admission: moderate
Beit Eliahu (Eliahu House), home of the founding commander of Haganah, Eliahu Golomb, is a memorial to his life and times. Models and tableaus bring to life the history of Israel's armed forces, from their clandestine origins in 1907, through the creation of diverse undercover groups, to the creation of the Israel Defense Forces in 1948.

▶ Historical Museum of Tel Aviv–Jaffa 114B3

27 Bialik Street (tel: 03-5173052)
Open: Sun–Thu 9–2. Admission free
This round-fronted Bauhaus building, once Little Tel Aviv's Town Hall, recalls the creation and growth of the new city (see side panel), using old photographs, models and a film.

Patriotism rules at the Haganah Museum

GUIDED WALKS IN TEL AVIV

Rothschild Boulevard, a relaxed but animated place of leisure for all the family, is a delightful historic avenue curving through the heart of Tel Aviv. For its entire length, the two traffic lanes are separated by a broad walkway shaded by leafy trees. A stroll along Rothschild and its side turnings, admiring the Bauhaus architecture, is one of a dozen Tel Aviv guided walking tours offered by city expert Yona Wiseman (yonawise @netvision.net.il) For a range of other guided walks in the city, contact the tourist office or see www.visitelaviv.org.il.

▶▶ Independence Hall 114B2

16 Sederot Rothschild (tel: 03-5173942)
Open: Sun–Thu 9–2. Admission: moderate

The city's first mayor, Meir Dizengoff, lived in this austere bunkerlike concrete building. On 14 May 1948, his home was the setting for the historic declaration that brought the State of Israel into being. The house has since become a fascinating museum (part of the Eretz Israel Museum, see page 118) recalling that momentous day and the events that led up to it. Many other exhibits are concerned with the establishment of the city of Tel Aviv.

Among many extraordinary displays is a photograph showing sections of the sand dunes north of Jaffa being awarded, lot by lot, to anyone who wanted one. Another photo is of the United Nations in session in November 1947 voting to partition Palestine, and a third shows the meeting at which David Ben-Gurion announced the creation of Israel. Intriguing maps include one showing which countries voted for partition, and another showing the borders of the Jewish state as proposed by the UN—which was to consist of three small sections located between Tel Aviv and Haifa.

Alongside the hall in which the proclamation was made, the **Hall of Documents▶▶▶** is a small annex displaying a collection of original documents. One shows the draft proclamation with the name of the country still undecided—just days before the announcement. Penciled-in possibilities included Zion and Western Eretz Israel.

In the street outside, the white memorial and fountain is known as the **Founders' Monument▶**. It names those who founded the city and depicts the story of Tel Aviv in three bas-relief panels. The first shows laborers levelling the sand by hand, and starting to build while harassed by snakes and jackals. A second depicts important early landmark buildings, including the first Hebrew secondary school. The third captures the modern city showing the port, art museum, theater, the home of the national poet Bialik, and apartments behind.

Commemorating the founding of Israel

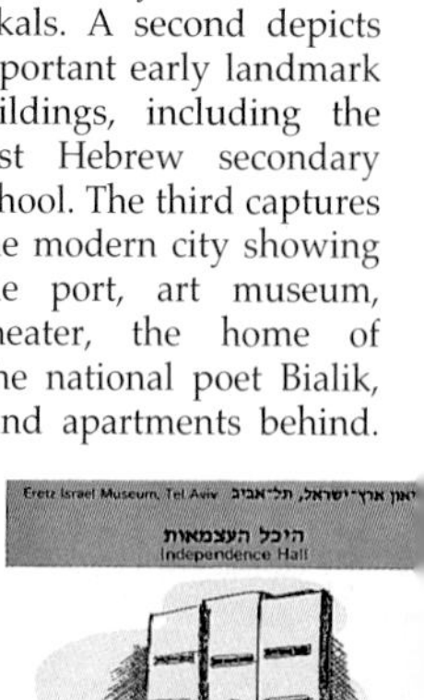

Walk

Multicolored fountain at the center of Dizengoff Circle

Dizengoff Street

No downtown avenue typifies the life and atmosphere of Tel Aviv as well as Dizengoff, named after the city's first mayor. To walk the entire length—stopping to window-shop and see the sights—could take a morning. It could require longer still if you break for refreshment at one of the many snack bars. As it continues northwards, the street's character changes to reflect different faces of the city and its people. The street's shaded west side is the more appealing (for map see page 114).

Dizengoff starts behind the modern **Mann Auditorium▶**, home of the Israel Philharmonic Orchestra, and the national **Habimah Theater▶**, focal points of the city's thriving highbrow culture. **Dizengoff Center** is Tel Aviv's main indoor shopping center. **Dizengoff Circle▶▶▶** (correctly Kikkar Zina Dizengoff, named after the mayor's wife) is a popular, often crowded, plaza with cinemas and cheap eateries. All around are Bauhaus buildings, one of them, a former cinema, is now a chic hotel. Here is also an area raised above the street where a gaudy multicolored **fountain▶** puts on a weird fire-and-water show to computerized music (11–1 and 7–9 daily).

From the Circle northward for several blocks, the street has a pleasant atmosphere. It's busy and crowded, lined with snack bars, juice bars, fashion boutiques and jewelry shops, and shaded by large trees.

After crossing **Arlosoroff**, things quiet down as Dizengoff enters the more prosperous **North Tel Aviv** area. There are more food shops, clothes shops take on a pricier, more exclusive look and cafés become more stylish. Beyond the pleasant **Nordau** junction, Dizengoff narrows. Near the street's north end, by the **Yirmehahu** junction, there is another cluster of smart boutiques and eateries. Just beyond this point, the Nahal Yarkon (Yarkon River) marks the official city limit.

Along Dizengoff's northern stretch

Little over a century ago, Hebrew was not a spoken language at all. Most non-Jews thought it was a dead language like Latin, and most Jews reserved it for prayer and ritual. Then Eliezer Ben-Yehuda arrived in Palestine from Lithuania. For him, it was imperative that Jews speak their ancestral tongue in their own land.

ONE OF THE PEOPLE
Eliezer Ben-Yehuda was not the only East European Zionist who wished to re-establish the Hebrew language. Russian Zionist Asher Ginsburg (1856–1957) also had a vision of Hebrew as the everyday language of the Jews, wherever they lived in the world. He ardently wanted the State of Israel to be created, but only as a spiritual and cultural centre for world Jewry. He himself did not envisage moving there, although he eventually did so in 1922. His vision attracted few followers, and he was an aloof, wealthy character, living an almost aristocratic lifestyle—in contradiction of his pen-name of Ahad Ha'Am, literally "One of the People." He is buried in Tel Aviv's Old Cemetery.

Nobel Laureate, Shmuel Yosef Agnon

Acclaimed writer, Max Brod

Ben-Yehuda's "crazy idea," as some described it, struck a chord with many people. By 1910, there were demonstrations calling for Hebrew to become the Palestinian Jews' official language. In 1924, the first Hebrew university opened. In 1966, a novelist writing in Hebrew, S Y Agnon, won Israel's first Nobel Prize for Literature.

New language, old language Today, as you walk in the bustling, lively streets of Israel's cities, passing newspaper stands piled high with different dailies and weeklies, all expressing varied viewpoints, or as you browse in the popular bookshops, listen to the radio or watch television, you will encounter Hebrew everywhere.

The early Zionists assumed that Yiddish, the Jewish language based on medieval German and spoken by two-thirds of all Jews before the Holocaust, would be Israel's national language. True, the country does have some

Yiddish publications, just as it has Russian and English papers. But, above all, the life of Israel is conducted in Ivrit, as modern Hebrew is called. This is so closely based on biblical Hebrew that any Israeli schoolchild can read the ancient scriptures with ease. Similarly, Moses, King David, or Solomon would be able to read a modern Israeli newspaper. Yet Ivrit includes many European constructions and English-based vocabulary, making it a functional modern working language for everyday use.

The revival The inspiration behind Hebrew's renaissance was Eliezer Ben-Yehuda (1858–1922), who came from Lithuania to Palestine in 1881. This fanatic announced on arrival that he would not talk to his Yiddish-speaking wife and child except in Hebrew. He spoke to puzzled storekeepers in Hebrew, wrote the first Hebrew dictionary, and in 1890 founded the Hebrew Language Committee. Later the committee became the Academy of the Hebrew Language, final arbiter on all matters of vocabulary. At first dismissed by the Zionist authorities as a crank, he eventually led a mass movement they could not ignore. By 1900, many East European Jewish writers were using Hebrew with great effect, notably Chaim Bialik (1873–1934), the brilliant poet, fiction writer and translator who moved here from Russia in 1925.

Dots, capitals, roots A Semitic language, written from right to left, Hebrew has no upper or lower case (capital or small letters), and words such as "the" (Ha) are joined to nouns as prefixes. Also, it has in effect two alphabets —one used in printing and one for handwritten script. Then, more difficult, the all-important dots and dashes underneath consonants, used to indicate vowel sounds, are rarely shown. Lastly, there is no agreed way of expressing Hebrew sounds in English. The guttural *h* is often written *ch*. The sound *ei* is also written *e* or *eh* (as in Eilat). The letter *tzadik*, pronounced *tz*, is often written as *z* or even *s* (as in Sefat or Masada). The common word *beit*—a house or institution—can be written *bet* or *beth*.

A nation of readers and theatergoers Israel has more bookstores per capita than any other nation. A UNESCO survey showed that the proportion of Israelis who regularly buy books is among the highest in the world, way ahead of the US and Britain. The world's literature, classic or modern, is avidly read in Hebrew translation. Shakespeare is constantly performed on the stages of Tel Aviv and Jerusalem, as are other great playwrights and contemporary Israeli works. The longest-running play on the Israeli stage was not a comedy, but Arthur Miller's *All My Sons*.

Writers of today Israel has produced a crop of novelists, dramatists and poets of its own (though few were born in Israel). In 1966, Shmuel Yosef Agnon (1888–1970), writing in German, Yiddish and Hebrew, was the first Israeli to win the Nobel Prize for Literature. A far better-known Israeli author is Amos Oz (born 1939), whose Hebrew novels and short stories have been widely translated. Other distinguished Israeli writers include Max Brod (1884–1968) and Ephraim Kishon (born 1924).

ON THE STAGE

HaBimah means "the stage." The platform on which the Torah is read aloud in a synagogue is also called the *bimah* and Israel's national theater is called simply Habimah Theater. It is housed in a large round modern building (in Kikkar HaBimah) beside the Mann Auditorium, the superb 3,000-seat concert hall (in Kikkar HaTizmoret) that is home to the renowned Israel Philharmonic Orchestra.

Israeli author Amos Oz

▶▶▶ Jaffa (Yafo) 114A1

The oldest working port in the world has become a suburb of Israel's newest city. Approached along the seashore promenade or boulevard, Jaffa lies only a short distance from its neighbor Tel Aviv. Inland, the two are joined and, since 1950, have been a single municipality. In 1960, the Jaffa Development Corporation set out to revive the squalid remnant of the town, and turned it into a place of entertainment and leisure. On Friday and Saturday evenings the atmosphere can be wonderfully vivacious and exciting. The crowds gather by the clock tower, or in Kedumim Square, to stroll, to talk in the balmy air, or to eat at outdoor restaurants. The view along the seafront to Tel Aviv is superb.

Modern Jaffa conveys little sense of its long history. The earliest remains here date back to the 18th century BC. In the 12th century BC, Jaffa became part of the Israelite kingdom, and scripture makes mention of the town several times. Under Solomon it was developed as the principal port for the Jewish capital, Jerusalem. The 12th and 13th centuries AD saw frequent invasion as successive Crusaders, including Richard the Lionheart, were beaten off. From that time up until the British entered Jaffa in November 1917 (with the exception of Napoleon's destructive foray in 1799), Jaffa was resolutely Arab and, despite its ups and downs, remained a busy port up until modern times.

The 20th century led to far-reaching change, in some ways bringing Jaffa's history to an end (other than as a leisure district of Tel Aviv). By the start of that century, a few Jewish refugees had settled among the Arabs of Jaffa. They were made unwelcome, and, in any case, they aspired to better housing.

In 1909, a group called Ahuzat Bayit built a suburb on barren sands north of the port, the start of Tel Aviv. From then on, the building never stopped. In 1921, 1929 and 1936 Jaffa's Arabs rioted against the Jews, each time killing several people. The response of the British Mandate authorities was to cut avenues through the tangle of narrow streets in order to control civil disturbances. A new port was constructed in Tel Aviv, which soon replaced the port at Jaffa; within months of the 1936 riots, the ancient port was closed down.

The bizarre 1947 UN Partition Plan placed Jaffa in an Arab state and Tel Aviv in a Jewish one. Following the

POT LUCK

Inside the Jaffa Museum you can see a copy of the Harris Papyrus, which describes the conquest of the town in 1500BC by the men of Pharaoh Thotmes III. Under their general, Tehuti, they entered the town by ship, concealed in hundreds of large earthenware cargo pots. Tehuti ceremonially announced himself to the governor of Jaffa, saying he had fled Egypt with a huge stolen treasure. Delighted, the governor invited him to a banquet while the pots of treasure were unloaded. Tehuti accepted, killed the governor over dinner, and seized the palace, while his men attacked the city.

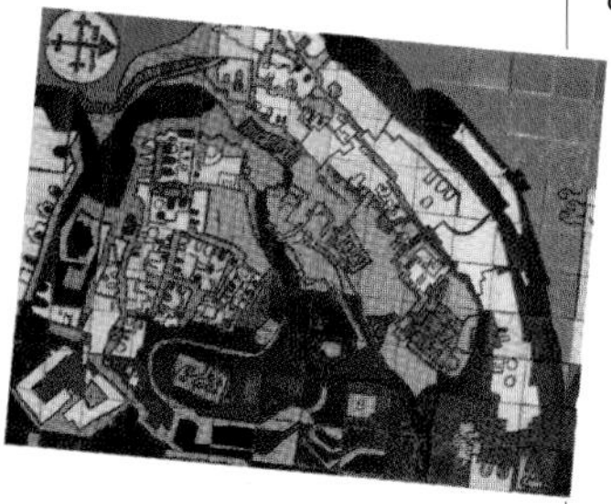

The historic port city of Jaffa

Archeological finds date Jaffa's origins to the 18th century BC.

DOCKLANDS
Jaffa's historic docks, famous throughout the ages, have been turned into a curiously down-market, but atmospheric, pay-to-enter family entertainment area. The quays are lined with big old waterside warehouses, some of which have been converted to contain cheap shops and stalls or restaurants overlooking the harbor. In the water are pleasure boats (some with eating places on board) and a few fishing trawlers.

1948 Proclamation of the State of Israel, Jaffa's Arabs launched a military attack on Tel Aviv. They were defeated and many fled. Large areas of unsanitary alleys and lanes were swept away. Today only a minority of residents are Arabs—Christian and Muslim—but Jaffa retains an Oriental flavor. Much of this comes from the many Jews from Arab countries living here.

The center of activity is **Kedumim Square▶▶▶**, a pleasant open plaza paved in pale stone. Around the square are places of entertainment, a nightclub, eateries and a large Catholic church. Steps dive below street level to the **Visitor Centre▶▶▶** (*Open* Sun–Thu 9am–10pm, Fri 9–2, Sat 10–10. *Admission free).* It is, in fact, a simple little museum revealing what lies under the square—mainly walls and structures dating from around 300BC. Off the square is the **Artists' Quarter▶▶▶**, a strangely quiet, picturesque district of narrow lanes with attractive Turkish-style dwellings.

The green **Abrasha Park▶▶**, rising from the square, is part of Tel Jaffa. At its summit, there's an observation point with fine sea views. There is more history at the small **Jaffa** (or **Antiquities**) **Museum▶▶** Rehov Mifratz Shlomo (*Open* Sun–Thu. *Admission: moderate*) part of the Eretz Israel Museum (see page 118). This museum has an astonishing range of finds spanning the millennia, though it is difficult to follow the layout of the five halls and their contents. Just below, close to the waterfront, rise the minaret and two colorful domes of **Mahmudiye Mosque▶**. Nearby stands the un-Arabic looking **Clock tower▶**, Jaffa's famous landmark, erected in 1906 to honor the rule of Turkish sultan Abdul Hamid II.

On the other side of Yefet Street are the squalid but busy streets of non-tourist Jaffa. Off Beit Eshel Street, and near the Clock tower, are the atmospheric alleys and lanes of the extensive **flea market** (Shuk HaPishpeshim)—which is Jewish, not Arab (*Closed* Shabbat).

Attractive Turkish-style dwellings in Jaffa's Artists' Quarter

WHO RETURNED?
Although every Jew has the right to choose to live in Israel, in practice most immigrants have been refugees, driven from their homes by force or under pressure of persecution or discrimination. Some 61 percent have come from Europe, and 18 percent from Africa, almost all of them from North African Arab states that expelled Jews from their homes. Others left South Africa after the start of apartheid. Some 15 percent came from Asia, notably those who fled penniless from Yemen. Only 6 percent have come from the Americas. Currently the population is being increased by thousands of new arrivals every year migrating from the former Soviet Union. Between 1989 and 1998 (latest figures) about 800,000 former Soviet Jews settled in Israel, adding over 13 percent to the total population of the country.

OLD AND NEW
Tel Aviv was the Hebrew title of Theodor Herzl's seminal Zionist work, *Altneuland* (literally, "Old-New Land"). The name is a play on words: a tel is a mound made by civilizations piled one upon the other. The word implies great antiquity. *Aviv* means springtime and newness. So the city's name could mean Hill of Spring, or Old and New. According to the Bible (Ezekiel 3 and 15), this is not the first town to be called Tel Aviv: There was one in ancient Babylon.

▶▶▶ Museum of the Jewish Diaspora (Beth Hatefutsoth) *114C6*

At Tel Aviv University (Gate 2), Ramat Aviv (tel: 03-6408000; www.bh.org.il)
Open: Sun–Tue, Thu 10–4, Wed 10–6, Fri 9–1.
Admission: expensive

Ranging over several floors of an unattractive modern building, but set in pleasant parkland in the university grounds, this museum is essential viewing during a visit to Israel, illuminating both the country and its people. It takes a full day to visit—perhaps longer.

In a succession of rooms, each dedicated to a particular theme, visitors wander down the generations, glimpsing the life of Jews in 80 different nations around the world (and "speaking 100 different languages," according to a display caption), scattered since the destruction of the Temple in AD70. The overall theme is the combination of Jewish diversity with Jewish commonality. The thesis of the museum is that tenacious adherence to traditions—especially observance of the Sabbath, rituals and festivals, and the constant focus on the idea of Eretz Israel—enabled the Jews to remain as a single people and eventually to return to their homeland. Hand in hand with this uniformity of tradition and belief, a great deal of diversity developed in the different Jewish communities.

This "uniformity with variety" is explored in scores of intriguing displays of ritual objects and clothing, books, photographs, models of housing and synagogues, videos, sound recordings and much else. The rooms are entitled **Family▶** and **Community▶▶**, **Faith▶▶** and **Culture▶▶**, **Among the Nations▶▶**, the **Return to Zion▶▶▶** and **Remembrance▶▶▶**. There is also an interesting room devoted to the theme of **Synagogue Architecture▶▶▶**. More recent periods are covered in **Jewish Theater▶▶** and **Jews in Arts and Sciences▶▶**. In many exhibits, modern Jewry and Reform Judaism are contrasted with more ancient forms; frequently the links and similarities are striking.

A variety of other **short films▶▶▶** deal with Jewish life in Eastern Europe, Greece, and Morocco. A longer audiovisual show, called the **Chronosphere▶▶** (lasts about 30 minutes), explores the Jewish Wandering, or Diaspora. Other films are shown on such subjects as Yiddish and

the other Jewish languages. Fascinating and ingenious push-button displays and tableaus bring to life important episodes in Jewish history.

A number of sections on the Yiddish-speaking world in **Eastern Europe Before the Holocaust▶▶▶** are painful to observe, revealing, as they do, the vibrant population and culture that was eliminated by the Holocaust. The **Jewish music▶▶▶** of different places and periods can be heard, including the rousing pioneer songs of the socialist Second Aliyah (1904–14).

Within the museum, the **Dorot Jewish Genealogy Center▶** runs an ambitious project to record the family data of as many Jews as possible from all over the world. For the benefit of future generations and for the purpose of reuniting dispersed family members, the project will give people the chance to see if anything is already known about their family and its history.

For deeper research, there are also study areas where you can view films on topics related to diaspora life. (Note that photography is not allowed and you must leave cameras at the door.) The museum can also advise on particular subjects, and has a musicologist on the premises.

On the ground floor the pleasant self-service cafeteria has good food. Customers are frequently entertained by live traditional Jewish music. The museum's shop sells an unusual range of CDs and tapes of Jewish music.

THE RIGHT TO RETURN
"Every Jew has the right to immigrate to Israel."
—*The Law of Return*, July 5, 1950

Zodiac signs and mystical symbols adorn the ceiling of this mid-17th-century synagogue from Poland

THE OLD CEMETERY
A high wall of stone blocks encloses Tel Aviv's first cemetery, started in 1903, even before the town was created. It served the Jewish setlers of Jaffa. Many of the early Zionist leaders, politicians and artists are buried here, including Nordau, Dizengoff, and the poets Bialik and Tcherninchovsky. (*Trumpledor Street, off Pinsker. Admission free. Closed Shabbat.*)

▶ Palmach History Museum (Beit HaPalmach) *114C6*

10 Haim Levanon Street, Ramat-Aviv (tel: 03-6436393)
Guided tour (90 mins, must be pre-booked. English translation on headphones. No under 6s). Admission: moderate
Beit Hapalmach is an entertainment as well as a museum, with multimedia simulations of 1940s Israel and actors playing the young men and women of the Palmach, elite of Israel's pre-State combat forces. The building is of architectural interest. Exhibits, in underground chambers, show a unit, training, carrying out operations and more.

▶ Rubin Museum (Beit Rubin) *114B3*

14 Bialik Street
Open: Sun–Thu. Admission: moderate
Bialik Street is the heart of the 1920s' Little Tel Aviv district. This former home of the artist Reuven Rubin (1893–1974) is now an enjoyable museum of his dream-like, highly personal paintings and drawings.

Old Cemetery, Tel Aviv

Walk

Old Jaffa

This is an easy stroll around a small area. Old Jaffa today exists mainly as a tourist attraction, yet it has plenty of charm and plenty to see. You could enjoy a full day of unhurried strolling and exploring (for map see page 114).

Start at the 20th-century Ottoman **Clock tower▶** (see page 125), in Yefet Street, which looks like an incongruous piece of Victoriana. Around it there is a strong Middle Eastern feel, yet many of the Oriental snack bars, such as the Tunisian café, turn out to be Jewish and kosher. Turn right at a sign to the "Old City of Jaffa." Pass by the domes of the **Mahmudiye Mosque▶**. Mifratz Shlomo (no entry for vehicles) rises up, with a wooded park on both sides. To one side lies a little square with the **Jaffa Museum▶▶** (see page 125) in an old stone building. Behind it, pass the old **Hammam▶** (Turkish bathhouse), now a theater-restaurant, and climb to **Abrasha Park▶▶**, on the slope of a tel (settlement mound) excavated 1955–74. Descend the hill, crossing a wooden bridge, to the traffic-free and beautifully paved **Kedumim Square▶▶▶** (see page 125).

Meander through the **Artists' Quarter▶▶▶**, off the square. Street names here are based on zodiac signs: for a simple route, follow Mazal Dagim (Pisces) to the end, and double back on Mazal Arie (Leo), which reaches a length of **ancient city wall▶▶**. Emerge at the foot of broad steps, but cross straight over to narrow Shimon Habursekai Street. Follow this, passing "Simon the Tanner's House" at No. 8, home of a family who claim that St. Peter stayed in this house.

Go downhill on Mazal Keshet (Sagittarius). To visit the **port▶** (see page 125), turn left at Nativ HaMazalot (Zodiac) and go down covered steps to the waterside. Return along Nativ HaMazalot, below lofty buildings, including the Greek Orthodox church and Catholic St. Peter's. Take a path into the delightful **HaMidron Gardens▶**, passing below the domed former Jews' hostel (now a restaurant) and above the evocative pale minaret of the **Sea Mosque**. Reaching the Mahmudiye Mosque, return to the Clock tower.

Old Jaffa's traffic-free lanes invite unhurried exploration

HEALTHY TAKEOUTS
Fresh juices are made to order at dozens of stands in downtown Tel Aviv. The "menu" generally runs the gamut of fruit varieties, including watermelon, peach, kiwi, prickly pear, orange, or a cocktail of several mixed together.

►► Tel Aviv Museum of Art 114C3

27 Shaul HaMelech Boulevard (tel: 03-6077020; www.tamuseum.com)
Open: Mon, Wed, Sat 10–4, Tue, Thu 10–10, Fri 10–2.
Admission: expensive (includes Helena Rubinstein Pavilion)
The imposing modern building of Israel's leading art museum is a world-famous showpiece of 20th-century art and esthetics. From the architecture of the museum itself—with its exterior sculptures and light, open interiors—to the distinguished exhibitions of 20th-century painting, video, photography, music and film, this is an important focal point of modern high culture. **Permanent exhibitions►►►**, representing the major 20th-century schools of painting, are arranged in a series of rooms, and include works by Braque, Klimt, Kandinsky, Picasso, Léger and Mondrian. **Temporary exhibits►►►**, often long-term, cover contemporary painting and photography, on loan from international galleries and museums. **Special exhibitions►►►** cover subjects relevant to Israel.

Despite specializing in the modern, the museum does not ignore everything that occurred before 1900. There are collections, temporary and permanent, of the art of past centuries, and many of the evening **concerts►►►** feature classical music—while others feature jazz. The **Helena Rubinstein Pavilion for Contemporary Art►** (6 Tarsat Boulevard) is part of the Museum of Art. It shows work by guest artists from Israel and abroad.

As an unusual diversion from the typical museum visit, the Museum of Art offers a free guided **Bauhaus tour►►►** by bus through the 1930s areas of Tel Aviv, a showcase for this simple and functional architectural style. The tour takes all morning (the bus will pick you up at your hotel). Although the tour is free, the museum will charge its usual entrance fee; after the tour, you can visit the museum without further payment. Tel Aviv is a fascinating city of many architectural styles, but it is these modernist (or Bauhaus) apartment complexes, many influenced by Le Corbusier, that give their character to the "White City."

Expressionist mural, Helena Rubinstein Pavilion

The Tel Aviv Museum of Art specializes in 20th-century art and sculpture

Visitors soon notice certain obvious facts about Israeli music: most street musicians play classical violin music and most of Israel's contemporary pop music is terrible. More interesting, traditional Jewish folk rhythms from Eastern Europe, North Africa, and the Middle East are fusing with other Mediterranean styles to create a genuinely new Israeli sound.

A mix of traditions When Jews fled to Israel from Eastern Europe, North Africa and Arabia, they brought their instruments and musical traditions with them. Indeed, they have come from every continent, bringing the multitude of diverse styles which can be heard today in Israel.

Perhaps the most recognizably Jewish music is the lilting clarinet-and-fiddle of *klezmer*, the sound of celebration and festival in the destroyed Jewish world of Eastern Europe. Few of the old players have survived, but the style lives on. Most *klezmer* today comes from America, though you will hear plenty of it in Israel, including a variant called Hasidic rock. Similarly, traditional Oriental Jewish music has settled in Israel, become more upbeat and is growing in popularity.

New sounds After a slow start—with a repertoire often limited to rousing, singalong tunes from religious, kibbutz and army life—Israel has started to produce world-class pop and rock. Apart from the bland harmonies of the annual Eurovision Song Contest, won in 1999 by flamboyant Israeli transsexual star Dana International, the country produces talented rock singers like Noa (known as Achinoam Nini in Israel), an intriguing mix of Yemen and New York, rock-blues artists like Shlomo Artzi, and outstanding folk-rock singer-songwriters like Chava Alberstein. Another influence comes from nearby Greece. You'll often hear Israeli recordings that join traditional Jewish musical ideas to a Greek sound, reflecting Israel's East Mediterranean location.

A symphony of orchestras In classical music, Israel really excels. People say, only half in jest, that every police station and every factory has its symphony orchestra. Certainly there is an astonishing number (the Tel Aviv suburb of Ra'anana, for example, has its own), including several of high standing. At the national level, Israel's Chamber, Symphony, and Philharmonic orchestras, and its National Opera, are all acclaimed worldwide—a remarkable achievement, since the population of Israel is only six million.

MUSICAL MOVEMENTS
Music is such an integral part of life in Israel that almost every community has its orchestra, often reaching professional standards. One Israeli joke has it that two in every three Russian immigrants arrive with a violin case tucked under their arms. What about the third? He's the pianist.

Classical street entertainer

SHABBAT AND FESTIVALS
Although things grind to a halt, or at least slow down, for Shabbat (Sabbath) each week from Friday afternoon to Saturday evening, and also on certain festivals and holy days, the one place where you can still expect to find things working more or less as normal is a hotel. Only at religious hotels (which make a point of informing guests of the restrictions on arrival) will you find that there are no reception staff on Sabbath—but even here you will usually be able to get a meal.

Hotels line Tel Aviv's coastal road

FRIDAY NIGHT SPECIAL
Many hotels, even those that are not especially observant of Jewish ritual, offer something special for Friday night dinner, the big meal of the week for Jewish families. Usually, there are candles by the entrance so observant Jews can light them at the start of Shabbat (Sabbath). *Hallah* (the tasty Sabbath bread) and *kiddush* wine will be on the table. Typically, the main dish will be *cholent* (pronounced chilunt), the meat stew popular on Friday night among East European Jews. In the larger hotels there are also Shabbat elevators, programed to stop automatically on every floor so the observant do not have to push buttons—"work" is forbidden during Shabbat.

Accommodation

Comfort plus a sea view Altogether, Tel Aviv and its suburbs have a total of over 6,000 hotel rooms, ranging from the de luxe to the budget, most close to the seashore. This is a new city, and almost all its hotels are modern, comfortable and well-equipped. At most of them, a superb buffet breakfast comes as standard. Some Tel Aviv hotels aspire to (and reach) a high level of service and facilities while remaining relaxed and informal—children are welcome. Widely accepted as the best in the city is the Dan Tel Aviv (on the corner of Frishmann and HaYarkon). This is the best location, for beach access, eating out, entertainment and downtown shopping. Even if you cannot afford the Dan, it is a good idea to stay in this area.

In the right place The main hotel district lies along HaYarkon Street, between Trumpledor and Ben-Gurion. Here you will find the Dan Tel Aviv, Carlton, Renaissance, Yamit Park Plaza and Sheraton hotels among others. These are all on the sought-after west side of HaYarkon. But there are also hotels on the other side of the street, or in side streets. Among the best are the Basel and the City. Although a few paces farther from the beach, they are nevertheless comfortable, convenient and more modestly priced.

Off the beaten track A few beach hotels lie outside this hotel district. A little farther from the center of things, they can represent good value. Examples are the Hilton, north of the main beach but overlooking a sandy bay, and the family-oriented Dan Panorama, opposite Clore Park at the southern end of the main beach. A free shuttle minibus connects the Dan Panorama to the Dan every few minutes throughout the day.

Eating out

Out and about Sightseeing, strolling or shopping, you will pass dozens of places—some smart, some simple—offering cakes, pastries and falafel, or shwarma, in pita crammed with salad. The many juice stands are a delight and offer a delicious and healthy liquid meal. Street nibbles include bagels, bigger and breadier than the familiar Ashkenazi bagel, and nuts —plain, salted or honey-roasted.

Dinner Most big hotels have restaurants. In the hotel area—near Dizengoff Circle, in Ben-Yehuda Street, and along HaYarkon—eateries span the range from French cuisine, to the cheap-and-cheerful. Spicy, tasty Yemenite cooking can be sampled in the Yemenite quarter, for example at Shaul's Inn (Eliashiv Street). Beside the sea, lines form at Yotvata Dairy Restaurant. The huge London Restaurant fills the pedestrianized section of the seafront promenade north of Frishmann—its prices reflect the lovely setting. While the food itself is nothing special, tables are rarely wiped, it has a big menu, big portions and service with a smile.

Shopping

Where to shop, what to buy Tel Aviv's main shopping streets are Dizengoff and Ben-Yehuda, and there are indoor shopping centers like the Azrieli Center, Dizengoff Center and Opera Tower (corner of Allenby and the promenade) with fashions, music, jewelry, and high-quality Judaica. Kikar HaMedina, the big circle in the north of the city, is a designer-label zone. For creative, elegant clothes, jewelry and Judaica, check out boutiques in northern Dizengoff Street. The southern part of Dizengoff is good for shoes and sandals. If you are wealthy enough to want diamonds, there is no better place than the Israel Diamond Exchange, Maccabi Boulevard, Ramat Gan. At the opposite extreme, try Bograshov Street for low-cost street fashion. For unusual gifts and crafts, take a stroll in Carmel Market.

NOT KOSHER, BUT TASTY
Only a handful of Tel Aviv eating places attain a really high standard, despite the ubiquitous "gourmet" boast. Even so, most are perfectly adequate for an enjoyable evening out, and a surprising number offer live entertainment. Observant Jews need to know that the majority are not kosher. The tourist office has restaurant listings, such as *Tel Aviv Menus*.

Cheap and cheerful cafés line Dizengoff Street

NIGHT OWLS
Like other big cities, Tel Aviv has its share of all-night shops and services. Five supermarkets, a dozen petrol stations, and (more surprisingly) half a dozen little confectioners who specialize in nuts and candies stay open in the Tel Aviv area. There are also a dozen different locations where you can hire a video for 24 hours from an automatic machine. Details and addresses of late-night shops are listed in *This Week in Tel Aviv*, obtainable from the tourist office or in hotels.

Nightlife

Nightclubs The racy end of late-night Tel Aviv is mainly concentrated in the south and east of the city center, along and off Allenby Street, and close to Jaffa Port. There are some 20 nightclubs for the youth market, offering disco, techno, and house music, and most kick off after midnight. Another 20 or more specialize in ethnic music styles—generally Oriental, Turkish or Greek—and are aimed at adults, rather than disco-hungry teenagers.

Tel Aviv's nightlife is livelier than in the capital, Jerusalem

JUST HANGING AROUND
For an easy and relaxing evening, sometimes the best thing of all is to walk, talk and sit outdoors. Scores of cafés and bars (often misnamed "pubs") open until well after midnight on Dizengoff, Rothschild, Ben-Yehuda, HaYarkon, and the waterfront promenade.

Live music Most big hotels have bars with easy-listening live music (often just a piano) until the small hours. For something more special, there are performances almost every evening by the New Israel Opera (Tel Aviv Performing Arts Center, 28 Leonardo da Vinci Street, tel: 03-6927777), the Israel Chamber Orchestra (10 She'erit Israel Street, Jaffa, tel: 03-5188845, www.ico.co.il), or the Israel Philharmonic (Mann Auditorium, tel: 03 6290193). Other important spots for concerts are the Tel Aviv Museum of Art (tel: 03-6077020) and the Israel Music Conservatory (19 Stricker Street, tel: 03-5173711). Big-name rock concerts are often staged at Yehoshua Gardens (Rockach Boulevard, close to the university).

Dance and drama Tel Aviv is home to most of Israel's quality theater. Simultaneous English translation (on headphones, every Tuesday) makes a play at the Cameri Theater (19 Shaul Hamelech Boulevard, tel: 03-6061900; www.cameri.co.il) enjoyable and accessible. Performances here consist of classics and serious modern drama. Yiddish-speakers will enjoy the Israeli Yiddish Theater, frequently on stage in Tel Aviv, usually at the ZOA House (1 Daniel Frisch Stteet, tel: 03-6959341). The Habima Theater (Habima Square, tel: 03-5266666, www.habima.org.il) is the home of Israel's National Theater Company. For modern or classical dance, try the Suzanne Dellal Center (tel: 03- 5105656, www.suzannedellal.org.il). The Hasimta Theater, in Old Jaffa (tel: 03-6834709), puts on performances by Israeli artists in a café-theater ambience.

Practical points

Information The city has two tourist offices, one on the waterfront (46 Herbert Samuel Street, tel: 03-5166188. *Open* Sun–Thu 9.30–5.30, Fri 9.30–1) and the other in the front lobby of City Hall (69 Ibn Gvirol Street, tel: 03-5218500. *Open* Sun–Thu 9–2. They can provide information, free maps, help with bookings and copies of the latest editions of *Tel Aviv Today* and *This Week in Tel Aviv*, which contain useful listings, telephone numbers and advertisements.

Getting around Buses, into or out of town, are inexpensive. Rides within Tel Aviv cost about 5NIS. Bus stops have brief route details in English, and all bus drivers speak English. For local bus information call Dan Buses, 03-6394444 (English spoken). Services run between 5am and midnight, except on Friday (services stop an hour before sunset for the Sabbath) and Saturday (no service until the end of Sabbath, an hour after sunset). Buses leave every few minutes from the city's two bus stations to towns and cities all over Israel. A ticket from Tel Aviv to Jerusalem costs 18NIS (enquiries to Egged, tel: 03-694888).

Far more expensive are taxis, called "special taxis," which wait outside hotels. Agree the fare in advance of your ride, or, insist that the meter be used. Check before setting out, for instance at your hotel desk, what the fare should be to your destination. The cheaper *sherutim* (singular: *sherut*), or shared taxis are convenient and can be hailed on main streets anywhere along their set route.

Emergencies Unlike almost any other city in the world, crime is not a problem in Tel Aviv. Violence is very rare. Do take precautions, nevertheless, against simple theft (for example, of bags on the beach). Noisy, horn-tooting people are probably the worst hazard. In an emergency, call: Police 100; Ambulance 101; Fire 102.

PEOPLE OF THE BUS
Egged, Israel's main bus line, despite being a workers' co-operative and operating solely within Israel, is the world's second-largest bus com-pany (after Greyhound). Over a million passengers a week pass through Tel Aviv's New Bus Terminal in Levinski Street. That's about a fifth of the country's entire population. They catch comfortable if crowded air-conditioned buses that depart very frequently to destinations all over Israel from 5am to midnight. Tel Aviv likes to boast that the New Bus Terminal (opened 1993) is the largest bus station in the world, but that's because most of the multistory building is in reality a down-market indoor shopping, commerce, and entertainment center. If not the biggest, the terminal could claim to be the most chaotic and confusing. As if that were not enough, Tel Aviv has two bus stations! The other, a simpler terminal, is beside the train station.

Popular transport

While the whole world may have heard of the Ten Commandments, few realise that the scriptures contain a total of 613 commandments (or mitzvot) *concerning every aspect and nuance of behavior. Attempting to obey them is "religious observance." Ignoring them completely is to be "totally secular." Most Israelis fall somewhere in between, and regard the* mitzvot *not as commandments but as traditions.*

RELIGIOUS OR SECULAR?

16 percent of women regularly attend *mikveh* (ritual baths).
22 percent of men keep their head covered at all times.
25 percent regularly wear *tefillin* (prayer boxes containing scriptures).
55 percent read from a prayer book sometimes.
66 percent mark Sabbath with some kind of ritual, usually the lighting of candles.
66 percent eat only kosher food at home.
71 percent fast all day on Yom Kippur.
72 percent light Hanukka candles.
78 percent attend a *seder* (ritual dinner) at Passover.
90 percent keep kosher part of the time.
92 percent circumcize their sons according to Jewish ritual.
98 percent have a *mezuza* scroll on their doorpost.
—Guttman Institute

Religious observance Tel Aviv's Diaspora Museum suggests that religious observance facilitated nationhood by preserving Jewish identity during the diaspora. In today's Israel schools recognize Jewish holidays and teach the Bible (albeit as part of the nation's annals rather than as Holy Writ). Yet many Israelis know little about traditional Judaism, and the many immigrants from the former USSR are overwhelmingly secular. Even so, Israelis are proud of their heritage. And religious political parties' show of strength in elections underscores the continued importance of Judaism in Israel.

A secular Zion In the early years of the twentieth century, the pioneering Zionists who made the journey to settle in Palestine and struggled to re-create the Jewish homeland were, almost without exception, socialists and atheists. They wholeheartedly rejected religion, just as they rejected every other inheritance from the past, even family life. They considered the Jewish people to be no more, and no less, than a nation exiled from its land, and defined Jewishness in purely cultural, historical terms. Instead of the biblical injunction to be "a light unto the nations," they wished only that Israel would be "a nation like any other."

The people of Israel The existence of Jews as a separate people rests on their attachment to Israel, which lies at the heart of the Jewish religion. Unlike Christianity, which is based on belief (of God in Man, the Messiah), Judaism is literally a question of getting down to earth. At the cornerstone of the religion is the principle of Israel as the promised land, the land to which the Jews returned after the exodus from Egypt, the land conquered by Joshua in fulfilment of God's promise. These events are not mythical but historical (if embellished). The only sacred place in the world, for Jews, is Temple Mount in Jerusalem. Synagogue prayers, today as always, refer to the Jews simply as Israel. For millennia, Israel meant the land of the Jews, of the Jewish religion and of the Temple. That is why Diaspora Jews wanted to return to Israel, and why even the

Burning yeast before Passover

most secular Jews in Israel are part of, and the product of, a religious heritage.

The not-so-great divide A recent nationwide survey of Hebrew-speaking Israeli Jews showed that 21 percent consider themselves to be "totally secular." About 39 percent are "strictly observant" or "observant to a great extent." In between are the roughly 40 percent who pick and choose which customs to keep and which to ignore. To some extent, the division is illusory, because Jewish festivals, such as Hanukka, Pesach (Passover), Purim, Sukkot, are now as much national as religious holidays, observed even on secular kibbutzim. Shabbat (Sabbath) still brings the country to a standstill—for religious and secular alike. Survey figures show that being religious or secular is not an absolute: Most Israelis obey some religious commandments, seeing them simply as part of their inherited traditions.

A cause for conflict The big Sabbath shutdown rankles some Israelis, especially in a predominantly non-religious city like Tel Aviv. There is resentment that the Orthodox authorities, backed by religious political parties (which sometimes hold the balance of power in the Knesset), can wield such a pervasive influence over the life of the secular. Examples range from the lack of any form of civil marriage to the fact that El Al, the state airline, cannot fly on the Sabbath. But no government that depends on religious party support can risk liberalization. Anger about this has led many Israelis, including the many who are observant to some degree, to regard "the religious" with contempt. The antagonism is mutual.

A VOTE FOR PLURALISM

It is partly due to Israel's electoral system that the religious/secular divide is so sharp. The ultra-Orthodox, who routinely hold the balance of power in the Knesset, have used this position to win government funding and to ensure their grip on certain areas of life. This works against Judaism's non-Orthodox Masorti and Reform streams which are denied funding or places on local religious councils, and whose rabbis are not recognized. If the proportional representation rules are altered, requiring parties to garner a certain minimum percentage of the vote before gaining a Knesset seat, ultra-Otrthodox representation in the Knesset would lose most of their seats and their influence. Non-Orthodox and partially observant citizens would then be in a position to win much-needed civil rights and respectability.

Lighting Hanukka candles

SWEET CONSUMPTION
One thing that Israel's Jews and Arabs have in common is a sweet tooth. Israelis are the world's largest consumers of halva, the hard, sugar-packed sesame confectionery. They consume a phenomenal 1.5kg (3.3lbs) per person per year on average. Most of the country's Arab neighbors are not far behind in the halva consumption league.

▶▶▶ Akko *113B4*

This large, industrial Arab town (population 46,000), sitting on a spit of land projecting from the Galilee coast, contains at its heart a striking Old City with thick, sturdy fortifications and imposing towers. These superb 18th-century **ramparts▶▶▶** (free access), now breached by newer roads, were originally entered only through the Land Gate, not far from the shore, or the Sea Gate, on the harborside. Today access to the top of the walls is from the steps by the law courts.

The historic waterfront quarter, a mass of stone structures, beautiful archways, evocative alleys and green-roofed mosques, makes a magnificent sight. There is squalor too: you will find groups of youths hanging around, and unwashed children in the dirty squares and alleyways. In the past, Akko (known to English-speakers as Acre) figured large on the map of the world and even today carries the mark of its former standing. Above all, though later restored and reconstructed, the walls and stonework recall an era of bloodthirsty medieval struggles between the Crusaders and the Arabs for control of the land of Israel.

Akko's history dates back far beyond those times. Remnants of a Canaanite settlement on the site of the **Tel▶** (settlement mound), about 1 mile (1.5km) inland, have been dated to 3000BC. Taken, lost and retaken by Egyptian pharaohs, it became a Phoenician city. Joshua, the Israelite leader, was unable to conquer it in 1300BC and the Israelite tribe of Asher, in whose territory Akko was, also failed. The Phoenicians were eventually expelled in 640BC. The town passed between Persians, Assyrians and Egyptians, and in 219BC became part of the Seleucid

Akko: modern port and Crusader city

kingdom of Syria, which wisely allowed it to remain an independent city-state. When the Hasmoneans forced the Syrians out of the rest of Israel in the 2nd century BC, they too were unable to take Akko, which survived as a non-Jewish town. Rome succeeded in conquering it, and the town served as their campaign base for crushing the First Jewish Revolt (AD66). Akko remained a busy port under the Byzantines, and after the 7th-century Arab conquest became the seaport of Damascus.

After years of trying, the Crusaders eventually took Akko in 1104, made it the stronghold of the Knights of St. John and renamed it St. Jean d'Acre (Saint John of Acre). When the Arabs took Jerusalem (1187), Akko became capital of the Crusaders' Kingdom of the Holy Land. The town's finest spectacle is still the wonderfully preserved **Crusader city**►►► (*Open* daily. *Admission: moderate*) headquarters of the Knights Hospitallers. It is a vast, impressive complex of offices, halls, refectory and hospice, all now lying underground because the 18th-century Citadel was raised on top of it. Built largely in the 12th century, in the transition from Romanesque to early Gothic, the Crusader city's stone-paved floors and vaulted ceilings retain a simple but majestic elegance and dignity.

From antiquity, Akko flourished as a port, and for a thousand years it was the biggest and busiest in the eastern Mediterranean. It was also notorious as a place of vice and decadence, which worsened under the Crusaders as the town grew. Densely populated, it was divided into quarters given over to different "nationalities"—in fact mostly Italians from the city-states of Genoa, Pisa, Venice and Amalfi. These districts were often in conflict, sometimes breaking into open warfare. The population was mainly Christian, and there were dozens of churches.

In 1187, Salah ed-Din wrested Akko from the Crusaders but in 1191 it was reconquered by Richard the Lionheart. When the Fifth Crusade reached Palestine in 1290, full of naïve zeal about driving Islam out of the Holy Land, they slaughtered the Muslim traders resident in Akko—much to the chagrin of the town's Christian citizens, who were more interested in commerce than conquest. The massacre caused the Mameluke Sultan Qalawun to attack the city mercilessly, carting off thousands of Christians as slaves. The Knights Templar fought on

Akko's Gothic arches have lasted much longer than the fragile Crusaders' Kingdom that built them

THE GREAT ESCAPE

During the British Mandate, the authorities put Akko's medieval citadel to use as a high-security prison for Jewish guerrillas: Several were hanged here. In a spectacular raid on the citadel in May 1947, the Irgun group dynamited a hole in the ancient wall, went inside, overpowered the guards, and freed 30 Irgun and 11 Lehi prisoners. The citadel now contains the **Museum of Heroism**, honoring the prisoners who were held or executed here.

AKKO'S BEACHES
Just outside the walls, Akko has one extremely dirty and unappealing public beach. For something a little better, head farther south from the city to Hof Argaman (or Purple Beach). This lies a 15-minute walk along the seafront. Alternatively, you can drive along the Haifa road as far as the Argaman Motel. You must pay to use the beach, but it has good facilities and an excellent view of the city.

Ahmed al Jazzar Mosque (above and below)

until the massive wall of their fortress was brought crashing down, symbolizing the end of two centuries of Christian rule in Palestine.

From 1291, Akko was resolutely Arab, sinking into almost total obscurity and poverty. Druze emirs revived it in the 17th and 18th centuries, and between 1775 and 1805, under Ahmed el-Jazzar (literally, "the Butcher"), there was much grandiose building. The Crusader city was covered and above it the mighty **Citadel▸** (*Closed* Shabbat. *Admission: inexpensive*) was constructed. Later, the British used this as a prison for Jewish guerrillas: A poorly arranged **museum▸▸** inside contains photographs, papers, and the gallows on which the Jews were executed. Beside the Citadel, on the site of the Crusaders' Cathedral of the Holy Cross, stands the **Ahmed al Jazzar Mosque▸** (*Closed* during prayers. *Admission: inexpensive*), with its geometric marble patterns, tall minaret, and rococo architecture. Close by in Ahmed's handsome **Turkish baths▸▸** (*Open* daily. *Admission: moderate*), a museum covers the story of the town, explaining how, in 1799, the British came to Ahmed's aid helping to repel an attack on the town made by Napoleon.

Under Ottoman rule, the walls of Akko were restored and new defences were constructed. Despite this, the British seized Akko in 1918. The residents staunchly defied both the British and Jewish presence in Palestine. In 1948 Akko came fully under Jewish control.

Around the Old City, you will find much of interest: the **souk▸**, the narrow streets full of fragrances; the huge *khans* (enclosures built as caravansaries), notably the columned **Khan el-Umdan▸▸** by the water, with the landmark clocktower beside it; the **quayside▸▸** with its fish restaurants.

Some 1.2 miles (2km) north of Akko, the extensive and exquisite **Bahá'i Gardens▸▸** (*Open* daily 9–4. *Admission free*) contain the burial shrine of Bahá'u'lláh (literally, "God's glory," 1817–92), the title of the founder of the Bahá'i religion. Here, too, is the cottage in which he lived during his last years, having been exiled to Akko in 1868. The shrine is the holiest place in the world for members of the Bahá'i faith (see panel page 152).

The new country of Israel was won after a hard struggle, involving determination, courage, even ruthlessness. Born of centuries of yearning, Israel is still grateful to the men and women who brought it into being. Some were intellectuals, others soldiers, others farmers who tackled swamps and deserts. They are honored everywhere. Streets, towns, kibbutzim, hills and valleys, not to mention children, have been named in their memory.

Theodor Herzl (left)

Creators of a nation The rebirth of Israel is regarded by many Jews, and not a few Christians, as one of the greatest events to have occurred in two millennia. For some, it is nothing less than the hand of God at work. Others see it as the result of painstaking struggle by individuals of courage and vision. And for yet others, it is a combination of both of these. After all, according to the Bible story, even when God gave the Land of Israel to the Jews, they still had to go out and conquer it for themselves. All those who made this modern, political and diplomatic miracle happen tend to be regarded with sincere admiration by Israelis.

The early days Few towns are without a boulevard, main street or central square named after Theodor Herzl (1860–1904), founder of the Zionist movement. His successor as Zionist leader, Chaim Weizmann (1874–1952), who became the first President of Israel, also has many mentions. The hardliner who led the Revisionist group within the movement, Vladimir Jabotinsky (1880–1940), is also recalled as a hero, as is Josef Trumpledor (1880–1920), founder of the Hehalutz Zionist movement in Russia, decorated for bravery by the Russian and British armies, who died defending a Galilee farming settlement from Arab attack. More recently, David Ben-Gurion (1886–1973) was the tough and shrewd Zionist veteran who became Israel's first prime minister. All were born in Eastern Europe.

Writers and scholars Eliezer Ben-Yehuda (1858–1922) gained huge admiration for reviving and revitalizing the Hebrew language. Shmuel Yosef Agnon (1888–1970) was the first Hebrew writer to win the Nobel Prize for Literature. Haim Nachman Bialik (1873–1934), author of many early Zionist songs and also considered the greatest modern Hebrew poet, is another name held in the highest esteem by Israelis.

THE FOUNDER OF ZIONISM
Theodor Herzl (1860–1904), born in Budapest, grew up to be cosmopolitan, intellectual and entirely non-religious. He spoke several languages and studied for a doctorate at Vienna University in a period of daily anti-Jewish rioting in the city. Finding work as a journalist, he was made Paris correspondent of the Austrian *Neue Frei Presse*. In 1895, he witnessed the public humiliation of the Jewish army captain Alfred Dreyfus, who—in a wave of anti-Jewish feeling that swept France—was convicted on a trumped-up charge of treason. The evidence is known to have been forged. The sight had an electrifying effect on Herzl. He at once wrote *Der Judenstaat* (*The Jewish State*) and in 1897 convened the first Zionist Congress. This called for "the creation for the Jewish people of a home in Palestine." He campaigned tirelessly to further that cause until his untimely death. Within 50 years his extraordinary dream had come true. His body was transferred to Mount Herzl, in Jerusalem, in 1948.

▶▶ Ashkelon and Ashdod *112B2–B3*

These two modern, rapidly growing, industrial beachside towns (with a combined population of 165,000) were founded in the 1950s on the sand dunes not far from the Gaza border, and are major absorption centers for new immigrants. There is a boomtown feeling in the air, as construction work carries on at a frantic pace. Ashdod's successful port now rivals Haifa's.

Similarly, the two towns also have a long history. Both were among the five Philistine cities on Israel's Mediterranean coast (Joshua 13:3). When the Philistines captured the Ark of the Covenant, they took it first to Ashkelon, then installed it in the temple of Dagon in Ashdod. A multitude of conquerors came and went during the centuries, including Egyptians, Assyrians, Persians, and Romans. The towns were taken by the Crusaders in the 12th century and, when retaken, largely destroyed in the process.

Ashdod▶▶ has a beach and a couple of modest hotels, but plans to turn it into a big holiday resort seem fanciful. Its earlier settlements were at **Tel Ashdod▶**, 3 miles (5km) south. Later it became an Arab village, hostile to Jewish immigration, with a British army base. During the 1948 War of Independence, the Egyptians advanced this far into Israel before being forced to retreat.

Between the two towns stretch 9.5 miles (15km) of dunes and citrus groves. **Ashkelon▶▶**, though sprawling, has more appeal for visitors. Its pleasant sandy beach and waterside hotels lie at the southern end of town near **Ashkelon National Park▶▶**, a popular picnic area with remnants of several periods. The ruined churches, fortifications and collapsed towers, where rather forlorn fragments of stonework lie on the sand, were built by Crusaders. Within the site, the earliest remains date back to Canaanite and Israelite times, and there are Roman ruins. North of the park is a 3rd-century Roman tomb.

This part of Israel's Mediterranean coast lies surprisingly close to the desert and to southern Israel, which are within easy reach for day trips.

GAZA

Down the road from Ashkelon and Ashdod is another ancient city—Gaza ("Azza" in Arabic), main town of the Gaza Strip. Entry into the terrirory is controlled by the Palestinian Authority. Measuring 31 miles (50km) by 3.7 miles (6km)—hence its description as a "strip"—this is one of the world's most densely populated areas. Most of the 1.6 million inhabitants are grandchildren of those who fled Israel when the Arab states failed in their promise to wipe out the new state in 1948. Gaza, previously part of the Turkish Ottoman Empire, became part of the British Mandate of Palestine in 1918. With the end of the Mandate in 1948, Gaza was invaded and annexed by Egypt, which held it until the 1967 Six Day War in which Israel took control of it, establishing 25 settlements and military bases. Even these failed to prevent Gaza becoming a chaotic, violent region in which Islamist terrorist groups flourished unchecked. In 2005 Israel abandoned Gaza, handing over the administration to the Palestinian Authority.

Ashkelon (right)
Roman statue of Isis (below)

Atlit's sunset beauty belies its tragic history

▶▶ Atlit (also known as Ma'apilim Atlit Camp) *113B3*

About 0.5 miles (1km) from the sea, around 5 miles (8km) south of Haifa beside Highway 2 exit signposted "Apilim" (tel: 04-9842913).

Notorious Atlit Camp was the British detention center, established in 1938, used for holding illegal Jewish immigrants to Palestine during the pre- and postwar periods. When Jews were trying to escape from Nazi Europe, a succession unseaworthy and overloaded ships put ashore on Israel's beaches. The occupants were rounded up by the British authorities, brought here, and held in crowded dormitories until they could be deported. Tens of thousands of would-be immigrants passed through the camp.

You can walk between the high barbed-wire fences where Holocaust survivors, including children whose parents had died in the extermination camps, were detained. Some were returned to Germany or other parts of Europe, and many were forwarded to other British prison camps in, for example, Cyprus or Mauritius. This camp was restored in 1970, but of the original 80 dormitory huts only two remain. These are filled with models to give an idea of the life and conditions endured by the inmates. The camp is dominated by the Disinfection Building where detainees were stripped naked on arrival, segregated by sex, and herded in to be sprayed with disinfectant liquid from showers, in an uncanny echo of the procedures at the Nazi gas chambers. Also on the site is a ship in which some of the illegal immigrants arrived.

Atlit is geared to group visits, of which there are many, but individuals are also welcome with advance notice. A very moving audiovisual presentation is shown.

▶ Bat Yam *112B4*

This beach resort, 3 miles (5km) south of Tel Aviv, is a suburb of its larger neighbor. It has an attractive setting, a nice, well-maintained beach, and many leisure facilities including a sports center, swimming pools, three art galleries and several moderately priced hotels.

THE LAST CASTLE

Now within a military base, the huge ruined castle which can be seen perched on a promontory near Atlit was built by the Templars in 1200 following their expulsion from Temple Mount in Jerusalem. They called the new fortress Pilgrims' Castle. After the loss of Akko in 1291, the Templar presence in the Holy Land looked unlikely to survive. The fall of Tortosa Castle, in Syria, in the same year left only Pilgrims' Castle at Atlit in their possession, and the Templars decided to leave before being driven out. The castle subsequently fell into ruins. It was excavated in the 1930s, but is not open to the public.

ALEXANDER ZAID
The statue of Alexander Zaid, on the highest point of Beit She'arim, honors a founder of HaShomer (the Watchman), the undercover organization that provided armed guards for Jewish farmers and that evolved into the Haganah (see page 42). Zaid is said to have discovered the Beit She'arim necropolis while secretly patrolling in 1936. He was eventually killed during the 1938 anti-Jewish riots.

▶ Beit She'arim 113B3

(Tel: 04-9831643; www.parks.org.il)
Closed Shabbat. Admission: moderate
This archeological site at the foot of Mount Carmel, some 11.5 miles (19km) east of Haifa, contains the remnants of a Galilean town which acquired enormous importance in Jewish religious life in the centuries after the destruction of the Temple in Jerusalem. With the crushing of the Bar Kochba Revolt in the 2nd century AD, Beit She'arim grew to be a large, religious town. Rabbi Yehudah Hanassi moved here with his seminary, and under him it became the seat of the Sanhedrin, the "supreme court" of Jewish law. Hanassi spent his time here writing and codifying the Mishna (still known today as the Oral Law), which was to become part of the scriptural works that Orthodox Jews believe to be God-given.

Hanassi was buried in the **Necropolis▶▶** (or Necrophos), which is a remarkable network of underground tunnels, stairways and caves. These catacombs were already well known as a burial site, but after Hanassi's burial they became the most important Jewish burial place in Israel, taking over from the Mount of Olives, which the Romans had closed to Jews. The Necropolis was, and is, entered through landscaped courtyards. Of the 20 burial chambers inside, two are currently open to visitors. Inside, it is eerie and atmospheric. The decorated sarcophagi—now empty—have inscriptions in Hebrew, Aramaic and Greek. There is also a museum inside the larger of the two catacombs.

Above ground, there are traces of private dwellings and other structures dating from the 2nd to the 4th centuries AD, including ruins of a **synagogue▶**, a **basilica▶**, a **glass factory▶** and an **oil press▶**—all that remain of the city, which was ravaged by the Romans in the 4th century.

Beit She'arim, site of the Sanhedrin, or Jewish Supreme Court

Some Jewish holidays date back to the Bible, others commemorate events in Jewish history. Many are national holidays celebrated by all Israelis, both religious and secular. Dates vary from year to year. Christian festivals also attract crowds of visitors, as do Muslim festivals, although to a lesser extent.

Spring and summer Pesach, or Passover—the seven-day festival of abstinence from bread and other leavened food, commemorates the Exodus from Egypt. It is mainly a family affair. The big moment is the *seder* ritual festive meal, when the Haggadah, a text containing the Exodus story, is read aloud. Christian Holy Week, with processions along the Via Dolorosa in Jerusalem, and Easter occur at about the same time—Jesus' Last Supper was a *seder*. Holocaust Day, Remembrance Day, Independence Day and Jerusalem Day, recalling the pain and joy of 20th-century events, follow soon after. Lag b'Omer (April/May) is a day of picnics, one month after Pesach. Shavuot, 49 days after Passover, celebrates Moses receiving the Torah; it is traditional to eat dairy products. The Tisha b'Av fast (July), when people gather at the Western Wall, is the day on which both the First and the Second Temples were destroyed.

Autumn The month of Tishri (September/October) starts with Rosh Hashanah (New Year), a happy but thoughtful time. The 10 Days of Awe that follow are also a time of reflection, ending with the solemn fast of Yom Kippur (Day of Atonement). A joyous note returns with the seven days of Sukkot (Tabernacles), a harvest celebration that commemorates the years spent by the Jews wandering in the wilderness after the Exodus from Egypt.

Winter Hanukah ('Dedication') recalls the Maccabean victory in 167BC, and the miracle that occurred when the Temple was rededicated (one day's lamp oil lasted for eight days). People light *hanukkiot*, the eight-branched candelabrum, lighting one candle each evening until all eight are lit. Latkes (fried patties), donuts and other fried foods are eaten at this time.

Christmas draws huge crowds, especially to the city of Bethlehem. Purim (February/March), a zany day of fun, recalls the Jewish escape from an ancient Persian plot to kill them. The story of Esther is read in synagogues, and children try to drown out the name of the villain, Haman.

MERRY CHRISTMASES

In Israel, Christmas does not come just once a year: it is celebrated on different dates by different Christian denominations. The Catholics, Latin churches, and Protestants proclaim the birth of Christ on December 25. The Eastern Orthodox churches celebrate his birth on January 6 and 7. The Armenian Church has its Christmas on January 18 and 19.

Lilies for Christ's Resurrection (top)
The fruit and palms for Sukkot, the Jewish harvest festival (left)

ANYONE FOR GOLF?
For visitors or Israelis who crave a round of golf, Caesarea Golf Club has no rival—not because it is so good, but because it is the only golf course in Israel. Established in 1980, the club has an 18-hole course covering 395 acres (160ha), including 62 acres (25ha) of grass—no mean achievement in this terrain. The course is open all day, every day, including Saturday. In fact, Saturday is the most popular day, and reservations are advisable.

VISITING CAESAREA
To best appreciate this extensive site, follow one of the five marked paths, according to how much you want to see, how far you want to walk and how much time you have. The shortest (just 545 yards/500m) takes in the Ramparts Observation Point, the Caesarea Experience and Time Tower, a multimedia journey back through history. The longest route (1 mile/2km) leads to all the site's points of interest.
Open: summer, Mon, Wed–Thu 9–6, Tue 9–8, Fri 9–5, Sat 10–8; winter, Mon–Thu 9–5, Fri 9–4, Sat 10–5. *Closed* Sun (excl National Park 8–4).

Caesarea: Corinthian capital (right) and theater (below)

▶▶▶ Caesarea *113A2*

(Tel: 972-4-617444; www.caesarea.org.il)
Admission: expensive.

One of the great cities of the ancient world, Caesarea was a port from the 4th century BC onwards, and the Roman administrative capital of Judaea for hundreds of years. As an archeological site, it is dramatic, extensive and accessible. Excavations began within three years of the founding of the State of Israel, and still continue. Today, one sees an area of superimposed walled cities—Herodian, Roman, and Byzantine—overlaid in part by the Gothic remains of a medieval Crusader fortress town. The best-represented periods, dominating the site visually, are the Roman and Crusader cities. A short distance from the archeological site, modern Caesarea consists of a coastal area of high-quality holiday and leisure facilities, including hotels and restaurants, as well as some of Israel's best and most expensive private housing.

The first port at Caesarea was set up by the Phoenicians and conquered 100 years later by the Greek army of Alexander the Great. In 22BC, the Roman city was born under Herod. This large walled town encompassed the 20,000-seat **hippodrome▶** (or racetrack) and a splendid **theater▶▶▶**. Water was carried in on a fine beachside **aqueduct▶▶**; its ruins remain impressive. Through taxes and trade, the town became a source of wealth for Herod and Rome. It drew many Jews and pagans, and was above all a cosmopolitan, commercial town. From AD6,

Judaea became a Roman province, with Caesarea as its administrative center. It was here that, in AD69, Vespasian was proclaimed emperor. At about this time, according to the Acts of the Apostles, St. Philip baptized the Roman centurion Cornelius and later established a Christian community. In AD135, following the defeat of the Bar Kochba Revolt, the great scholar Rabbi Akiva was tortured to death at Caesarea.

Minaret in Caesarea, relic of Turkish rule

The town continued to be an important Christian centre, and the seat of a bishop, right through the Byzantine period. New walls were erected, enclosing a much more compact area, and the port town prospered. The **Byzantine street (Cardo)**►►, lined with shops, is the evocative remnant of this era.

After the Persian invasion of 614, the commercial life of the town came to a complete end, and it fell into obscurity. A succession of Muslim rulers held the town until the arrival of the Crusaders in 1099. Two years later, in 1101, the Crusaders turned their attention to Caesarea, moving in and reviving the site. They constructed numerous substantial new buildings, reusing many pieces of Roman and Byzantine masonry. In 1254, the Crusaders, under the French King Louis IX, constructed their imposing **fortifications**►►►, of which the splendid walls and moat of the Crusader citadel survive. They enclose only a small, rectangular part of the ancient Caesarea, which can be reached by passing through a Gothic gatehouse into the ruined city. Dusty walls and arches, vestiges of houses with their water cisterns, and skeletal remnants of other buildings are sufficient to kindle the imagination. The three apses of the Crusaders' cathedral remain standing.

The Crusaders' presence was abruptly terminated in 1275 by the Mamelukes, and again the city fell to ruin. During the four centuries of Turkish rule, until 1917, there was increasing decay and destruction, apart from an odd episode in which Muslim refugees from Bosnia were accommodated on the site. They built the 19th-century **mosque** beside the Crusader cathedral and put up warehouses by the **Old Harbor**►►, which had originally been constructed by Herod and was later reconstructed by the Crusaders. Today, the attractions of the restored harbor district include several eating places and a pleasant pay-to-enter beach area.

A TALE OF TWO CITIES

"If you hear that Caesarea thrives, but Jerusalem suffers—believe it. If you hear that Jerusalem thrives, while Caesarea suffers—believe it. But if you hear that both Jerusalem and Caesarea are thriving—don't believe it." This ancient saying reflects the rivalry between the two great "capitals" of Judaea. Jerusalem was the spiritual, Jewish capital. Caesarea was the temporal, Roman capital. Caesarea attracted pagans and was devoted to wealth and luxury. Jerusalem was pious and dominated by the Temple. Caesarea became an early stronghold of Christianity. Jerusalem was the bastion of Judaism. Even today, Jerusalem remains the religious and national capital, while Caesarea has the country's wealthiest inhabitants, best housing and most secular atmosphere.

The widespread use of the word kosher—as in "a kosher business deal"—is very close to the real meaning. Other words related to kosher mean such things as honest, wholesome, to legalize a doubtful situation, to be worthy of an honor, to succeed. "Kosher" refers to more than food. It means that things are right, correct, as they should be, and in particular, that they satisfy the requirements of Jewish law.

FORBIDDEN FOODS
"The camel, because he cheweth the cud but parteth not the hoof, he is unclean unto you. And the rock badger, because he cheweth the cud but parteth not the hoof, he is unclean unto you. And the hare, because she cheweth the cud but parteth not the hoof, she is unclean unto you. And the swine, because he parteth the hoof and is cloven footed, but cheweth not the cud, he is unclean unto you. Of their flesh ye shall not eat, and their carcass ye shall not touch. Whatsoever hath no fins nor scales in the water, that is a detestable thing unto you. And these ye shall have in detestation among the fowls; they shall not be eaten, they are a detestable thing..."
—Leviticus 11:4–13

A right way The body of Jewish law and ritual concerning food and drink is called *kashrut*. On restaurant menus and in food stores, you may notice the three Hebrew letters of the word "kosher." That is to let people know, especially religious Jews, that all the food sold there is acceptable to eat. If it is not kosher, food is usually called *trefa* (or *treif*, in Yiddish), meaning impure, incorrect.

Some examples *Kashrut* forbids certain foods entirely, such as pork and shellfish. Commercially prepared foods may be acceptable if free from forbidden ingredients—they generally require the seal of rabbinical approval. Meats must be from animals killed in the prescribed manner so that they have not a drop of blood in them. Jews must never consume any blood. *Kashrut* also reflects the biblical injunction that "You shall not seethe a kid in its mother's milk." Perhaps this was meant to be taken literally; perhaps it was meant metaphorically as a way of saying that, even when animals are killed for meat, they should not be humiliated or treated with contempt. Over the years, however, this has come to be defined as a law that forbids eating dairy products and meat products at the same time—or even within several hours of each other. For the strictly Orthodox, they cannot even be cooked in the same pans. For the more strict, they may not be eaten off the same plates, and for the stricter still, the utensils may not even be cleaned in the same sink or dishwasher. It also means that cheese cannot be made with animal rennet and that you cannot put milk in your coffee after a meat meal.

Sabbath bread (top)
Sign of approval (above)

Bon appetit You probably won't notice any of this unless you simply cannot live without a chicken breast sauteed in butter or a shrimp cocktail. You won't find them easily, and there is very little call for cheeseburgers in Israeli fast-food bars. However, food in Israel, despite *kashrut*, tends to be very good, and the whole country is equipped with a wide range of vegetarian or "dairy" restaurants (where fish is usually served as well).

▶▶ Haifa 150/151

Undoubtedly the most appealing of Israel's three large towns, Haifa is full of views and is beautifully situated on a promontory that projects into the Mediterranean, rising steeply to the south, on the slope of the Mount Carmel upland. A popular Israeli saying has it that Jerusalem prays and Tel Aviv plays, but Haifa works. The city has industrial areas on the northeastern side, a university, a science and research institute of worldwide importance at the top of the Carmel slope, and a major port near the town center.

Haifa is also a town with a mixed population. Predominantly Jewish, it also has many Druze, Muslims and Christian Arabs. Between the different groups, there seems to be no strife or friction at all, merely a pragmatic desire to work together amicably and have a peaceful life. The city is also the world center of the Bahá'i community (see page 152), whose Shrine of the Bab, with its gilded dome, makes a striking landmark.

Haifa has attractions of considerable interest to the visitor. The Mediterranean shore, extending alongside the western sections of the town, has a good, long **beach▶** and promenade, within sight of the Haifa–Tel Aviv highway. The beach curves around the headland, almost reaching the **Old City▶**, a mainly 18th- and 19th-century harbor district at the foot of the hill. Up the slope lies **Hadar HaCarmel▶▶▶**, the center of Haifa. Here you will find scores of inexpensive eating places, including Sephardi snack bars selling Middle Eastern dishes.

Downtown Herzl Street is the busy main thoroughfare, for shopping or eating. Parallel to it runs a pleasant pedestrian mall, Nordau Street, which has a quieter atmosphere and scores of open-air restaurant and café tables. As the city heads up the steep Carmel hill, a striking feature is the **stepped alleys** linking street to street. Farther up, near the crest of the hill, **Central Carmel▶** is the more stately, well-to-do, residential and academic neighborhood. A **funicular railway▶** with six stations, from Kikkar Paris at the bottom to the hotel district of Central Carmel at the top, joins the three sections of the city center.

History Archeological studies show settlements on and around present-day Haifa dating back to the 10th century BC. The busy port town with a large *yeshiva* (a school devoted to the study of sacred texts) was taken by Crusaders in 1099 and largely destroyed.

Haifa survived only as a quiet village until the 19th

Continued on page 152…

HERZL'S DREAM

Theodor Herzl, the 19th-century founder of Zionism, once said that he had a dream—no metaphorical Utopian vision, but a real sleeping dream—in which he saw Haifa transformed, with white buildings rising up the hill and great liners in the harbor. His dream has come true with astonishing accuracy, though in Herzl's fantasy, the liners were cruise ships. In today's Haifa, a century later, they are cargo vessels laden with goods.

THE TECHNION

Another dream of Herzl's was that Israel would one day possess a center of scientific research that would be the envy of the world. Haifa's Technion (the Israel Institute of Technology), the country's first university, opened in 1924, with Albert Einstein as its first president. Even before the creation of the State of Israel, the Technion had made major leaps in knowledge and technology in the fields of construction, water management and agriculture. In 1954, the Technion moved to its present Mount Carmel campus. Since then it has made great advances in aviation, chemistry, agriculture, electronic communications and medicine. Its medical school, engaged mainly in developing new techniques, is a world leader.

Haifa, city of views

Map: Haifa

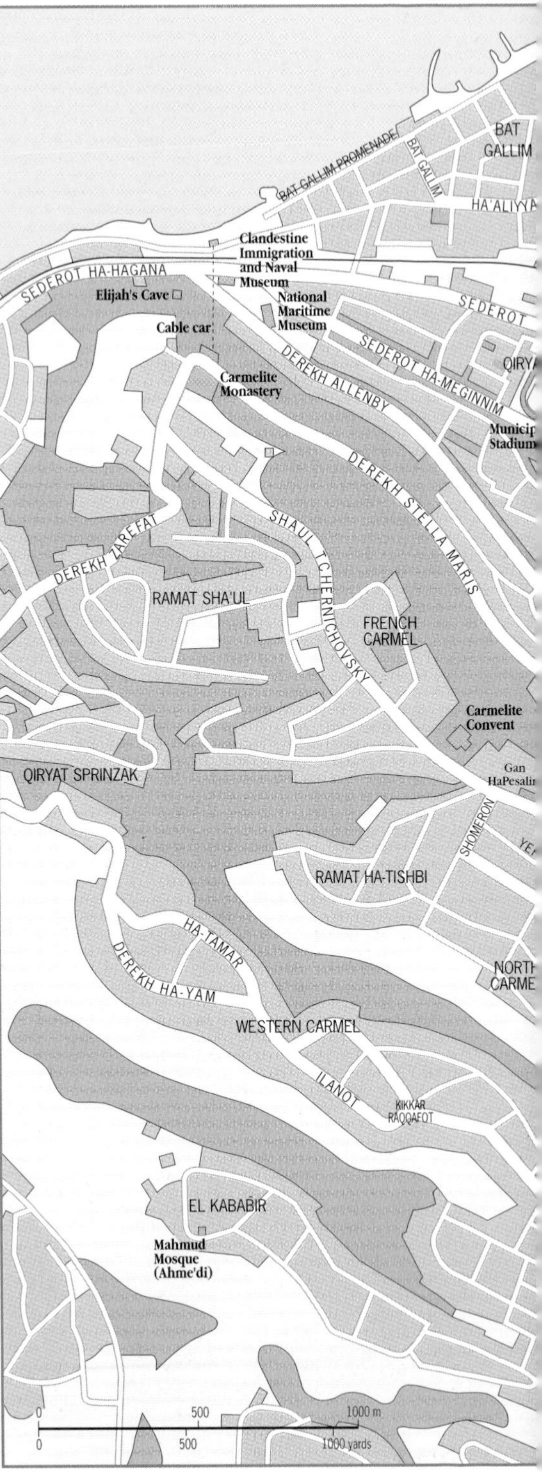

EXODUS
Originally called *The President Warfield*, the 1,800-tonne river steamer was renamed *Exodus*. Packed with Holocaust survivors, it set sail for Palestine in early July 1947, from the French port of Sète. On 18 July, on the approach to Haifa, British sailors boarded the ship and overcame the crew, killing three passengers and injuring 28. The British government ordered all passengers returned to the French port. On arrival, the refugees refused to disembark, and the French refused to use force against them. They stayed on board until the British decided to take them back to Germany. Here they were forcibly removed from the ships in September and transferred to camps for displaced persons.

Bahá'i Shrine, Haifa

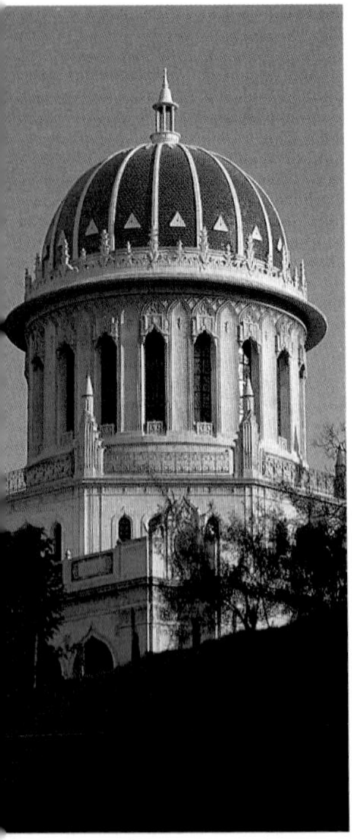

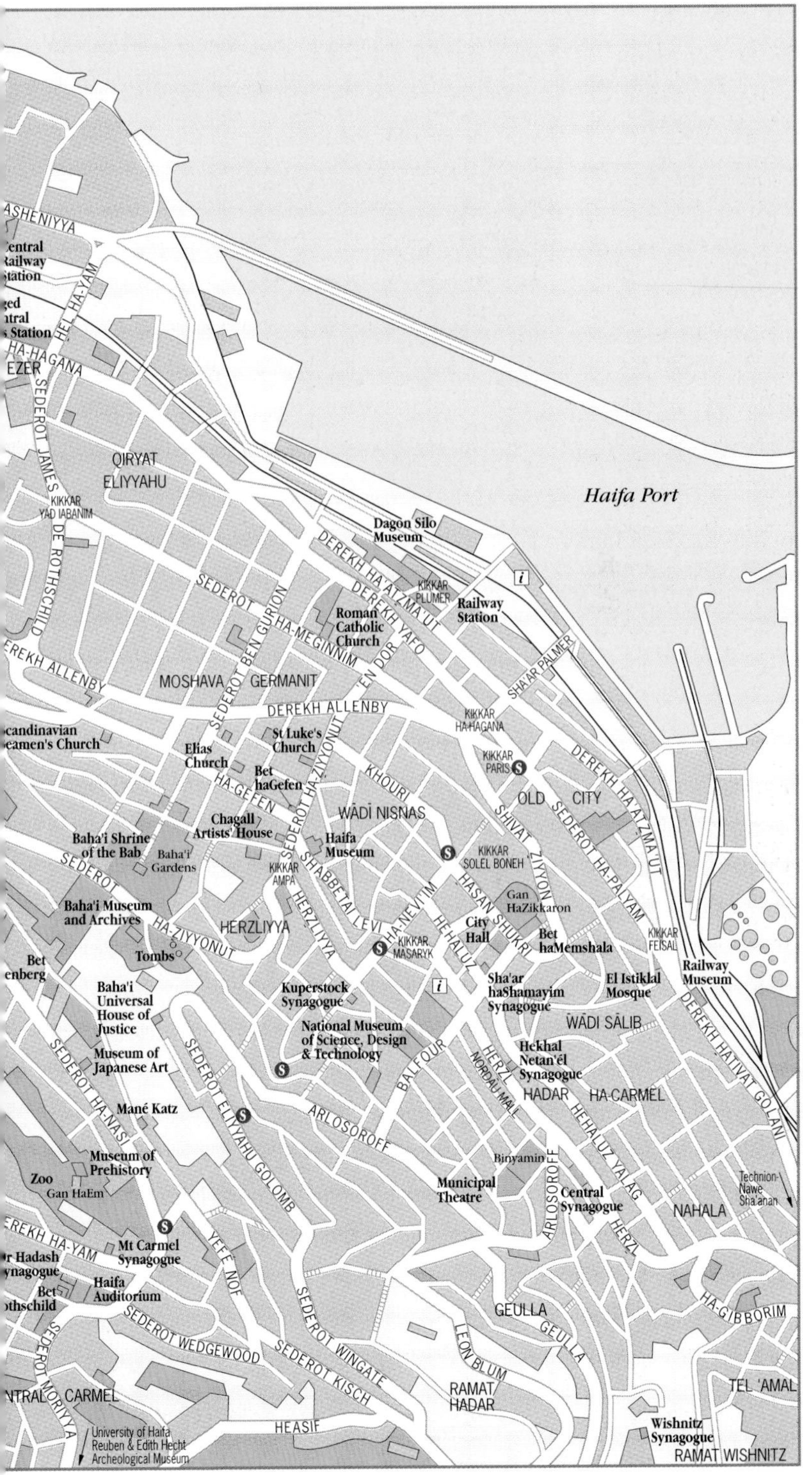
Haifa Port
Dagon Silo Museum
KIKKAR PLUMER
Railway Station
Roman Catholic Church
DEREKH HA'ATZMA'UT
DEREKH YAFO
'EN DOR
SHA'AR PALMER
QIRYAT ELIYYAHU
KIKKAR YAD IABANIM
SEDEROT JAMES DE ROTHSCHILD
SEDEROT HA-MEGINNIM
SEDEROT BEN GURION
MOSHAVA GERMANIT
DEREKH ALLENBY
HA-HAGANA
HEL HA-YAM
St Luke's Church
Elias Church
Bet haGefen
HA-GEFEN
SEDEROT HA-ZIYYONUT
KHOURI
KIKKAR HA-HAGANA
KIKKAR PARIS
OLD CITY
SHIVAT ZIYYON
SEDEROT HA-PALYAM
WĀDĪ NISNAS
Chagall Artists' House
Haifa Museum
Baha'i Shrine of the Bab
Baha'i Gardens
KIKKAR AMPA
SHABBETAI LEVI
KIKKAR SOLEL BONEH
HASAN SHUKRI
Gan HaZikkaron
Baha'i Museum and Archives
HA-ZIYYONUT
HERZLIYYA
HA-NEVI'IM
KIKKAR MASARYK
HEHALUZ
City Hall
Bet haMemshala
KIKKAR FEISAL
Railway Museum
Tombs
Baha'i Universal House of Justice
Kuperstock Synagogue
Sha'ar haShamayim Synagogue
El Istiklal Mosque
WĀDĪ SĀLIB
DEREKH HATIVAT GOLANI
National Museum of Science, Design & Technology
Museum of Japanese Art
SEDEROT HA-NASI
SEDEROT ELIYYAHU GOLOMB
BALFOUR
HERZL
NORDAU MALL
Hekhal Netan'él Synagogue
HADAR HA-CARMEL
Mané Katz
ARLOSOROFF
HEHALUZ YALAG
Museum of Prehistory
Zoo
Gan HaEm
Binyamin
Municipal Theatre
Central Synagogue
NAHALA
Technion-Nawe Sha'anan
Mt Carmel Synagogue
YEFE NOF
Haifa Auditorium
SEDEROT WEDGEWOOD
SEDEROT WINGATE
SEDEROT KISCH
GEULLA
LEON BLUM
HA-GIBBORIM
RAMAT HADAR
TEL 'AMAL
CARMEL
SEDEROT MORIYYA
HEASIF
University of Haifa Reuben & Edith Hecht Archeological Museum
Wishnitz Synagogue
RAMAT WISHNITZ

...*Continued from page 149.*

century when its port grew to accommodate steamships. The first half of the 20th century saw a huge amount of Jewish settlement. The Technion, the scientific research institute, was founded (see page 149) and various Zionist-run commercial and manufacturing enterprises were opened. Histadrut, the all-pervasive workers' union, to this day a pillar of the Israeli establishment, based itself in the town. Haifa also became the principal entry port for clandestine Jewish immigrants to Israel.

The seafront areas are the oldest part of town. Behind Haifa's slightly seedy **port**, crowded little **Wadi Nisnas▶** Arab district centers on its busy market streets. Along Ben-Gurion Avenue, the quaint **German Colony▶▶** of red-roofed stone houses was founded in 1868 by a German Christian sect. German family names are still inscribed over some doors. Today the area is being restored, with shops, cafés and restaurants opening.

The **Clandestine Immigration Museum▶▶▶** (*Closed* Shabbat. *Admission: inexpensive*) at 204 Allenby Street catches the eye of every passing motorist. This building, close to the beach and a little out of the heart of town, envelopes an entire ship. It combines the functions of memorial and archive, recording through displays and documents the organized struggle that brought 107,000 "illegal immigrants," including Holocaust survivors, to Israel from Europe during the years 1934 to 1948. Heartrending exhibits include the story of the 1947 clandestine ship *Exodus* (see page 150). The ship on display shows what the interior would have been like.

Close by, is the **National Maritime Museum▶** (198 Allenby Street), a record of shipping throughout the ages (*Open* Sat–Thu. *Admission: moderate*). Opposite, and up steep steps, is the atmospheric, if historically dubious **Elijah's Cave▶** (*Closed* Shabbat. *Admission free*).

A steep staircase of 300 steps cut into the hillside continues up and across an attractive heath with superb sea views to the handsome **Carmelite Stella Maris Monastery▶▶▶** (*Open* Mon–Sat. *Admission free*). Inside, a circular domed chapel encloses another reputedly holy and miraculous cave where Elijah is said to have lived and died. Across the road, the Stella Maris Lighthouse stands on a 19th-century Ottoman villa. The easy way to reach the monastery is to take the cable-car from close to the Clandestine Immigration Museum.

The conspicuous gilded dome rising grandly over central Haifa belongs to the exquisite **Shrine of the Bab▶▶▶** (*Open* daily 9–12; closed most of Aug. Gardens 9–5. *Admission free*), completed in 1953. This is, without doubt, the best cared-for and most elegant holy site in Israel. The rather meditative, private style of worship takes place in two small and silent white rooms, laid with rich carpets. The shrine stands in immaculate gardens looking across Haifa.

Haifa Museum▶ (26 Shabtai Levi Street) brings together a wide range of exhibits on ancient and modern art, folklore, ethnography and Jewish ritual art (*Open* daily in morning, Tue, Thu and Sat afternoons also. *Admission: moderate*). Almost opposite is **Chagall House▶** (*Open* Sat–Thu. *Admission free*) another art museum hosting special exhibitions of work by contemporary artists.

THE BAHA'I FAITH

Followers of the Bahá'i religion believe in a single deity, in the essential unity of all human beings and religions, and in the continuous revelation of an evolving, yet fundamentally unchanging, divine truth through a series of prophets ("Divine Educators"). In particular, adherents pay homage to the "Martyr-Herald" (or "the Bab"), who announced his beliefs and his mission in Persia in 1844 and was executed in 1850 (aged 31) as a result, and the "Founder of the Faith" (Bahá'u'lláh), who was exiled to Akko in 1868 and died there under house arrest in 1892. Haifa is the administrative capital of the religion, and the Universal House of Justice is its supreme institution. But while the magnificently beautiful Shrine of the Bab is in Haifa and is seen by more visitors, the lovely Shrine of Bahá'u'lláh, at Bahjá, near Akko (see page 140), is actually the more sacred site.

CARMELIM – A NEW REGION

The warm, green and wooded Mediterranean hills of Mount Carmel, the wine country around Zichron Yaakov, and the narrow coastal plain flanked by a long ribbon of sandy beach have together been dubbed Carmelim by Israelis. This beautiful part of Israel's coastal strip, reaching from Haifa to Caesarea, contains an exceptional legacy of history and culture.
For tourist information tel: 04-984 5239;
web: www.carmelim.org.il.

▶ Herzliya — 112C4

Named after the "Father of Zionism," Theodor Herzl, Herzliya is a busy working town. Quite separate is its beachfront area, correctly called **Herzliya Pituach**. This has a wide white beach backed by high-quality hotels and apartment houses. South of the Acadia Hotel is a superb modern marina. The resort is one of the smartest in Israel.

▶ Lod (Lydda) — 112C4

Beside Ben-Gurion International Airport, Lod dates to the Israelite conquest in 1300BC. The Acts of the Apostles records that St. Paul miraculously healed a bedridden man here. It is also claimed as the birthplace of St. George, the Roman tribune sacred to Christians and to Muslims. He is buried here, in a building that is both church and mosque, on the site of a 6th-century basilica and 12th-century Crusader church.

▶▶ Lohamei HaGhetaot — 113B4

(tel: 04-995 8044; www.gfh.org.il)
Open: daily, early closing Fri. Admission free

The name of this kibbutz, built beside a Byzantine aqueduct on the edge of Akko, means "The Ghetto Fighters." It was founded in 1949 by Holocaust survivors and former ghetto resistance fighters. At the entrance is their massive, gaunt **Holocaust Memorial and Museum▶▶▶**. This deals in clear displays with the Jewish history of Lithuania, the growth of Zionism there, Jewish youth movements, the Warsaw Ghetto Uprising, and much more. A display on the Nazis' death camps includes a large-scale model of Treblinka, and deals with the extermination of two different historic Jewish communities, the Dutch and the community of Salonika in Greece. Among the disturbing photos on display are the terribly sad faces of child victims of Nazi medical "experiments." **Yad Layeled (The Children's Memorial)▶▶▶** is housed in a separate building, an award-winning structure in which visitors follow a spiral of vivid exhibits that evoke the Holocaust through the eyes of its child victims. Yad Layeled is suitable for child visitors.

BEHIND THE SCENES
Perceived by most visitors simply as one of Israel's quieter beach resorts, Herzliya has a successful "clean industries" zone generating an income of US $300 million, and accounting for 25 percent of Israel's science-based exports.

Lod, claimed as the birth and burial place of St. George

DUNES AND SWAMPS
Israel's coastal strip is a region of infertile dunes that, apart from the Carmel upland, used to be backed by the hot swampy Plain of Sharon. Right into this century, the area was notoriously unhealthy and unworkable. On top of the other problems, it was inhabited by crocodiles. The great Levantine highway of the ancient world, later to become the Romans' Via Maris (the Coast Road), had to divert away from the swampy, treacherous coastal hinterland. The British Mandate authorities were the first to set about drainage and bridge-building to make the area more accessible. With the founding of the State of Israel, a mammoth effort was made to build new towns along the coast. The marshes were drained and the main north–south highway put through. The Sharon Plain has since been turned into one of the world's most productive citrus-growing areas.

Carmel National Park (right and below)

▶▶▶ Mount Carmel *113B3*

Some of the most beautiful countryside in Israel falls within the Carmel National Park. The Carmel range – consisting of the Carmel escarpment itself and the smaller Mehallel, Shoker, and Sumak peaks—rises from the surrounding coastal lowlands in the form of a triangle. The triangle's northern apex pushes into the sea at Haifa and its sides plunge down to the Kishon Valley and Yizre'el Plain on one side and to the Mediterranean Sea on the other. The base of the triangle fades gradually into the lower Sharon countryside, creating an attractive landscape of rock and abundant, varied scrub rolling across the Mediterranean hinterland.

Despite the name, Mount Carmel is no mountain. The highest point, only 550m (1,804ft), hardly rises above the rest of the Carmel ridge, along which runs the road from Haifa. The range covers a tiny area (14 miles/23km from end to end, and only 6 miles/10km at the widest). Yet it has the feel of a world apart, with a character and history distinct from that of the lower-lying country all around.

In Canaanite times, these hilltops were adorned with shrines dedicated to Ba'al. The cult's appeal was such that it continued to thrive long after the Israelite conquest. Its end in the 9th century BC is described in the biblical account (I Kings 18) where Elijah wins a public contest to see whose god could make spontaneous fire for their sacrifices. Elijah called on the people to slaughter the 450 "prophets of Ba'al" and to turn instead to the God of Israel. Since that time, Elijah's name has been associated with Carmel—interestingly more among the Christians and the Muslims than among the Jews.

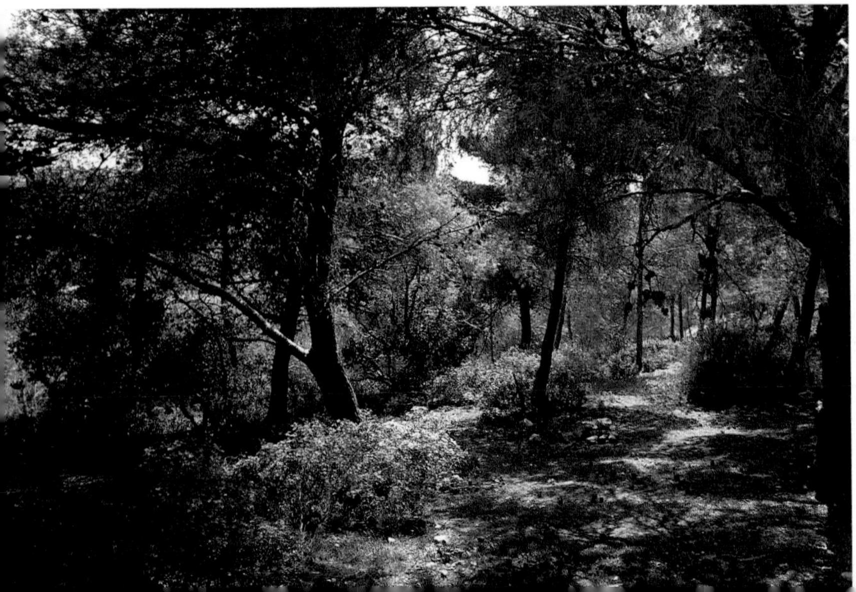

Drive

Carmel scenery

Mount Carmel's Mediterranean countryside, of limestone hills covered with fragrant evergreen vegetation, is full of historical and human interest. There are Druze towns to visit, plus religious and historical sites, an artists' village, and local wine to taste (for map see page 113). *Allow all day.*

From **Haifa**, take the steep road to the **university**, dominated by the intrusive **Eshkol Tower**, a monstrosity designed only to be as tall as possible. Leave the city on the tranquil hill road to **Isfiya▶**, a small town of Christians and Druze. The road winds steeply down to larger **Daliyat▶▶**, where the people's dress and local architecture are more noticeably Druze. Its main street has a fascinating Middle Eastern atmosphere, with open-fronted stores and snack bars. **Oliphant's House▶**, a memorial to Druze soldiers who died for Israel, was the 19th-century home of an Englishman whose Jewish secretary, N H Imber, wrote *HaTikva,* Israel's national anthem. A turn leads to the hilltop monastery at **Muhraka▶** (or Keren Carmel), traditional site of the meeting between Elijah and Ba'al's prophets. Follow the main road to **Zichron Ya'akov▶▶** (see page 160), where wine-tasting and a tour of the cellars is available at the Winery Visitors' Center.

On the coast, **Kibbutz Nahsholim▶** has a museum, in a former wine-bottle factory. The kibbutz also offers simple beachside accommodation. The archeological site of **Tel Dor▶** was a Phoenician port town thousands of years ago. Take the Haifa highway, and turn into the **Nahal Me'arot Reserve▶▶▶**, where several big caves were inhabited by humans as far back as 200,000 years ago. These can be toured with a guide. The reserve also offers a choice of marked hiking trails through lovely natural vegetation.

Ein Hod▶, to the north, is a hillside "artists' village" of meandering lanes, scattered houses, pretty gardens, art galleries, and open-air sculptures. A left at the crossroads leads to **Atlit▶** (see page 143) while the right turn winds through beautiful rocky hills to **Carmel Forest▶▶**. The sign to **Hai Bar Carmel▶** leads down a dirt road to a reserve where once-indigenous animals are being reintroduced. Continue to the junction and take a left to get back to Haifa.

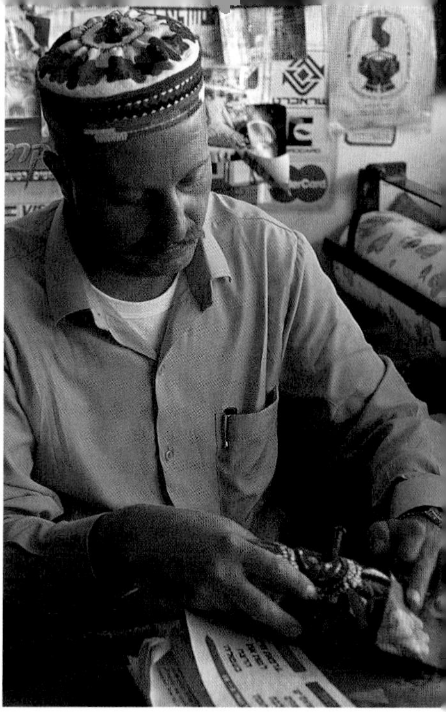

Traditional Druze skullcaps for sale in Daliyat.

The open-fronted stores of Daliyat's main street

In ancient Israel, wine in moderation was the usual drink before, during and after meals. Jewish coins of the Second Temple period depict bunches of grapes. Grapes or vine leaves can often be seen in the mosaics and stone carvings of post-Temple synagogues. With the return to Israel, the winemaking industry has been revived with great success, and is currently flourishing.

WINE AND RITUAL
"Blessed are you Lord, our God ruler of the world, who created the fruit of the vine." This blessing over wine is said (in Hebrew) before every meal on the Sabbath, starting with the Friday night dinner. A glass of kosher wine is then drunk—usually just a tiny glass of the extra-sweet Kiddush wine.

Sacred and profane Israelis are not big drinkers. There is no breath-testing here for motorists, simply because excessive drinking is almost unknown. Observant Jews thank God for the fruit of the vine on the Sabbath, yet no one could be more abstemious. Things have obviously changed since biblical times when the people of Israel grew grapes in abundance, were fond of wine, and—to judge by references in the Scriptures—sometimes drank a great deal of it.

Jews are supposed to drink only kosher wine. Rabbis decided that any contact with a non-Jew would render wine non-kosher unless the wine was boiled. Of course, boiling is not the ideal way to preserve a wine's finest qualities, and kosher wine came to be regarded with derision by wine-lovers. There is also an ultra-sweet blended wine specially produced for Kiddush, the ritual blessing that sanctifies all sorts of occasions. Such wine seems to be intended to dissuade drinking—yet when the sages decreed that the Sabbath be sanctified over a cup of wine, the reason given was precisely that wine brings joy and festivity.

Products of the Golan Heights Winery

The new approach Even Israelis do not think of themselves as a wine-producing nation. They are mistaken, for in recent decades Israel has rediscovered its great wine tradition. In keeping with the Talmudic injunction to ensure that the wine is kosher, only Jews may be involved in its production at every stage. The most modern techniques are used, and many different grape varieties have been planted, crossed, or combined, in the search for higher quality and an authentic Israeli style of fine wine.

Some have been a great success, especially the elegant dry white Chardonnay and Sauvignon Blanc and the classic, full-bodied red Cabernet Sauvignon. Blander and sweeter Emerald Riesling is the most popular with Israelis. Richly sweet Muscat is grown, as is the tangy California

Mural celebrating Baron Rothschild's introduction of viticulture to the Carmel region

variety zinfandel. The main wine areas are in southern Carmel, the district south of Tel Aviv around Rishon-l'Tsion, and the Golan Heights in the north, with smaller wineries around Ashkelon and Beersheva. Less expensive labels include the Segal and Baron wineries.

Carmel It is said that the name Carmel probably means God's Vineyard (Kerem El). A century ago, Baron Edmund de Rothschild had the whole area, from Zichron Ya'akov down to Binyamina, planted with vines, under the direction of French agronomists. The Carmel Mizrachi Winery in Zichron Ya'akov is now the country's largest wine producer, and visitors are welcome for tours and tasting.

Rishon l'Tsion The name (also spelled Rishon le Zion) means "First In Zion." It means, in other words, the first Jewish settlement of modern times, established in 1882. Five years later, the struggling pioneers were bailed out by Baron Rothschild, who again planted vineyards, with tremendous success. The Carmel winery here, recently modernized, offers guided tours and tasting. Its wines have improved enormously in recent years.

Golan Heights Winery Acclaimed as Israel's best are the wines produced on the Golan Heights, just outside Katzrin. The vineyards, tended by settlements and kibbutzim over a wide area of the Golan, are run as a co-operative together with the winery itself. This launched Israel's dramatic rediscovery of winemaking, and it's the only winemaker in the world to have won the Chairman's Trophy of Excellence at the trade's important Vinexpo exhibition three successive years. Golan's soils and drainage are perfect for wine, and, because of poor rainfall, the water supply is controlled by irrigation. The wines, in a wide range of styles, are marketed under three labels: Yarden (the best), Gamla and Golan. The winery, the only one in Israel growing Merlot grapes, also makes a fine sparkling dry white.

Netanya's beach

Open-air entertainment

SUMMER NIGHTS
Open-air entertainment takes place in Netanya's main square every night of the week (except Friday) right through July and August. The atmosphere is jolly, participatory and good-humored. In a typical week you could expect a disco on Sunday, folk dancing on Monday and Saturday, magicians, puppets and clown shows for children on Tuesday, and community singing on Wednesday and Thursday.

► Nahariya 113B4

The waterfront area Nahariya on Galilee's Mediterranean coast, 20 miles (32km) north of Haifa, enjoys a good beach, a pleasant frontage, a wide range of leisure amenities, and a calm, tranquil air. Farther back from the sea lies a busy working town, founded in 1934 by Jewish refugees from Germany. **Museums►** of art, archeology and local history can be found in the town hall. The resort is a good base for excursions and tours. About 3 miles (5km) north are the seashore ruins of **Akhziv►►**, now a national park. It was an important Canaanite, Phoenician and Israelite town and renowned for the purple dye produced from its shellfish. Some 2 miles (3km) south of Nahariya, 4th- and 5th-century Byzantine mosaics and other archeological finds can be seen at **Kibbutz Evron►** and at **Moshav Shavei Zion**, which also has a good hotel.

►► Netanya 113A1

Spreading comfortably alongside the seashore, but not far inland, this big, likeable and unpretentious town is peaceful, almost sedate, and has dozens of decent mid-range hotels and moderately priced eating places. The clifftop is laid out in gardens and parks that form a series of beautiful pedestrian promenades with glorious views out to sea. A public elevator on the central Harishonim Promenade makes it easy to get from the clifftop direct to the main beach, called Sironit, which has year-round restaurants and beach facilities. In addition, 6 miles (10km) of sandy beaches head in both directions.

One focal point for visitors is **Kikkar HaAtzma'ut** (Independence Square), which fronts onto the clifftop above Sironit beach. Another gathering place is the main street, **Rehov Herzl**, where tourists and locals stroll in the pleasant evening air. Behind its leisurely facade, Netanya is a productive commercial town. Diamonds have been among its most lucrative specialties since World War II, when the jewelers of Antwerp moved here to escape the Nazis. The **National Diamond Centre►►** at 90 Herzl Street shows an interesting video about diamonds, gives a guided tour of a diamond factory, and offers a chance to buy at discount prices (*Closed* Shabbat. *Admission free*).

►► Ramla *112C3*

Almost unique in that it came into being during a period of Arab rule, Ramla was founded in 716 by Caliph Suleiman and became a large city of Muslims, Christians and Jews. In 1936, the Jews were forced out by the Arabs, who in 1948 largely fled in fear of reprisals. The population of 50,000 now consists mainly of Jews driven in turn from their homes in Arab countries, along with several thousand Israeli Arabs. It is also a center of the Karaites, a small Jewish sect that accepts the Torah but rejects subsequent rabbinic comment. The town is attractive and friendly, with a strongly Middle Eastern character.

The **Great Mosque►** (off Herzl Street), reflecting the town's mixed history, is a 12th-century Crusader church topped by a white minaret and transformed into a mosque. The landmark Gothic stone **White Tower►►** is gaunt, square and rises 88.5ft (27m). Napoleon, who in 1799 stayed overnight in Ramla, enjoyed the view from the top, and General Allenby, in 1917, found it a useful military observation post. Also known to Christians as the Tower of Forty Martyrs, and to Muslims as the Tower of the Prophet's Companions, it was built in 1267 by the Mameluke Sultan Baibars. It adjoins an extensive walled area, along one side of which are the remnants of an 8th-century **mosque►**. Just off Herzl Street, **St. Helena's Pool►** is an impressive 8th-century reservoir.

► Rehovot *112C3*

Zionist leader Chaim Weizmann (1874–1952), Israel's first President, lived here at the end of his life. In his honor, the distinguished **Weizmann Institute** research centre was founded in 1944 (tours by arrangement), near **Weizmann's home►** (open to visitors). He died here and is buried in the garden.

CHAIM WEIZMANN (1874–1952)
Besides being a leading Zionist, Chaim Weizmann also persuaded Balfour to write the famous Declaration (pledging Britain's support in setting up a Jewish homeland), was president of the World Zionist Organization, and first president of Israel. Born near Pinsk, in Russia, he studied chemistry in Germany and Switzerland, and in 1916 was made director of the British Admiralty Chemical Laboratories. Although devoting much of his energy to diplomacy and politics, he had an international reputation in the scientific world for his discoveries in organic chemistry. He made historic advances in the study of carcinogens and his many other discoveries included the making of synthetic rubber from organic substances.

Blue and white Israeli flags in front of the Weizmann Institute

DOR
Located on the coast close to Zichron Ya'akov and next to Nachsholim, Dor was a Phoenician port in 2000BC. Though seized by the Israelites and then by the Assyrians, it was recaptured by Phoenicians and remained an independent city until the Roman conquest. From the 4th to 7th centuries it was a Christian town, destroyed in the Arab conquest. Crusaders built a castle on the shore here in the 12th century, but within a hundred years it had been destroyed by the Mamelukes. Dor was revived in 1949 as a *moshav* (co-operative village) set up by immigrants from Greece. It has a beautiful beach and plenty of reminders of its long history.

The white cliffs of Rosh HaNikra

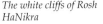

▶▶▶ Rosh HaNikra *113B4*

The coastal hinterland climbs as it approaches the Lebanese border, which runs along a high ridge in Israel's northwestern corner. Rosh HaNikra is essentially a frontier post on this ridge of mountain where white cliffs plunge straight down into the blue Mediterranean. At the top, thrilling views run down the Mediterranean shore. The border bristles with defenses, and both UN and Israeli soldiers continually cross through the gate here.

The area's biggest attraction is the **Rosh HaNikra Caves▶▶▶** at the bottom of the cliffs, which can be reached, except on Shabbat, by an expensive cable-car. Here the sea has eaten into the soft pale sandstone like moth grubs into wool. The cliffs are riddled with little holes and tunnels that wind through the rock from one opening to the next—and at each the azure water hammers in as if to bring the whole cliff tumbling down into the waves.

▶▶ Zichron Ya'akov *113B2*

The name means "In Memory of Jacob" and refers not to the biblical character but to the 19th-century banker, Jacob de Rothschild. The town was named in his honor by his son, Baron Edmond de Rothschild (also known as Benjamin or Binyamin). A pleasant small town on high ground at the edge of the Carmel hills, it looks down towards the sea in one direction, and into the Valley of HaNadiv—"The Benefactor"—in the other. The benefactor was Baron Rothschild, who purchased this valley and its surrounding country in the 1880s in order to establish new settlements and bail out existing ones. His intentions were Zionist but not always entirely philanthropic. The settlements were expected to pay their way and cover their costs.

Zichron Ya'akov was founded in 1882 by Romanian Jews, who floundered and fell into serious difficulty. Half of them died, and the others were ready to quit. Rothschild then came in with an offer to buy up the settlement lock, stock and barrel and employ the residents on a salaried basis. They agreed. The baron then brought in non-Jewish agronomists from the south of France and asked them what could be produced there successfully. Their answer was wine. Other Jews came and, desperate for work, were employed here. Zichron Ya'akov became the most important of the little wine-growing towns of Israel. Today, the main attraction is a tour of the co-operatively owned

Carmel Oriental or **Carmel Mizrachi Winery▶** (*Closed* Shabbat. *Admission: moderate*). After a visit to the cellars, you can taste the several varieties of wine made here. The town center is also worth a stroll. On the main streets, HaNadiv and Mayasdim, pioneer houses can still be seen and, at the central junction, the pioneers' synagogue. **Beit Aaronsohn▶** (*Closed* Shabbat. *Admission: inexpensive*) was the home of the distinguished agronomist and botanist, Aaron Aaronsohn (1876–1917). He created and led, with his brother Alexander and sister Sarah, the Nili spy ring which operated for the British against the Turks in World War I. The group was eventually uncovered by the Turks, who captured and tortured Sarah for several days before allowing her to commit suicide. Alexander was executed. Aaron later died in a plane crash. Their home, on Mayasdim Street, the ring's headquarters, has been preserved just as it was in 1917 with the addition of an audiovisual show explaining more about the Aaronsohn (or Aharonson) family.

Memorial to Rothschild, "the Benefactor," who turned Zichron Ya'akov into an important wine town

The road south leads through vineyards to another wine settlement, **Binyamina**, reflecting the baron's Hebrew name. Between the two towns, an access road leads to **Ramat HaNadiv▶▶▶** (Hill of the Benefactor), the beautiful memorial park dedicated to Baron Edmond de Rothschild and his wife. In the park is their massive and dignified burial chamber. The two lie under a single slab of black marble in a mausoleum open to the public.

Cable-car to Rosh HaNikra caves

REGION HIGHLIGHTS

Basilica of the Annunciation, Nazareth *page 193*

Church of the Beatitudes *page 189*

Church of the Primacy of Peter, Tabgha *page 202*

Hula Valley *pages 178–179*

Old Synagogue, Peki'in *page 195*

Roman and Byzantine spa, Hamat Gader *page 176*

Sea of Galilee *pages 196–198*

Sefat *pages 200–201*

Synagogue, Capernaum *page 171*

Tel Dan *page 203*

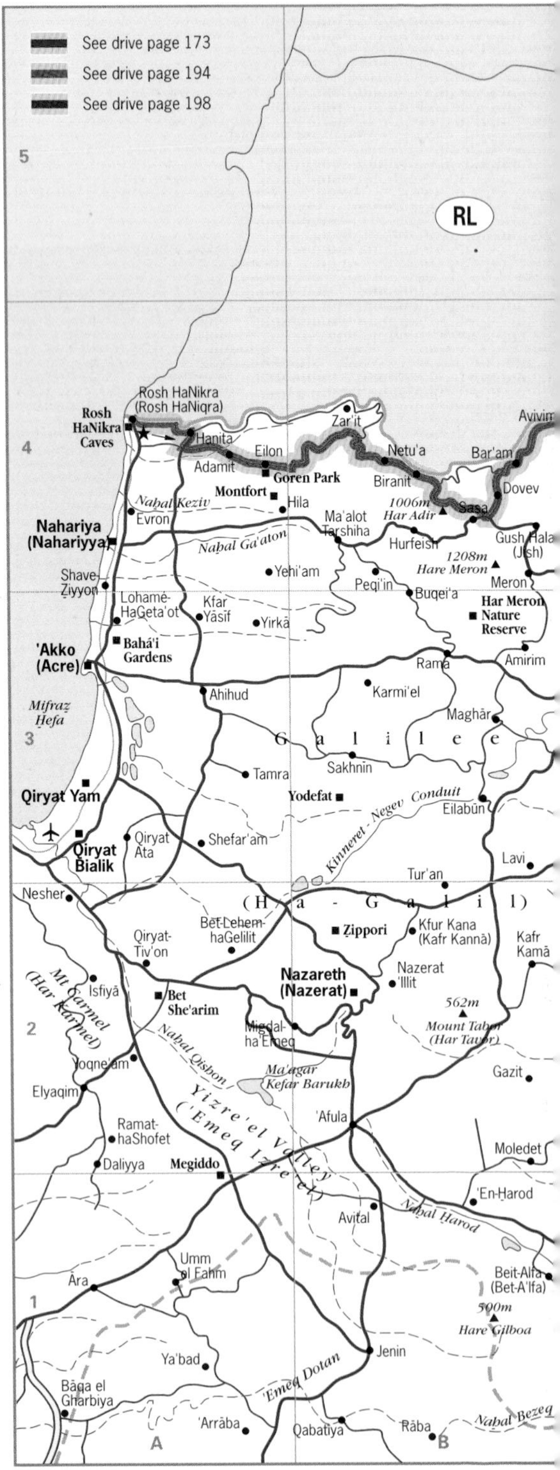

Galilee and the North

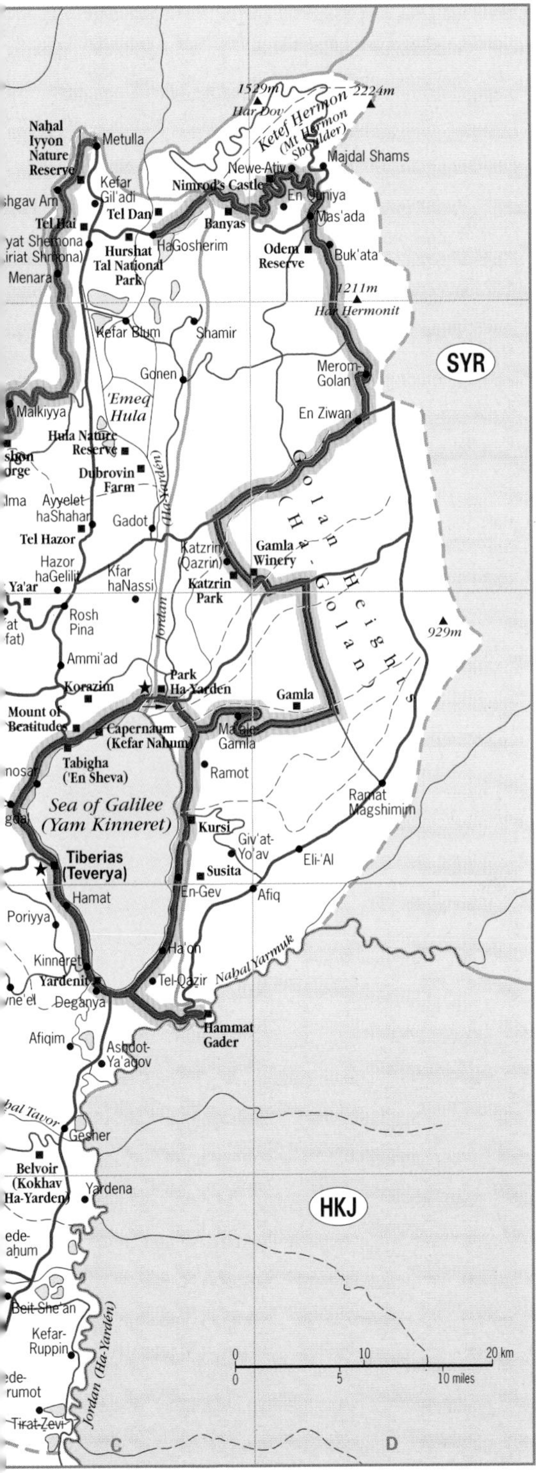

Sign advertising the Jordan River baptismal site

THE DISTRICT
The Hebrew name for Galilee, HaGalil, simply means "the District." Originally it was HaGalil HaGoyim, meaning (more or less), "the Non-Jewish District." That is because, from the 8th century BC to the Hasmonean conquest in the 2nd century BC, the region was not part of the Israelite kingdom. Instead it was a possession of the Assyrians, Babylonians, Persians and Seleucids. Under Roman rule it was reunited with Judaea. Yet the name has rarely been accurate. Jews have always been numerous here, and this northern region has historically been a stronghold of Jewish nationalism as well as a centre of Jewish religious learning.

Galilee and the North The hills of Galilee, on Israel's warm, northern borders, are startlingly green. Here, the rocky landscape is clothed in natural or planted forests. Farms produce an extraordinary range of crops. The northeast corner, around Dan, on the slopes of Mount Hermon and in the upper Hula Valley, enjoys a wealth of plant, bird and animal wildlife.

Images of Israel as a Middle Eastern country can be misleading. Essentially, this is a Mediterranean land, tied by history, culture, geography and climate entirely to the waters of the classical, Mediterranean world, rather than to the sands of Arabia. No part of Israel strikes the eye as so utterly and familiarly Mediterranean as the Galilee.

The Galilee forms a narrow band stretching from the sea in the west to the Jordan River. The east is dominated by the Sea of Galilee, while to the south it is bounded by the Jezreel Plain. The region is blessed with an exquisite climate that is a few degrees cooler than in the beach resorts further south. Snow falls on the heights in mid-winter, but fine weather lasts from May to October.

A place of pilgrimage The fact that Jesus lived in Galilee—and walked on its waters, miraculously fed the multitudes, taught that we should love one another, and recruited his disciples from among the Galilee fishermen—is accepted by Christians around the world. Many travel to see the spots where all this happened. The fact that the sites have been disputed, or are symbolic rather than historically proven, seems not to matter. Stand beside the tranquil shore of the Sea of Galilee, and it is easy to believe that you are indeed standing where he stood, seeing the serene landscapes where he wandered in prayer and in thought. Dozens of simple churches and grand basilicas commemorate the significant events of his three-year public ministry.

It is now more widely understood among Christians that Jesus was an observant Jew, learned in the Scriptures and concerned only that his fellow Jews should obey the spirit, rather than just the letter, of the Law. Galilee, far from the Temple in Jerusalem, was perhaps an ideal place for his teachings. Yet within a few years of his death, after the crushing of the First Jewish Revolt and the destruction

Christ recruited his disciples from the fishermen of Galilee (right) Christians from around the world (below) come to trace Christ's ministry

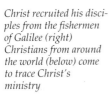

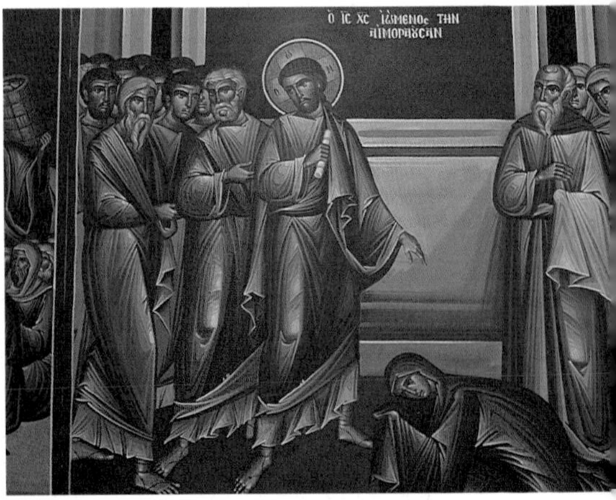

The Sea of Galilee

of the Temple, the eastern Galilee was to become the greatest centre of Jewish learning. The Mishna and Talmud (commentaries on the ancient Scriptures) were both written here. Two of the four Jewish holy cities – Sefat and Tiberias—are in Galilee. The region again became the focal point of Jewish culture after the expulsion of the Jews from Spain in 1492. The tombs of the great Galilean scholars and sages of the biblical and medieval periods attract numerous Jewish visitors.

Golan Mediterranean scenery also rises to the east, in the Golan hills. These sparsely inhabited uplands rise to a high plateau overlooked by the majestic snows of Mount Hermon. All this countryside formed part of the biblical land of Israel and has extensive remains from that era. Coming under Arab control in the Middle Ages, Golan formed part of Syria until Syria invaded Israel in 1967. Six days after the invasion, Syria was defeated and driven east. Israel took the Heights and created a buffer zone, which Syria still claims as its own.

Cultural diversity For more than a century, Jews have been drawn to the Galilee as an ideal place to settle and cultivate. Many of their most difficult struggles, both with the land and with the Arabs, have taken place here. Today, there is a good degree of harmony between the different cultural groups, and certainly for a tourist it is safe (and interesting) to visit Israel's non-Jewish communities. The largest Arab town in Israel is Nazareth, where most of the residents are Christian. Several other Galilee towns have a Christian Arab population, though of course many other smaller Arab towns and villages are Muslim. Almost all the members of Israel's 40,000 Druze population live in the western Galilee and on the Golan Heights.

WHERE'S THE BEEF?
Israel has an exceptionally large proportion of vegetarians, and the Galilee, in particular, seems to have become the capital of the meatless lifestyle. Jewish dietary laws require meat and milk to be kept separate—to the point where some believe they cannot be eaten within several hours of each other. For many, the problem of keeping meat and milk apart could be avoided most easily by becoming vegetarian. That is why nearly all factory cafeterias in Israel are vegetarian. Many other Jews chose to become vegetarian for reasons of compassion towards animals, which is a biblical precept. As well as its famous vegetarian village, Amirim, the Galilee has a good meat-free hotel (the Sea View, near Rosh Pina) and an unusual cheese restaurant (Ein Camonim, near Parod).

Byzantine-era frieze in the Golan Archeological Museum

WHO ARE THE DRUZE?
Bnei Maruf, the Children of Grace, is how the Druze refer to themselves. Members of this distinctive community wear striking black-and-white attire and live in their own well-kept villages scattered over Galilee and Golan. They originated as an 11th-century breakaway group from Ismailism, a branch of Islam. The tenets of the religion are kept a closely guarded secret, with a body of arcane knowledge known only to the initiates or the *Ukal*. The rest of the Druze population are the *Juhal*, the ignorant.

Israel's Druze have been keen supporters of the Jewish state because it gives them full religious freedom, unlike any of the Islamic countries where the Druze are to be found. As a community, they have accepted the obligations of army service (for which, as Arabs, they could have asked to be exempt), and many have distinguished themselves fighting to defend Israel.

▶ Amirim 162B3

High in the Galilee hills (Amirim means "Treetops") this tranquil agricultural *moshav* (co-operative village) is entirely vegetarian. Just a short drive from historic Sefat, it offers tremendous views to west and east, as well as south to the Sea of Galilee. Half of Amirim's 100 families take paying guests (including some or all meals), and the vegetarian restaurant is very popular.

▶▶ Banyas (Hermon National Park) 163C5

(Tel: 06-6902577)
Open: daily 8–5, (to 4 in winter). Admission: inexpensive

At the foot of Mount Hermon, this lush, delightful park is one of the sources of the Jordan River. With gushing waters, shaded picnic tables and benches, and extensive classical ruins, it attracts many visitors. An enjoyable footpath (about 1.5 hours' walk) makes a circle through rich vegetation, crossing and recrossing the turbulent Banyas stream on wooden walkways, with an optional extra kilometre (half-mile) walk to a lovely **waterfall** that thunders into a pool enclosed by greenery that is perpetually moist.

Banyas was once perhaps the most important pagan shrine in Israel. The park entrance opens into an impressive Greek archeological site, with pools and statuary. Previously sacred to the Canaanite god, Ba'al, the shrine was rededicated to Pan (Paneas in Greek, from which the name Banyas is derived) when it became part of the Hellenistic kingdom of Antiochus III of Syria in the 3rd century BC. In those days the spring poured from the mouth of a cave above the shrine; now it emerges from a crack below. Niches around the cave originally held statues, and scores of Greek carvings have been found here.

The Romans, on taking control of Palestine, rededicated the site to Pan and Zeus, greatly enlarging it. Herod's son Philip made Banyas his capital, renamed it Caesarea Philippi and turned it into the biggest city in northern Israel. It later passed into Arab hands and the city died away. It was held by Crusaders from 1129 to 1135. By the 1967 Israeli takeover, its population was just 200.

Gushing rivers and ancient caves in Banyas National Park

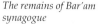

A LONG TWO WEEKS
In late 1948, Israeli forces, fighting desperately against invading Arab armies, arrived at the Christian Arab villages of Biram (now Bar'am) and Ikrit, on the Lebanese border. The Israelis were welcomed and, to assist the soldiers, the villagers agreed to leave for an estimated period of two weeks. But the continuing state of hostilities after the war left the Israeli government wary of Arab villages on the border, and the residents were never allowed back. Ikrit was destroyed in 1951 and Biram in 1953. Many of the villagers, and now their children, live in nearby Rama and Jish, but they have not abandoned hope of returning to their homes and lands.

The remains of Bar'am synagogue

The Gospel of Matthew (16:13–20) relates that, while visiting Caesarea Philippi and walking beside the water, Jesus asked his disciples who they thought he was. Simon for the first time declared Jesus to be the Messiah (Christos in Greek), whereupon Jesus called him Petrus, saying, "...upon this rock I will build my church." Banyas remained important to Christians and was the see of a bishop from the 4th to the 7th century. The white-domed Weli el-Hader on the hillside, built in honor of the prophet Elijah, is sacred to the Druze (see panel, page 166).

►► Bar'am National Park *162B4*

(Tel: 06-6989301)
Open: summer, daily 8–5; winter, daily 8–4.
Admission: inexpensive

Dating from the 2nd century AD, the well-preserved remains of the fine synagogue here include two walls of huge stone blocks, stone columns forming three aisles, a flagstone floor and an arched entrance facing Jerusalem.

Until the 1948 War of Independence, the synagogue was part of a small Maronite Arab village friendly to the Jewish forces. During the fighting—which was intense here, so close to the Lebanese border—the residents were asked to leave "temporarily." Instead, their homes were largely destroyed. Not far from the synagogue, on higher ground, is the villagers' church and their ruined houses. Their children, now adults, use the church for weddings and ceremonies, and have campaigned for the return of the village. Distinguished Israelis have supported the cause, and the authorities now seem likely to agree.

SOMETIME, NEVER
Among the sayings and legends attached to Banyas is the Talmudic statement that the Messiah will come only "when the Banyas turns red." This seems to relate to the old Yiddish expression, that you can have the gift you want or do the thing you want "when Moshiach (the Messiah) comes." In other words, probably not in our lifetime.

MARRIAGE MADE IN HEAVEN

Not far from Bat Ya'ar, in a pretty vale of pine and olive groves outside Amuka village, stands a small domed building housing the tomb, blackened with candle flame, of Rabbi Yonatan ben Uzziel. The building is divided into men's and women's sections. Here Hasidim and Sephardim flock to pray for a marriage partner or that they might become pregnant. Obscure and tenuous rabbinical remarks account for the practice. Yonatan himself was very preoccupied with the importance of the marriage bond, and later rabbis commentated that the need for a wife, and the way to find one, was "deep" (*amuka*—which happened to be where Yonatan was buried). You might think that only a few hopeless cases would be found here, but among the worshippers are many pretty young women and handsome young bachelors. Glances between the men's and women's sections lead to many a friendly conversation later, and often subsequently to a wedding—thus proving the efficacy of a prayer at the tomb.

▶ Bat Ya'ar *163C3*

(tel: 06-692 1788; fax: 06 6921991)
Open: daily 8–2. Admission free

This popular activity center, close to Amuka, Sefat and Rosh Pina, is set in a clearing in the midst of Israel's largest forest, the Birya. All planted by the Jewish National Fund, these tall, refreshing woodlands consist mainly of Jerusalem pine, cedar and cypress. Offering activities and excursions lasting from an hour to a week, by pony, jeep or on foot, Bat Ya'ar is well placed for off-road tours into the Upper Galilee countryside. The 3-hour jeep tour (*Admission charge*) travels through farmland planted with crops ranging from apples to bananas; wildlife encounters could include anything from foxes to gazelles to bee-eaters.

The center also stages children's entertainment, dance and open-air music shows. It attracts many lunchtime visitors to its ranch-style restaurant, which serves generous salads, steaks and homemade breads, with a view across the Hula Valley to the snowy summit of Mount Hermon.

▶ Beit Alfa *162B1*

Located between Heftsiba and Beit Alfa, two neighboring kibbutzim at the foot of Mount Gilboa, 40km (25 miles) from Afula, the ruins of the Beit Alfa synagogue were discovered in 1928 during the digging of a kibbutz irrigation channel. Its beautiful mosaic floor is divided into three panels. One depicts religious emblems and the Ark of the Covenant. Another shows a zodiac circle with the astrological signs named in Hebrew, the moon and the stars, four women symbolizing the seasons and a youth riding a horse-drawn chariot. The third represents the sacrifice of Isaac, as described in the Bible. Unusually, the work is dated with an Aramaic inscription: "This floor was laid down in the year of the reign of Emperor Justinus." Justinus ruled Palestine from AD518 to 527.

▶▶ Beit She'an *163C1*

Archeological site (Beit She'an National Park (tel: 06-6587189)
Open: Sat–Thu 8–5, Fri 8–3. Admission: moderate

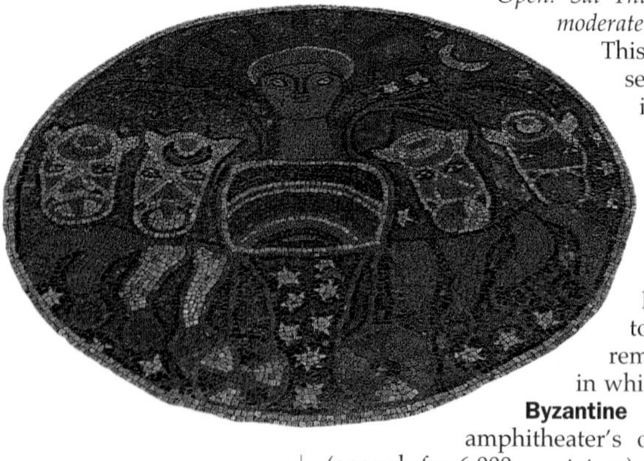

The Chariot of the Sun, Beit Alfa synagogue

This charmless little town seems modern but has been inhabited for 5,000 years. It is the site of Scythopolis, mentioned in Egyptian documents as long ago as the 19th century BC. Its excavations are among Israel's most impressive. In the middle of the new town, a large site contains remnants of a **Roman theater▶** in white stone, and a 5th-century **Byzantine street▶** in black. Of the amphitheater's original 12 rows of seats (enough for 6,000 spectators), three rows have survived.

Downhill lie the remarkable principal **Scythopolis excavations**, where work is still in progress. Steps lead to the summit of the **tel▶▶**, where 18 successive towns have been unearthed. A circular trail gives a good overview of the

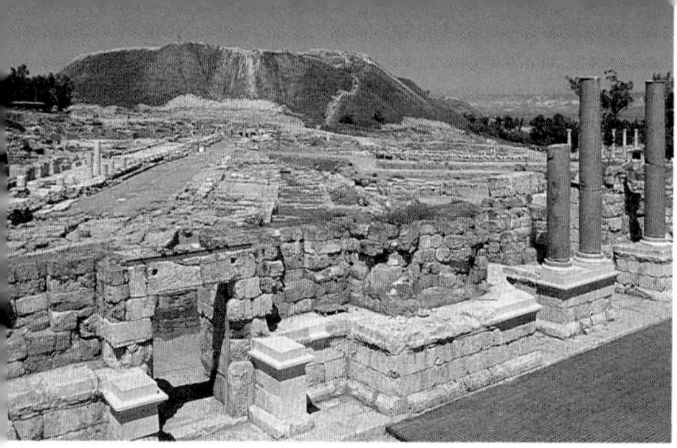

Byzantine main street, Beit She'an

whole site, and the remains of the imposing buildings that once stood in the centre. White and black stone make a dazzling contrast here as well. White columns, now being re-erected, lined the black-paved Byzantine **cardo▶▶▶** (main street). Black walls enclose a superb white **Byzantine amphitheater▶▶▶** (also seating 6,000), and there is a huge 4th-century **bathhouse▶▶**, with marble columns rising from a mosaic floor. Tragically, an entire 6th-century mosaic floor was stolen from the site in 1989.

▶▶ Belvoir (Hebrew: Kokhav HaYarden) *163C2*

Open: Sat–Thu 8–4, Fri 8–3. Admission: inexpensive

A steep side road climbs to these substantial hilltop ruins of a powerful French Crusader castle, with views across the Jezreel Plain and the Jordan Valley to the Jordanian mountains. The remains consist of a five-sided outer wall, seven towers and a wide moat on three sides. Inside, a square inner castle has the remains of the storerooms, kitchen and dining room. Built by Knights Hospitallers in 1168, the castle was twice attacked unsuccessfully by Salah ed-Din in 1182–83. A third seige, from 1187 to 1191, ended in victory for the Muslims, who allowed the Crusaders to retreat to Tyre. The Sultan of Damascus then ordered the castle to be partially dismantled. Crusaders returned in 1241, but were unable to reconstruct it.

CONSERVING WATER
The Jordan Valley, from Belvoir to Beit She'an, and the valley of the Beit She'an, a tributary of the Jordan, have been chosen for a massive water conservation program. Water shortages are the biggest threat to Israel's future life and livelihood. Most of the country's water comes from the Sea of Galilee, but this is proving inadequate. Winter downpours result in huge runoffs into the Jordan. The Jewish National Fund has been building a network of 40 reservoirs in the two valleys designed to capture this water. Hopefully it will solve some of the problems, and add some 65 million cubic yards (50 million cu m) to the country's water supply.

The basalt walls of Belvoir Castle

Greek Orthodox church, Capernaum

JESUS AND CAPERNAUM

"Now when Jesus had heard that John [the Baptist] was cast into prison, he departed into Galilee; and leaving Nazareth, he came and dwelt in Capernaum, which is upon the sea coast, in the borders of Zabulon and Nephtalim."
—Matthew 4:12–13

"After [the wedding at Cana] he went down to Capernaum, he, and his mother, and his brethren, and his disciples."
—John 2:12

▶▶ Capernaum (Hebrew: Kfar Nahum) *163C3*

Open: daily 8.30–4. Admission: inexpensive

Little remains of "the town of Jesus," except for the ruins, enclosed within black basalt walls. It has been excavated by Franciscan monks for the last 100 years. According to Matthew's Gospel (4:12–14), Jesus moved to Capernaum, from Nazareth to fulfill the words of the prophet Isaiah (9:1–2). John's Gospel (6:42) implies that Jesus was already well known in Capernaum, as were his parents (see side panel). Here, all the Gospels agree, Jesus encountered first Simon and Andrew, then James and John, all of them fishermen working on the nearby Sea of Galilee. They became his first disciples. He then began preaching "in the synagogues throughout all Galilee," as Mark's Gospel tells us, but mostly in and around Capernaum, where he performed numerous miracles.

Enlarged by refugees from Jerusalem after AD70, the town thrived until it was devastated during the 7th-century Arab conquest. Franciscans acquired the ruins in 1894 and began a program of excavation that continued into the 1960s. Today the site is an open-air museum. On the right, inside the entrance, is an impressive frieze of carved white stone, and on the left the ruins of simple **houses▶** in black stone.

Ahead rises the ugly modern roof of the octagonal **St Peter's Memorial**, erected over the black-stone ruins, below ground level. The monks claim this is the **home of St Peter▶▶**. All around are traces of several similar dwellings, all from about 200BC to AD700.

Adjacent to St. Peter's is the substantial reconstructed ruin of a fine **synagogue▶▶▶**. It is imposing in black-and-white marble, with Roman-style façade, pillars, and carved capitals and lintels. The stonework depicts Jewish symbols, such as the Star of David and the seven-branched menorah (candelabrum), as well as non-Jewish images, such as a half-man, half-fish. The synagogue, dating from the 2nd century AD, is not old enough to be the one where Jesus urged his neighbors to "eat of my flesh and drink of my blood" (John 6:54), though it probably stands on the same spot. For their skepticism, Jesus said the people of Capernaum faced eternal damnation.

▶ Deganya "A" Kibbutz *163C2*

On the Sea of Galilee's southern shore, by the Jordan outflow, Deganya "A" (founded in 1909) is Israel's oldest kibbutz. At the gate stands a small **Syrian military tank▶▶**, one of a whole column that was halted by kibbutzniks armed with old rifles and Molotov cocktails during the 1948 War of Independence. Within the kibbutz but entered from the main road, the **A D Gordon Institute▶** (*Open* Sun–Thu 9.30–4, Fri 8.30–12, Sat 9.30–12. *Admission: inexpensive*) is a museum and study center devoted to local history, archeology and natural history.

▶▶▶ Gamla *163D3*

Open: summer, daily 8–5; winter, daily 8–4.
Closed during military exercises. Admission: moderate (ticket gives discount at Qasrin Antiquities Park)

A rough 1.5-mile (2.5km) driveway leads to this dramatic, soaring, exposed site. Its name—"the camel" in Aramaic—derives from the humped terrain. The viewing area beside the parking lot gives a stark impression of the ruined city on its barren hill. Difficult trails lead up to the ruins. Gamla was one of many Golan towns founded after the Maccabean revolt against the Seleucids (168BC). Some 250 years later, during the First Revolt against Rome, the people of Gamla supported the rebel Zealots. As other Judaean towns were subdued or surrendered, Gamla's population of 5,000 doubled as Zealots flocked here. Some 15,000 Roman troops gathered below, but most were slaughtered in the first battle, which resulted in a surprising victory for the rebels. Three more Roman legions (60,000 men) arrived to besiege the fortress town for a month before unleashing a second attack. This time Gamla was taken. Thousands of residents and rebels were captured and killed, but 4,000 others chose suicide. Gamla was totally destroyed. To see artifacts from the site and a film about Gamla, visit the Golan Archeological Museum in Katzrin (see page 183).

▶▶ Ginosar Kibbutz *163C3*

Beside the western shore of the Sea of Galilee, the kibbutz is home to the **Yigal Allon Museum of Man in the Galilee▶▶** (tel: 06-6721495. *Closed* Shabbat. *Admission: moderate*) with its **2,000-year-old fishing boat▶▶** (see side panel). Nof Ginosar Kibbutz Hotel, next door, has superb grounds.

BEIT GABRIEL

Almost opposite Degania, "the mother of kibbutzim," stands the attractive Beit Gabriel. On the main road beside the Sea of Galilee, this is a cultural center open to the public, with a theater, restaurant and auditorium for concerts and a variety of other performances.

THE ANCIENT BOAT

The small fishing vessel found at Ginosar gives a great insight into biblical passages in which the disciples are described fishing or cowering during a storm, or in which Jesus is described preaching from a boat to a crowd assembled on the shore. The boat is 19.5ft (6m) long and 7.5ft (2.3m) wide. It is made entirely of wood, the planks being held together by mortise-and-tenon joints. The frames were installed after the hull had been constructed, rather than the more usual practise of building the hull around the frame. It appears that the boat was crewed by five people, using a sail and two pairs of oars.

HA'AM IM HAGOLAN
All over Israel you will see bumper stickers, posters and even banners hanging from apartment balconies declaring, in Hebrew, Ha'Am im HaGolan (The people are with the Golan). The slogan opposes any deals with Syria that might involve giving back any part of the Golan region. Opinion polls show that only 5 percent of Israelis are willing to return Golan in its entirety, but a majority would be prepared to let Syria have some of the territory.

Basalt columns in the Hexagonal Pool at Nahal Meshushim, in the Golan Heights

►► The Golan Heights *163D3–D4*

The rolling Golan hills, often known as the Golan Heights, rise steeply from the Sea of Galilee (656ft/200m below sea level) to the Mount Avital plateau (3,936ft/1,200m above). Airy and open, these agreeable uplands have spacious, uncultivated areas of heath and grassland cut by deep plunging wadis, as well as some pretty farming districts and important historical sites. A popular outing is to the Kuneitra viewpoint, which looks deep into Syria.

From 1948 until late 1994, Syria officially maintained a state of war against Israel. Until the Six-Day War of 1967, Syrian big guns located on the Golan Heights regularly bombarded kibbutz homes in Israel. When Syria invaded Israel in 1967, it rapidly lost control of Golan. An attempt to regain it in 1973 caused Syria to lose even more ground. In 1981, Golan was formally annexed by Israel. However, Syria still vigorously lays claim to the territory, and the Golan Heights remain a bargaining chip in Israel's quest for lasting peace with its neighbor.

In 1967, the population of the region stood at 12,000 and was almost entirely Druze (there are no Muslim or Christian villages). The establishment of new kibbutzim, and the town of Katzrin, have since attracted 12,000 Jews to the Golan, which has a considerable Jewish heritage. To the surprise of many visitors, there is no tension here, and no danger—though hikers should, of course, not climb into fenced-off military enclosures and training grounds.

A shepherd works in the Golan Heights—a scene unchanged for centuries

Drive

The Golan Heights

(for map see page 163)

Israel's influence on the lower slopes, close to the Sea of Galilee and the Hula Valley, is now complete. There are well-established communities, large and small, productive farms, and tourist facilities. Higher altitudes remain relatively deserted, and the presence of army and United Nations personnel is a reminder that Syria is not far away. *Allow a full day.*

Cross the Jordan River into Golan on the unceremonious **Arik Bridge**, a simple army construction of wooden planks. Beyond the bridge, an access road on the left leads into the pleasant **Jordan River Park▶**, where you can rent a kayak, have a picnic, or visit the excavations at **Tel Bethsaida**. At a fork, turn right (marked "Bet Shean, En Gev"). At the next left, turn uphill. Reaching higher ground, pass the new settlement of Ma'ale Gamla, press on to a junction and turn left onto the Golan's high plateau road. Soon after, an unpaved road leads to the impressive, rugged site of ancient **Gamla▶▶** (see page 171).

Just before Katzrin, and indicated simply by a sign saying "Industry," is the outstanding **Gamla Winery▶▶**. It is collectively owned by Golan's winegrowing kibbutzim and produces some of Israel's best wines, under the Gamla, Yarden and Golan labels. You can drop in for a tasting. **Qasrin Antiquities Park▶▶** (see page 183) lies in woods off the road. New **Katzrin▶▶** (see page 183), a pleasant, planned modern town, is Golan's capital, containing half the region's Jewish population. Do not miss its excellent **Golan Archeological Museum▶▶** (see page 183). The **Dolls Museum▶** (see page 183), opposite, uses models to portray Jewish history.

Drive up to **Kuneitra Viewpoint▶**, at the crest of Golan, to gaze across the now abandoned village of Kuneitra, towards Damascus, 15 miles (40km) away. Israel seized Kuneitra in repelling Syria's 1973 attack, but has since given it back. The UN base separating the two nations can be seen in the foreground.

Turn north toward snow-streaked Mount Hermon, rising in the distance. You skirt the lovely oak forest of the **Odem Reserve▶** and pass the **Druze villages▶** of Buk'ata, Mas'ada, and Ein Kuniya. Zigzagging across the foot of Hermon, you will reach **Nimrod's Castle▶▶** (see page 195), **Banyas▶▶** (see page 166) and **Tel Dan▶▶▶** (see page 203), enjoying extensive views over the **Hula Valley**, before leaving Golan.

Important warning

❑ If you get out of the car and walk in the Golan border areas, do not be tempted to climb over fences. And never enter an area with a blue triangle warning sign —this signifies the presence of unexploded mines. ❑

View to Mount Hermon

Despite changing values, the kibbutz (plural, kibbutzim), surely Israel's best-known institution, is still dedicated to shared effort, mutual aid and the simple life. Only some 2 percent of the population live on kibbutzim, yet many top army officers, government ministers and senior officials in all fields have been drawn from a kibbutz background.

KIBBUTZ HOTELS
Around 50 kibbutzim, most of which happen to be in resort areas, have opted to make tourism a major part of their income. Thirty of these are members of the highly professional Kibbutz Hotels Chain, which has its own Tel Aviv head office. Some, like Ramat Rachel in Jerusalem, offer top-notch accommodations not unlike other city hotels. Others are simpler guest-houses in rural settings.

A typical kibbutz canteen (above right), where kibbutz members eat all their meals together
A man herding beef cattle (below) in the zibbutz fields surrounding the wine-producing town of Zichron Ya'acov

Many young visitors first encounter Israel through working as a kibbutz volunteer. For some this is rewarding; for others it is a shock to find that this is no easy going holiday with time off. Kibbutz life involves hard work and few luxuries. These tightly knit villages are run on principles very different from those that reign beyond their metal gates and sturdy perimeter fences.

For outsiders who do not really want to roll up their sleeves and earn breakfast by the sweat of their brow, another way to glimpse kibbutz life is as a paying guest. Most of Israel's 270 kibbutzim have tourist accommodations, which vary in style, quality and price from basic guest rooms to large, high-quality hotels.

To look at, a kibbutz is an assortment of unostentatious dwellings and public buildings. Within its grounds are footpaths rather than roads, while all around lie its fields, plantations, orchards and gardens, animal sheds, workshops, maybe even a factory. Many also have a theater, museum and other visitor attractions, marked on tourist maps.

The kibbutznik, though partly a figure of fun for having such plain and unsophisticated ways, is almost everywhere revered as the ideal Israeli, tough, down to earth forthright and hardworking, the product of a pioneer movement which literally drained the swamps, watered the desert, and settled the land. Since the earliest days,

kibbutzim have played a vital security role because of their strategic locations, public shelters and good defenses.

Origins The kibbutz movement started during the Second and Third Aliyahs (1904–14 and 1919–23). Thousands of socialist Russian Jews fled to Palestine under often cruel and difficult conditions—some came all the way on foot. They were ardent Zionists who believed just as passionately in the ideals of shared ownership and the virtue of labor. The egalitarian communes they created were not like anything seen before in the world. Decisions were made communally, no one possessed any private property, and children lived together separate from their parents. Though keenly aware of their Jewish identity and heritage, these early kibbutzniks were fiercely anti-religious. The first kibbutz was founded at Deganya in 1909 and is still going strong (see page 171).

Even today, new kibbutzim are being established. In fact, more have been established in the last 25 years than in the first 25 years of the movement. Although communal living has been largely abandoned, each kibbutz is still run by its elected committee which provides members with free education, health care, child care, laundry and free meals in a communal dining room. They have diversified from farming into dozens of other ways of earning a living, including manufacturing and tourism. "Children's houses" were scrapped as children have been found to thrive better with their parents. A tolerant attitude to Jewish traditions has replaced strict secularism—and several observant religious kibbutzim have been set up.

The *moshav* In 1920, the first *moshav* (literally "seat," plural, *moshavim*), or co-operative village, was started. Today this is the commonest form of village or rural community in Israel. By the standards of any other country, even the *moshav* is Utopian. *Moshav* members — applicants to join are rigorously vetted—live as families on their own income. They lease, rather than own, their homes and land, and are not allowed to employ outside labor without permission. *Moshavim* are run by elected committees, and many free services are provided for the community by its members. A *moshav* is not the same as the similarly named *moshava* (plural, *moshavot*), which is more like an ordinary non-communal village.

BEYOND THE KIBBUTZ
The kibbutz movement has its own institutions of higher education and scientific research. It also boasts its own chamber orchestra, theater groups, highly acclaimed dance group, art galleries and large publishing houses. This enables kibbutz members to bypass the private sector in many areas. www.kibbutz.org.il/eng/

Farm workers on a kibbutz in the 1930s express the pioneering spirit of the original movement

BLESSINGS AND CURSES
The track that rises from the Roman spa baths to the 5th-century synagogue ruins passes the burial site of the local Arab ruler who was given Hamat Gader in 1918 by the British Mandate forces. The inscription on his tomb reads: "He who honors Hamat Gader shall be blessed in eternity. He who desecrates Hamat Gader shall be cursed in eternity."

►► Hamat Gader *163C2*

Hamat Gader Park Information Center (tel: 04-6659965; www.hamat-gader.com)
Open: Mon–Thu 7am–9.30pm, Fri 7am–11.30pm, Sat–Sun 7–6.30. Bathing Sun 7–5, Mon–Fri 7am–11pm, Sat 7am–10pm. Makhvat Restaurant and Siam Restaurant Mon–Sat 12–4.
Admission: expensive

According to the Byzantine empress Eudocia, these were the finest spa baths in the whole Roman world. Even the ruins are considered among the most impressive anywhere, and as there are also modern hot baths, eating places, picnic tables and other attractions, this is a popular place for a day out. Located in the Yarmuk Valley at the meeting point of Israel, Jordan and Syria, the area bristles with army patrols. From the main car-park, hiking trails lead through the attractive park-like grounds.

Steps descend to the extensive Roman and Byzantine spaPPP, for six centuries (2nd to 8th) a grand bathing resort. Much survives of the opulent bathhouses built in black and white stone, with numerous pillars, vaults and statues. You can walk from one pool room to the next, passing the small Lepers' Pool, the well-preserved Oval Pool, the imposing Pilaster Hall, with huge windows in the form of a triumphal arch, and others. An outdoor pool beside the bathhouses contains oily-looking water from a hot spring, veiled in sulphurous steam.

Four mineral springs and a freshwater spring emerge at Hamat Gader. A few paces from the Roman baths are the attractive **modern hot baths**►►, laid out as a series of open-air swimming pools, also smelling strongly of sulphur. The hottest is a constant 108°F (42°C), and bathers are officially advised that it can be dangerous to stay in for longer than 10 minutes.

At the covered central baths, all sorts of spa treatments

Roman baths, Hamat Gader

CROCODILE CREEK
"The crocodile still lingers in one corner of Palestine, at the northeast corner of the Plain of Sharon, under Carmel, in the marshes of the Wadi Zerka (Crocodile Wadi). One was brought to me measuring 11 feet 6 inches. I still possess its head and bones. This is the only spot beyond the limits of Africa where it is found."
The Natural History of Palestine, by the Rev Canon Tristram, FRS, 1892

are available, including four different kinds of massage. The separate Spateva is a tranquil spa complex, while the child and teen Splash area has water features and music.

Remnants of an **ancient synagogue▶** stand beside a high **observation point▶**. The abandoned mosque is recent. In front of it is a children's play area. As an added amusement, mainly for children, there is also an interesting **alligator farm▶** at Hamat Gader. A wooden walkway crosses an area of naturally warm water, where dozens of alligators and crocodiles can be seen basking.

Reared for meat, feathers and entertainment: ostriches at Ha'on Kibbutz

PRAYING FOR RAIN
If there is a drought while you are in Hatzor, go along to the Cave of Honi HaMe'agel, near Ayelet Hashahar. Named for a famous "rainmaker" of Second Temple times, the cave is still considered by the credulous as one of the most effective places to pray for a downpour.

▶▶ Hazor National Park (Tel Hazor) *163C4*

Opposite Kibbutz Ayelet Hashahar, Route 9 (tel: 06-6937290)
Open: Apr–Sep 8–5; Oct–Mar 8–4

This, the largest tel, or settlement mound, in Israel, consists of separate Upper and Lower sections and overlooks the southern Hula Valley. In total, 21 layers of civilisation have been uncovered here and key biblical passages verified. Joshua, leading the Jews into Canaan after the years of desert wandering, set about conquering the "promised land." In the 13th century BC, having destroyed other Canaanite city-kingdoms, he took on Hazor, the largest city in northern Canaan. Its king, Jabin, rallied other local chiefs against the Israelites. He chose the difficult Hula swamps, with which only his men were familiar, for a pitched battle. Against the odds, the Israelites won a phenomenal victory, killing Jabin and destroying Hazor by fire. Later, the Jewish king Solomon restored the town as a fortified royal residence.

That much can be read in Joshua 11, Judges 4, and I Kings 9. Each part of the biblical accounts has been confirmed in the excavations, led by Professor Yigael Yadin between 1955 and 1959. He also uncovered Canaanite temples. Traces of structures dating back as far as 400 years prior to Joshua were found. By comparison, the constructions made by Solomon appear almost recent. Perhaps the most remarkable discovery was King Ahab's tunnel, built in the 9th century BC. It is reached by 123 spiral steps down a 125ft (38m) deep shaft. The Bible records (II Kings 15) that in 732BC the Assyrians completely destroyed the town. A large number of finds from the site is on display at the **Hazor Museum** (*Closed* Shabbat. *Admission: inexpensive*) on the other side of the road.

JOSHUA'S TRIUMPH
"And Joshua at that time turned back, and took Hazor, and smote the king thereof with the sword: for Hazor beforetime was the head of all those kingdoms. And they smote all the souls that were therein with the edge of the sword, utterly destroying them: there was not any left to breathe: and he burned Hazor with fire. And all the cities of those kings, and all the kings of them, did Joshua take, and smote them with the edge of the sword, and he utterly destroyed them, as Moses the servant of the Lord commanded."
– Joshua 11:10–12

YESUD HAMA'ALA

The first attempt to tackle the problem of draining the Hula swamp was part of a venture of almost reckless idealism. It started at a *shtetl* (Jewish village) in Poland, when several young people decided to leave together for Palestine. They bought a section of the uninhabitable, uncultivated swamp and in 1883 started to build their new village here. They named it, using an evocative phrase from the Bible, *yesud hama'ala*, ("he began to go up"), describing Ezra's first steps on the road to Jerusalem at the head of the Jews returning from captivity in Babylon. Lacking in knowledge, under attack from Arabs, and brought low by the malaria that thrived in the swamps, the young pioneers might have failed if not for the intervention of Baron Rothschild: he suggested, and provided, eucalyptus trees—which can consume vast amounts of water—to plant all around the settlement.

►►► Hula Valley (Emek Hula) 163C4

The green landscape of Hula, wide and flat under an immense sky, makes a glorious sight when viewed from the higher country at its margins. From this viewpoint, a number of small lakes can be seen, each lying beside the canalised Jordan River. The most southerly of these, Lake Hula, lies at the centre of an interesting nature reserve and has an information centre about the region.

The name of the valley is misleading: there is no Hula River, and neither is this a valley. In Hebrew it is more often called Emek Hula; literally, the Hula Plain. The flatland of Hula lies in a rift basin between the steep Naftali and Golan hills north of the Sea of Galilee. Several rivers and streams run into or through the valley. In the Bible it is referred to as "the waters of Merom" and, until the early 1950s, was a huge area of malarial swamp and fetid waterways. The Arabs used to say that through its reeds it was impossible for even a wild boar to make its way. Perhaps this is an exaggeration, for wild boar certainly lived here, as did water buffalo and hundreds of bird species, some rare. The reed varieties included papyrus, this being the northernmost boundary for the wild plant, from which an early form of paper was made.

The draining and cultivation of Hula began in 1883, with the setting up of Yesud HaMa'ala village (see panel and Dubrovin Farm opposite) by Jewish refugees. They drained their settlement by planting eucalyptus. In 1934, the Hula valley was purchased by the Jewish National Fund (JNF), which, after the creation of the State of Israel, began to transform the swamps. The work, completed in 1957, involved changing and channelling the course of the Jordan River. The result was nearly 14,820 acres (6,000ha) of new land being opened up for cultivation, as well as the eradication of malaria from the region.

But even before it was completed, the original drainage work gave cause for concern about its environmental impact. This brought about the birth of the Society for the Protection of Nature in Israel (SPNI), now a powerful national pressure group with a decisive consultation role

Hula wetland reserve

Dubrovin Farm, a fortified 19th-century pioneer settlement, preserved and restored

on all major environmental projects. The first act of the new SPNI was to set aside Lake Hula as a nature reserve. However, the diversity of the region's flora and wildlife was drastically reduced, while the populations of certain other species—rats, for example—exploded. Worse still, the drained terrain was transformed into a dry and peaty organic material, easily eroded by wind and liable to spontaneous fires in summer. The dried-out terrain began to sink at the rate of 3 inches (80mm) per year, and wind-blown Hula peat polluted the Sea of Galilee.

In 1994, the JNF rediverted the Jordan into the drained marshes, deliberately reflooding some 494 acres (200ha) as part of a wildlife conservation scheme. The reflooding scheme is intended to enlarge Lake Hula, and a further 1,976 acres (800ha) of land, in a 37-mile (60km) long strip, will be returned to peat bog. There is public access to the area, and there are plans for a large new nature reserve where marsh fowl and animals will be able to breed. The existing **Lake Hula Reserve▶▶** (tel: 06-6937069. *Open* daily 8–4. *Admission: moderate*), the country's first nature reserve, gives a good idea of how the swampland looked before 1957. There are picnic areas and an easy walking trail – partly on boards over swamp – allowing visitors to see (if they are lucky) wetland species including water buffalo, wildcats, mongoose, beaver, boar, coypu and numerous migratory and resident bird varieties. From October through March the reserve is full of birds. The **Visitor Information Centre▶** has a museum dedicated to explaining Hula's flora and fauna, and shows a short film about the region.

Dubrovin Farm▶ (tel: 06-6937371. *Closed* Shabbat. *Admission: moderate*), just south of the reserve and originally part of the 19th-century settlement of Yesud HaMa'ala, has been reconstructed to show how a pioneers' fortified farm once looked. The buildings of the farmyard are ranged around a spacious enclosed courtyard. The family home, smithy and gardens are the main attractions, but many visitors go simply to enjoy the Dubrovin Farmyard Restaurant, specializing in its own smoked meats and trout, where good food is served in a rough-and-ready stone-built outhouse.

KIBBUTZ CONCERTS

In the middle of the pastoral landscape of the Hula Valley, at a plain and simple kibbutz, a week of civilised entertainment is held every summer during the Kfar Blum Chamber Music Days. The Voice of Israel radio station, the Galilee Council and the Ministry of Education jointly sponsor an annual classical music extravaganza. Nowadays the event has widened, with typically around 25 concerts and some 50 musicians, a choir, and a program that includes baroque music on period instruments, lieder and even jazz and chamber music. The Chamber Music Days take place usually at the end of July or beginning of August.

The fact that Israel is turning the desert green is a cliché—and one that does not bring fully to mind the many types of terrain that exist here, or the extraordinary transformation that is taking place. Even more startling than desert irrigation are the millions of acres of forest plantations and nature reserves.

WHO OWNS ISRAEL?
Some 92 percent of the land in Israel is publicly owned, to ensure that it remains a possession of the Jewish people as a whole. This has been a deliberate policy since 1901, when the Jewish National Fund (JNF) began to buy land from (mostly absentee) Arab landowners. Almost all of Israel had been purchased before the setting up of the State, and almost all by voluntary contributions from Jews all over the world. The State owns 78 percent of Israel directly, while the JNF owns 14 percent. The JNF also administers most of the rest of the country's non-urban land.

A drive along Israel's border road with Lebanon shows the stark contrast between the wooded hills of Galilee and the infertile rocky landscape on the other side of the frontier, where goatherds lead their animals in the constant search for vegetation. At the time when Israel came into being, the two landscapes were identical.

Jewish households around the world are familiar with the "blue boxes" of the Jewish National Fund (JNF), in which coins have been collected since 1901 to raise money for planting trees in Israel. During that time the JNF has planted 79,040 acres (32,000ha) of woodland—over 200 million trees. These forests, mostly of pine, are crisscrossed with public footpaths and bridle paths, often linking places of historic interest, and some provide considerable leisure opportunities. More importantly, their main purpose is to create topsoil and oxygen, to provide a habitat for threatened animals and birds, and to bring about a lasting change in the terrain.

One of the longest forest belts in the country is the 4,940-acre (2,000ha) Bar'am, Ein Zeitim and Biriya woodland, planted by the JNF in the 1950s on treeless mountain ridges surrounding the historic Galilee town of Sefat. It has been argued that it was a mistake to use only pine, and new planting includes many other tree varieties. The

Some of the ancient oak trees of Hurshat Tal National Park

green belt created by the JNF around Jerusalem on the formerly barren Judaean hills, for example, has been planted with acacia, pepper, myrtle, laurel, oak, cedar and carob, as well as pine. Areas with any natural woodland—such as Goren Park, around Montfort Fortress—are carefully tended and being enlarged.

A popular JNF scheme allows donors to pay for and plant a tree in Israel with their own hands. You can do this at the JNF's Jerusalem Planting Centre, which enables visitors to make a personal contribution to the capital's green belt or to other new forests around the country.

National parks Israel's forests are intended to change the land, the national parks to conserve it. There are 40 national parks in total, scattered across the country from Galilee to Negev and from the Mediterranean shore to the stony banks of the Dead Sea. Some peaks contain beautiful woodlands, but others are stark desert and wilderness. The National Parks Authority mainly cares for areas of great historical interest—major archeological sites, for example. Part of the authority's job is to open up such places to the public while protecting them from the damage that millions of visitors each year might cause.

Most national parks are relatively small, such as the ancient ruins of Bar'am, Nimrod Castle, Kursi and Tel Hatzor, while others cover larger areas, such as Carmel Park near Haifa, Hurshat Tal and Masada. Other properties could hardly be called parks at all—for example, the Jerusalem city walls.

Nature reserves The 160 nature reserves in Israel are something different again. Totaling about 9.880 acres (4,000 ha), they concentrate on protecting the country's astonishing diversity of flora, fauna and landscape. This adds up to over 3,000 species of plants (150 exclusive to Israel), 430 kinds of birds, 70 mammals, and as many as 80 types of reptiles. Terrain varies, from lush river valleys and springs like Tel Dan, to the dry, leafless desert of Timna Park.

Access to forests is free at all times, but national parks and nature reserves are supervised and charge entry fees. The reserves are open every day of the year, except Yom Kippur. The parks are well-marked, and equipped with restaurants and picnic areas.

Carmel Park protects sacred sites and a lovely Mediterranean landscape

FOR MORE INFORMATION
If you want to plant a tree while in Israel call the Jewish National Fund (Keren Kayemet l'Israel) on 02-6707411. The head office of the National Parks and nature Reserves Authority is in Tel Aviv on 03-5766888.

White oryx in the Negev desert

The hilltop town of Jish, in the 1st century an important Jewish stronghold, is now a Christian Arab community

THE MIRACLE AT CANA
"When the ruler of the feast had tasted the water that was made wine, and knew not whence it was (but the servants which drew the water knew), the governor of the feast called the bridegroom, and saith unto him, Every man at the beginning doth set forth good wine, and when men have well drunk, then that which is worse. But thou hast kept the good wine until now."
—John 2:9–10

►► Hurshat Tal National Park *163C5*

(tel: 06-6942440)
Open: Sat–Thu 8–5, Fri 8–4. Admission: moderate
Situated between Tel Dan and the Hula Valley, this pleasant woodland area, whose name means "Forest of Dew," is watered by the Dan River. Scores of mighty, ancient oaks grow here. Legend has it that 10 of Muhammad's messengers paused here for the night and, finding nowhere to tether their horses, stuck stakes into the ground. In the morning they awoke to find their stakes had sprouted into these fine trees. An artificial swimming lake, restaurant and picnic site, as well as a nearby riverside campsite, make this a popular spot. Adjacent Kibbutz Hagoshrim, part of the Kibbutz Hotels Chain, has attractive grounds and offers high-quality accommodation.

► Jish (Hebrew: Gush Halav) *162B4*

This hillside village of Christian Arabs was an important town during the Second Temple and Talmudic periods, associated with the learned Jewish community based around Meron (see page 185). During the First Revolt against Rome (AD68), it was a rebel stronghold. Revolt commander Yohanan came from here. The tombs of 1st-century sages Shemai'a and Avtalion lie in a domed building by the road below the village. Remnants of small 3rd- and 4th-century synagogues were found 1.2 miles (2km) east of the village, and also at the neighboring *moshav* (cooperative village) of Sifsufa.

► Kfar Kana *162B2*

St John's Gospel names the (now Arab) village of Cana, near Nazareth, as the place of Jesus' first miracle: turning water into wine at a wedding feast. The Franciscans claim that their church, built in 1881, stands on the ruins of the house where the miracle occurred. It does stand on the remains of a 6th-century church or synagogue with a 3rd-century mosaic floor beneath it (an Aramaic inscription honoring the craftsmen who made the mosaic). Other Catholic and Orthodox churches in Kana also claim to be built on sacred sites.

Daniel in the Lions' Den: Byzantine frieze in the Golan Archeological Museum

VOLCANIC GOLAN
The Golan summit was volcanic until the Upper Pleistocene period (40,000 years ago), and the terrain is rich in signs of volcanic activity. Massive basalt boulders, areas of lava flow, deep craters and remnants of volcanic cones characterize the Heights. The Golan's largest extinct volcano is Mount Avital, near Kuneitra. Its crater is now cultivated.

▶▶ Katzrin (Qazrin) *163C4*

This attractive, well-laid-out town, built in 1967, is now the capital of the Golan region. Its population of 6,500 accounts for half the Jews in the Golan. The town makes a good base for exploring local antiquities. The **Golan Archeological Museum▶▶** (*Open* daily. *Admission: inexpensive*) has extensive displays of relics from the region, especially coins, domestic items and stonework. There are many relief carvings of menorahs (ritual candelabra) dating from Temple times and the Roman and Byzantine periods. It is worth seeing the short but very stirring film about the Roman conquest of Golan's former capital, Gamla. Almost opposite is the **Dolls Museum▶** (*Open* daily. *Admission: moderate*) which tells Jewish history through a succession of charming tableaus made of little models.

Just outside the town on the southeastern side, a sign saying "Industry" indicates the way to the **Golan Heights Winery▶▶** (tel: 04-6968409, 04-6968435; www.yardenwines.com, www.golanwines.co.il). *Closed* Shabbat. *Admission with tasting: moderate*), a leading name in Israel's quality wines. A full range of wines is produced, from dessert wines to white *methode champenoise*, with a choice of award-winning Chardonnay and Reisling whites, and Cabernet and Merlot reds. The finest are branded as Yarden, the second rank as Gamla, and the most affordable as Golan.

Nearby are the remains of the 4th-century **Ancient Synagogue▶** in the **Qasrin Antiquities Park▶▶** (tel: 06-6962412. *Closed* Shabbat. *Admission: moderate*), an open-air museum. Reconstructions give an impression of life in Talmudic times alongside the archeological site of the original town.

Talmudic obelisks in Qasrin Antiquities Park

▶ Kiryat Shmona *163C5*

The name meaning "eight men and women," commemorates Joseph Trumpledor and his seven comrades who died defending the nearby Tel Hai settlement in 1920 against Arab attacks from Halsa village. After the defeat of the Arabs, Halsa was transformed into this development town.

HONORING RASHBI
Thousands of Orthodox Jewish pilgrims make their way to Meron every year for the joyful early-summer Hilula Rashbi procession. It's held on the eve of Lag b'Omer (the 26th day after Passover). The pilgrims carry Torah scrolls from Sefat to Meron. On arrival, two bonfires, and countless candles, are lit at Rashbi's tomb. Riotous music and dancing and noisy picnics take place through the night. The following morning, three-year-old boys—who, until then, have been allowed to let their hair grow long—receive their first haircut.

▶ Korazim *163C3*

(tel: 06-6934982)
Open: Apr–Sep daily 8–5; Oct–Mar daily 8–4.
Admission: inexpensive

Built of dark basalt and now all in ruins, Korazim is 2.5 miles (4km) from the Sea of Galilee's northern shore. According to Matthew's Gospel (11:21), this was one of the Galilee towns that Jesus reproached because its citizens refused to repent after he had performed "mighty works" there. The town continued to prosper for four centuries more, and was praised for its wheat. The **synagogue▶▶** was constructed in the 2nd century, and substantial remains can still be seen of the walls and floor and of the pillars that divided the building into three aisles. Remnants of **houses▶▶** (some partly restored) and an **oil press** also survive. East of the site, **dolmens** confirm that the area was inhabited in prehistoric times. Abandoned in the 5th century, Korazim was revived as a Jewish village in the 16th century. Just west is the popular riding center and "Guest Farm" tourist complex of **Vered Hagalil▶**.

▶▶ Megiddo National Park *162A1*

(tel: 06-6522167)
Open: summer, daily 8–5; winter, daily 8–4.
Admission: moderate

MEGIDDO AT THE END OF DAYS
"And he gathered them all together into a place called in the Hebrew tongue Armageddon. And the seventh angel poured out his vial into the air; and there came a great voice out of the temple of heaven, from the throne, saying, It is done. And there were voices, and thunders, and lightnings; and there was a great earthquake, such as was not since men were upon the earth, so mighty an earthquake, and so great. And the great city was divided into three parts."
– Revelation 16:16–19

The fortified hill of Megiddo is a remarkable tel (settlement mound) where 20 layers of civilization have been uncovered since excavations began in 1903.

The English corruption of Har Megiddo, or Megiddo Hill, is Armageddon. Here, according to the New Testament (Revelation 16), God will gather everyone at the end of days and pour out his wrath in earthquakes, storms and a hail of stones. The hill, long considered worth fighting for, controlled a pass on the route between Egypt and Assyria. Of military and trading importance, this highway became the Romans' Via Maris. The French (in 1799) and the British (in 1917) defeated the Turks at Megiddo. One of the titles granted to Commander-in-Chief Allenby was Lord Allenby of Megiddo. In 1948, Jews defeated Arab forces here.

In about 4000BC, Canaanites took over the Neolithic settlement here and remained for some 2,000 years. A **Canaanite temple▶▶** and **fortifications▶▶** survive. In 1479BC, Pharaoh Thutmose III attacked the city. Hieroglyphs describing the battle, carved on the walls of his temple in Upper Egypt, are the first historical reference to Megiddo. When Megiddo was conquered by the Israelites under Joshua in the 13th century BC, the name of the town first enters the Bible. Philistines subsequently held the city for 100 years, but it was retaken by King David in 1000BC. Solomon enlarged the city, and many vestiges remain from that period. After a 9th-century BC Egyptian attack, it was rebuilt by King Ahab, who added an impressive **underground shaft and water tunnel▶▶** 118ft (36m) deep and 71 yards (65m long). On the site of Solomon's Palace he built **chariot stables▶▶** for 450 horses, chariots and riders. In front is a large circular **grain silo▶** built in the 8th century BC. Conquered by Assyrians in 733BC, the site frequently changed hands and was abandoned from 538BC. A Roman camp was later set up on the adjacent site, which became the Arab village of Lejun (from "Legion") and is now the Kibbutz Megiddo.

Remains of Roman houses, Korazim

SACRED NUMEROLOGY
Kabbala is an esoteric Jewish form of mysticism whose aim is reunification with God, achieved by following specific paths to wisdom. One of its mystical practises involves using assigned numerical values of the Hebrew alphabet to discover hidden meanings within the verses of the Torah (e.g. alef = 1, bet = 2, and so on). For centuries, the study of Kabbala was limited to devout married men over the age of 40, to discourage dabblers and self-seeking enthusiasts. A prime kabbalistic work, the *Zohar*, is often attributed to Rashbi, especially by devout Hasidim and Sephardim. But many scholars believe the book was in fact written by several people, probably in medieval Spain, and based on earlier works stemming from Sefat and Meron.

► Meron *162B4*

In Second Temple and Talmudic times, Meron became a great centre of Jewish learning, as well as a focal point for rebellion against Roman rule. In 1949, a new Meron, an Orthodox religious settlement, was founded in the same place. Several 1st- and 2nd-century tombs survive, including the domed mausoleums, set within a walled enclosure, of the renowned **Rabbi Shimon bar Yochai►►►** (also known by his acronym as Rashbi) and his son, Eleazer. Rashbi is claimed by the Orthodox to be the author of the *Zohar* (one of the principal books of the mystical kabbala). Some scholars assert that Rashbi was not the author of this work although Meron and Sefat can still be considered the birthplace of Jewish mysticism (see side panel). North of the tomb stands the magnificent rock-carved façade of a 2nd-century **synagogue►**. Little else remains of the building. Several other revered rabbis are reputedly buried in rock-cut tombs here, including the great 1st-century sage **Hillel►**, his less liberal rival **Shammai**, and the 2nd-century **Rabbi Yohanan** "the shoemaker."

ARMAGEDDON VILLAGE
The settlement of Mishmar HaEmek (literally Guard of the Plain) stands next to Megiddo, or Armageddon. Founded in 1927, it was the first modern community to be established in the Valley of Jezreel. The scene of much prolonged fighting, especially during the 1948 war, it is better known today for its striking Holocaust memorial.

THE GOOD FENCE
Close to Metulla is the only place where civilians (with correct documents) can cross the border between Israel and Lebanon. There are broad views over the Lebanese hills from here. Most of the permitted border traffic consists of Lebanese workers employed in Israel. The name "Good Fence" comes from the Israeli medical post here, which Lebanese citizens can attend free of charge.

A WRONGED WOMAN?
The word "magdalen" has come to mean a reformed prostitute, or a home for such women, through its association with Mary Magdalene. Yet the Scriptures give no reason to suspect Mary Magdalene of being a prostitute. It used to be thought that the "woman which was a sinner" (Luke 7:37), who anointed Jesus' feet and wiped them with her hair, could be identified with Mary Magdalene, but the text does not suggest this and modern scholars reject the idea. Later, Jesus encounters "Mary called Magdalene, out of whom went seven devils," as if for the first time. The name Mary Magdalene means simply "Mary, woman of Magdala."

Spring comes to Mount Hermon: the view from Metulla

▶ Metulla *163C5*

Enclosed on three sides by the northern border with Lebanon (you can see Arab laborers working the fields across the frontier), this small agricultural town has a cool, tranquil hill setting overlooked by the snowy crest of Mount Hermon. Metulla was settled a century ago on land purchased by Baron Rothschild. Since 1976, it has been best known as the HaGader HaTova (the Good Fence), an opening in the border between Israel and Lebanon through which Lebanese people pass freely to obtain medical supplies or even to work in Israel. The town's main avenue, **Settlers Street▶**, gives visitors a chance to glimpse those early days with its Farmer's House Museum and a few surviving older buildings. The town's Canada Center is a modern leisure complex with high-quality sports facilities, indoor and outdoor pools, squash, tennis and basketball courts, a complete football pitch and the largest ice-skating rink in Israel. Between the town and the frontier lies the **Nahal Iyon Nature Reserve** (see page 191).

▶ Migdal *163C3*

On a hillside beside the Sea of Galilee and within an hour's walk of Jesus' home at Capernaum lie the ruins of ancient Migdal (the name means "a Tower"). This was the supposed birthplace of Mary Magdalene, the woman from whom Jesus drove out "seven devils" and who became one of his most ardent followers. Migdal was a thriving small town until about the 2nd century. Remnants of paved streets, a villa, a pool and a synagogue have been uncovered. Above the old village rises the new, which has plenty of guest accommodation.

▶▶ Montfort Castle *162A4*

This majestic ruined Crusader fortress, soaring on a high crest enclosed by an immense natural forest, is best seen from **Mitzpe Monfort▶▶▶** (*mitzpe* means viewpoint) in **Goren Park▶**. The park, located 9 miles (14.5km) inland from Nahariya, is a natural forest of oak, carob, almond, arbutus, and the purple-flowered Judas tree. To reach the castle, you must follow a series of steep narrow paths for about half an hour, first down to the attractive **Kviv stream▶**, then up again to the fortress. It can also be approached on a longer walk, equally steep, from the village of Hila.

Built in the 12th century by French Crusaders, Montfort Castle (*free access*) is the largest ruin in western Galilee. Reconstruction is under way, consisting of the repair of the remnants of inner and outer ramparts, great blocks of fallen stone, roofless sections of sturdy walls, and broken Gothic arches. These vestiges are all that survive of a once huge fortress. Its lofty position provides a stirring view over rolling woodland. Shortly after completion, Montfort (which means "Strong Mountain" in medieval French) was destroyed by Salah ed-Din in 1187. The shell was then sold in 1220 to the Knights of the Teutonic Order, who rebuilt part of the fortress and renamed it Starkenburg (Strong Castle). They occupied it until 1271, when they were expelled by Baibars, the Mameluke sultan. He allowed them to take their archives and treasury, and the castle has remained abandoned ever since.

▶▶ Mount of Beatitudes 163C3

This lovely grass-covered hillside, rising behind the sites of Tabgha and Capernaum, has long been considered the place where Jesus delivered the Sermon on the Mount. The view from the top of the slope, taking in the calm blue expanse of the Sea of Galilee with blue-tinted hills behind, is serene and inspiring.

Did Jesus really preach his sermon here? The weight of tradition points to this as the likely hill. The church at the summit is modern; previously the event was commemorated by a church nearer to Tabgha. The official Catholic view is that the hill, and the church, should be understood only as commemorating the sermon, not marking the site. But for millions of pilgrims, this is the very hill where Jesus inspired the multitudes with his message of purity of spirit, humility and peace.

The Sermon on the Mount, fully recorded in Matthew's Gospel (chapters 5–7), marks the start of Christianity's departure from Judaism. The nine Beatitudes are Christ's assertion that nine categories of people are blessed and will receive a heavenly reward. He named in turn the poor in spirit, the meek, mourners, those who hunger for righteousness, the merciful, the pure in heart, peacemakers, those persecuted for righteousness' sake, and those persecuted for Jesus's sake. The remainder of the sermon praises those who lead a simple, virtuous life according to Jewish law. Much of the sermon restates ancient commandments, although he also departs from them by, for example, prohibiting divorce, redefining adultery to include looking lustfully, and warning of hellfire for calling one's brother "Traitor." He adds to the original "Love thy neighbor" the far more difficult precept "Love your enemies." The sermon ends with a Jewish text that sums up his message: "Be ye therefore perfect, even as your Father in heaven is perfect."

Luke's Gospel (chapter 6) briefly describes what is probably the same sermon, but says that it was delivered at the foot of the hill, "in the plain," after Jesus had spent all night on the mountain in prayer, and chosen and named 12 of his followers as Apostles. He then descended the hill with the Apostles to preach to the multitude. Jesus "looked up" to address the crowd, so they stood on the

HOW TO FEEL TOWARDS YOUR ENEMIES

"It has been said that thou shalt love thy neighbor and hate thine enemy" (Matthew 5:43). These words of Jesus during the Sermon on the Mount have caused controversy, since it was *not* part of Jewish Law that people should "hate" their enemies. Leviticus 19:17–18 states: "Thou shalt love thy neighbor as thyself." It also states that it is all right to "rebuke thy neighbor" (though not in public) but "not to take vengeance nor bear any grudge"; and "Thou shalt not hate thine brother in thy heart." Some of the earliest Bible passages urge humanity and restraint with respect to enemies: "If thou meet thine enemy's ox or his ass going astray, thou shalt bring it back to him again" (Exodus 23:4).

higher ground, and urged them to "love your enemies and do good to them which hate you; unto him that smiteth thee on the cheek offer also the other."

The **Church of the Beatitudes▶▶▶** (*Open* daily 8–12, 2.30–5) on the hilltop, an octagonal arcaded structure under a dome, belongs to Italian Franciscans. It is one of the most attractive works of Antonio Barluzzi, architect of some of the finest 20th-century Galilean churches and basilicas. Built in 1937 (the date in the church floor being given as Year 15 of the Italian People—in other words the Fascist regime), it elegantly contrasts white and dark stone and stands among palm trees in delightful gardens. Each of the eight sides of the church is dedicated to one of the first eight Beatitudes, written in Latin inside the church. The ninth Beatitude (blessing those who suffer persecution for the sake of Jesus) is symbolized by the dome itself, reaching to heaven. Around the altar of the church are representations of the seven virtues (Justice, Charity, Prudence, Faith, Fortitude, Hope and Temperance).

Close by is the Franciscans' **Mount of Beatitudes Hospice▶**. Glorious views can be had by walking down the slope from the summit of the mount to Tabgha. The walk takes a more circuitous 2.5-mile (4km) route by road.

THE SERMON ON THE MOUNT

"And seeing the multitude, he went up into a mountain. And when he was set, his disciples came unto him, and he opened his mouth and taught them."
—Matthew 5:1–2

Church of the Beatitudes, atop the mount where Christ laid down some of the basic tenets of Christianity

Mount Tabor's Basilica of the Transfiguration

THE TRANSFIGURATION
"And after six days Jesus taketh Peter, James, and John his brother, and bringeth them up into an high mountain apart, and was transfigured before them: and his face did shine as the sun, and his raiment was white as the light. And behold, there appeared unto them Moses and Elias talking with him. Then answered Peter, and said unto Jesus, Lord, it is good for us to be here: if thou wilt, let us make here three tabernacles."
—Matthew 17:1–4

▶ Mount Hermon (Har Hermon) *163D5*

The snow-covered peak of Israel's highest mountain (9,069ft/2,765m) is visible over much of Golan and north-eastern Galilee. The mount makes a dramatic contrast to the Mediterranean sunshine, landscape and vegetation below. Only a small slice of the Hermon massif belongs to Israel, the rest forms the barrier between Lebanon and Syria. Its snow and springs deliver much of Israel's water supply. **Neve Ativ▶** (or the Mount Hermon Ski Centre) is a small winter sports resort high on its slopes. It has a ski lift from 5,412ft–6,560ft (1,650m–2,000m), equipment rental, excellent accommodations and reliable snow from December through to April. The runs range in difficulty, the longest run being 1.5 miles (2.5km).

▶▶ Mount Meron Nature Reserve *162B3*

Occupying a high ridge at the heart of Upper Galilee, the wooded Meron heights can be reached on steep but fairly easy footpaths from near the Druze village of Hurfeish (on the western side) or from Meron (on the eastern flank). The paths climb through attractive but thorny Mediterranean scrub and low woodland, where you may see several of the curious *katalav* trees, with their smooth bark resembling polished copper. At the rocky wooded summit (3,936ft/1,200m), you will find a radar base, a tiny stone pool enclosed by a stone terrace (actually a 2,000-year-old winepress), and immense vistas to the north, with Sefat visible to the east.

▶▶ Mount Tabor (Har Tavor) *162B2*

This striking fortified plateau, rising from the Jezreel Plain, is taken to be "the high mountain apart" on which Jesus was "transfigured" in the eyes of Peter, James, and John. According to the Gospels, "His face did shine as the sun, and his raiment was white as the light. And behold, there appeared unto them Moses and Elias talking with him. From a cloud came a voice, saying 'This is my beloved son, in whom I am well pleased'" (Matthew 17: 1–5; Mark 9:2–7; Luke 9:28–35). These were almost the same words that a voice from heaven had uttered when Jesus was baptized in the Jordan (Mark 1:11).

Over the centuries, several churches were erected on or near the site of the apparition, especially during the Crusader period, and their ruins now adorn the mountainside. The slopes are covered with vegetation, notably Tabor oak. A twisting road winds up to the top of the hill. At the summit stands the Franciscans' handsome **Basilica of the Transfiguration▶▶** (*Open* Sun–Fri 8–12, 2–5; *closed* during services), with its two sturdy square towers, built by Barluzzi in 1921 and incorporating the remains of 6th- and 12th-century churches. The basilica encloses three grottoes, or chapels, recalling the three tabernacles that Peter suggested should be put here for Jesus, Moses and Elijah (Elias). The Grotto of Christ contains a mosaic pavement dating from before the year 422 (after which date it was forbidden to put the shape of the cross in any position where it could be walked upon). In the upper part of the church, a fine mosaic depicts the Transfiguration. Close by stands the Greek Orthodox **Church of Elias▶**, built in 1911 on the ruins of a Crusader church. A **Canaanite shrine▶** also stands on the summit.

During the period of the Israelite conquest of Canaan, the judge and prophetess Deborah (12th century BC) gathered 10,000 men here. She led them in a victorious attack on the men and chariots of Sisera, one of the generals of Canaanite king Jabin of Hatzor (Judges 4).

▶ Nahal Iyon Nature Reserve *163C5*

One mile (2km) from the small northern border town of Metulla (see page 186), this reserve lies in the Iyon Valley beside the Lebanese frontier. It has pleasing tree-shaded water pools and seasonal waterfalls. The **Tanur Waterfall▶** can be found 1km (0.5 miles) from the town. It is dry in summer, gushing in winter, and its name, meaning "oven," is based on its shape and the impression of smoke given by the fall's billowing misty haze.

NEBI SABALAN

From the village of Hurfeish the path up Mount Meron first skirts Mount Larom. At the top stands Nebi Sabalan, a large structure enclosing a small cave, together with a pilgrims' inn. Sacred to the Druze, this became a holy site in 1948. The Druze claim that their prophet, Sabalan, lived as a hermit in the cave, studying and composing religious texts. One day, Muslims discovered him and dispatched a force to kill him. When they tried to climb Larom from the Kziv stream at its foot, Sabalan prayed for divine assistance. It came in the form of a dam which blocked the stream and caused the area to be temporarily flooded—just long enough to drown his pursuers. When the water subsided, he moved on to Mount Lebanon, where his tomb can be seen today. Every year on September 10, the Druze make a pilgrimage to Nebi Sabalan, where there are lodgings and provisions for slaughter and sacrifice. Non-Druze are not welcome.

Galilee from Mount Tabor

THE CHILDHOOD HOME OF JESUS

The evangelists do not agree as to where Mary and Joseph lived before the birth of Jesus. Luke says that Nazareth was where the angel Gabriel appeared to Mary, and that she and Joseph set out from Nazareth to register in Bethlehem for the census. They also returned "to their own city Nazareth" after presenting Jesus in the Temple. Matthew, on the other hand, implies that Jesus' birthplace in Bethlehem was not a temporary dwelling but the family home of Joseph (a native Judaean) and Mary (by tradition the daughter of a Temple priest, and so living in or near Jerusalem). In his account they fled from Bethlehem to Egypt, then, fearing to return to Judaea, they went to dwell in Galilee, eventually settling in Nazareth. Mark only states that Jesus, having reached manhood, "came from Nazareth of Galilee and was baptized of John in the Jordan." John simply has Nathaniel, a Galilean, astonished to be told that the man the prophets wrote about came from Nazareth.

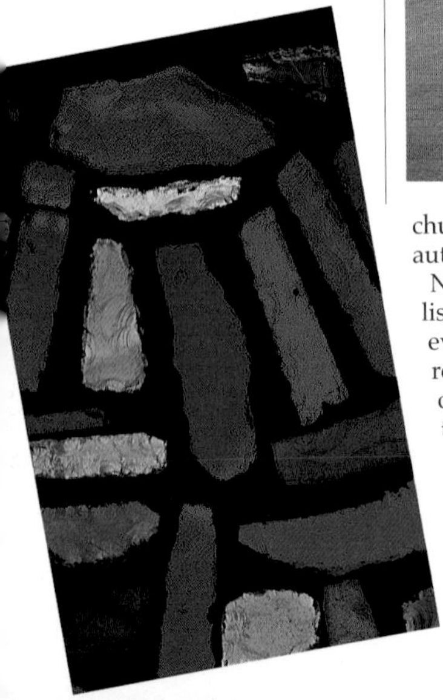

▶▶ Nazareth (Hebrew: Natzerat; Arabic: En-Nasra) *162B2*

The largest Arab town in Israel (population 60,000) is sprawling, noisy and chaotic. The population is 40 percent Christian and 60 percent Muslim, with a separate Jewish new town (Natzaret Illit, or Upper Nazareth) of 45,000 growing alongside. Friction between the Arab communities has been sparked by the building of a new mosque close to the Basilica of the Annunciation. Since the time of the Gospels, Nazareth has been regarded as the childhood home of Jesus. The town bristles with

churches: but the seeming lack of spirituality, or sense of authenticity, sometimes disappoints Christian pilgrims.

Nazareth gets no mention in Josephus' comprehensive list of towns and villages of the Galilee. Archeological evidence finds scant trace of habitation at the time he refers to, although there are vestiges of older structures on the site dating from 2000BC. From the 3rd century AD there was a Christian settlement here, destroyed by Persians in the 7th century. It was revived in 1099 by the French Crusader Tancred, then seized by Mamelukes in 1263. All Christians were banished until 1620. Nazareth once again became popular as a center for Christian worship in the 19th century, when it became a focal point for Christian Arabs.

All the Gospels agree in suggesting that Jesus spent most of his childhood in Nazareth, though how many years is unclear. There is disagreement as to whether Joseph and Mary lived there before the birth of Jesus. According to Luke (1:26), they did: he asserts that it was here that the Archangel Gabriel spoke to Mary, telling her that she was to give birth to a son who "shall reign over the house of Jacob forever, and of his kingdom there shall be no end." Matthew (1:18–21) relates that Joseph, learning Mary was pregnant, planned to divorce her but was dissuaded by an angel in a dream.

Early Christians worshipped at this place, which was known later, as the Grotto of the Annunciation. The first of Nazareth's churches was built there, in a style that resembles a synagogue. With the growth of devotion to Mary, and to the image of Jesus as an infant, even greater importance became attached to the grotto where Gabriel addressed Mary.

Three more churches, erected in the 5th, the 12th and the 18th centuries, were built at the grotto long before today's **Basilica of the Annunciation▶▶▶** (*Open* Mon–Sat 8.30–11.45, 2–5, Sun for services only) was constructed between 1955 and 1969. The main entrance is in Casa Nova Street, the heart of the older part of town. This pleasing modern edifice, by the Italian architect Giovanni Muzio, is built of pale stone, arranged in bands of lighter and darker shade, under a dark conical dome surrounded by delicate white stonework. Some of the walls stand on top of the ruined 12th-century Crusader walls, and the Crusader's triple apse at the east end has been brought into the new building. Thus it ingeniously combines the past – represented by the lower levels and the grotto itself – with the present, the two being linked by stairs at the west end. A large opening in the floor beneath the dome gives a view down through the centuries to the grotto and the relics of earlier churches. The upper church is decorated with images of the Madonna and Child from around the world.

Other churches (*Open* daily) lie nearby, reached via teeming narrow streets and an open-air market. **St. Joseph's▶** (1914), in Casa Nova Street, stands above a grotto known since the 17th century as Joseph's Workshop. **Synagogue Church▶**, stands on traces of a 6th-century synagogue which, despite the date, Greek Catholics claim was the one Jesus attended. **Mensa Christi Church** (1918), west of the Synagogue Church, contains a slab of rock that Franciscans claim was the table at which the risen Christ ate with his disciples. A mile or so (1.5km) out of town, on the Tiberias road, **Mary's Well▶** or the Fountain of Mary has four waterspouts set in a modern circular stone surround. This is another place where some claim that Gabriel appeared to Mary. Many believe the waters to have miraculous healing powers. This new Mary's Well replaces the older one in the crypt of beautiful **St. Gabriel's Church▶** nearby.

TOURING NAZARETH
The town is hot and crowded, built up a steep hill, bus services are not geared to tourist sights and the maze of streets is short of signs. If you are not prepaired to deal with these challenges join an organized tour. Hotels and tourist offices all over Galilee can provide details of these.

Greek Orthodox rites at St. Gabriel's Church

Left: Basilica of the Annunciation

Drive

The Northern Road

(for map see pages 162A4–163C5)

The northern road takes a quiet, peaceful course along a crest of forested hills. There are good views into Lebanon, with its relatively barren terrain, and across the Galilee, where a hundred years of tree-planting have sharply altered the scenery. Along the way the drive passes a string of old pioneer kibbutzim and appealing, small-scale relics of history, ancient and modern. *Allow a full day.*

Start at the high chalk cliffs of **Rosh HaNikra▶▶** (see page 160). On the clifftop is the scruffy frontier post with Lebanon but there are also magnificent views down to the coast. At the foot, reached by cable-car, spectacular white caves lie half submerged in the sea. The winding road descends through natural and planted woodland towards **Kibbutz Hanita▶** (founded in 1938), with its small antiquities museum. Among the trees nearby is **Hanita Tower and Stockade▶**, a well-preserved example of the simple wooden watch-towers used by early settlers. The border road continues east beside the frontier. For greater interest take the parallel route through the attractive maple and terebinth woods around **Eilon▶** and **Goren Park▶▶**, south of which rises the Crusader fortress, **Montfort Castle▶▶** (see page 186).

Back on the border, **Netua▶** and **Biranit▶▶** give great views into Lebanon. Cross the high **Har Adir** plateau, descending to the superb ancient synagogue at **Bar'am▶▶** (see page 167). After **Avivim**, where 11 children were killed in a PLO attack on the school bus in 1970, the **Dishon Gorge▶** on the right has a drivable trail at the bottom. Suddenly, ahead you will see a broad view of the Naftali hills, reaching to the Hula Valley. The fence of **Mishgav Am Kibbutz** forms the national boundary. In 1980, five PLO men captured the nursery and ended up shooting a 2-year-old and her teacher in front of the other children.

Continue to **Metulla▶** (see page 186) via the **Good Fence▶▶** border crossing, so named because of the free Israeli medical clinic run here for Lebanese citizens.

A landscape under transformation: forests have been planted on the once-barren Lebanese frontier

▶ Nimrod's Castle National Park *163D5*

(tel: 03-7762186)
Open: Sun–Thu 8–5, Fri morning. Admission: inexpensive
The huge, ruined hillside fortress 2 miles (3km) east of Banyas was named after Nimrod, the "mighty hunter" (Genesis 10:8–9). It dates largely from the 13th century. Built by Crusaders in 1129, it was immediately seized by Syrian Arabs. Held again by Crusaders from 1140 to 1164, it was taken and enlarged by Ayyub sultans in 1220, and by Mamelukes in 1260. It was later abandoned.

▶ Peki'in *162B4*

Now mainly Druze, this village claims an impressive Jewish history. The revered 2nd-century Rabbi Shimon bar Yochai (see page 185) lived in a cave here with his son for 13 years, hiding from the Romans. A possible candidate above the village has been marked **Rashbi Cave▶**. Walk down past the ornate village fountain and balconied houses to the attractive **Old Synagogue▶▶**, on its original 2nd-century foundations. It has a simple interior, a floor of huge stone blocks, and fine stonecarving. Other sights in Peki'in include the olive presses, flour mill and Jewish cemetery. Two snack bars face each other on the main Haifa road. Both make excellent pitas and local dishes.

▶▶ Rosh Pina *163C3*

Its name means "Cornerstone," and this village on Mount Canaan was the first Zionist settlement in Galilee. Head up the steep main street to **Rosh Pina HaAtika (Old Rosh Pina)▶▶▶**. Here the road surface has been stripped off to reveal handsome cobbles, while to either side restored pioneer houses of pale stone survive from the original hilltop settlement site of 1882. The community today has an arty feel, and some of the old buildings are appealing restaurants. Nearby **Kibbutz Kfar Hanassi** makes high-quality herbal remedies from its own gardens (tel: 06-6914833). Roadside viewpoints on the way to Sefat include **Mitzpe HaYamim▶**, where both the Sea of Galilee and (hazily) the Mediterranean can be seen.

ECHOES OF THE PAST
When the Israelites conquered Canaan in 1300BC, the area that would become Galilee was shared between the tribes of Asher and Naftali. The Menasseh tribe had the Golan. The tribe of Dan was given the foot of Mount Hermon. Many of today's place names recall this remote past. The Naftali hills overlook the Hula Plain. Ancient Dan lies half a mile (1km) away from the Dan of today. Sefat stands atop Mount Canaan.

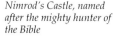

Nimrod's Castle, named after the mighty hunter of the Bible

BELOW THE RED LINE
The banks of the Sea of Galilee lie 695ft (212m) below true sea level. From north to south, the lake measures 13 miles (21km), and its width reaches a maximum of 8 miles (13km). The total area is 65 sq miles (168sq km). On average it is 161ft (49m) deep. The lake is Israel's principal reservoir, and the National Water Carrier pipeline pumps water directly from the shore near Capernaum to smaller reservoirs across the country. The "red line" is a theoretical water level below which the lake's surface should not drop—but it has done so frequently in recent years, causing anxiety about the quality of the water and the effect on its fish.

►►► Sea of Galilee (Hebrew: Yam Kinneret) *163C2-C3*

Not really a sea, of course, the exquisitely beautiful and tranquil body of water that Israelis call Lake Kinneret astonishes the eye, lying blue under a pearly sky, enclosed by hills that also seem blue-tinted. The name Kinneret comes from *ginnar*, meaning a harp, because of its shape. Certainly its size and shape are ideal. Wherever you stand, whether on a distant viewpoint or on the very shore, the countryside can be seen rising steeply on the other side. All along, the gently lapping waters disappear enticingly around folds in the landscape.

This is, of course, no ordinary lake. It exists as much in faith and legend as in reality, and holds a central place in the hearts of millions of people around the world. This, more than anywhere else, is the land of Jesus. He lived on the lake shores, his disciples were its fishermen, and many of his miraculous works were performed around its banks. If the Gospel account is not a metaphor, he even walked on its waters. What is more, the Jordan River, of hymns and prayers and Gospel songs, that richly symbolic frontier of the biblical Promised Land, flows in one end and out of the other.

Not surprisingly, many visitors find here not only water and sunshine, but also the very spirit of Jesus and echoes of his ministry. However, beware. Many pilgrim sites, even those hallowed by centuries, rest on scant historical evidence. Theologians have decreed that this does not matter, that one should regard the sites as commemorative. But for anyone with simpler, Sunday School notions of "The Holy Land," a few places associated with Jesus could prove quite surprising, and even disappointing. Although many New Testament stories were never intended to be taken literally anyway, shrines, exquisite churches or opulent basilicas mark every spot.

Yet Israel is not a storybook: It is a real country, inhabited by Jews for whom the greatest miracle is their return to this land after their 1,800-year exile. For them, the most wonderful thing of all about the Sea of Galilee is that it is a vast, clean lake in a Mediterranean country with few

Still waters of the Galilee shore

CHANGING NAMES
In the early Scriptures, the Sea of Galilee is called Sea of Chinneret. Both Numbers 34:11 and Joshua 13:27 explain that its eastern shore forms the edge of the Promised Land. By the time of the Book of Maccabees – which is not included in the Jewish and Protestant Bibles – the lake is called the Sea of Ginnosar. This evolved to Lake Gennesaret in the New Testament (Luke 5:1), though Sea of Galilee (Matthew 4:18, Mark 1:16) and Sea of Tiberias (John 6:1, 21:1) are also used. Sea of Tiberias seems to have been current in the 1st century – the time of Jesus – as both the Talmud and the historian Josephus use that name.

Oleander in full bloom

other sources of fresh water. The sea is full, too, of edible fish—20 different species, notably the unique St. Peter's fish. Its shores are fertile and eager to yield their produce. Most of its shoreline remains wonderfully undeveloped, but kibbutzim and moshavim (co-operative villages) are scattered all around the lake. The fields grow the whole gamut of fruit: apples, avocados, beans and bananas. Most people are involved in fishing or fish farming.

The lakeside kibbutz hotels make excellent places to stay —or merely stop for a meal. They have parklike settings and a more restful atmosphere than conventional hotels. Among the most appealing are the well-placed **Nof Ginnosar** (see page 171), on the northwestern shore and the religiously observant (though non-Jews are very welcome) **Kinar**, facing it on the northeastern bank.

On the whole, the northern half of the lake offers superb tranquility. Most of the places associated with Jesus are here: **Capernaum▶▶** (see pages 170–71) and, within a few minutes of Capernaum, the **Mount of Beatitudes▶▶** (see pages 188–89), **Tabgha▶▶** (see page 202), **Migdal▶** (see page 186), the home of Mary Magdalene and ancient **Kursi▶** (see page 198).

The southern half of the lake tends to appeal to a livelier crowd. **Tiberias▶▶** (see page 204), Galilee's little capital, stands on the edge of the water and invites you to swim in it, ski on it, or take a trip on it—either in a mock-biblical boat or in a modern pleasure cruiser equipped with disco. Or you can soak in its hot spa, famous since Roman days. At the southern tip of the Sea of Galilee, where the Jordan River pours out of the lake at **Yardenit▶** (see page 205), you can even be baptized in its waters.

WATER FOR PEACE
Under the 1994 peace accord, Israel provides Jordan with 196.5 million cubic yards (150 million cu m) of water per year by allowing extraction from the Yarmouk River, which flows into the Sea of Galilee. These days, the amount of water now pumped out of the Sea of Galilee each day to meet the needs of Israel's own population is more than the total for all of 1948.

Drive

The Sea of Galilee

(for map see pages 163C2–C3)

This circular tour of the lake offers plenty to do and see. *Allow all day, and take a swimsuit.*

From the lake's biggest town, **Tiberias▶▶** (see page 204), head south. After 3 miles (5km) you pass the Roman and modern spa baths of **Hamat Tiveria▶▶** (see page 205) and, on the hill slope opposite, two beautiful **old synagogues▶**. Nearby is the tomb of Rabbi Meir Ba'al Haness, revered by many Sephardi Jews. Turn right beside the Jordan River to the **Yardenit▶** baptismal park (see page 205). Almost next door, **Deganya▶** (see page 171), founded in 1909, is Israel's oldest kibbutz. A right turn leads from the lake to **Hamat Gader▶▶** (see page 176), site of extensive spa baths and an alligator farm. If alligators are not to your taste, try the ostrich farm at **Ha'on Kibbutz▶** (see page 177).

Kibbutz Ein Gev▶, founded in 1937, lies just within the pre-1967 border. This was where the first Jews in modern times cast their nets again into the Sea of Galilee. On the stony hill above is ruined **Susita▶** (Hebrew for "horse," named after the hill's saddle shape), which, as the seat of a Byzantine bishop, flourished until the 7th-century Arab conquest. Nearby **Kursi National Park▶**, the biblical Gergesa, contains what was once Israel's largest Byzantine monastic church. The 5th-century building, partly reconstructed, traditionally marks the place where Jesus cured the man possessed by a 'legion' of unclean spirits; they entered a herd of some 2,000 pigs, which promptly ran down to the water and drowned (Mark 5:1–20). **Kinar▶**, a religious kibbutz, has a hotel and restaurant on delightful lakeside grounds.

The road recrosses the Jordan on the wooden planks of **Arik Bridge**, and straight away reaches **Amnun Beach▶**, a very agreeable spot for a dip. Just minutes away, several important places in Jesus' ministry lie close together: **Capernaum▶▶** (see page 170), **Tabgha▶▶** (see page 202), and the **Mount of Beatitudes▶▶** (see page 188 and opposite Walk). Do not miss the **ancient boat▶▶▶** at the **Man in the Galilee Museum▶** which can be found beside the attractive **Nof Ginnosar Kibbutz Hotel** (see page 171). Last comes ancient **Migdal▶** (see page 186), just 2.5 miles (4km) from Tiberias.

Green and scenic Galilee, site of many events in Christ's life

The Chapel of the Primacy of St. Peter

Walk

In the footsteps of Jesus

Most of Jesus' ministry took place within a small area around Capernaum. This attractive countryside, dotted with churches, makes for enjoyable, easy walking. Wear a sunhat, take drinking water and dress modestly for access to churches. *Allow 1.5 hours.*

Start by visiting Capernaum's ancient synagogue and dwellings, including the one said to have been St. Peter's House (see page 171). Jesus lived at **Capernaum▶▶**, where he preached and soundly reproached the townsfolk for not taking his message to heart.

From the site, take the access path back to the main road. Almost opposite, paths lead on through the fields to the **Mount of Beatitudes▶▶** (see pages 188–89), a possible site of the Sermon on the Mount. Climb to the summit (0.5 miles/1km), where the lovely domed **Church of the Beatitudes** (or Basilica), set in gardens adjacent to the **Hospice**, commands a fine view.

Descend on the path that heads in the direction of Tabgha (0.5 miles/1km). You meet the road almost opposite the grounds of the **Church of the Primacy of Peter**. Walk to the simple chapel, which stands on the shore of the lake. The chapel was built on the spot where the risen Christ appeared to his disciples, who were fishing on the lake. They did not recognize him until he told them to cast their nets on the other side of the boat, whereupon their nets were full. Peter then miraculously walked on the waters of the lake to reach the shore. Over breakfast Jesus asked Peter three times if he loved him. On replying yes, Peter was made head of the Church.

Turn along the road away from Capernaum. On the right are remains of the 4th-century **Monastery of the Sermon on the Mount**, held, at that time, to mark the site of the Sermon. Continue for 150 yards (140m) to the modern **Church of the Multiplication of the Loaves and Fishes**, the third church on this site. It is traditionally associated with the feeding of the multitudes with loaves and fishes. Return along the road to Capernaum.

THE ARI
Sefat's Ari Ashkenazi Synagogue is supposed to stand on the spot where the nature-loving Yitzhak Luria, known as Our Master Rabbi Yitzhak, or the Ari (an acronym that means "the Lion"), would greet the Sabbath. The six psalms and chanted blessing that he and his followers recited have become the familiar Friday evening *Kabbalat Shabbat*. The Ari also established the popular Tu b'Shvat festival, the "New Year for Trees," now celebrated by Jews all over the world. The Ari was Sephardi, but the congregation today is Ashkenazi—hence the synagogue's name.

►►► Sefat (Hebrew: Tsfat or Zefat) *163C3*

One of Israel's most picturesque towns, Sefat (see panel for other spellings) stands 3,280ft (1,000m) high in beautiful hills north of the Sea of Galilee, with superb views. This has been a center of Jewish learning for centuries and was, with **Meron►** (see page 185), a birthplace of kabbala (Jewish mysticism). It's one of the four holy Jewish cities. Many strictly observant Jews live here, but it is a focus of secular Jewish culture as well. Every July, Sefat hosts its popular festival of *klezmer* (East European Jewish music).

Café-lined **Yerushalayim (Jerusalem) Street►►►**, is the old city's main street and is set on the slope of a steep hill. Pick up a map at the tourist office, located a few paces from the **Davidka►**, a home-made cannon; its noise alone is said to have helped the Jews conquer Sefat in 1948. At the hill's summit, there is a park and the remains of a **Crusader Citadel►►**. On the northern slope, the **Israel Bible Museum►** (*Closed* Shabbat. *Admission free*) houses art depicting biblical scenes. More interesting, **HaMeira House►►** (*Closed* Shabbat. *Admission: inexpensive*) has material on 19th-century Sefat. It is near the top of **Ma'alot Olei HaGardom►**, a remarkable flight of hundreds of stone steps down the hill. Also at the top of the steps is the **Police Station►**, built by the British to separate Jewish and Arab neighborhoods. It is still pitted with bullet marks.

North of the steps, wander among the attractive cobbled lanes, stairways and courtyards of the **Synagogue Quarter►►►**. The ornate little 16th-century synagogues (some rebuilt in the 18th century) are very much in use. These synagogues welcome non-Jewish visitors, though modest dress is expected (see panel, page 99). Do not miss

Sefat's ancient Abuhav Synagogue

the **Ari Ashkenazi Synagogue▶▶▶**, a tiny white stone building in a quiet stone courtyard, with its detailed hand-carved ark. Also not to miss are **Abuhav Synagogue▶▶**, with its three arks and **Yosef Caro Synagogue▶▶▶**, named after the Spanish-born rabbi who arrived here in 1535. Caro wrote the still-authoritative work on Jewish law, the Shulhan Aruch.

South of the steps lies the charming **Artists' Quarter▶▶**, a former Arab district taken up in the 1950s by an artists' collective. This area is packed with studios and open-air sculpture displays. Farther south is the town's fascinating **Ancient Cemetery▶▶**, which has the graves of many distinguished 16th-century rabbis. Also buried here are the victims of two tragic PLO attacks—the 22 Sefat high school pupils killed at Ma'alot on a school trip, and the 11 younger children from Avivim, whose school bus was attacked.

After the First Revolt (AD66–73), the town grew as Jews fled here from Jerusalem. Crusaders drove the Jews out

Lions and doves in the Artists' Quarter

and constructed the citadel in 1140 (they dubbed the town Safed—still a popular version of its name). It was taken in turn by Salah ed-Din (1188), the Knights Templar (1240), and the Mamelukes (1266). In 1517 all Israel came under Ottoman rule. Jews returned, including many expelled from Spain in 1492. The new arrivals brought with them a rich culture; they built the synagogues and, in 1578, set up the region's first printing press. An earthquake in 1759 caused great damage, after which many Sephardim (Jews of Spanish origin) moved elsewhere. However, Ashkenazim arrived from Russia and took their place, bringing with them their own mysticism and Yiddish culture. In 1837, another earthquake and epidemic killed over 5,000 people, and the town went into decline. Arabs moved in, and in the 1929 anti-Jewish riots they killed 21 Jews and wounded 80.

In the 1948 War of Independence, Sefat was an Arab stronghold with a population of 12,000, including a fighting force of 6,000. When the Arabs entered the Jewish quarter, with its population of 1,500 mainly elderly Hasidim, a group of 35 men in the Palmach elite Jewish fighting force arrived. The fact that such a small number of men managed to defeat the Arab forces and take the whole town is now widely celebrated in Jewish history. It is known as the Miracle of Sefat (see panel).

THE MIRACLE OF SEFAT

When the Jews won Sefat in the 1948 war, the chief rabbi of the town gave it as his opinion that the victory had been due to two things: the natural course of events, and a miracle. The natural course of events was that Jews prayed and God answered their prayers. The miracle was that the Jews were prepared to stay and fight for their city when so heavily outnumbered.

HOW ARE YOU SPELLING THAT?

The name of the hilltop town north of the Sea of Galilee is spelled in Hebrew with the three letters *tsadi, feh, taf,* pronounced approximately as Tsfat. Foreign efforts to say this, or transliterate it into different European languages, have led to a multitude of alternative spellings. As well as Sefat, the town's name is commonly written as Sefad, Safed, Zefat, Sfat and Tsefat.

Modern walls on Roman columns in the Church of the Multiplication of the Loaves and Fishes

JOSEF TRUMPLEDOR
Born in Russia in 1880, Trumpledor served in the Tsar's imperial army, lost an arm in battle and was decorated for bravery, and yet still had to endure the anti-Semitism sweeping Russia at the time. He founded the Zionist Hehalutz (Jewish Pioneer) movement, and in 1912 went to live in Palestine. There he founded the Zion Mule Corps and, despite having only one arm, fought with the British at Gallipoli, after which he was again decorated for bravery. On his return to Palestine in 1917, he joined with others to purchase and cultivate the land they called Tel Hai, the "Hill of Life." In 1920, Arabs attacked the settlement, which was vigorously defended. Eight settlers died, including Trumpledor, whose last words were: "It is good to die for our own country." His grave attracts many visitors, especially on the 11th day of the Jewish month of Adar, which has been set aside for the commemoration of Tel Hai Day.

► Shibli *162B2*

This village on the north slope of **Mount Tabor** (see pages 190–91) is one of several Bedouin communities in this area, which until recently provided donkeys and refreshments for Christian pilgrims going up the mountain. Of Israel's total Bedouin population of almost 200,000 about one third live in this region. The huge Bedouin Tent at the entrance to the village is a focal point for visitors, a heritage, meeting and welcome center.

►► Tabgha *163C3*

Not a village, but a small, fertile valley on the Galilee lakeshore, its name derives from the Greek *hepta pegon* or "seven springs." The springs emerge by the Church of the Primacy of Peter. Just 2 miles (3km) from Capernaum, Tabgha lies at the foot of the **Mount of Beatitudes►►** (see page 188). At the bottom of the hill the **Church of the Multiplication of the Loaves and Fishes►►►** (*Open* daily till 5) commemorates the feeding of the multitudes. This attractive modern building was constructed in 1982 for the German Benedictines, whose 1956 monastery stands next door. The church stands on the site of its 4th- and 5th-century predecessors, and encloses a beautiful cloister in white stone. Inside, visitors must remain quiet, which creates a tremendous atmosphere. In the transepts, exquisite **ancient mosaics►►** retrieved from the two earlier churches depict Egyptian imagery, common in early Christian art. A mosaic in front of the altar shows the two fishes and the basket of loaves (four, not the biblical five) with which Jesus fed the 5,000 (Mark 6:30–44).

Next door, the small, black **Church of the Primacy of Peter►►►** (*Open* daily till 5) built in 1933 on traces of a 4th-century church, marks the site where Jesus appeared to his disciples after his resurrection, according to the Gospel of John (21). The church is in a superb setting on the shore of the Sea of Galilee. Inside, modern colored glass contrasts with the black basalt. The simple interior is built around the waterside rocks, with one great rock emerging from the tiled floor. Known as Mensa Christi, it is claimed to be the "table" at which the risen Christ sat and ate bread with the disciples. Beside the church, steps carved into stone lead down to the water. These steps date from the 2nd century, but many believe that the risen Christ appeared to his disciples on them. On that same occasion, he named Peter head of his church.

▶▶▶ Tel Dan *163C5*

The ancient city of Dan, standing on the largest of the three sources of the Jordan River, marked the northern limit of the biblical Land of Israel ("from Dan to Beersheva"). It is now located within a glorious 99-acre (40ha) **nature reserve▶▶▶**, still on Israel's northern border. Rising above the spring, the adjacent **Tel▶▶** gives a dizzying sense of history. The site of Laish, a city mentioned in Egyptian records of the 19th and 15th centuries BC, it was conquered by Joshua in the 13th century BC and occupied by the Jewish tribe of Dan, which, the Bible notes, had a bad record of idolatry. About 200 years later the city was destroyed by the Assyrian king Tiglath-Pileser III and never rebuilt.

Kibbutz Dan▶, half a mile (1km) away on a panoramic ridge, has views of the Hula Valley and the summit of snow-covered Mount Hermonr. The kibbutz runs a field studies center with residential classes and guided walks. Its **Beit Ussishkin▶▶** (*Open* daily. *Admission: inexpensive*) (Ussishkin House) houses an information center and museum of the wildlife of Golan, Hermon and Hula. The displays and video can only hint at the region's variety of over 2,000 plants and 400 species of birds to be seen here.

▶ Tel Hai *163C5*

North of Kiryat Shmona, Tel Hai (the Hill of Life) is a simple encampment preserved as a museum of the pre-State Haganah underground militia. Josef Trumpledor (see panel opposite) and others of the "eight people" (*kiryat shmona*) died here in March 1920 while defending the land they had purchased in 1917. Trumpledor's grave is at the **military cemetery▶**. To the north, **Beit HaShomer▶** (*Open* daily. *Admission: inexpensive*) at Kibbutz Kfar Giladi is a museum of the HaShomer (literally, "the Watchman"), another early Zionist militia.

JESUS APPEARS

"But when the morning was now come, Jesus stood on the shore, but the disciples knew not that it was Jesus."
—John 21:4

"DAN TO BEERSHEBA"

"And this shall be your north border: From the great sea you shall point out for you Mount Hor; From Mount Hor you shall point out your border unto the entrance of Hamath; and the limits of the border shall be to Zedad; And the border shall go on to Zifron, and its limits shall be at Hazar-Enan; this shall be your north border."
—Numbers 34:7–9

The Tel Dan Nature Reserve, believed by some to be the Garden of Eden

MAIMONIDES
Rabbi Moshe ben Maimon, also known by the sobriquet Rambam, or as Maimonides, was born in Spain in 1135. The leading scientist and physician of his day, he became the personal doctor of Salah ed-Din and wrote important commentaries on biblical matters that have now become standard works. He died on December 13, 1204, and was buried as he wished, at the holy city of Tiberias.

WISH YOU WERE HERE?
In the year 985, Arab writer El-Mukadassi had this to say about life in Tiberias: "For two months a year they gorge themselves upon the fruit of the jujube bush which grows wild and costs nothing, for two months they struggle with the numerous flies, for two months they go about naked because of the heat, for two months they suck sugarcane, for two months they wallow in mud because of the rain, and for two months they dance in their beds because of the legions of fleas."

►► Tiberias (Hebrew: Tiveria) *163C3*

Galilee's little capital (population 37,000), one of the four holy Jewish cities, runs downhill to the edge of the Sea of Galilee. The traffic-free *tayyelet*, or waterfront promenade, with its palms, strolling crowds, fish restaurants and Oriental-looking food stalls, has a pleasant, convivial air and a curious mix of the plush and the tacky. There is a lot of entertainment for visitors, including evening lake cruises with dinner and dancing on board. Away from the shore, the town degenerates into squalor and appalling traffic jams. Most residents and tourists live in new districts high above the old city, but even the lakeside old quarter is marred by a mishmash of modern architecture.

History In AD20, near the ruins of ancient Rakkat, Herod Antipas built an opulent palace and synagogue which soon attracted numerous religious scholars. The Mishna was compiled here about AD200, codifying the so-called Oral Law, the traditional interpretation and practice of the Written Law. From then until AD429 (when it was abolished by Emperor Theodosius II), this was the seat of the Sanhedrin, the supreme court of Jewish law. The Palestinian or Yerushalmi Talmud (Book of Law) might be better termed the Tiberias Talmud, as it was written here around AD400. Jewish life thrived until the 7th-century Arab conquest. Crusaders took the town in 1099 and Salah ed-Din in 1187. Under the Ottomans, Druze Emir Daher revived Tiberias, resettling it with Jews. The First Aliya (1882–1903) dramatically increased its population, and the town has continued to grow ever since.

Sights Waterfront amusements include the **Galilee Experience►** (tel: 04-6723620; www.thegalileeexperience.com. *Closed* Shabbat. *Admission: moderate*), a stirring multimedia "edutainment" packing the region's 4,000-year story into a shmaltzy 40-minute family show. Remains of the black basalt **Crusader fortifications►** are on the north side of the old town. The handsome **St. Peter's Monastery►** (*Open* daily 8–11.45, 2–5), close to the waterfront, also stands on Crusader ruins. Off the main HaGalil Street, the **tomb of Maimonides►►** (the renowned 12th-century Rabbi Moshe ben Maimon, also known by his acronym Rambam) lies beside a small garden. The tomb is reached

Modern fishermen follow in the footsteps of St. Peter

The tomb of Maimonides

by steps lined with black pillars. The large rounded pale stone tomb, set within a black stone enclosure, is covered by a ramshackle metal roof. Rambam's wife's square tomb lies to one side of the enclosure. Beyond are several imposing rabbinical tombs, including those of 1st-century Yohanan ben Zakai, the eminent scholar and founder of the Yavne Academy. Also here is the tomb of revered scholar, 2nd-century Eliezer "the Great." The white **tomb of Rabbi Akiva▶▶**, spiritual leader of the Second Revolt against the Romans (AD132), is higher up the hill.

Nearby Romans flocked to enjoy the hot baths at **Hamat Tiveria▶▶**, 3 miles (5km) south of town. The spa now occupies a modern complex and the emphasis is more on pleasure than health. Ancient buildings were found on the hillside opposite; relics can be seen in the **Lehman Building▶**. Travel up the ramp to a paved esplanade where steps enter the domed interior of an ancient **Sephardic synagogue▶**, still in use. Above, on the slope, is the blue-domed **Ashkenazi synagogue▶**. Both provide access to the low vaulted chamber of the **tomb of Rabbi Meir Ba'al HaNess▶**. This 2nd-century scholar is revered by Sephardim as a miracle worker.

THE *TAYYELET*
Until 1934, the waterfront of Tiberias was densely populated, with houses descending to the edge of the lake. A huge storm in that year caused mud, water and rock to pour through the city, demolishing hundreds of homes at the foot of the hill. Many people were killed. In the aftermath the ruined homes beside the water were swept away. In their place was constructed the town's *tayyelet*, or waterside promenade.

▶ Yardenit *163C2*

(tel: 04-6759111; www.yardenit.com)
Open: Sat–Thu 8–6, Fri 8–5
Kibbutz Kinneret's baptismal park is on the banks of the Jordan, south of the Sea of Galilee. It has attractive grounds and water terraces, where devout Christians come to be immersed in the biblical river. (The traditional site of Jesus' baptism in the Jordan near Jericho has been closed for several years.)

▶▶ Zipori (or Sepphoris) *162B2*

North of Nazareth, this remarkable **archeological site▶▶▶** consists of ruins from the First Temple period, remnants of a complete pre-Roman Jewish town and a Roman theatre. A reconstructed Roman villa contains its original Dionysian mosaic floor. A woman's face in the design has been dubbed the "Mona Lisa of the Galilee." Zipori's 12th-century **Crusader fortifications▶** are a reminder that the Crusader armies gathered here in 1187, before marching to the Horns of Hittim to take on Salah ed-Din. The former's crushing defeat ended the Second Crusade.

Crusader fortress rising above Roman theater ruins at Zipori

Judaea and Samaria (The West Bank)

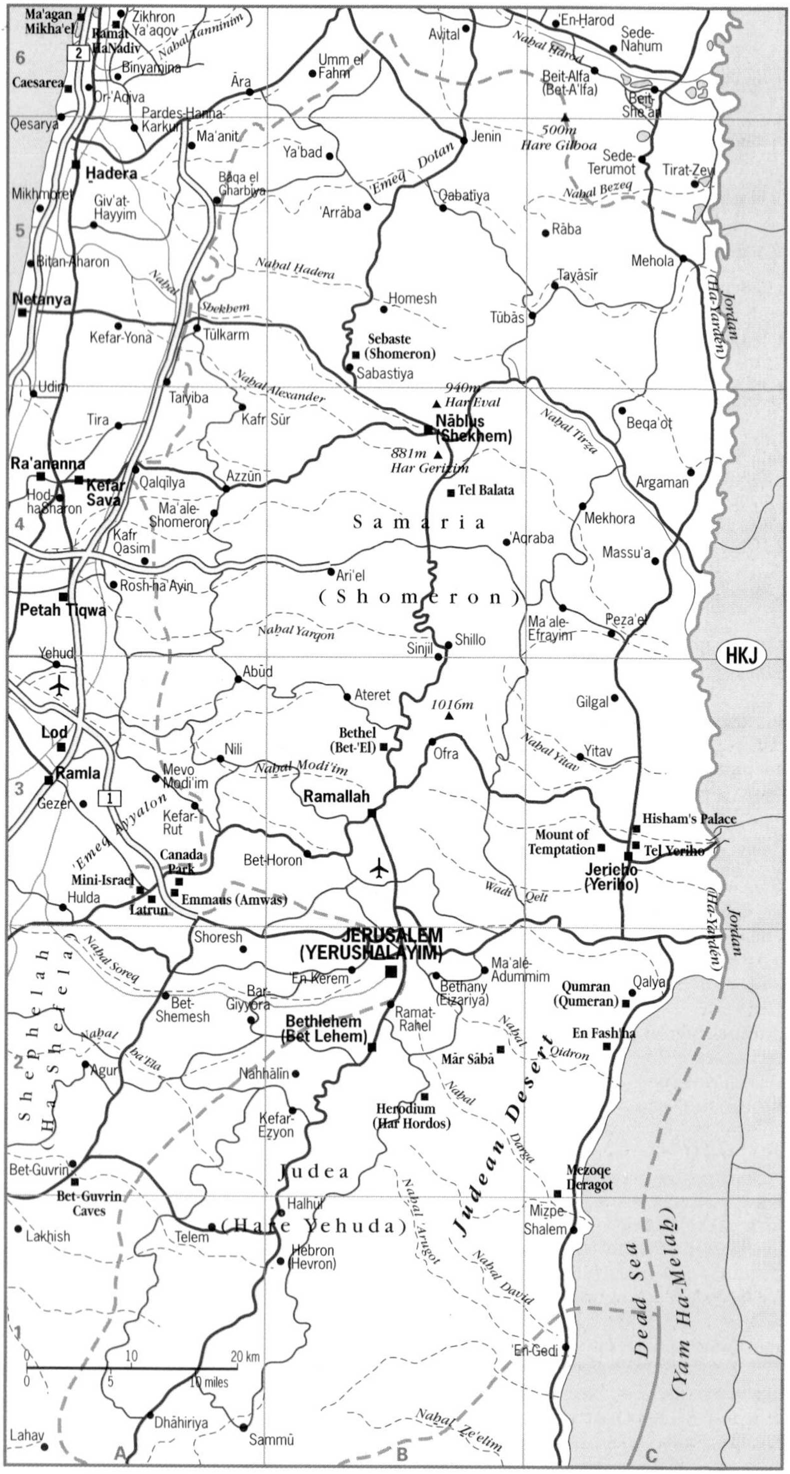

Judaea & Samaria (The West Bank)

Palms and greenery in Jericho, the oldest town in Israel, and with a relatively calm atmosphere

JUDAEA AND SAMARIA (THE WEST BANK) In Hebrew, this region, including the Jerusalem Hills within the borders of Israel, is known as Yehuda and Shomron. Arab residents call the area Al Defa al Gharbia, literally, the West Bank. Most of Judaea and Samaria lies outside the State of Israel but part is likely to become Israeli territory after a settlement with the Arabs. These two ancient Jewish kingdoms have been disputed territory since 1948. Technically, the territory is part of no country, although, since the setting up of the Palestinian Authority in 1994 most of the region is under their administration.

The term West Bank used to refer to all lands west of the Jordan river. Currently, "the West Bank" suggests only the land placed under Israeli military rule after the 1967 Six-Day War. Worldwide, it was dubbed the Occupied Territories even after the handover to the Palestinian Authority; Israel too has come to view its presence as a burdensome occupation, while at the same time, arguing that, under international law, only land properly belonging to another country can be described as occupied. Either way, it remains a divided, disputed region, a remnant of Palestine that ended up in neither Israel nor Jordan (see page 209 for travel advice).

A HARD PLACE A narrow ridge of rocky hills, reaching from Galilee to the Negev, passes through Judaea and Samaria and forms the greater part of the terrain. On their eastern slopes the hills fall sharply down into the Jordan Valley. Certain parts of Judaea fall within the borders of Israel proper such as Ein Gedi on the Dead Sea, Masada and Arad, and the capital itself, Jerusalem, which also includes "the mountains that are round about" the capital (Psalm 125:2).

JUDAEA WEEPS
After quelling the Jewish Revolt and destroying Jerusalem, the 1st-century AD Roman emperor, Vespasian, issued celebratory coins showing a palm tree, a man in chains and a woman weeping, and bearing the words: *Iudaea Capta* (Judaea taken).

DISAPPOINTMENT
"What public relations can do for a river!" —Henry Kissinger, on seeing the West Bank of the Jordan River in 1980.

JERUSALEM HILLS
Not all of Judaea is in the West Bank. Parts of the area covered in this chapter are within the state of Israel, or are likely to become so. The Jerusalem Hills west of the Israeli capital are mainly within the boundary of the state of Israel. They include a West Bank enclave around Latrun, which is on the main Tel Aviv to Jerusalem highway. Some popular Israeli attractions are here, including Mini-Israel.

Previous page (bottom, right): Detail at the entrance to the Milk Grotto Sanctuary

St. George's Monastery at Wadi Qelt, near Jericho

Occupied Judaea lies south and east of Jerusalem, with Samaria to its north. Together they are less than half the size of Northern Ireland. Both districts are stony, mountainous, and largely infertile, though the Samarian hills are terraced and planted with crops. A large proportion of Judaea consists of uninhabitable desert, yet Judaea and Samaria lie near the heart and soul of Jewish history and heritage. Judaea (in Hebrew, Yehuda or Judah) actually means "the Land of Jews." This is the country in which Abraham wandered, where he and the other patriarchs—and the matriarchs—of the Jewish nation lived and died. Jewish towns and places of pilgrimage grew around their tombs. Later, some of these became Muslim holy sites as well.

WHOSE LAND? In 1947, as the British were about to withdraw, the UN debated the future of Palestine. The Arab Higher Committee in Palestine, chief representative body of Palestinian Arabs, declared that "Palestine is part of the province of Syria." At the same time, the new kingdom of Jordan claimed sovereignty over all of British Palestine, while the Egyptians formed their own All Palestine Government to fill the vacuum left by the British departure. In 1948, the war between the Arab states and Israel left the region partitioned between Jordan, which annexed the entire West Bank, and the new State of Israel. With its defeat in the 1967 Six-Day War, Jordan lost the West Bank, which Israel occupied but did not annex.

After 1987, Israeli rule was challenged directly by the First Intifada (literally "Throwing Off"), an uprising of West Bank Arab residents, some opposed to Israel's presence in the West Bank, others opposed to the State's very existence. Partly through their inability to contain the Intifada, Israelis moved towards the idea of quitting the West Bank. Under Prime Minister Rabin's government agreement was reached with the PLO, which set up the Palestinian Authority in 1994 and took over Gaza and parts of the West Bank. However, in 2000, PLO leader Yasser Arafat rejected the "Two State Solution," instead launching the second Intifada. The brutal chaos of the Intifada proved self-destructive; it ended in 2004, leaving the West Bank economy, social order and infrastructure in ruins. After Arafat's death, moves resumed to hand over the West Bank to Palestinian rule.

►► Bethany (Arabic: El Azaria, Eizariya) *206B2*

A small town just over the crest of the Mount of Olives, Bethany is only 3 miles (5km) from Jerusalem. The Gospels of Luke and Matthew record that, before riding into Jerusalem on his final journey, Jesus sent two disciples to Bethany to fetch "a colt [of an ass]...whereon yet never man sat." The animal had been tied up for him there—possibly by Lazarus and his sisters Martha and Mary, friends of Jesus who lived in Bethany.

In Aramaic, Bethany means "house (or place) of poverty," but the Arabic name means "the (place of) Lazarus." Lazarus is revered by Muslims as well as Christians. Lazarus had died from an illness, John's Gospel relates, and "lain in the grave four days already' before Jesus arrived. Jesus wept and called out, 'Lazarus, come forth'." The dead man came out, still bound with strips of cloth (John 11:1–44).

Lazarus' Tomb►►, near the mosque, is the principal sight. Difficult steps descend to a dark cavern, which leads to the low tomb where Lazarus is thought to have lain. The area north of the church was a cemetery in the 1st century AD, and the tomb has been popular with pilgrims since the 4th century. Mark makes no mention of Christ raising Lazarus from the dead, although the evangelist does have Jesus and the disciples going to Bethany on that day. In his story, Jesus is hungry and pauses at a fig tree. Finding it without fruit (because, as the Gospel states, Passover is not during the fig season), he curses the tree and tells it that no man shall eat fruit from it forever. Tourists are sometimes shown what is said to be the very tree, although Matthew (21:19) says that after Jesus' curse "the fig tree withered away" instantly.

Jesus stayed with his friends again "six days before the Passover" (John 12:1), on which he was to be crucified. The various Gospel accounts differ in their details of what happened on that day. John's gospel tells of Lazarus' sister Mary anointing Jesus' feet with "a pound of spikenard, very costly," and wiping his feet afterwards with her hair. Matthew's gospel says that a woman came with precious ointment in an alabaster box and anointed his head. These anointments, Christian authorities have claimed, were the ritual verification of Jesus as the Messiah. The word messiah, or *moshiach* in Hebrew, meaning "the anointed," is used several times in the Old Testament to describe Jewish kings or leaders.

In Matthew's Gospel (26:6–13), the anointment of Jesus takes place not at the home of Martha and Mary, but in the home of a leper called Simon. Not far from Lazarus' Tomb is the ruined **House of Simon the Leper►**. Formerly known as the Castle of Lazarus it was once part of the defences for a nunnery. The nunnery was founded by Milicent, wife of the Crusader-era King Fulke. Similarly, the so-called **House of Mary and Martha►** is the remains of the medieval nunnery. A blocked-off recess in the **Church of Mary and Martha►** forms another entrance to Lazarus' Tomb.

According to Luke's Gospel (24:50), Bethany is also the site of Christ's ascension. There are other Christian associations nearby: about 6 miles (10km) out of Bethany, on the Jericho road, is the inn of Jesus' parable about the Good Samaritan (Luke 10:25–37).

►►► REGION HIGHLIGHTS

Bethlehem *pages 212–14*

Herodion *page 214*

Jacob's Well, Nablus *page 220*

Latrun *page 218*

Mini-Israel *page 219*

TRAVEL IN THE WEST BANK

Two well-supported, well-funded and well-armed Palestinian guerrilla organizations are at war with Israel: Hamas and Islamic Jihad. Their presence in the West Bank makes it dangerous to travel here. The stoning of cars with Israeli license plates (including rental cars) is commonplace. Shootings have also taken place, resulting in the deaths of numerous drivers and passengers.

This being said, the main roads to popular tourist sights are considered safe and have good security cover (for example, the Jerusalem to Qumran and Jericho road, or the Dead Sea road to Ein Gedi). Arab buses will not be attacked, and the Arab-run buses based at the East Jerusalem bus station travel to towns and villages throughout the West Bank. *Organized tours are the safest way to see the sights. West Bank tours are usually organized by Arab companies, with Arab guides traveling in Arab buses.*

The Palestine Liberation Organisation (PLO) was created in 1964 with the aim of destroying Israel. Its leader, Yasir Arafat (known to the Arabs as Abu Amr, Father of War), never seen without his traditional keffiye *headdress and a pistol strapped on to his battle fatigues, became a media figure lauded by Western radical groups and Soviet-bloc client states.*

THE SECURITY BARRIER
There is no natural border between the West Bank and Israel. From 2000 to 2003, more than 100 West Bank suicide bombers crossed unimpeded into Israel, where they killed almost 900 people. In 2003 the Israeli government began constructing a "security barrier" around the West Bank to end the attacks. Progress was slow, as the Supreme Court heard challenges to the fence which sometimes had to be re-routed following court rulings. By the end of 2005, two-thirds of the barrier was complete, yet infiltration by terrorists was already so impeded that attacks had been cut almost to zero.

Protesters (below) are fenced in by police

Until 1993, the many factions within the PLO were bound together by a common aim: To destroy Israel and set up an Arab republic in all of Palestine. On September 13, 1993, Yasir Arafat took off his gun and held out his hand in peace to Israeli Prime Minister Yitzhak Rabin on the lawn of the White House in Washington. In 1994, the Israelis began the process of handing over territory to the PLO, henceforth to become the ruling "party" of the Palestinian Authority. This did not bring an end to the Palestinian war against Israel. The PLO was an uneasy alliance of guerrilla factions. The head of Al Fatah, Yasir Arafat, became chairman of the Palestinian Authority. Even as the PLO appeared ready to negotiate for a "Two State Solution," no-quarter groups like Hamas, Hezbullah and Islamic Jihad, funded by Iran, Iraq and Syria, were winning the hearts of those who still dreamed of seeing Israel utterly destroyed. The Palestinian Authority walked a tightrope between a conciliatory tone for the West, and anti-Zionism for the Islamic world. In 2000 Israeli premier Ehud Barak offered Yasir Arafat almost all of the West Bank, including East Jerusalem. Arafat opted to continue the armed struggle. Prime Minister Ariel Sharon tackled the violence by reoccupying the West Bank, assassinating guerrilla leaders and confining Arafat to his HQ at Ramallah. Arafat died in 2004, bringing a new hope of peace between Israel and the Arabs.

History In the Arab world, resolute opposition to the setting up of a Jewish state in Palestine goes back a long way. Before and after Israel came into being in 1948, Arab states set up anti-Zionist armed groups. *Fedayeen* (terrorist) attacks ran at a high level through the 1950s. In 1964 the Arab League (a pan-Arab inter-government forum) met in Cairo to create the Palestine Liberation Organization as an umbrella for these forces. They declared the PLO was "the sole legitimate representative of the Palestinian people." Al Fatah joined in 1967 and became the dominant faction. In 1968, the PLO wrote its Covenant, in which for the first time Arabs living in Palestine were defined as a separate nation—the Palestinians. Through the 1970s, terrorist acts around the world were sharply escalated as the PLO attacked Israel and Israelis. By focusing on Israel's occupation of the West Bank rather than the aim of destroying Israel, the Palestinian cause won huge support worldwide. By the 1990s Arafat's support for Saddam Hussein lost the Palestinians some international backing.

Hamas rally (top)
Former Iraqi president Saddam Hussein and the late Yasir Arafat (left)

A new era A new reality prevails in the region. The demise of Saddam Hussein—a key backer of the anti-Zionist cause—and pressure on the Arab world to stop supporting terrorism, is marginalising the extremists. Yet while Arab states are coming to terms with the idea of a Jewish state, in the Arab streets hostility is as great as ever. Opposition has increasingly come under the wing of violent Islamist organizations, leading to the landslide victory of Hamas in the Palestinians' 2006 elections. However, even such hardliners face a need to accept the new realpolitik if there is ever to be a Palestinian state.

ZIONISM
Arabs hostile to Israel brand it "the Zionist entity." Their influence enabled a vote to be passed year after year in the UN Assembly affirming that "Zionism is Racism," a Soviet-sponsored motion only rescinded with the collapse of the Soviet bloc. In fact, Zionism is the political movement whose objective is to create (and now to maintain) a Jewish homeland in Israel. Most political organizations and parties in Israel, even those advocating total withdrawal from the West Bank, consider themselves Zionist.

Clashes often involve youths and children

▶▶▶ Bethlehem (Hebrew: Beit Lechem; Arabic: Bet Lacham) *206B2*

For devout Christians, a visit to this large Arab town, 6 miles (10km) from Jerusalem, is the experience of a lifetime. The focal point is the **Church of the Nativity▶▶▶** (tel: 08-2742440. *Open* Apr–Sep daily 6.30am–7.30pm; Oct–Mar 5.30am–5pm. *Closed* Grotto Sun am) in Manger Square, known to the world as the birthplace of Jesus.

History Bethlehem first appeared in the Scriptures nearly 2,000 years before Jesus as the burial place of the matriarch Rachel, wife of Jacob. The events of the Book of Ruth took place locally, and a young shepherd boy from Bethlehem, David, son of Jesse, was anointed King of Israel here by Samuel (I Samuel 16:1–13). The richness of its fields and pasture are reflected in its name: The Hebrew Beit Lechem means "House (or Place) of Bread," while the Arabic name means "House of Meat."

Christian beliefs Jesus' birth in Bethlehem is attested to by two of the evangelists. The gospels of Matthew (2:1) and Luke (2:4–7) relate what has become the traditional Nativity story (neither Mark nor John refers to the birth of Jesus). They give no details of the exact location, except that Jesus was lain in a manger. Tradition has it that a certain cave was the exact place of his birth as animals were often quartered in such places. Many older Bethlehem houses have caves behind them to this day. According to the 4th-century St. Jerome, the cave and site had, since Hadrian's time (AD135), been a shrine to Adonis, the youthful paramour of Venus who symbolized the winter solstice. Hadrian's choice of this site, it has been suggested, may have been motivated by a desire to interfere with the veneration by Christians.

The first church When St. Helena, the mother of Emperor Constantine, visited in the 4th century, she was shown the cave, told the story and promptly ordered a church to be built. In the 6th century Emperor Justinian replaced this with a larger structure. His church was left standing by the Arab invaders of the 7th century. It also remained untouched in the 11th century when many churches were destroyed by invading Muslims. Jesus is named in the Koran as one of the Holy Prophets, and the destructive force of the Muslims was quelled by the thought that this was his birthplace. Justinian's church remains essentially that which exists today, except for alterations carried out by the Crusaders, who captured it in 1099.

Power struggle When the Crusaders left, the church went into decline. Warring Christian factions divided it into sections and each defended their own patch, while Mamelukes and others took everything of value. Later, in the bitter struggle for ownership of the church, Napoleon intervened on behalf of the Roman Catholics, securing a portion for them. Armenian, Greek Orthodox and Catholic monasteries and churches were built abutting the Church of the Nativity, with entrances directly into it. When the church was damaged by earthquake (1834) and fire (1869), disagreements between the factions made it impossible to carry out repairs or replace lost furnishings.

CHRISTMAS IN BETHLEHEM
Those who wish Christmas would come more often should be taken to Bethlehem. The three denominations controlling the Church of the Nativity celebrate the birth of Jesus on different days: Catholics on December 25, Greek Orthodox on January 7, and Armenians on January 19.

CHRISTIAN INFORMATION CENTER
For information on visiting Bethlehem and other Christian sites in the Holy Land, contact the Christian Information Center, just inside Jaffa Gate in the Old City of Jerusalem. PO Box 14308, 91142 Jerusalem, tel: 02-6272692; email: cicinfo@cicts.org

SOLOMON'S POOLS
South of Bethlehem, on the main road to Hebron, three large and ancient reservoirs are attributed to Solomon (Ecclesiastes 2: 6). Herod brought water from them to Herodion, and Pontius Pilate ran their waters into Jerusalem.

BEWARE OF TOUTS
On arrival in Manger Square, visitors are usually set upon by groups of would-be guides of all ages, who shout and pull at the tourists while offering their "services." To employ one might be an act of charity, but for a more enjoyable visit to Bethlehem, it is wise to refuse.

Bethlehem's Church of the Nativity

Under British and then Israeli rule, pilgrimages to the church revived. Israeli soldiers have several times had to separate fighting Christians, notably in 1984 when armed Greek and Armenian clergymen fought a fierce battle. A worse incident occurred in 2002, when 200 armed Islamic guerillas escaped Israeli forces by occupying the Church of the Nativity for 39 days, besieged by the soldiers. Troops shot and killed seven who emerged from the building. After neogitiations, the guerillas were allowed to leave unharmed on condition that 13 left the country. They were given asylum in Cyprus.

Church of the Nativity today Despite an unattractive, buttressed, fortress-like Crusader outer wall, the church is a good example of early Christian basilican construction. It is entered by crossing a large paved courtyard to reach the tiny 6th-century doorway, which Crusaders made even smaller, apparently for ease of defence. By contrast, the interior is large and open, almost free of any decoration or furnishing. Inside are two double rows of red limestone pillars beneath an oak ceiling (a gift from Edward IV

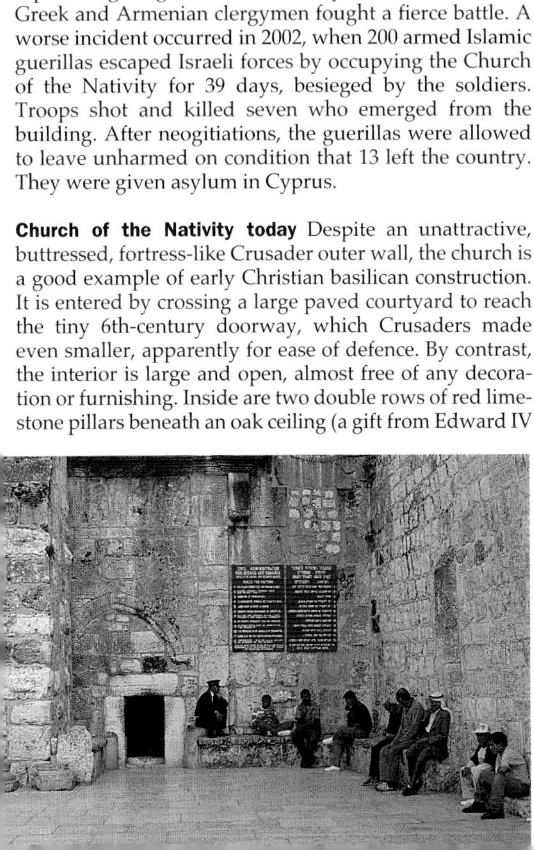

Visitors entering the church bow in submission and humility through this low door

HERODION
This magnificent archeological site (*Open* Sat–Thu 7.30–6, Fri 7.30–5. *Admission: moderate*), set on a high hilltop in the Judaean wilds south of Bethlehem, preserves substantial and impressive remains of the palace which Herod constructed for himself in 24–15BC. He flattened the summit and ringed it with defences to enclose his luxurious circular Mountain Palace. The Lower Town, at the bottom of the hill, was built for Herod's staff. In both the First and Second Jewish Revolts, the palace was seized by rebels and used as their fortress and operations Centre. Later, Byzantine monks built a monastery on the slope among the ruins of the palace annexes. From the summit, there is a fantastic view of Bethlehem and the Judaean hills.

of England and Duke Philip of Burgundy in 1482). During Crusader times and after, this austere interior was beautifully painted and gilded. Trapdoors in the floor open to show remnants of the **mosaic floor►** of Helena's original church.

Site of the Nativity Beside the ornate Greek Orthodox altar at the east end, steps lead down to the **Grotto of the Nativity►►►**. The marble-lined cave is small—8ft (2.5m) high and less than 13ft (4m) across—and rather overpowering, with its warm, heavy atmosphere of incense and lamps. Some visitors are visibly moved. Groups on religious tours often break into carols or hymns. Below the little curtain-fringed Altar of the Nativity, a large silver star overhung with lamps supposedly marks the spot on which Mary gave birth, though the position was chosen in the 17th century. Across from the altar, three steps lead into the **Chapel of the Manger►**, where Mary is said to have placed her newborn baby. The Grotto, a Greek Orthodox possession, is part of a labyrinth containing altars, chapels and the tomb of St. Jerome, with separate access from the Catholic side. To the right of the Grotto is the Greek Orthodox Monastery, and to the left the pleasant 19th-century Franciscan **Church of St. Catherine►** (*Open* summer, daily 5–12, 2–6; winter, daily 5–12, 2–5).

The Church of St. Catherine

Where shepherds kept watch there is now a modern shrine

The other sights Leading off Manger Square, Milk Grotto Street passes the **Chapel of the Milk►** (*Open* daily 8–11.45, 2–5) where, it's said, drops of Mary's milk fell while she was breast-feeding Jesus, turning the ground white. Running parallel, Shepherds' Street leads out of town to the cultivated **Field of Boaz►**, where Ruth gathered the gleanings left by her future husband (Ruth 2). Just 1 mile (2km) away is the walled **Shepherds' Fields►**, now an olive grove. A small cave in the center has become the **Grotto of the Shepherds►**, a shrine stated to be the place where the "shepherds watched their flocks by night." Six miles (10km) farther south, **Herodion►►►** is the well-kept remnant of Herod's majestic hilltop palace (see page 213).

Out of Bethlehem on the Jerusalem side, **Rachel's Tomb►** (*Closed* Shabbat) is a well-established place of prayer for the Jews. A large tomb here, shrouded in cloth, is supposed to cover the grave of the matriarch, second wife of Jacob. **Beware of youths stoning cars on the way to all of these out-of-town sites.**

▶ Hebron (Hebrew: Hevron; Arabic: El Khalil) *206B1*

Be careful if you intend to visit this notorious trouble spot. It is a town with a large population (70,000) and a devout Islamic center with a tradition of violence (see page 209 for advice on traveling in West Bank trouble spots). Hebron is a harsh town without warmth, bars or theaters, but it does have a powerful, fervent atmosphere. Among the world's oldest cities, occupied continuously since Canaanite times, this is also one of the four Jewish holy cities. It was here, as Genesis details, that Abraham made his covenant with God, here that Abraham and Sarah, Isaac and Rebecca, Jacob and Leah, founders of the Jewish nation, lived, died and were buried. Here David was anointed Saul's successor as King of the Jews; he made Hebron his capital before Jerusalem. As a national shrine, the town has been vitally important ever since. The Bible also calls the town Kiryat Arba, and that is the name of the heavily defended, tough-minded new Jewish district (population 5,000). This replaced the old and peaceful Jewish quarter (population 700), emptied by Arab rioters in the horrific 1929 massacre and demolished during the Jordanian occupation.

Sights The town is dominated by the fortress-like structure (largely 13th- and 14th-century, but with Herodian elements dating to 20BC) built over the **Cave of Machpela▶▶** (*Open* Sun–Thu approx 8–4; restricted access Fri and Sat). Also called the Tomb of Patriarchs (in Arabic: Haram el Khalil—literally "Tomb of the Friend"), this tense, divided shrine is where Jews and Arabs both pray. It stands on the south side of town, not far from the busy souk. The cave itself is sealed; 9th- and 14th-century cenotaphs in the building and courtyard are said to stand above the graves of Abraham and Sarah. Koranic script decorates the walls. The shrine has been a synagogue, a mosque and a church before reverting to the Muslims, who from 1267 to 1967 banned Jews from entering. The Yitzhak (or Isaac) Hall is still reserved for Muslims. A synagogue has been placed between the cenotaphs of Abraham and Sarah. It is quite probable that this really is the site of their graves. Less plausible is the popular idea that Adam and Eve are also buried in the cave. Adam's footprint, Abraham's oak tree, and other doubtful tombs and relics are among the town's sights.

MASSACRE IN HEBRON
Hebron had an almost unbroken Jewish presence for thousands of years up to August 1929, when Arabs besieged the Jewish quarter, killing 67 people and forcing the rest to abandon their homes. After the 1967 Six-Day War a group of Jews returned and created the new Kiryat Arba district. In May 1980, as a group of Jewish students came out of the Cave of Machpela, Arabs opened fire on them, killing six and wounding 17. In 1993 and 1994, following the Israel–PLO accord, there were many attacks on Jews, and Jews have sometimes responded in kind in the Hebron area. In February 1994 a Jewish doctor, Baruch Goldstein—previously considered a dutiful servant of both communities—opened fire on Arabs praying at the Machpela cave, killing 29.

The cave of Machpela is a place of prayer for both Jews and Muslims

The walls of Jericho come tumbling down

►► Jericho (Hebrew: Yericho; Arabic: Er Riha) *206C3*

The lowest town in the world (820ft/250m below sea level), and the oldest, Jericho has a shabby charm and a relatively calm atmosphere. It's a relatively safe excursion from Jerusalem. There are lots of places to eat and a striking abundance of greenery and flowers. It was the first West Bank town transferred to Palestinian rule under the 1994 agreement, and was the first to be handed over as Israeli troops withdrew from the West Bank in 2005.

LAND WITH NO NAME
Israelis often talk about "across the Green Line" when referring to the West Bank territories. They are also known officially by an acronym, Yesha, from Yehuda-Shomron-'Azza (Hebrew names for Judah, Samaria, Gaza). The name West Bank, first coined by the American CIA, was brought into general use by the Jordanians.

History The "oldest town" claims do not really apply to present-day Jericho—only the tel (settlement mound) on the northern boundary is ancient. This was, the Bible vividly records, the first town in the Promised Land taken by the Israelites under the command of Joshua. Following God's instructions, Joshua encircled the city, and when the priests blew their trumpets, the walls came tumbling down. He then cursed the city and any man that would rebuild it. All this and more is told in ripping style in the Book of Joshua. The curse was not taken too seriously by his fellow Israelites, who immediately rebuilt Jericho as a Jewish city. Despite a succession of foreign rulers this is how it remained, with a few breaks, right through the millennia up to the Arab conquest in the 7th century AD. Its location has varied slightly.

Jericho makes numerous other appearances in the Bible, and its life seems to have been entwined with that of Jerusalem. Temple priests had homes here, and it was said that trumpets blown at the Temple could be heard in Jericho, 21.5 miles (35km) away. In 30BC, the city became the personal possession of King Herod, who enlarged and aggrandized it, building a winter palace here. It was the Herodian city that Jesus knew and to which he came prior to the Crucifixion.

Knot window from Hisham's Palace

Herod's city was virtually destroyed by the Romans during the Second Jewish Revolt, but reappeared on its present site under the Byzantines. Arabs took control in AD638, then the Crusaders, who were driven out in 1147. The town then dwindled away; at the British takeover it had a population under 3,000. This changed dramatically in 1948, when 70,000 Arabs, fleeing from the new State of Israel, settled here in refugee camps. After 1967, they came under Israeli rule and again fled, this time to Jordan. In 1994, under the gaze of the world's TV cameras, Jericho became the first independent Palestinian city on the West Bank. There's a casino here, and tourists are welcome in town.

Sights Most things worth seeing lie north of modern Jericho. Start with **Tel Yeriho▶▶** (*Open* summer, daily 8–6; winter, daily 8–5. *Admission: inexpensive*), where 23 layers of civilization have been found, dating back to 8000BC. The whole of the mighty encircling defences of Canaanite times have been excavated, together with traces of the rampart which fell at the sound of Joshua's trumpet blast. Despite its importance, however, the tel does not convey a great deal to the layman. At its foot, and across the road, Elisha's Spring (Nahal Elisha), also known as Sultan's Spring (Ein es-Sultan) provides the abundant fresh waters which have given the area its greenery and fertility. Close by, in a private house, ruins of an **Ancient Synagogue▶▶** (*Open* daily 8–4. *Admission: moderate*) have a lovely 6th-century patterned mosaic floor featuring a menorah (candelabrum) and the inscription "Peace on Israel."

Some 545 yards (500m) east, the ruined **Hisham's Palace▶▶** (*Open* Sat–Thu 8–5, Fri 8–4. *Admission: moderate*) was probably built by Caliph Hisham of Damascus as a winter palace in 743. Four years later, it collapsed in an earthquake. Even so, much survives, including massive columns, a sumptuous bathhouse, exquisite mosaics, and delicate stonework. About 1 mile (2km) farther north, the **Mount of Temptation▶** is where Orthodox churches claim that Jesus was "led into the wilderness to be tempted of the devil" (Matthew 4:1–11). An impressive Greek **monastery** (*Open* Mon–Sat) hangs onto its barren, rocky slope. West of town, at the start of Wadi Qelt, are the ruins of **Herod's Palace▶**. Here, Herod entertained during the winter and, occasionally, got up to darker deeds—he drowned his brother-in-law in the swimming pool here.

JESUS' BAPTISM

The Jordan River east of Jericho is where Jesus was baptised by John, according to Matthew's Gospel. The reputed site (chosen by Byzantines), though signposted, has remained closed for a number of years. However, a visit is possible for members of the Greek Orthodox Church at Epiphany (January) and for Roman Catholics on the third Thursday in October. The Christian Information Center at Jaffa Gate, Jerusalem, has more details.

This harsh desert is typical Judaean terrain

THE SAMARITANS
A tribe and sect descended from the tribes of Ephraim and Menasseh, which broke away from mainstream Judaism around 400BC, the Samaritans hold that only the Torah (the first five biblical books) is sacred, rejecting all subsequent oral and rabbinic law. In that respect they resemble the Karaites. However, the Samaritan Torah contains variations from the Jewish text, including its own version of the Ten Commandments, one of which requires God's followers to build his sanctuary on Mount Gerizim. Samaritans say the original holy Scriptures were altered by Ezra, for which there is some historical evidence. There are no lay teachers, and all ritual remains in the hands of the hereditary priests and Levites (assistants to the priests). Savagely persecuted by Romans, Jews, Muslims and Christians, Samaritans today number only about 600, all living at either Holon or Nablus.

PALESTINIAN POST
In 1994, the Palestinian Authority issued its first postage stamps, initially priced in the British Mandate currency of mils. They were then re-issued in Jordanian currency of fils. Significantly, the Palestinian stamps depicted locations which had not been transferred to Palestinian rule, including Temple Mount and the Tower of David, in Jerusalem.

▶▶▶ Latrun *206A3*

This monastery, fort, wooded park and ruined village is located on the main highway, midway between Jerusalem and Tel Aviv, overlooking the Ayalon Valley. It has become an integral part of Israel and is very unlikely to be given over to Arab rule. Latrun sits in a corner of land that saw some of the worst fighting in 1948. Many lives were lost as Jews struggled to keep the road to the capital open, and Arabs struggled to close it. The abandoned building on the hill above the road was the British police station which had previously overseen this trouble spot. Like many other British military emplacements and police stations, it was handed over to the Arab Legion in 1948. The Ayalon Valley, now blooming with new settlements, has a long history as a battleground. When Joshua came this way and urged the sun and moon to remain still, to prolong the day and give him more time to slaughter the Amorites, they obligingly did as he asked (Joshua 10:12).

On the left-hand side of the road (coming from Jerusalem), the attractive French **Trappist monastery▶▶▶** (*Open* daily) of 1927 stands among its flourishing gardens and crops. The monks produce good wine, spirits and olive oil (on sale by the entrance). Early Christian stonework can be seen in the monastery gardens. On top of the hill behind stand the ruins of a 12th-century **Crusader fort▶**. To the right of the road is the ruined village of Amwas, known in the Bible as **Emmaus▶**. It was here, according to the Gospel of Luke, that Jesus appeared to two disciples after the Resurrection. The ruins of an old church remain, while above it are a monastery and the ruins of a Crusader-era basilica, erected on the site of a Roman villa. Here, the **Canada Park▶** forest makes a pleasant place for a walk and a leisurely picnic.

▶▶ Mar Saba (St. Sabas) Monastery *206B2*

Open: daily 7–11, 1.30–5
The watchtower of this remarkable historic Greek Orthodox monastery lies at the end of a long road that passes through barren hills. West of it rises the sheer Kidron Gorge, pockmarked with caves. A sect of hermits used to reside here, each man living in his own cavern. One of them, arriving here in AD478, was a monk called Sabas, who originally came from Cappadocia. In 492 Sabas founded a monastery on the slope opposite his cave. Sabas became an influential figure, persuading Emperor Justinian to rebuild Bethlehem's Church of the Nativity. After his death in 532, the monastery

of St. Sabas, and the saint's grave, both became popular places of pilgrimage.

Only male visitors may enter the monastery. Women are permitted to enter the Women's Tower on an adjacent hill, but there is a superb view from here!

▶▶ Mini-Israel 206A3

Kibbutz Nachson, tel:08-9222444; www.minisrael.co.il
Open: Sat–Thu 10–6, Fri 10–2. Admission: expensive

This hugely popular family attraction, south of Highway 1 a few minutes from the Latrun exit, displays hundreds of models of major buildings and important sites and landscapes all around Israel. Everything is on a scale of 1:25, with exquisite precision and detail. All is in a lovely setting of miniaturized vegetation. The thousands of human figurines stand about 2.7 inches (7cm) tall. There are restaurants and a shop on the site.

▶▶ Mount Gerizim 206B4

The holy place of the Samaritans rises to 2,890ft (881m) just south of Nablus. The mountain gives glorious views over Nablus and the surrounding countryside. Below the summit are dwellings which the Samaritans use at Pesach (Passover), which they observe as a pilgrim festival, fulfilling every detail of the biblical injunctions concerning the sacrificial slaughter of sheep (carried out at a ceremonial site just off the road). On the same mountain, Samaritans believe that Abraham prepared to sacrifice Isaac.

CASTLES AND ROBBERS

The name Latrun has an odd history. For centuries Christians have held that it comes from the Latin *latro*, robber, and that this was the home of the "Good Thief" crucified alongside Jesus. However, Latrun is probably the Arabic form of the medieval French name, Le Toron des Chevaliers (Knights' Hill), so called because of the Crusader fortification built here in the 12th century. Later the fortress ruins became known as Castrum Boni Latronis (Castle of the Good Thief), compounding the confusion.

Surviving against the odds: the 5th-century Mar Saba monastery

SAMARITAN ISRAELIS
Although Samaritans are not considered Jews, their relationship with Israel is a special one, and their religion is closely connected with Judaism. That is why the Israeli High Court has ruled that Samaritans have the right to become Israeli immigrants with full citizenship. The court was responding to a petition from Samaritans wanting to leave Nablus (on the West Bank) and live at Holon (near Tel Aviv), the other Samaritan population center.

▶ Nablus (Hebrew: Shechem) *206B4*

Nablus is a beautifully located commercial and industrial town, the largest on the West Bank (population 75,000). It is also a passionate center of Palestinian nationalism, with a recent history of violent unrest and political killing. **This is a place to visit with the utmost care, after checking the current situation**.

Nablus is the successor to the biblical city of Shechem, demolished by the Romans in AD70 and replaced in AD72 by Neapolis, literally the "New City." Its name became corrupted to Nablus after the Arab conquest. The small **Samaritan quarter▶** lies in the western part of town.

About 1 miles (2km) southeast of Nablus, **Tel Balata▶▶** is the site of the original Shechem, the place where Abraham was told by God, "Unto thy seed will I give this land." Here Abraham erected his first altar before heading farther south.

Returning from Mesopotamia, Jacob set up camp here. An unfinished Greek Orthodox church, built on top of Crusader foundations, now encloses **Jacob's Well▶▶** (*Open* daily 8–12, 2–5. *Admission free*), set within an elaborate, arched chamber hung with lamps. This is probably the very same well dug by Jacob, on land where he had pitched his tent outside Shechem (Genesis 33:19). It is also the place where, in John's gospel (4:1–42), Jesus asked for a drink from a Samaritan woman, who convinced the townsfolk that he was the Messiah.

Just a few hundred yards north, a white dome covers the reputed **Tomb of Joseph▶** (Joshua 24:32), whose remains were brought here from Egypt.

▶▶ Qumran National Park 206C2

(tel: 02-9942235)
Open: Apr–Sep daily 8–5; Oct–Mar daily 8–5.
Admission: expensive

Famous as the place where the Dead Sea Scrolls were found in 1947 (see page 222), mystery still surrounds Qumran's archeological site, which lies 12 miles (19km) south of Jericho. Built in 150BC, but destroyed in AD70, its stonework is well preserved, with several rooms still enclosed by high walls. Its watch-tower gives an excellent overview of the site. The scrolls were found in almost inaccessible caves (indicated by signs) in the adjacent hillsides. The mystery is that so little is known about Qumran, and theories and questions abound. Was it a community? There are no bedrooms. Just a library? There is a large cemetery. A military fortress, a religious retreat, a factory? Many of the scrolls detail the practices and structure of a rigid, rule-bound community. The prevailing view is that this was a community of some 200 to 400 Essenes (see page 223) who hid their writings to save them from the Romans.

▶▶ Sabastea 206B5

Open: Sat–Thu 8–5, Fri 8–4. Admission: inexpensive

In 876BC King Omri founded the hilltop city of Samaria, or Shomron (I Kings 16:24). Capital of the Northern Kingdom and notorious for abandoning Judaism in favor of Ba'al, it was destroyed in 721BC by Persians, who built a non-Jewish city here. Taken by successive conquerors, it was eventually left deserted. Today there is a small Arab village below the ruins of the ancient city where the most impressive parts date from the Herodian period.

Qumran's ruins continue to mystifiy scholars

MA'ALEH ADUMIM
About 4 miles (6.5km) east of Jerusalem on the main Jericho road, the gleaming white modern blocks of this large new Jewish town (population 20,000) make a stark contrast with the surrounding scenery. At the heart of town is a major archeological site with the dramatic ruins of the Byzantine **Martyrius Monastery▶▶** (*Closed* Shabbat). The largest such structure on the West Bank, it has a display of well-preserved mosaic floors.

SINJIL AND SHILOH
Between Nablus and Ramallah is the village of Sinjil. It was named after St. Gilles, a small town in southern France and ruled by Raymond, Count of Toulouse and St. Gilles, who built the fortress here. On the other side of the road, a turning leads to the site of ancient Shiloh, where the Ark of the Covenant was housed in its Tabernacle during the early days of the Israelite conquest. From here the Ark was seized by the Philistines. Little survives from that period, though there are traces of an even older Canaanite temple, as well as some Byzantine mosaic floors.

In 1947, he didn't remember in which month, a Bedouin shepherd boy named Muhammad ed-Dhib scrambled into a cave near the (then unexcavated) site at Qumran and found strange-looking earthenware jars containing fragments of parchment and leather. It was to prove the most dramatic discovery of ancient Hebrew documents ever found.

NOW READ ON...
Scores of books have been written about the Dead Sea Scrolls, some sensational, some academic, some religious. For a balanced, intelligible overview, authoritative and academic yet accessible, read *The Dead Sea Scrolls* by Geza Vermes (Penguin, 1999).

The caves (top) that held the Dead Sea Scrolls and the jars (above) in which they were stored

What are the Scrolls? After the initial find, a dozen more Qumran caves yielded a vast hoard of ancient manuscripts in Hebrew, and occasionally in Aramaic, ranging from scraps to scrolls. Among them were two complete Books of Isaiah, parts of all the other Hebrew holy books (except for Esther), books of the Apocrypha and Pseudepigraphia (both excluded from the Jewish Bible), and other nonbiblical works such as the Book of Jubilees and the Book of Enoch.

There were prophetic and visionary Jewish books not previously known, and biblical commentaries offering unfamiliar interpretations. The Temple Scroll described the Holy Temple in detail. The enigmatic Copper Scroll discusses hidden treasures. Perhaps most interesting, many scrolls—including at least one written in poetic form—spelled out the Qumran sect's customs and beliefs: the Community Rule (beliefs and rituals), Statutes (practices and laws in detail), the War Scroll (concerning the perpetual struggle between Good and Evil) and dozens more.

Important for Jews The discovery of the Scrolls, the oldest Hebrew texts ever found, revealed two complementary and contradictory things. First, that the Hebrew Scriptures have remained essentially unchanged for at least 2,000 years. Second, parts of the Bible have existed in several versions. Some of the Scrolls resemble later Greek editions, some are like the Samaritan Torah, some contain the Masoretic text used today.

The Qumran scribes also worked on and from other scriptural writings that are no longer part of Jewish liturgy. Individual scribes felt free to "reinterpret" or "edit" texts, showing that they considered the Scriptures a product of the human hand and human mind, albeit perhaps guided by God. Only after the destruction of the Temple did a group of Pharisee rabbis set the seal on a limited and censored body of holy literature, conforming to the Pharisee viewpoint. This included compilation of oral traditions, which they then declared to be the word of God. They thus created a unified, unchallengeable "Orthodoxy" that has, arguably, served well as a survival mechanism during the Diaspora years.

Important for Christians At an early stage in the study of the Scrolls, excited attempts were made to read them as Christian documents. Some wanted to believe that Jesus was the Teacher of Righteousnesss mentioned in various Scrolls, others that it was John the Baptist, or Jesus'

Professor Bieberkraut has devoted his life to conserving the scrolls

kinsman, James. Several agreed that Paul was the Wicked Priest. None of these notions stood up to further study. Instead, it became clear that the Essenes—their ideas predating Jesus by a century or more—had many beliefs that reappeared in the New Testament. The hierarchical community devoted to religious study under a learned leader presaged the monastic and church system. The Essene idea of a Holy Spirit became part of Christian doctrine. Jesus' celibacy and his emphasis on sharing and communality—all these echoed Essene dogma.

Essenes practiced baptism to symbolize a new beginning in religious awareness, as did John the Baptist. Miracle cures associated with forgiveness of sins were well-known among the Scroll writers. One of the Scrolls, the Prayer of Nabonidus (set in the 6th century BC) is about just such a cure. To this extent, the Scrolls show that Jesus' ideas were not new. It is interesting, too, that the New Testament reviles all the other Jewish groups but makes no mention of the Essenes. But Jesus himself was no Essene. Their rigid, structured, and exclusive community prepared itself for the end of days, while Jesus opened his arms to the common people and a new age.

THE ESSENES

The Essenes numbered about 4,000 people and they lived in the period 2nd century BC to 1st century AD. Much has been learned about the Essene sect from the contemporary Roman writer Pliny and the Jewish writer Josephus. Both greatly admired their austerity, asceticism, and firmness of purpose. The Essenes at Qumran (see page 221) were vegetarian, probably celibate and preoccupied with a high degree of ritual purity. They lived communally but under a hierarchy with a Teacher of Righteousness at its head, and believed that they alone were the chosen, the "Sons of Light," who would soon be led by the Messiah to victory over the "Sons of Darkness." They were vehemently opposed to the Hasmonean dynasty, to the Pharisees, the Saducees, the Romans, and to the Temple priests, whom they felt had betrayed and defiled the Temple. They revered the descendants of King David's high priest Zadok as representing the pure line of the priesthood, supplanted by the Hasmoneans.

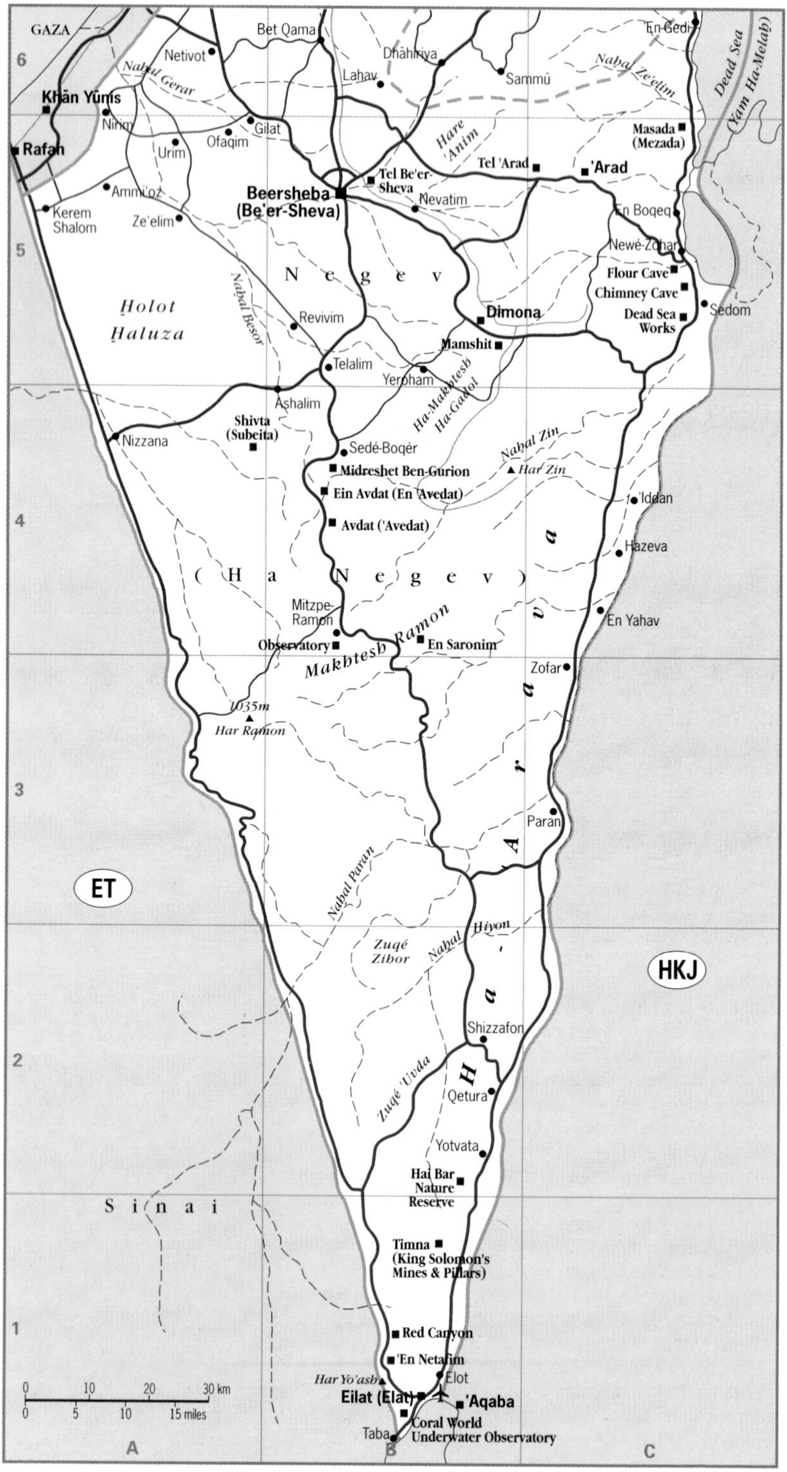
GAZA
Khān Yūnis
Rafah
Netivot
Nahal Gerar
Nirim
Bet Qama
Lahav
Dhāhiriya
Sammū
'En Gedi
Nahal Ze'elim
Dead Sea (Yam Ha-Melah)
Masada (Mezada)
Gilat
Ofaqim
Urim
Hare 'Anim
Tel 'Arad
'Arad
Ammi'oz
Kerem Shalom
Ze'elim
Beersheba (Be'er-Sheva)
Tel Be'er-Sheva
Nevatim
En Boqeq
Newé-Zohar
Flour Cave
Chimney Cave
Dead Sea Works
Sedom
Negev
Holot Haluza
Nahal Besor
Revivim
Dimona
Mamshit
Telalim
Yeroham
Ha-Makhtesh Ha-Gadol
Ashalim
Shivta (Subeita)
Nizzana
Sedé-Boqér
Midreshet Ben-Gurion
Nahal Zin
Har Zin
Ein Avdat (En 'Avedat)
Avdat ('Avedat)
'Iddan
Hazeva
(Ha Negev)
Mitzpe-Ramon
Observatory
Makhtesh Ramon
En Saronim
En Yahav
Zofar
1035m
Har Ramon
Paran
Ha-'Arava
ET
HKJ
Nahal Paran
Zuqé Zibor
Nahal Hiyon
Shizzafon
Zuqé 'Uvda
Qetura
Yotvata
Hai Bar Nature Reserve
Sinai
Timna (King Solomon's Mines & Pillars)
Red Canyon
'En Netafim
Har Yo'ash
Elot
Eilat (Elat)
'Aqaba
Coral World Underwater Observatory
Taba
0 10 20 30 km
0 5 10 15 miles
A B C
1 2 3 4 5 6

The South

Scorched rock eroded by wind-blown sands

THE SOUTH More than half of Israel is desert, including the whole of the southern half of the country, which is taken up with an awesome expanse of scorched rock and raw, naked mountains and scored by arid bone-dry valleys. This is the Negev, picture-book desert, where the harsh dryness, consuming heat and intense light can thrill you—or kill you. Anyone exploring off the beaten path here, or even stepping out of their car for a quick look around in some desert location, will realise within seconds that it is vital to take precautions.

LIFE Yet the Negev is no sterile, lifeless zone. This part of Israel has its tough and resilient flora and fauna, and it also has a human history. Nations have thrived in the Negev, nourished by a body of practical knowledge – of how man can live in such an environment. This has been all but lost. Three thousand years ago, the trade routes of the Nabateans ran through the Negev between the ports at Gaza and Eilat and the Nabatean capital at Petra, in what is now Jordan. Their camel trains carried perfumes and goods of all types, many imported from Europe.

The Nabateans, originally a nomadic Arab people, built caravansaries, even small towns such as Avdat, in this empty land. Water cisterns were placed in flood valleys to catch the runoff after rare desert rains. It has been estimated that a Nabatean settlement collected enough rain in half an hour to provide water for three years. The Romans, conquering Palestine, took over the Nabatean settlements, then fortified and enlarged them. Following the Arab conquest, civilization here disappeared, leaving only the nomadic, pastoral Bedouin as the last people of the desert. A thousand years later, Jewish kibbutzniks arrived.

The serenity of the desert at dawn

►►► REGION HIGHLIGHTS

Dead Sea *pages 230–1*

Eilat *pages 232–37*

Ein Gedi Kibbutz *page 231*

King Solomon's Pillars *page 252*

Masada National Park *pages 242–43*

Nahal David Nature Reserve *page 231*

Observatory, Mitzpe-Ramon *page 246*

DESERT CITIES
Despite annual rainfall of less than 8in (200mm) a year, five Nabatean cities once thrived in the Negev. Taken over by the Romans and later occupied by Byzantines, they continued to prosper right up to the Arab conquest in the 7th century. Four were destroyed. The fifth, Shivta, was occupied by the Arabs but abandoned two centuries later. Known as the Negev Pentapolis, the five desert cities were Avdat, Kalutza, Nitzana, Mamshit and Shivta.

LANDSCAPE The Negev is a region within a much larger arid desert zone reaching into Jordan, Egypt and Saudi Arabia. It is a hard land, consisting mainly of bare granite mountains and dry valleys scattered with sand or stones. The rock faces are streaked through with shades of red, yellow, purple, and even stark black and white. Visually, it is highly dramatic. On the map, the Negev forms a vast upside-down triangle, its point at Eilat on the Red Sea, its base running across Israel from Gaza to the Dead Sea. On its eastern edge, the Dead Sea and the Arava rift valley score a deep frontier between Israel and Jordan. The rather arbitrary border with Egypt's Sinai desert marks the western side. The flatter Arava, where the main road links Eilat to the rest of Israel, is less interesting than the mountainous interior.

LEISURE There is a tremendous amount to see, learn, explore and experience in the Negev—this is Israel's vast, natural adventure playground. Hiking, birdwatching, climbing, riding, jeep tours and camel tours—even sight-seeing—are excitingly different in this terrain. Although even a quick glimpse can be intriguing, you need something more than the usual brief tour taken by every visitor to Eilat to get the best of it. Far more rewarding is to stay in the heart of the desert itself—for example at Mitzpe-Ramon, or at a Dead Sea spa resort such as the lovely Kibbutz Ein Gedi. Remarkably, there is plenty to see in the Negev, including Roman and Nabatean ruins, and a reserve for rare desert animals such as oryx and addax.

THE FUTURE It is an old Zionist dream that towns will prosper in the midst of the Negev. Several kibbutzim shock the eye with their lush fields lying like vivid green rugs on the rocky desert floor. So far, though, attempts to break and harness the spirit of the Negev have met with only limited success. Some Israelis want to keep it that way. Others would like to see the whole place green and cultivated. Inevitably, some parts of the Negev will be developed. Water conservation will become more advanced so that small towns, industry and agriculture may indeed flourish here, but this vast area of heat and rock will never be tamed, never lose its haunting spirit.

►► Arad *224C5*

Arad, the town nearest to the Dead Sea, was founded in 1962 as a base for archeologists and for scientists working in connection with Dead Sea industries. The thriving town has attracted medical staff because of the allergy and asthma treatment that goes on here, as well as university people from Beersheva who like living in modern and civilized Arad. The WUJS (World Union of Jewish Students) based here attracts students of Jewish studies.

The town perches on the hilly ridge just west of the Dead Sea. Immediately noticeable is the tangible cleanliness of the air. There is no pollen at all—all planting in the area is controlled—so the place is a boon for asthmatics. The Margoa Arad Hotel's clinic caters specifically to sufferers.

For visitors, Arad makes an ideal base for touring the northern Negev, the Dead Sea and the wild Judaean hills. The **Visitor Center** is well informed on local antiquities and desert walks and includes the **Arad Museum►** (tel: 07-9954409. *Open* summer Sun–Thu 9–5, winter Sun–Thu 9–4; year round Fri morning. *Admission: moderate*) displays collections of finds from nearby **Tel Arad►** (see page 250). Around the edge of the town are several Bedouin encampments where, despite the unrelieved aridity of the area, sheep and goats are somehow grazed. The Bedouin, who have very good relations with the locals, find casual work in the town.

ARAD FESTIVAL
Arad's usual peace and quiet are broken in July during the huge neo-hippy and hippy-revival rock fest lasting for four days and four nights non-stop. About 200,000 visitors (most aged under 20) gather to enjoy Israeli rock and folk music. During the festival, some 120 performances are staged in the town or under the desert stars at nearby Masada.

►► Avdat National Park *224B4*

(tel: 07-6586391)
Open: daily, summer 8–5; winter 8–4. Admission: moderate

The walled, ruined desert city of Avdat stands on a rocky ridge of high ground just off the main Negev interior road (Route 40), 40 miles (65km) from Beersheva. Built in 300BC by the Nabateans (who called it Obodas, after a king they worshiped as a god), it flourished under Roman and Byzantine rule, but—after becoming a Christian settlement—was abandoned following the Arab conquest in the 7th century. The town has survived remarkably well and has benefited from sensitive and intelligent restoration. It retains superb relics of each period in its history, especially the Roman era, with remnants of streets, dwellings, water cisterns, houses, a Roman bath, temples, basements and wine cellars. Its irrigation system was studied by the Israelis in 1948 and successfully copied at new Negev settlements.

OPENING TIMES
Opening times differ slightly from those in the north, and many sites remain open on the Sabbath. Museums and attractions in the south are usually open 8.30–4.30, with slightly shorter hours on Friday and Saturday.

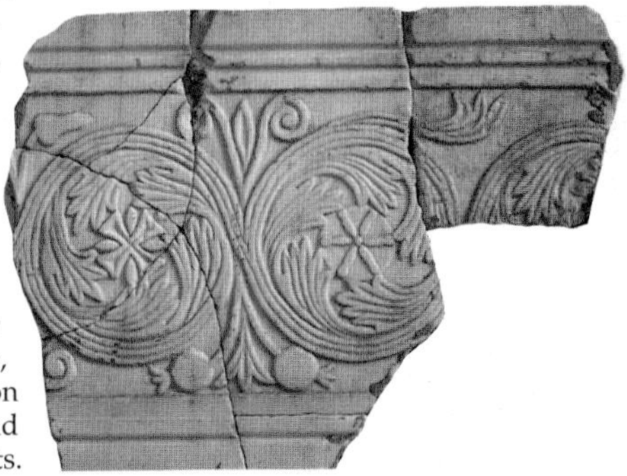

Byzantine frieze, Avdat

Avdat's rock-cut wine cellars and basements

ABRAHAM FOUNDS BEERSHEBA
"And Abraham planted a tamarisk tree in Beersheba, and called there on the name of the Lord, the Everlasting God."
—Genesis 21:33

The Negev Museum, Beersheva

Abraham's Well

▶ Beersheva (Hebrew: Be'er Sheva) *224B5*

The capital of the Negev stands on the desert's flat northern edge, where irrigation and water conservation have dramatically reduced the aridity. The town's picturesque Turkish is animated and appealing. The sprawling newer neighborhoods around the town, which has mushroomed in the last 10 years and continues to grow rapidly (current population: 170,000), are fresh and modern, if less atmospheric. There is also a university and a desert research center. New Russian immigrants make up much of the population.

The town's roots run deep into the pages of the Bible. Cave dwellings of 4000BC and an Israelite town of 1100BC have been found 2.5 miles (4km) east at **Tel Sheva▶** (*Open* daily 9–5. *Admission free*) which has a museum. The patriarch Abraham settled at Beersheva and paid for a well with seven lambs (*be'er sheva* means both "well of seven" and "well of the oath"). Here he was called by God to sacrifice his son Isaac, and here he drove out the Egyptian maidservant, Hagar, with his other son Ishmael, who grew up in the desert and married an Egyptian (Genesis 21 and 22). In the next generation, Jacob left Beersheva on his own journey to Egypt. Later, Beersheva was named the southern limit of the Land of Israel (Judges 20:1).

The **Old City▶▶** dates only from 1907, when the Ottoman Turks revived the town as a Bedouin market. After 1948, Jewish settlers were drawn to the place and developed it. Today it is an attractive area of the city, with pedestrian sections, pavement cafés, and a marked walking tour. The Old City runs to **Abraham's Well▶** (*Closed* Shabbat. *Admission free*). The well is an Ottoman invention, with no known connection to Abraham. In a former mosque off HaAtzmaut Street, the **Negev Museum▶▶** (*Open* Sun–Thu 10–5, Fri–Sat 10–1. *Admission free*) displays artifacts from the town's prehistoric origins.

The town's most interesting feature is the continuing Bedouin presence. However, the **Bedouin market▶▶**, held every Thursday, has been marred by tourism and modernization. Permanent **Bedouin encampments▶▶** can be seen south of the town: Big, dark tents among which human beings, camels and dogs go about their business together under the desert sky.

Abraham was a nomadic herdsman. To understand something of his way of life, and that of the other patriarchs, take a look at the Bedouin who still wander through the harsh desert scenery, far from food or water and accompanied only by a herd of animals that somehow find enough pasture to survive.

Tribal lands Just as the people of Israel comprised 12 tribes, so too are the Bedouin divided into several tribal sub-groups, each with its own territory. In 1946, when the British created the Kingdom of Transjordan (now Jordan), almost 40 percent of its population were described as Bedouin. A report of that year stated: "There are constant seasonal migrations of the Bedouin from Transjordan into Palestine, from Arabia into Transjordan, and back again." The Bedouin are true native inhabitants of these uncultivated regions, former pagans who embraced Islam when it arrived in the 7th century.

Lifestyle Like Abraham, the "nomadic" Bedouin do not in fact wander constantly. They have home ground and they have seasonal territories in which they pasture their herds of sheep, goats and camels. They move according to the seasons and the needs of their animals. Like Abraham, they live in spacious tents, in extended family groups. They are subject to their own tribal laws, enforced by their tribal sheik (chief), which the state recognizes as valid for minor disputes.

The future The official Israeli view of the Bedouin is that they should be housed in modern, well-equipped dwellings as soon as possible and be offered tempting alternatives to this ancient lifestyle. New Bedouin small towns and neighborhoods have thus come into existence. At the same time, Bedouin culture is changing spontaneously. Many tribes have started to erect their own stone dwellings for more permanent habitation on the desert margins. However, the nomadic way of life is enduring and adaptable, and it is unlikely that the Bedouin will be persuaded to abandon it altogether.

BEDOUIN ISRAELIS
Most Bedouin consider it in their interest to support the State of Israel. They distinguished themselves during the War of Independence and assisted the army in later wartime desert operations against neighboring Arab states.

Sociably gathered around a glowing fire (above) Preparing to move on (left)

Pillars of salt

Floating free

THE DEPTHS
At 1,312ft (400m) below true sea level, the shores of the Dead Sea are as low as you can get on the surface of the earth. It is said that the additional 1,312ft (400m) or so of atmosphere filters out enough ultraviolet radiation to help prevent sunburn—but it is not worth running the risk of exposing yourself unnecessarily to find out whether this is true.

►►► The Dead Sea (Hebrew: Yam HaMelach) *224C6*

Dramatic rocky desert surrounds this blue lake, the saltiest on earth and located at the lowest point on earth, at more than 1,312ft (400m) below sea level. It is so salty that the human body floats like a cork and you can sit in the water reading a newspaper. Try it—almost everybody else does!

The saltiest The Hebrew name means Salt Sea, and it is the high level of salts—nearly 10 times the proportion in the Mediterranean—that makes it the Dead Sea. Life is impossible in these weird waters. The Jordan trickles down from the Galilee to the Dead Sea, and gets no farther. The water evaporates, leaving minerals behind. The process has been going on for countless millennia, so the concentration of salt is greater than ever.

At its southern tip, mushroom-like excretions of minerals have formed a bizarre white landscape. This "salt" is not the table condiment variety, but is composed of a mass of minerals. Salt pans in the south draw off magnesium, potassium and sulphates for a multimillion dollar industry. In this same place the biblical cities of Sodom and Gomorrah, synonymous with moral decadence, were situated. According to Genesis (18:16–19:29), when God determined to destroy the cities, he first allowed Lot to flee with his wife. She looked back with regret and was turned into a pillar of salt.

The healthiest The mineral-rich waters, together with hot springs, have given rise to a number of thriving spa resorts. These are nothing new: Cleopatra, Herod and Solomon all visited the Dead Sea for a cure. Their naturally warm waters are a proven help in the treatment of skin and rheumatic problems. It is claimed that the water is beneficial even to healthy skin. Be careful, though, when taking a dip; the salts are painful to the eyes, lips and mucous membrane. After bathing, the skin feels oily and sticky. Unless you are on a cure, it is far

Mineral-rich Dead Sea mud is good for the skin —and has entertainment value too!

more enjoyable to swim in a hotel pool. As a bonus, this arid zone is almost totally pollen-free—giving relief to people with hay fever or respiratory complaints.

South to north The sea measures 47 miles (76km) from tip to tip, and is never more than 10 miles (16km) across. Half of the Dead Sea's western shore is in Israel's Negev region and half in Judaea. The eastern shore is in Jordan. At the southern tip, erstwhile Sodom has been reborn in different guise as **Sedom**, center of the mineral extraction industry. The bleak little hot-springs spa resort of **Zohar▶** stands on the shore just up the road. From here an empty, uninhabited coast road clings to the shore, with a salty desert plain (formerly under water) and mountains to the left. **Ein Bokek▶** is another small waterside spa resort with hotels and a beach. Beyond the turn for **Masada▶▶▶** (see page 242), there is the concrete and glass **Ein Gedi Spa▶**, with showers, beach access, and Dead Sea mud for sale. A little farther is **Ein Gedi▶▶**, a waterside bathing area.

Above it, **Ein Gedi Kibbutz▶▶▶**, established in the 1950s by concentration camp survivors in the harshest environment they could find, is now a comfortable and prosperous community. It has a popular "inn," consisting of terraces of small, simple bedrooms in basic centers scattered about the attractive grounds. The self-service restaurant is of good standard. Most guests are here on spa cures. Ein Gedi's fantastic setting, and its amazing achievement—the lush, florid greenery of the kibbutz bursting from a hillside of barren red desert rock overlooking the Dead Sea—make it a remarkable place to stay. Below Ein Gedi, the **Nahal Arugot▶▶** and phenomenal **Nahal David▶▶▶** nature reserves both consist of desert gulleys with hiking trails running alongside their seasonal riverbeds (see side panel).

Beyond here, the road crosses into Judaea. The scene changes little, and there are no further developments or interesting sights on the road until the area of **Qumran▶▶** (see page 221), near the northern end of the Dead Sea.

NAHAL DAVID

In this nature reserve, a footpath follows the narrow *nahal* (seasonal watercourse), which flows with water and bursts with lush greenery in contrast to the barren rocky cliffs either side. After some 20 minutes the path reaches a lovely waterfall splashing down from high rocks. Turn back here, or take a steeper path to the top of the waterfall, which emerges from a spring, close to which there is a cavern, called Lovers' Cave, and some ancient temple ruins. For a longer walk, leaving most other visitors behind, continue up the *nahal* past two more springs and into the desert canyon beyond. A marked path in the "dry canyon" takes all day to complete; above the springs it can be moist and even muddy underfoot, and winter can bring flash floods. Several animal species thrive in the reserve: little hyrax (or rock rabbits) dash across the path, and there is an ibex observation point. Wild leopard live in the western part of the reserve, but are rarely seen.

Dolphin Reef

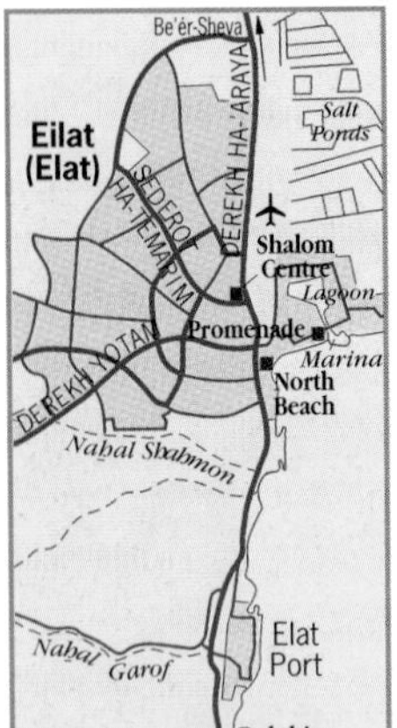

▶▶▶ Eilat 224B1

It's the setting of Eilat (pronounced Ay-*lat*) that makes it so special. Jagged rose-tinted mountains rise up on three sides, forming ridge after ridge of barren rock fading back into scorched wilderness. In front lies the sea, reflecting those red peaks under a blue sky like shimmering silk. The desert air is warm and dry, and there is a sense of immense space, of enormous distances. Eilat feels like a land apart, separated from the rest of Israel not just by the Negev desert, or by time and distance, but also by attitude. It is alive, with a taste for pleasure and action. This southern outpost was, for years, a rough and ready place with a Wild West feel to it. Even though Eilat is now a civilized beach resort with a whole string of good hotels, the old pioneering spirit and taste for adventure linger on in the atmosphere, and in the look of the town. Even so, Eilat is not as new as it looks. It even gets a mention in the earliest books of the Bible. However, almost everything is open on the Sabbath: Eilat must be just about the least religious town in the whole of Israel.

The town center The heart of Eilat remains surprisingly small and easy to explore. There are some good shops, especially the enjoyable indoor Mall Hayam near the beachfront. In Eilat Israel's usual 17 percent VAT is not charged. To discover the finer things in life, look in the hotels and in the beach areas, a little separated from the rest of town.

North Beach Within easy walking distance of the town center, Eilat's main leisure district is **North Beach▶▶▶**, which runs along the tip of the warm Gulf of Eilat (or Gulf of Aqaba). The beach is of mixed sand and pebble, lined by palm and tamarisk trees, as well as bars and watersports equipment rental shops. Running alongside is a paved promenade, with a few good restaurants as well as a string of cheap, tacky stalls. North Beach ends at the **marina and lagoon▶▶**. A humpback pedestrian bridge crosses the water to another promenade area, which turns to follow the lagoon waterside, with shops and eateries alongside. Most of Eilat's leading and popular hotels are clustered around here. On the seafront beyond North Beach, the two **Lagoons▶▶** include a swimming lagoon with beaches. The **Royal Promenade▶▶** pushes the resort eastwards towards the Jordan border, via the Royal Beach and Dan hotels.

Kings City▶▶ At the end of Eilat's promenade, near the Eastern Lagoon, the spectacular family attraction, King's City, is a lavish, over-the-top Bible-themed leisure park showcasing traditional stories of ancient times. Rides and adventures are put on at, for example, the Cave of the Bible, Cave of Wisdom, the Cave of Illusions and the good ship Solomon. The kitsch Las Vegas-style re-creations of the Egypt of the pharoahs is good fun for everyone. King's City has fast-food restaurants and several shops. (*Open* 9–1, 6–10. *Admission: expensive.*)

Coral Beach To find Eilat's marine nature reserve, drive out of town and down the Taba road on the western shore of the Gulf. Pass by the unusual **Red Sea Star** restaurant, standing in (and below) the water (*see Restaurants, page 283*). Just after the port is **Dolphin Reef▶▶** (*Open* daily 9–5; www.dolphinreef.co.il), a delightful pay-to-enter sand and pebble bay with an enjoyable beach bar-restaurant. There are also several large enclosures in which you can "swim with the dolphins." Or, if you prefer, you can

PETRA AND AQABA
With the opening of Eilat's Arava border crossing into Jordan, Petra makes a superb excursion. The amazing desert capital of the Nabateans, with its temples, treasury, tombs, amphitheater and monastery all cut out of the pink sandstone cliffs, can be visited with an overnight stop. Allow time to linger in Aqaba, Eilat's unassuming neighbor on the Red Sea shore, and an entirely non-touristic Arabian town. Inclusive trips from Eilat are bookable through all hotels.

Artistic efforts point the way

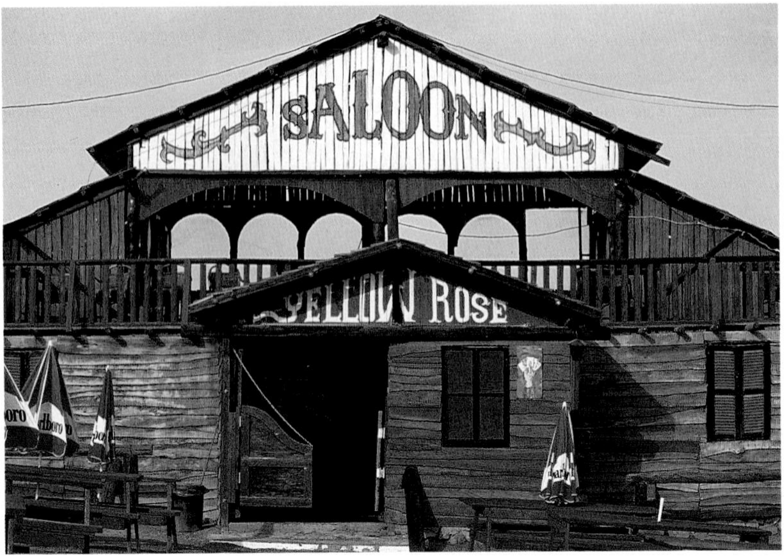

Bring the children to Texas Ranch

Coral Beach gives access to the underwater coral reserve

watch from floating pontoons as the endearing dolphins—along with sea lions and turtles—frolic in the water. Farther down the road, on the right, is the **Texas Ranch▶** (*Admission: moderate*), a mock Wild West town that children will enjoy. Just south, the pay-to-enter **Coral Beach▶▶▶** (*Open* summer, daily 9–6; winter 9–5. *Admission: moderate*) and its offshore waters form an unusual and important nature reserve, a magnificent underwater garden of coral and warm-water fish (see page 236). This is one of the world's leading sites for diving and snorkeling. A visitor center on the beach is geared up to deal with divers' needs and give instruction (for children too). Marked "paths" under the water lead around the coral reef.

View the creatures of the deep by submarine or underwater observatory

At the southern end of Coral Beach is **Coral World Underwater Observatory Marine Park▶▶▶** (tel: 08-6364200; www.coralworld.com. *Open* Sat–Thu 8.30–4, Fri 8.30–3. *Admission: expensive*), the major Eilat attraction. This comes in several sections, with a recommended route indicated by directional arrows. First come the impressive aquariums, including a circular reef tank which visitors view from the middle, and a shark pool. An outdoor pool contains turtles and rays. The walkway then reaches the superb **Underwater Observatory▶▶▶**. This is no ordinary attraction, and should not be missed. Spiral steps descend to viewing areas, where you can literally walk under the sea, peering through thick windows at a seabed heaving and moving with strange life forms, like a bizarre jungle. There are no barriers or nets to keep the fish in. What you see is really living out there. The Observatory also rises high above the waves, giving magnificent views across the gulf, to the red mountains of Jordan and Saudi Arabia.

Also available at the Observatory, the **Oceanarium▶** (tel: 07-6376666. *Open* daily) is a virtual trip beneath the waves—a three-screen simulator where spectators move in hydraulically operated seats while watching a spectacular audiovisual show. For the real thing, a trip in the **Yellow Submarine▶▶**, called *Jacqueline* (Mon–Sat from 9am. Check in 45 minutes before boarding), takes visitors on a one-hour journey beneath the Red Sea, giving a close-up view of the exotic underwater world. The 75ft (23m-long), 10ft (3m) wide submarine descends to a depth of 60m, then gradually climbs to 98ft (30m), beside the coral reef wall.

Finally, walk through the intriguing **Marine Museum▶** for a closer look at some of the species that live here.

Taba The coast road continues from Eilat to the Egyptian frontier, established in 1989 after a long dispute over its location. The beach along this stretch is poor and the setting bleak, though the mountain views are dramatic. The Princess Hotel just before the crossing, is one of Eilat's most remarkable resort complexes.

ISRAELI FOLKLORE

Since Israel is hardly a half-century old, its "folklore" is necessarily something of a recent invention, but simple traditional Jewish dances and shows based upon Jewish themes and customs are a popular entertainment. The weekly Israeli Folklore Evening at Kibbutz Eilot, 2 miles (3km) from town, makes a good night out. It is held every Saturday evening, and the price includes a typical kibbutz buffet dinner, free drinks and transport from Eilat to the kibbutz, as well as a singing-and-dancing extravaganza under the desert stars.

The greatest treasure of Eilat is the water itself. Beneath its surface lies a whole spectacular world of color and coral, home to thousands of exotic fish, looking like rainbow fragments. For a closer encounter, dive in: The water is gorgeously warm (constantly around 70°F/21°C). No wonder this is a world capital for scuba and snorkeling.

MARINE RESERVE
Coral Beach is managed by Israel's Nature Reserves Authority. The area was studied over a period of years following the creation of the State of Israel, and declared a nature reserve in 1964.

Dali-esque fish drift among the vividly colored foliage. Tiny silver shoals like iron filings dart past as if towards a magnet. There are fish with pink dots, blue stripes, yellow patches and long feathery spikes. Is that a plant, a fish, or just a stone lying on the bottom? Seemingly all three, and it is called a stone fish. Whether for experts, amateurs or complete novices, diving at Eilat is a remarkable experience, and one not to be missed.

The reserve The Gulf of Eilat (or Aqaba), part of the Red Sea, is among the northernmost extensions of tropical ocean. The Eilat coral reef is the most northerly in the world. Starting just below the surface of the warm, lapping waters, the coral reef is 1,297 yards (1,190m) in length, reaches to within 12 yards (11m) of the high-tide line, and drops 20ft (6m) to the seabed at its farthest edge. The reserve extends out from this point on to the densely populated seabed where thousands of species of tropical fish and other sea animals can be seen.

Sea life The surface of a coral reef is a mass of living animals (mainly stony corals), while the rest consists of fossilized or dead corals from previous generations. The corals live for hundreds of years, growing at an incredibly slow rate, as they expand the existing colony or create new ones. Living among the hard corals are several species of soft coral, looking like brightly colored seaweeds, their delicate tendrils waving to and fro.

Eilat's coral reefs throng with colorful fish

Pretty as they are, corals can be dangerous, and it is best to avoid being scratched by them. One variety called fire coral (not a true coral but a similar life form) gives a burning sting that marks the skin. Sharing the seabed with the corals are weird molluscs and other invertebrates, such as giant clams and sea anemones. Other plant-like animals move around at night, including the sea lilies, sea urchins, and different kinds of starfish that hide during the

SCUBA HIRE
Scuba equipment can be rented from several firms in Eilat, mostly along the Coral Beach area. The tourist office and most hotels have the names of diving rental companies.

WARNING
Wear trainers or plastic shoes in the water. Swim, don't walk, except where indicated on marked pathways. Don't touch anything at all underwater, whether it seems to be a plant, fish, animal or rock. Some of these are in fact highly venomous creatures whose poison can injure or kill.

Diving at Eilat (left) leads to close encounters with Dali-esque fish (below)

day. Day and night, the coral throngs with dazzlingly hued fish. Pretty damsels and clowns, butterflies and parrots, blues and cleaners can be seen during the day, while darkness brings out the uglier, highly poisonous varieties, such as the lion, scorpion and stone fish. Most coral-dwelling fish are exceptionally thin, enabling them to slip in and out of the coral construction.

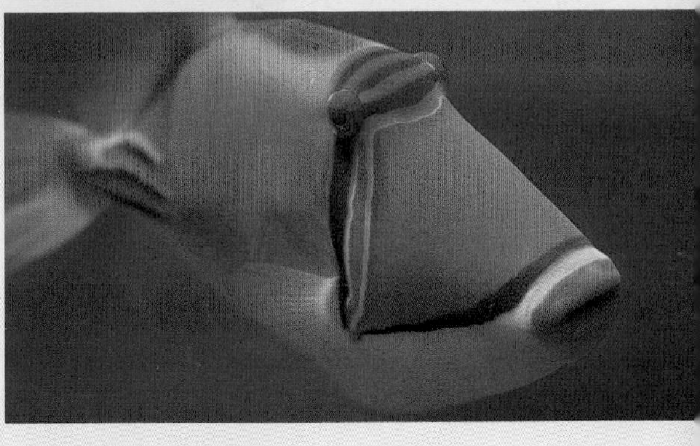

Snorkel and scuba It is possible to get a good look at all these creatures without even getting wet, from the Underwater Observatory (see page 235), the Red Sea Star restaurant (see page 283), or on a glass-bottom boat tour. For a more intimate look, get in the water at the Coral Beach marine reserve (see pages 233–4), one of the best places anywhere in the world for diving. If you want to scuba dive, bring certification card and log book in order to rentequipment. If you wish to learn, bring a medical certificate.

The Negev is no theme park. This is raw and dangerous wilderness, yet majestic and beautiful. No visit to southern Israel would be complete without an off-road excursion into this haunting, rocky terrain. The best introduction is by guided tour in a four-wheel-drive jeep—desert tours and excursions are referred to as "safaris."

WALKING IDEAS
Experienced hikers thinking of tackling a short outing in the southern Negev should ask the tourist office for its free booklet *Routes and Trails in Eilat Mountains.*

If you are hungry for something challenging, rest assured that an all-day trip into the desert, even with a group and a guide, will be something to remember. The vehicles do not offer pampered luxury. The ride is rough, entailing a certain amount of clinging on for dear life. As if that were not enough, there are two-day, even three-day trips, with nights spent under the stars. Trips on horseback, or even by camel, are available. It is also possible to see the desert on foot, perhaps combined with jeep touring; for this, it is even more important to have an experienced guide, except on short marked trails.

Desert encounter On closer inspection, you'll see that the desert is not totally barren. Isolated acacia trees spring from the solid rocks, red-berried mistletoe clings to the branches. Tiny sandbirds dart about. Ibex sprint with ease up near-vertical cliff faces. Caper bushes hang from granite clefts: The edible part is the flower bud, but the caper fruit can be eaten too—it tastes like mustard and, so Bedouin say, improves virility.

Desert safaris reveal that life exists in the wilderness

Around Eilat A quick four-wheel-drive trip into the desert is a popular excursion for Eilat tourists. There are outings that last an hour or two, all morning or all day. Most jeep tours, or "desert safaris," make their way into the wilderness from the Coral Beach area. There is plenty to see, even within just a few minutes: the incongruous, lush spring of **Ein Netafim**►► where animals and birds gather; the vivid sandstone of the amazing **Red Canyon**►, where there is an easy one-hour marked hiking trail between the rock

The majestic landscape of Sde Boker

faces. **Mount Yoash** offers a panoramic view reaching into four countries—Israel, Egypt, Jordan, and Saudi Arabia. Either do-it-yourself or guided trips on noisy "fun buggies"—small motorized all-terrain vehicles—can be a lot of laughs, but you will miss out on the magic, silence and beauty of the real desert experience.

The Arava Part of the Syrian-African Rift, the Arava is a deep lowland at the eastern edge of the Negev, marking the border with Jordan. A main road runs along it from Eilat to the Dead Sea, and offers the easy way to penetrate the desert while staying on a modern highway, virtually free of traffic. Sights along the way include **Timna▶▶** (see page 251) and, just a little further north, the **Hai Bar Reserve▶▶** (see page 240). For the more intrepid, there are several simple-to-follow three- to four-hour walking trails that follow desert canyons, signposted off the road, such as **Wadi Sh'horet▶▶**, **Nahal Barak▶▶** and the **Amran Valley▶▶**. Be aware, though, of current flash flood warnings.

Central Negev Several firms, notably the excellent market leader, Desert Shade (tel: 07-335377), run a range of long and short off-road drives. Some combine with walks through the immense and magnificent Makhtesh Ramon crater. Near Mitzpe-Ramon, you will find Nabatean and Roman ruins, strange flora, the tracks of strange fauna and other-worldly scenery. Other trips through the desert go to Avdat, the ruined Nabatean city, and to Sde Boker, the desert kibbutz where former Prime Minister David Ben-Gurion once lived. It can be cool in these higher regions in winter, and snow in winter is not unknown.

Eastern Negev Walks and drives from Ein Gedi include explorations of the Dead Sea hinterland and hikes up the steep, stony footpath to Masada (see page 242). There is also a great hike from Ein Gedi along the enclosed valley trail of the Nahal Arugot Nature Reserve to a waterfall and pool in the midst of desert.

TAKE WATER!
On any trip into the Negev, summer or winter, it is essential to carry adequate supplies of drinking water—you will need about 2 pints (1 litre) per person for every hour spent in the desert.

GET BACK TO WHERE YOU ONCE BELONGED
"At all times one should live in Israel, and not live outside Israel, even in a place the majority of whose population is Jewish."
—Maimonides, *The Laws of Kings* (5:9–12), 1197

"I call upon you, our brothers and sisters in the Diaspora, to send your children here."
—Ezer Weizman, President of Israel, Independence Day speech, 1997

The upper Zin ravine, cut by the Ein Avdat

►► Ein Avdat National Park 224B4

(tel: 07-6555684)

Open: daily, summer 8–5; winter 8–4. Admission: moderate

The Ein Avdat, or Avdat Spring, runs through the upper Zin ravine in the midst of the Negev. To either side, the ravine walls rise to crests of striking white chalk and dark flint. The spring and its surroundings form an oasis bursting with plant life surrounded by harsh, spectacular aridity. Trees even grow in places around the spring, and at the head of the ravine there is a single 250-year-old pistachio tree. Desert animals and birds gather here for food and drink. Two marked walks provide an opportunity to explore the area thoroughly. The longer route involves some steep climbing and the use of metal ladders. The shorter walk is much easier, but takes in all the main sights.

DINNER GUESTS

Numerous guided trips in the desert offer dinner or tea in a real Bedouin tent with a real Bedouin playing host. The Bedouin consider the whole thing just a game in which they win a few shekels from the gullible tourists, and the experience bears little resemblance to an authentic encounter with nomads. For all that, it is interesting and enjoyable to sit on the floor in a huge tent, eating meat and pita bread or being poured a cup of tea by a Bedouin in full traditional attire.

►► Hai Bar Reserve 224B2

Yotvata Hai Bar (tel: 08-6373057)

Open: daily 8–5 (4 in winter and Fri). Admission: moderate

On the Arava road, 22 miles (35km) north of Eilat, a side road on the right leads to this curious desert enclosure that mixes nature reserve and zoo, combining entertainment with serious conservation. Visitors may only explore the reserve by means of guided minibus tours, which include a walk. Most or all of the desert creatures that can be seen, have at some time been native to the Negev. The reserve's objective is to breed these animals for reintroduction into the wild, and to disperse some species throughout Israel's other 280 nature reserves. Many of the species here are not usually found in zoos and most visitors will never

have come across them before. For example, you will see the ongar (or Asiatic wild ass), an elegant, nervous little wild donkey like a miniature horse. Also to be seen is the grey Somalian wild ass, precursor to the donkey and the antelope-like oryx and white oryx, that can live for prolonged periods without any water at all. The walk takes you through small carnivore enclosures, where the species include the lovely fennec, like a little golden fox, the sand cat, the ancestral wild cat, and the caracal, like a small lioness. There are also lynxes, wolves, hyenas and leopards, as well as snakes, lizards and birds of prey.

▶ Mamshit (Arabic: Kurnub) *224B5*

(tel: 07-6556478)
Open: daily 8–5 (4 in winter and Fri). Admission: moderate
Mamshit is the most northerly of the five walled and fortified Negev cities of the Nabateans, located 4 miles (6.5km) from Dimona, southeast of Beersheva. Mamshit changed little during the Roman and Byzantine periods, and so preserves many elements of its original character. The fine, pale-stone ruins still possess a certain grandeur. At Mamshit, there are remnants of the main street, houses, arched lintels, stables, an imposing flight of steps and two Byzantine churches. Several tomb chambers have been excavated at the cemetery outside the town.

The nearby Camel Ranch is a fun desert-encounter and resort base, providing accommodations in a Bedouin tent. Bedouin hosts entertain with good food and traditional music. Guests can set off with guides to explore the desert by jeep, by camel or on foot.

A well-camouflaged caracal

OVER THE BORDER
The Negev continues, across the Egyptian border into the Sinai, where several intriguing sights can be found within easy reach of Eilat. Highlights are Ein Hudra (a beautiful oasis), the Nawamis (well-preserved Bronze Age burial sites), St. Catherine's Monastery, and Mount Sinai. In the other direction, trips can be made to Petra, the rock-carved Nabatean desert capital (see page 233).

Mountaintop Masada

▶▶▶ Masada National Park 224C5

(tel: 07-6584117)
Open: Apr–Sep 8–5 (4 on Fri) ; Oct–Mar 8–4 (3 on Fri).
Admission: expensive

A ruined mountaintop fortress in the desert overlooking the Dead Sea, Masada (pronounced Matzada) has become a potent symbol for the state and people of Israel (see side panel opposite). Israeli soldiers are sworn in here with the words, "Masada shall not fall again."

Reaching the top the easy way

Reaching the site From the parking areas, visitors climb dusty Snake Path to the mountain top —the walk taking about an hour. Alternatively, a cable-car carries visitors up the mountain, a marvellous ride with magnificent views, leaving but 80 steps to be climbed to the site entrance.

History The small Hasmonean fort at Masada assumed its present form under King Herod (40–4BC), who constructed the palaces and fortifications as a desert retreat. He did not make use of it, but a Roman garrison was always stationed here. In AD66, the knife-bearing Sicari, or Zealots, captured Masada from the Romans at the start of the First Jewish Revolt (AD66–73). As the revolt was crushed in other parts of the country, Zealots made their way here. Eventually the Romans besieged Masada with 15,000 men, and traces of their camps can be seen at the foot of the mountain. The Zealots and their families numbered about 967. The Romans built a ramp up the western side of the mountain and breached the wall on the first day of Pesach in the year AD73. They found everyone dead, except for one woman and her children.

She told them that when defeat seemed inevitable, the Zealot leader, Ben-Yair, made a rousing speech praising death above defeat and dishonor. Ten men were selected by lot to kill everyone else. Every family group lay down, and all were killed. Finally the 10 killed each other, one last man killing himself. She alone decided to live.

The Romans occupied Masada again briefly. Byzantine monks resided here in the 5th and 6th centuries, after which the site was abandoned.

Visiting the site Snake Path Gate passes through the citadel's original guardroom into the site, which consists of a vast space open to the sky, steep and rocky in places, with several ruined structures, the whole encircled by ramparts. A black line on the structures shows the height that remained standing until reconstruction work began in the 1980s. Turn right to follow the fortifications; the walls here are low, giving an impressive view across the flat red and white terrain to the Dead Sea. You will reach a small **quarry▶**, spacious **storerooms▶**, that held a year's supply of stores in big jars, and a **look-out▶▶**. Just beyond, projecting northwards on a rocky crag, is the **Northern Palace▶▶▶**, Herod's immense private dwelling. Built on three levels, it retains corridors with several large and small rooms leading off. There is also a splendid **bathhouse▶**, with traces of mosaic and frescoes, and several hot and cold pools. In front of the bathhouse, the **upper terrace▶▶** of the Northern Palace villa gives a fantastic view.

The marked path next follows the perimeter of Herod's Northern Palace, above a vertiginous precipice. From here the **Roman ramp▶▶** can be seen (on the Arad side). Leaving the palace on the southwestern side, there is an **administration building▶** and a **mikveh▶** (ritual bath), close to the **storerooms' watch-tower▶▶▶**, which gives a clear overall impression of the site.

Now follow the western rampart wall, where there are a number of interesting structures, including a 2,000-year-old **synagogue▶**, the oldest ever found. The **observation point▶** here marks the point where the Roman ramp reached the citadel. This is close to the Byzantine western gate, the point of entry for walkers from the Arad side (the walk up the ramp takes 20 minutes). The **Western Palace▶▶** here has a complex of small rooms, including baths, with mosaic decoration. Close by is a small Byzantine **church▶**.

A longer tour through the large, open southern section of the citadel reaches **bakeries▶**, **large pools▶** for bathing, a neat, circular **columbarium▶** (or dovecote) and a **water cistern▶**, probably all of the Herodian period.

Roman under-floor heating

VISITING MASADA

Signs for Masada lead from near the southern end of the Dead Sea and from the desert town of Arad (28 miles/45km east of Beersheva). It can be approached from either direction, but both roads end at car-parks at the foot of the mountain (after visiting Masada you must return the way you came). Here, stores, eating places, and toilets are available. A visit to the site takes several hours. Recommended routes around the site are marked. It is a good idea to wear a sunhat and take drinking water. Masada is open daily from dawn to dusk. Walk up, or take the cable-car (operates from 8 till 4).

HISTORY LESSON UNDER THE STARS

A *son et lumière* in the extraordinary setting of Masada is as dramatic as you might expect. Using the latest in light and sound techniques, the show is staged in an amphitheater at the foot of the Masada mountain and brings to life the story of the citadel from Herod's construction to the Roman conquest. The amphitheater lies on the Arad side of Masada, and the show takes place every Tuesday and Thursday in summer at 9pm.

That Israel has "made the desert bloom" is a cliché. Before Israel was created, much of this land was tough stony heathland, swamp and dunes. Travelers in the 19th century spoke of the appalling poverty of the land. Early Zionists set themselves the task of reclaiming it, draining the Hula, planting the hills of Galilee and Carmel, and irrigating the Negev.

ISRAEL IN THE TIME OF PLENTY
"For the Lord thy God bringeth thee into a good land, a land of brooks of water, of fountains and depths that spring out of valleys and hills; a land of wheat, and barley, and vines, and fig trees, and pomegranates; a land of olive oil and honey; a land wherein thou shalt eat bread without scarceness, thou shalt not lack any thing in it."
—Deuteronomy 8:7–9

Milk and honey Was Israel ever a land of milk and honey? When the British took it over from the Turks, it consisted largely of infertile and arid terrain, supporting a total population of under 700,000, most of whom scraped the most meager of livings. Yet the Bible records that 3,500 years ago fields of grain, vineyards and oak forests ran from Jerusalem to the sea. It seems likely that, as the generations passed, more and more forest was cut down to make way for fields. Without the tree cover to bind the soil, storms washed the surface away. Overgrazing by sheep and goats made it difficult for trees to re-establish themselves and the land became impoverished.

Reclamation The British and the early Zionists together started the process which proved the land could be drained, improved, planted and cultivated—or, in Zionist terminology, redeemed. The new State of Israel continued the task of reclaiming poor land. Kibbutzim and *moshavim*—communal settlements whose occupants were usually willing to undertake difficult tasks for little reward—played a vital role in this process, and still do. Scientific research has also contributed. The Rothschilds brought in agronomists from the south of France to help replant the Carmel as a vineyard region. Millions of trees have been planted by the Jewish National Fund.

The rewards These efforts have paid off. Israel is now completely self-sufficient in agriculture, and exports large quantities of produce. Previously uncultivated areas are now intensively farmed. The range of crops grown is astonishing, with bananas, apples, avocados and oranges growing alongside each other. The Sharon Plain has become one of the world's most productive citrus regions. Galilee farmers have prospered with terraced fields of grain. Cotton, cereals and beet thrive in the

Corn, vetch and poppies (top)—typical roadside wildflowers
Turf production (right)

Jezreel Plain. The sunbaked Arava, on the Negev border with Jordan, supports thousands of acres of tomatoes and vegetables. Vineyards again flourish on the slopes of Mount Carmel. Careful planning, mechanization and skillful use of water account for much of the success.

Water, water everywhere All over Israel, the land is being irrigated, mostly by the underground drip-feed system, which was invented here and is now used all over the world. The system allows tiny drops of water to cover a wide area, being channeled directly to the roots of crop plants. This process makes maximum use of a scarce resource—and water is very scarce indeed. The National Water Carrier pumps water from the Sea of Galilee to reservoirs all over the country. New reservoirs are always being built. Forty new reservoirs, built mainly to catch storm runoff, have been constructed in the Beit She'an and Jordan valley areas, south of the Sea of Galilee. Much of the water used for irrigation is brackish—not clean. It has been found that this actually yields much better results.

Natural riches Land reclamation is not all about agriculture. Israel has some 300 nature reserves and an extraordinary variety of flora and fauna, with more than 2,000 plant species, hundreds of types of resident birds and almost 100 different kinds of native animals. By setting aside over 579sq miles (1,500sq km) for wildlife reserves, it is hoped that this abundance and diversity will flourish throughout the country.

MILK AND HONEY
"If the Lord delight in us, then he will bring us into this land, and give it us; a land which floweth with milk and honey."
—Numbers 14:8

Ben-Gurion University research station: testing the tolerance of various plants

The road south of Mitzpe-Ramon crosses the floor of the huge Makhtesh, or crater

▶▶ Mitzpe-Ramon *224B4*

Mitzpe-Ramon means "Ramon Viewpoint." The settlement was built in the 1950s in the optimistic belief that it would grow into a prosperous desert city. It hasn't yet, and remains a rather bleak one-horse town. It does, however, have one astonishing treasure: Ramon Viewpoint.

The Makhtesh The town has a setting that few places can rival, standing on top of a dramatic cliff with an extraordinary view, a sight that simply compels awe. Spread out below the cliff is the immense desert canyon called Makhtesh Ramon, or Ramon Crater. A *makhtesh* is a gigantic canyon-like crater formed not by a river but by huge natural cracks in the Earth's surface. At 154sq miles (400sq km), it is the world's largest. On the far side, the canyon rises to barren mountainous uplands. The whole scene is raw, vast and unspoiled. If standing in the open air, on the teetering brink of a 3,000ft (915m) drop, does not appeal, go into the town's clifftop **Observatory and Visitor Centre▶▶▶** (tel: 07-6588691. *Open* Sun–Thu 9–5, Fri–Sat 9–4. *Admission: moderate*). This semicircle of glass, projecting over the cliff edge, gives a glorious opportunity to linger safely over the view. It also houses an excellent exhibition explaining what has been learned from the canyon, together with displays of what has been found in it, and an audiovisual show about its creation.

This gigantic cut in the surface of the globe has been uniquely valuable to geologists, providing a window into the planet's earliest history. The strata at the bottom of the canyon date from 200 million years ago, and successive bands of color on the cliffs show the eons rising to reach our own era. In its dizzying timescale, and in its sheer physical size, Makhtesh Ramon puts humanity into perspective.

Exploring the Makhtesh For rugged and experienced individualists, well equipped with maps, local knowledge and plenty of drinking water, there are several hiking trails through the Makhtesh. For a safer adventure, with all the benefits of having an experienced and capable companion at your side, book a guided four-wheel-drive

HAMSIN
An annoying feature of the Negev climate is the Hamsin, the uncomfortably hot and dry wind that blows occasionally in April, May, September and October. The name comes from the Arabic for fifty—supposedly the number of days the wind will blow once it starts.

tour, which can be combined with a walk. On a Makhtesh tour, footpaths and tracks reveal the astonishing character of the terrain. One trip passes through a dazzling white limestone ravine, narrow and echoing, the rock slashed and riddled with holes by rough weather in seasons long past. Leopard tracks run across the paths, and multicolored lizards bask nearby. Bedouin signs, made of stones or tied into a bush, are translated by your guide. Visiting the remains of past civilization and the natural wonders within the Makhtesh is like finding lost treasure: Such places are hard to locate without a guide. **En Saronim▶▶**, not far from the main road, is a 2,000-year-old caravansary. Such camel-train stopovers appear every 15 miles (24km) or so, the distance a loaded camel can walk in a day. Nearby is a gracefully arched water cistern, cool and fresh, which once held over 22,000gal (100,000 litres) of water. It could still be used today. Another high point is **Ktsra▶▶**, a ruined Nabatean fortress; from the hills above, vistas open up across landscapes of sometimes formless chaos, a world of chalk and flint, black and white swirling shapes, ridges, edges and clefts, leading to the incongruous sight of snow-covered peaks in Jordan.

Around the town Other sights nearby include the popular **Alpaca Farm▶** (*Open* daily 9–6. *Admission: moderate*), which makes for an interesting outing, entertaining for children. Not just alpacas, but llamas, angora goats, angora rabbits, camels, Pyrenean sheepdogs and Welsh border collies are reared here. The animals are all harmless, though at times alpacas show their irritation by spitting at visitors!

DESERT DELIGHTS
Hikers in the desert should cover up against the sun and take care to avoid some of the less welcoming inhabitants: highly venomous yellow scorpions, vipers, black widow spiders, and the sand flea, whose bite is said to be able to kill a dog.

The view from Mitzpe-Ramon looks far across an awesome scene of arid desert

Israel lies at the junction of several important bird migration routes between Europe, Asia and Africa. Literally millions of birds—including birds of prey, storks and pelicans—pass overhead twice a year, between February and May, and September and November, and one of the best places to come for birds is Eilat.

TAKING TO THE AIR
It is possible to take wing yourself in a motor glider, arranged by Eilat's International Birdwatching Centre (tel: 07-374276). With the engine turned off, you drift silently in the sky among the flocks, enjoying a close-up view of the migrating birds.

Bird highway More than 150 different species of bird pass through Israel on their migration routes. Birdwatchers have counted 750,000 buzzards and eagles alone passing over Eilat—10 times as many as in the world's other great birdwatching area, the Bosphorus. The birds' main route is the Arava/Jordan Valley, which takes them from Eilat, via the Dead Sea, to the Galilee, after which the different species take different paths into Europe and Asia. The Arava/Jordan Valley forms part of the Syrian-African rift, which guides the birds between continents on their long journey. On reaching Eilat after the unbroken flight from Africa, millions of the smaller birds touch down for a rest on the salt-pans beside Eilat and the fields of Kibbutz Eilot, 2 miles (3km) from town.

Watching the birds Free birdwatching walks depart from Eilat three times a week, led by a qualified guide. Held on Sunday, Tuesday and Thursday, they start at 8.30am from Marina Bridge; bring a hat, water and binoculars. The walks last three hours and follow an easy path via the beach to the extensive salt ponds and Kibbutz Eilot fields. For those who prefer to go on their own, a marked trail takes a similar route. The best times to watch bird-life are early morning and late afternoon. Numerous small waders and waterfowl, plovers and sandpipers, some migratory, some resident, will be seen. An interesting colorful bird to look for is the little green bee-eater. Coots, herons, stilts and flamingos wade in the shallows. Birds of prey, such as kites and hawks, try to pick off the smaller birds. In the Eilot fields, wagtails, warblers and pippits scamper down below, while millions of swallows and swifts fly overhead.

Pelicans (top); bird-watchers (below)

►► Sde Boker (Sedé-Boqér) *224B4*

This desert kibbutz (www.sde-boker.org.il) attracted the attention of Israel's rugged, no-nonsense first prime minister, David Ben-Gurion. He and his wife, Paula, became members in 1953. The kibbutz itself is a hard-working community cultivating fields and orchards, and manufacturing adhesive tape. Members, totaling just a few hundred, live in plain white bungalows, some draped with dazzling purple bougainvillaea. The **Ben-Gurions' 'hut'►►►** (tel: 07-6560320. *Open* Sun–Thu 8.30–3.30, Fri 8.30–2, Sat 8.30–2.30. *Admission free*) was originally only slightly superior to those of the other kibbutzniks.

A guided tour of the house, unchanged since the 1960s, reveals the little details of this gigantic character. His library, for example, contains 5,000 volumes on every subject, yet not one novel. In the kitchen is a list, pinned up by Paula, detailing her husband's medication and menus. We see that the pair slept in separate—and very different—bedrooms, his stark and spartan, hers adorned with personal mementoes; a place where she sat dreaming of living somewhere more comfortable.

A 15-minute drive from the kibbutz, you will find **Ben-Gurion College►**, a centre for desert studies and part of Beersheva University. Here, the college's solar energy center is open to the public. A pathway leads through a pretty, natural garden, to the **Burial Site of David and Paula Ben-Gurion►►►**. The tombs are marked by massive stone slabs, on a clifftop overlooking the Wilderness of Zin. Here is the barren heart of the Negev, where bleached cliffs plummet to a stony plain riven by wadis. **Ein Avdat►►** begins at the foot of the cliff (see page 240).

THE BEN-GURIONS AT SDE BOKER

Having visited Sde Boker in 1953, David Ben-Gurion wrote to the kibbutz expressing his huge admiration for the enterprise and his envy of the life of its members. Later the same year he retired from politics, age 67, and moved with his wife Paula to Sde Boker, both becoming kibbutz members. He was asked to return to public life in 1955 and agreed to do so, while remaining a kibbutz member. In 1968, Paula died, aged 76, and David returned to seclusion on the kibbutz. He died in 1973, aged 87, and was buried alongside Paula near Sde Boker.

David Ben-Gurion (left) and the cottage (below) to which he retired after 13 years as Israel's Prime Minister

BEN-GURION'S DREAM
"It is possible to settle even millions of Jews in the Negev. Some day two million can be settled there based on agriculture. If so, another three million can be based on industry."
—David Ben-Gurion, 1935

DESERT FRUITS
Scientists at Ben-Gurion University are working with Negev farmers to use brackish water from deep desert aquifers. The water, previously thought unusable, is proving highly effective for fish farms, tomatoes and exotic new crops like argan. Argan yields cooking oil, and pitaya is an edible cactus fruit that Israel has started selling to European supermarket chains.

►► Shivta (Subeita) 224A4

Free access

About 40 miles (65km) south of Beersheva, this impressive desert site was the only Nabatean city to escape destruction by the Arabs. Like others in the Negev Pentapolis (see page 226), the town was originally founded as a stopover on the Nabatean caravan route to Petra. It was taken over and improved by the Romans, later occupied and Christianized by the Byzantines. By the 4th century it was a substantial community thanks to the Nabateans' knowledge of water conservation. It continued to thrive until the Muslims invaded in the 7th century and settled here without causing much damage to the existing structures. However, as Nabatean know-how on water and irrigation was lost, the town went into decline and was abandoned completely in the 9th century. Shivta's location, well away from roads, enabled it to survive the centuries relatively unscathed. Buildings survive up to two or even three stories high, each with its water cistern. You can also see a wine press, paved streets, three churches with marble-clad walls and a mosque.

► Tel Arad National Park 224C5

(tel: 07-7762170)
Open: Apr–Sep 8–5 (Fri to 4); Oct–Mar 8–4 (Fri to 3). Admission: inexpensive

Some 20 minutes' drive west of the new city of Arad, these remnants of a walled Canaanite and Israelite settlement of 3500–1500BC lie on a desert hillside set back from the road. This was already an old, wealthy city when its king joined the struggle to keep Moses and the Children of Israel out of Canaan. Later, Israelite settlements on the site were simpler. Tel Arad's setting is glorious: gentle, undulating sand and rock, speckled by the dark tents of the Bedouin who administer the site. Ruins of streets, houses, wells, sacrificial altars, a synagogue and a palace in two separate excavation areas, vividly illustrate desert life in those times. From here modern Arad looks like a striking blanket of green thrown over the desert.

Timna National Park

►► Timna National Park 224B1

(tel: 08-6326555; http://timna-park.co.il)
Open: Sep–Jun Sat–Thu 8–4, Fri 8–1; Jul–Aug Mon–Thu, Sat 8–4, 6–10.30, Sun, Fri 8–1. Admission: expensive

Renowned as one of the great ancient Arava copper mines, Timna was once known as King Solomon's Mines. It is now a huge area (23sq miles/60sq km) of desert scenery and historic ruins set around the dry Wadi Timna and edged by a semicircle of hills. Lying off the main Arava highway, 20 miles (32km) north of Eilat, and reached by a long access road, Timna National Park is desert pure and simple consisting of bare red sandstone and limestone with a few acacia trees and tumbleweed, though an artificial lake has been added as an extra diversion for visitors.

About 1 mile (2km) into the park, turn right to the **mushroom rock►**, so called for its shape, and the **copper smelting plant►**, which dates from the 14th century BC and belonged originally to the Egyptians. Dwellings, workshops and stores survive, and a temple site of the same period nearby was probably built for the use of miners.

Continuing, the road reaches the extensive **copper mines►►►**, characterized by sandstone arches, caverns, shafts and tunnels. Archeological work in the 1960s showed that copper had been worked here as long ago as

Temple used by Egyptian miners, the first to exploit Timna's mineral wealth

ISRAEL'S FLAG
Israel's national flag is the same as the Zionist flag raised at the First Zionist Congress in 1897. The design, worked out by David Wolfsohn, subsequently World Zionist Organization president, simply placed the Star of David in the center of a Jewish prayer shawl. "That is how our national flag came into being," he said. "and no one expressed any surprise or asked whence it came, or how."

COPPER AT TIMNA
The name King Solomon's Mines is misleading because, although Solomon exploited this and other mines, Timna was known and used many centuries before (and after) his reign. Copper-mining continued at Timna under the Romans, and the Arabs also extracted from the site. Mining was resumed here from 1958 to 1976, but proved unviable. In 1980, copper mining started again at another site about 1 mile (2km) south of Timna, and the mine is still in operation.

YOTVATA IN THE CITY
Sweet and savory yoghurts, chocolate milk, flavored cream cheeses... If you are fond of Yotvata's imaginative milk products, you can also enjoy them in Eilat, Tel Aviv and Haifa, at the excellent Kibbutz Yotvata restaurants on the waterfront.

3000BC. The Bible records that Solomon exported copper from a port at Ezion-geber (near Eilat), and derived great wealth from the proceeds. In a crevice at the bottom of a cliff, reached by rock-cut steps from the mine, **rock drawings▶▶**, attributed to 12th-century BC Egyptians and Midianites, depict war scenes.

The road continues to the artificial lake. Here is a restaurant and picnic area. Beyond is the most enjoyable feature of the park, the natural phenomenon known as **King Solomon's Pillars▶▶▶**. Having nothing to do with Solomon, these rocky structures result from the erosion of a 164ft (50m) high sandstone hill, at the foot of which, on the east side, is a 13th-century BC temple dedicated to Hathor. The pillars are gigantic columns forming just part of a jumble of weird, weather-beaten rocks, monumental in size and eroded to fantastic shapes, that can be climbed on, in or through. Steps have been carved up the massive formations, sometimes by man, sometimes by centuries of wind. The red stone is covered with its own red dust. Openings between the rocks suddenly look out onto immense desert mountains and the dry plain. The latest attraction at Timna is **The Tabernacle▶▶▶**, a full-size exact reconstruction of the Israelites' original tabernacle as they wandered in the desert after receiving the Torah. Every detail of the extraordinary portable structure comes from the precise description in the Book of Exodus. An accompanying multimedia show tells the Exodus story.

▶ Yotvata *224B2*

Many of Israel's favourite milk products come from Kibbutz Yotvata in the Negev desert. Many passersby on the Arava road stop here for a snack in the self-service **Yotvata Tourist Restaurant▶**. There's a picnic area and a children's play area. At the **Yotvata Visitor Centre▶▶** is a permanent exhibition on the flora and fauna of the Negev. Set back further from the road is **Ye'elin Holiday Village▶**, with a pool and pleasant chalet accommodation under the shade of acacia and palm trees. Ye'elin has its own big cafeteria, open to non-residents, and is better than Yotvata's.

King Solomon's Pillars

Travel Facts

Arriving

Getting there

Entry formalities Visitors to Israel do not require a visa, but their passports must be valid for at least six months from the date of arrival. Travelers are normally granted a three-month stay. However, those entering by land from Egypt or Jordan may be allowed only one month (visitors wishing to stay longer must apply for a visa through the Ministry of the Interior; expect a certain amount of delay as Israeli bureaucracy is not fast-moving).

On arrival to and departure from Israel, allow plenty of time for formalities. Every visitor is closely questioned by highly trained staff who will also carefully scrutinize all documents. Answer all questions frankly—and do not try to be humorous. For those traveling to or from Israel by air, this is usually performed as part of the check-in procedure. If you enter the country by private car, you will also be asked to empty the vehicle of all luggage and the vehicle will be searched. Cameras may be opened, so you may want to remove film before passing through security checks. An entry permit will be inserted in your passport, to be returned on departure.

By air Israel has two international airports. Ben Gurion is 37 miles (60km) from Jerusalem and 12 miles (19km) from Tel Aviv (known as Tel Aviv Airport). Ovda is in the Negev desert, about 65km (40km) from Eilat (however, Ovda offers few facilities).

El Al, Israel's privatized national airline, offers regular non-stop departures from London, regional UK airports and major European cities. They also fly direct to Israel from New York and other US and Canadian cities. Many travelers choose nonstop El Al flights for security reasons. El Al's rigorous security procedures far exceed anything that other airlines have in place. All food on board El Al flights is kosher and their fares are generally the least expensive available. El Al flights can be combined with hotel accommodations (and other facilities such as car rental) by booking through their package vacation company Superstar Holidays.

In addition, other scheduled and charter airlines and package operators fly from European cities to Israel. July and August, and the periods around the major Jewish and Christian festivals, are the most expensive times to travel to central and northern Israel; winter is the peak season for Eilat.

For details of all El Al flights, call:

- UK House, 180 Oxford Street, London W1N 0EL (tel: 020 7957 4100).
- 120 West 45th Street, New York, NY 10036 (tel: 212/768-9200 or 1-800/223 6700).

Haifa, the biggest and busiest of Israel's ports

Catering to the visitors who come to Israel from all over the world

By sea Israeli ports feature in the itineraries of cruise ships. There are sailings from ports in Italy, Greece and Cyprus to both Haifa and Ashdod. The sea route from Piraeus, in Greece, takes about 58 hours.

By land There is, as yet, no border crossing between Israel and either Lebanon or Syria. Travelers may cross to and from Egypt at Taba (Eilat). There are three crossing points between Israel and Jordan: Arava (outside Eilat), the Allenby Bridge (east of Jerusalem) and Sheikh Hussein Bridge (south of the Sea of Galilee). Border procedures are slow, and exit fees are levied.

Departure Those traveling with El Al may reduce the long check-in time to just one hour by checking in their hold baggage at certain special El Al offices 24 hours before departure—most notably the offices opposite the Tel Aviv North train station and next to Jerusalem bus station.

VAT repayments VAT is a sales tax, currently at 17 percent, charged on all goods and services. Tourists are exempt from paying VAT on hotel meals (including meals charged to the bill), car rental, domestic air travel and guided tours, among other tourist services—be sure that you are not charged VAT for these. On leaving Israel, visitors may claim back VAT paid on individual purchases of greater than US$100 in value at shops designated by the Ministry of Tourism and displaying a sign to this effect. When making your purchase, if you plan to reclaim the VAT, you should ask for a Tax Refund Invoice. The cash can be refunded at the official "Change Place" tax refund desk as you leave Israel, for example at Ben Gurion Airport or at Haifa Port. The Tax Refund Invoice must be produced, together with your passport, and the refund can be in shekels, US dollars, or in the original purchasing currency if available. A commission is charged. For more information visit www.cpl.co.il/english.htm.

The calendar

❑ No fewer than four separate calendars are in use in Israel—the Jewish and Muslim lunar calendars, plus the Julian and the more familiar Gregorian (Western) solar calendars. For everyday and business purposes, the last is used. The remaining three are mainly of religious significance. However, the terms AD (*Anno Domini*, the Year of Our Lord) and BC (Before Christ) are not used. Instead, years are measured as Before the Common Era or during the Common Era (BCE and CE). Fortuntely, the Common Era is deemed to have begun at the birth of Jesus, so there is no need for conversion. ❑

Essential facts

Climate

Climatic contrast is one of the striking features in Israel. The country compresses four climate zones into a space half the size of Switzerland, ranging from Mediterranean to Saharan. All four can be experienced in a 20-minute drive through Judaea.

For much of Israel, the year is dominated by two seasons—hot, dry summer and a cooler winter with occasional showers. January temperatures in Jerusalem can drop to around 39°F (4°C). It is several degrees warmer on the coast. The Galilee enjoys a short and delightful spring (in March and April) before the hills are slowly parched by the sun. Most of Israel's rainfall occurs between November and April, with the Mount Hermon area getting up to 40 inches (1,000mm) a year. Eilat receives less than 2 inches (50mm).

The hottest areas are Eilat, with winter temperatures around 70°F (21°C), the Negev, the Jordan Valley below sea level, and the shores of the Sea of Galilee (in high summer) and the Dead Sea. A strong, dry, easterly wind—known as the Hamsin (see page 246)—blows during the brief spring, and again in the autumn, raising temperatures as well as tempers.

Note that the relatively short days of winter, coupled with reliance on solar heating, can leave some accommodations rather chilly.

National holidays

The system of public holidays in Israel is complex, as there are Jewish, Christian and Muslim festivals to be observed. Additionally, there are differences within the Christian community between the observance of Western churches (Roman Catholic and Protestant) and Eastern (Greek and Russian Orthodox and Armenian). Jewish, Muslim and some Christian festivals are timed according to the lunar calendar, and their dates in the more familiar Gregorian calendar vary from year to year. It is well worth checking for festival dates before you depart for Israel, as a lot of time can be wasted while shops and

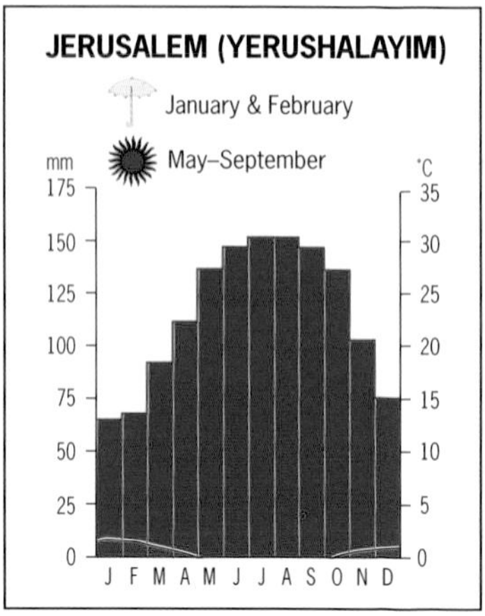

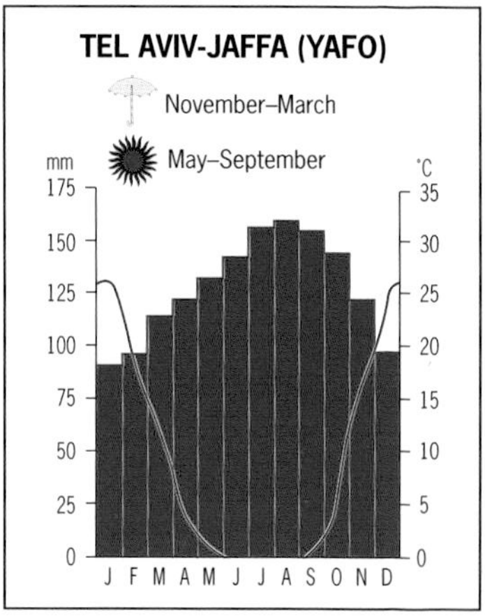

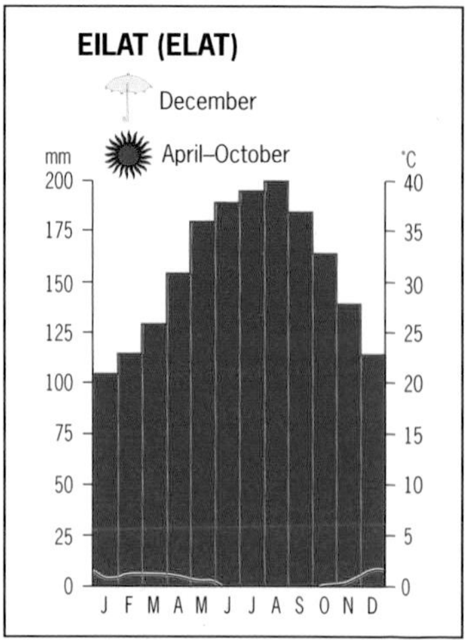

services are closed. Tourist sites are also frequently affected.

The Jewish Sabbath (Shabbat) almost literally brings Israel to a standstill. The only exceptions to this are the southern resort of Eilat, where many businesses ignore the Sabbath, and to a lesser extent, Tel Aviv. Elsewhere Jewish shops and services close on Friday afternoon and reopen on Saturday evening or Sunday morning. At these times, there is effectively no public transportation. If you are driving, you should avoid the ultra-orthodox areas of Me'a She'arim, in Jerusalem, and Bnei Brak, near Tel Aviv, where residents are hostile to Sabbath drivers. All Jewish festivals begin at sunset on the preceding day and end at sunset on the festival day. Christian shops and services generally close on Sunday. Muslim shops and services close on Friday.

The following list includes those festivals when some or all shops and services will be closed for all or part of the time. The dates are given according to the Gregorian (i.e. Western) calendar.

The list is not exhaustive

Eastern Orthodox Christmas; 7 January
Pesach (Passover); about April
Easter; a week, about March/April. Only Good Friday and Easter Sunday are holiday.
Shavuot (Pentecost); June/July
Tisha b'Av (fast day commemorating the destruction of the Temple); about August
Rosh Hashanah (Jewish New Year); about September/October
Ramadan (Arab areas only); one month, currrently starts September
Yom Kippur (Day of Atonement, religious fast day); 10 days after Rosh Hashanah.
Sukkot (Tabernacles); starts 4 days after Yom Kippur
Sigd (Ethiopian Jewish holiday); December
Catholic and Protestant Christmas; 24–25 December

Time

Israel is two hours ahead of Greenwich Mean Time (GMT) and seven hours ahead of Eastern Standard Time. Israeli Summer Time, a source of much controversy locally, operates from mid-April to the end of September, and is three hours ahead of GMT.

When to go

Although beach resorts are packed in summer, the weather then is not necessarily at its best. It is oppressively humid on the Mediterranean coast, and almost unbearably hot on the Dead Sea and at Eilat. Spring and autumn are perhaps the most comfortable times to visit Israel. Winter in Eilat can be delightful, with clear blue skies and temperatures usually in the lower 20s. The periods around the great Jewish and Christian festivals are expensive and crowded. Easter/ Pesach (Passover) in spring and Sukkot in autumn are both lovely times of year, but go just before or after the festivals to avoid the crowds.

Money matters

Currency The unit of currency is the New Israeli Shekel (NIS), known simply as the shekel, divided into 100 agorot. There are banknotes of 10, 20, 50, 100 and 200 shekels denomination. Coins are issued in denominations of 10 and 50 agorot and 1, 5 and 10 shekels.

Changing money Cash may only legally be changed through a bank, many of which have branches in the larger hotels, or through a licensed money changer. Only a few of the latter remain, but in Jerusalem many are to be found near the Damascus Gate of the Old City. They may give a better rate of exchange. The relative weakness of the shekel makes it preferable to change money in small amounts in Israel rather than abroad.

Credit cards Most major credit cards are freely accepted in Israel and credit card companies usually give a good rate of exchange.

Cashpoints
Holders of debit and credit cards can obtain cash from cash machines (ATMs) at many branches of Israeli banks. Check with your card issuer before leaving home to see if your card will work in Israeli cashpoints.

Payment in foreign currency Goods and services may frequently be purchased with foreign currency, although there is no obligation for businesses to accept this. The US dollar is most favored, but sterling and euros are also readily accepted. Many shops quote prices in dollars. Change will be given in shekels, so it is advisable to bring notes of small denomination. No VAT is applied to hotel, airline, car rental and other bills paid in overseas currencies, credit cards or by traveler's checks.

Opening times
Shops Traditional hours are Sunday to Thursday, 8.30am to 1pm and 4pm to 7pm; Fridays and days preceding Jewish holidays, 8.30am to 1pm. These days, many stay open all day. Additionally, many shops close on Tuesday afternoons, most hairdressers close on Monday afternoons, and travel agents close on Wednesday afternoons.

Banks Generally open 8.30am to 12.30pm Sunday to Thursday, 4pm to 6pm on Sunday, Tuesday, and Thursday, and 8.30am to noon on Friday. Some banks are open for longer hours in the afternoon and branches in hotels may keep hours to suit their guests.

Museums and archeological sites
Usually open Sunday to Thursday, 9 or 10am to 4 or 5pm. Typically they open mornings only on Friday and are closed all day on Saturday (any

exceptions to these opening times are noted in the individual entries in the A to Z section).

Post offices Hours vary considerably. Some main post offices are open from 7am to 10pm, others are open Sunday to Tuesday and Thursday, 8am to 6pm; Wednesday, 8am to 1.30pm; Friday, 8am to 1 or 2pm. Smaller post offices open Sunday to Tuesday and Thursday, 8am to 12.30pm and 3.30 to 6pm; Wednesday, 8am to 1.30pm; Friday, 8am to 1 or 2pm.

Fuel stations These are usually open all day and into the evening. However, only a few stations on main roads remain open on Friday afternoons and Saturdays, so remember to fill up before Shabbat (Sabbath) starts.

Government offices Usually open to the public from Sunday to Thursday between 8.30am and 12.30pm.

Pharmacies A list of pharmacies that take turns to remain open outside normal business hours is published

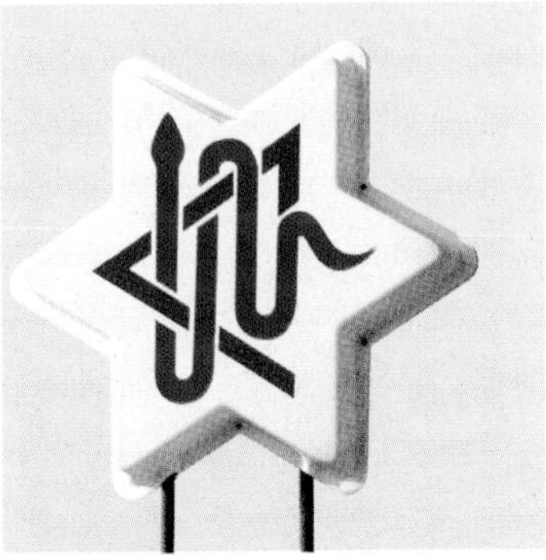

in the *Jerusalem Post*. It can also be obtained from hotels or from Magen David Adom (the Israeli equivalent of the Red Cross).

Customs and courtesies Israelis are remarkably casual in their dress and behavior, though immodesty by both sexes is frowned upon. Many Israeli people seem to regard excessive displays of courtesy with disdain. You should not, therefore, feel

affronted if your own attempts to be polite are disregarded. Accept that Israelis do not stand in line patiently or hold doors open for each other.

Do be aware of the customs of the Jewish Sabbath (Shabbat) and religious festivals. Observant Jews leave their cars at home on the Sabbath and on other festival days and they do not smoke on these days. For information on conduct in places of worship see page 269. Photography is forbidden within the enclosure at the Western Wall in Jerusalem.

Another feature of life in Israel is that daily life starts early (about 6am) and carries on until late (many restaurants and bars are open past midnight).

Getting around

Car rental

To rent a car it is necessary to produce your driver's license and be over 21, with at least one year's driving experience. Many international car rental companies are represented, and it is possible to book a car before departure from home, to be collected at the point of arrival in Israel. Several

Israeli companies also have offices abroad. Car rental desks at Ben Gurion Airport are open 24 hours.

Driving
An excellent road network, lovely and varied scenery, and short distances make touring Israel a pleasure. However, as in all areas of life, Israelis can be impatient and are not afraid to take risks when behind the steering wheel. Be cautious and drive defensively. Rush hours in major cities are hectic and traffic jams are frequent.

Traffic drives on the right, and the rules of the road are similar to those of Western Europe and North America. Signs are international and easy-to-understand, and street signs are in Hebrew, Arabic and English (although the type may be small and difficult to read if you are driving fast). Seat belts must be worn by all passengers at all times. Driving under the influence of alcohol is prohibited. Traffic approaching from the right has priority, except on main roads marked with a sign bearing a yellow square with a black and white border. These roads have priority over all side roads. All vehicles driving on roads between towns must use their headlights (note that parking lights are not enough) *at all times* between November 1 and March 31.

Emergencies Breakdown assistance can be obtained from the Automobile and Touring Club of Israel (MEMSI). The club offers free assistance to members of affiliated motoring organizations, such as the AA. Patrols operate around the clock, but a charge is made for assistance given between 5pm and 8am. Towing is free for distances under 15 miles (25km). Car-rental companies are often prepared to include short-term membership in the price or have their own emergency arrangements.

Parking This is strictly regulated in most town and city centers. Cars can be legally parked only in streets where the curbs are painted in blue and white stripes. A parking card (*cartise*) allowing five hours of street parking must be purchased from a post office or street kiosk and displayed on the windscreen. Between 7am and 5pm a car may be so parked for one hour. From 7pm to 10pm a longer period is allowed, and appropriate parking cards must be displayed. Overnight parking on blue and white striped streets is not regulated—but turn on your alarm clock! Find a car-park for longer stays in downtown areas. Do not park near red painted curbs: Cars will be towed away or

Fuel prices are slightly higher than many visitors are used to

clamped—often within minutes of their arrival.

Fuel Filling stations supply standard, premium grade lead-free, and diesel fuel. Prices are generally a little higher than in Europe and much higher than in the United States.

Speed limits Built up areas: (30mph) 50kmh; elsewhere: (50mph) 80kmh for cars, 35mph (60 kmh) for cars with trailers and 40mph (70 kmh) for motorcycles.

Public transport:
Air Israel's domestic airline, Arkia, has scheduled flights between Tel Aviv, Jerusalem, Haifa, Rosh Pina and Eilat. The under-an-hour flights from Tel Aviv to Rosh Pina or Eilat are much faster than driving (3–4 hours). Chartered flights to airfields, such as Masada, can be arranged through Arkia and other charter companies. Consult travel agents and Israel Government Tourist Offices.

Train Train services are run by Israel Railways along the coast between Nahariya, Haifa and Tel Aviv and continuing inland via Ben Gurion Airport to Jersalem. New stations, new track and new trains have greatly improved the service, and further improvements are in progress. Trains run from Sunday to Thursday between 6am and 11pm, on Fridays between 6am and 3pm and on Saturday evenings from the end of Shabbat until midnight. However, before committing yourself to rail travel, be aware that (for the time being) there are frequent rail cancellations, and that the Tel Aviv to Jerusalem train journey (1h20m) takes longer than the intercity bus. However the return fare is slightly less expensive (34NIS return). Israel Railways (tel: 03-5774000; www.isarail.org.il).

A station (above) on Haifa's underground system
Jerusalem railway station (below)

Bus Buses dominate public transportation in Israel. The nationwide Egged bus company provides a low-cost, comprehensive and efficient network of over 3,000 routes. These connect even the most isolated kibbutzim with the rest of the world. Intercity or long-distance buses are clean, comfortable, and, for the most part, air-conditioned.

Services start at about 5am and continue through the day until early

People waiting in line to buy tickets at Jerusalem's central bus station

Traveling by bus is part of the Israeli way of life

evening. Only the major routes between Tel Aviv, Haifa and Jerusalem continue until 11.30pm. Services also stop for the Sabbath on Friday afternoon and for religious festivals on the evening of the preceding day. Tickets can be bought at bus station ticket offices or, usually, from the bus driver. Town buses stop only when required, and passengers wishing to alight must press the bell to alert the driver. Bus drivers all speak at least basic English—it is part of their training.

There are several money-saving ticket options. The Israbus pass (costs vary) allows the holder to travel on all Egged buses for a specified period (7, 14, 21 or 30 days). It also entitles the holder to a range of discounts on tours, car rental, museum entrance fees, and restaurant bills. Multi-fare discount passes are valid for a month on urban routes only, and permit the holder to make a specified number of rides at a discount price. They can be used by more than one person. A simple round-trip ticket will also give worthwhile savings. Apart from anything else passes save you from having to wait in line for tickets, which can be a time-consuming and frustrating business, well worth avoiding at busy downtown bus stations! Tel Aviv city buses are run by Dan, and Egged passes are not valid here.

Various Arabic bus companies operate from the East Jerusalem bus station, serving Arab towns and villages in Judaea and Samaria (the West Bank). Their buses are painted blue and white or green and white. Arab buses tend to be crowded, cheap and rickety, but can be very useful for visiting these areas. They do run on Saturdays, unlike their Egged counterparts.

Taxis are fast and inexpensive but be cautious about overcharging

An easy and inexpensive way to see the sights is by taking an Egged guided tour in English. The national bus company runs trips lasting from half a day to a week, spent visiting all the country's places of interest. For information and bookings, go to any bus station in Israel, or contact Egged's head office in Tel Aviv, tel: 03-5375555.

Taxi and *sherutim* So-called "Special" (non-shared) taxis can be hailed on the street and are comfortable, fast and good value. Taxis are equipped with meters that are often not used, the driver simply stating his price for the journey. If you are not happy with the proposed fare, ask for the meter to be turned on instead. (Hotel reception staff may be able to advise what the correct fare should be for a given journey.) Note that at Ben-Gurion airport, taxis must be taken only from the official stand outside Arrivals—taxi drivers are not allowed to tout for fares inside the airport.

The *sherut*, or shared taxi, is the preferred choice of locals. These large cars, or minibuses, carry up to seven passengers, plying fixed routes within, or between, towns. All passengers pay a flat-rate fare (usually 20 percent more than the bus) and may alight at any point along the route. *Sheruts* operate from taxi stands and depart as soon as they have collected seven passengers. This usually does not take very long, as they are very popular. Fares are officially fixed, with supplements for night travel, and the drivers are generally helpful and honest, if not always friendly. The correct fare can be established by asking fellow passengers, or at the tourist office. *Sheruts* often run on Sabbath and festivals, but expect to pay a supplement. The addresses of *sherut* locations can be found in the local telephone book under "Taxi-cabs."

Boat Regular ferry services cross the Sea of Galilee between Tiberias, Ein Gev and Capernaum. Excursion boats can be chartered on the lake. For details, ask at local tourist offices. Red Sea excursions can be booked in glass-bottom boats, and there are ferries between Eilat and Taba. Details can be obtained from hotels or local tourist offices.

Ferry boats offer tranquil trips across the Sea of Galilee

Communication

Media

Israel has a thriving and extensive press, publishing in Hebrew, Arabic and many European languages. Papers cover the full gamut of opinions. The *Jerusalem Post* is a right-of-center English-language daily newspaper (no edition on Saturday) sold throughout Israel. It carries a full entertainment listings section on Fridays. Left-wing *Ha'Aretz* publishes a weekly English edition. Monthly magazines in Engish include the *Jerusalem Report*, a current-affairs magazine, and the *Israel Economist*. The *International Herald Tribune* and some British papers and magazines are also available. The Arab press produces some English-language publications, which are more readily obtainable in East Jerusalem.

Radio Kol Israel (Voice of Israel) broadcasts news in English every day at 7am, 1, 5, and 8pm on short wave (1170 kHz in the south and 576 kHz in the north). The 1pm news is followed by a 15-minute magazine programme. The Voice of America (1269 kHz) and BBC World Service (1323 kHz) can also be received and are much listened to by Israelis.

English-language news is broadcast by Channel 1 on Monday to Thursday at 6.15pm, Friday at 4.30pm, and Saturday at 5.30pm. In addition, cable television is available in most hotels, usually including BBC World and CNN. TV schedules appear daily in the *Jerusalem Post*. Jordanian television and cable channels such as Al-Jazeera are avidly watched by Israelis to gain an Arab slant on current events.

Post offices

These display a sign showing a leaping white stag on a blue background. As well as stamps, they sell telephone telecards, and some post offices also sell street parking cards (they also collect payment of bills and parking and traffic fines).

Main post offices in major cities are open from 7am to late (see page 259 for other post office opening times). The post office at Ben Gurion Airport is open 24 hours a day.

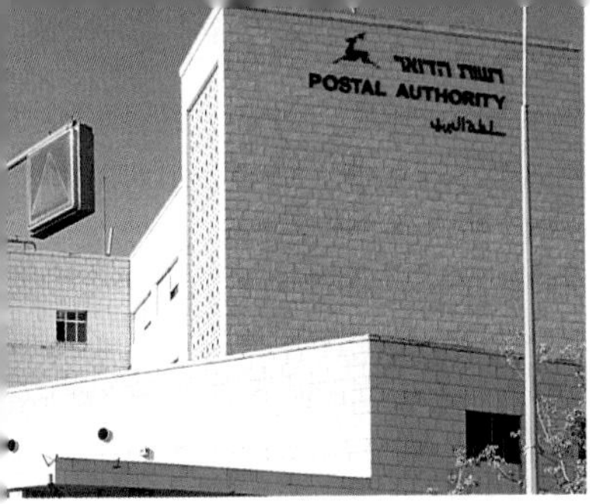

Typical main post office

Postboxes are red.

Stamps and telecards can be purchased at hotels and street kiosks. Stamps are also sold at bookshops and stationery and souvenir shops.

Visitors may receive mail through the *poste restante* (general delivery) service offered at main post offices (Jerusalem: 23 Jaffa Road; Tel Aviv: Rehov Mikve Yisrael Street); for details phone the Postal Authority's toll-free number: 177-0222131; or visit www.postil.com.

Telephones

Calls from public telephone booths must be paid for with a telecard (see above) for international as well as national and local calls. Different phone companies issue their own cards. Each company has its own code which must be dialed before the number you wish to call. For example, when using a Bezek phonecard, you must dial 014 before the international code and the number you wish to call. International calls can usually be made from your hotel room, but there may be a steep charge for this—check with reception.

Note that when calling a number within the same city, there is no need to dial the area code.

Mobile phones/cellphones Mobile (or cell) phones are called *telefon seloolar* in Hebrew, and often called "pelephone" after the name of a phone company. They are an essential part of daily life in this voluble and sociable country. You can use your own phone as normal while here, or rent one.

When calling abroad from your mobile, remember to dial the international code just as you do when calling from a land line.

Telephone services

Information: 144
International operator: 188
Time: 155
Telegrams by phone (up to 50 words): 171.

International dialling codes

United Kingdom to Israel: 00 972
United States or Canada to Israel: 011 972
Israel to the United Kingdom: 00 44
Israel to the United States or Canada: 00 1

When telephoning to or from a foreign country, omit the first zero of the local dialing code.

Language

The official languages of Israel are Hebrew (Ivrit) and Arabic (Aravit), with Hebrew being by far the most widely spoken. Most people dealing with tourists can speak, or at least understand, some English. This is particularly true of hotel staff. If this fails, it is always worth trying another language, as many Israelis are multilingual—French and Russian are very widely spoken, for example.

Street signs are usually in Hebrew, Arabic and English.

Basic vocabulary

hello (literally: Peace!)	*shalom*
good morning	*boker tov*
goodbye	*shalom*
yes / no	*ken/lo*
please	*bevakesha*
thank you (very much)	*toda (raba)*
good, fine	*tov*
sorry / excuse me	*sliha*
where is ...?	*aifo?*
how much?	*kama?*
do you have...?	*yeshlecha...?*
is (are) there any?	*yesh...?*
restaurant	*mis'adah*
museum	*muzaion*
synagogue	*beit knesset*
church	*knaissia*
hotel	*malon*
police	*mishtara*
station	*tahana*
tourist office	*lishkat hatayarut*
ticket	*kartis*
the check (bill)	*haheshbon*
passport	*darkon*

Emergencies

Crime
Israel is one of the safest countries in the world and experiences very little violent crime. A midnight stroll in any of the major cities is safer than it would be in broad daylight in most European or North American equivalents (the exception is East Jerusalem and parts of the Old City after dark). Violence may not be a problem, but theft of a casual nature sometimes can be. It pays to take a few elementary and commonsense precautions:
- Always carry money and valuables in an inside pocket or in a bag with a secure strap;
- Never carry your money and travel documents in the same wallet or bag;
- Never leave valuables visible in a parked car or unattended on a beach;
- Do not flaunt valuable jewelry;
- Pay particular attention to expensive cameras and video cameras.

For some years terrorist attacks were frequent in Israel. Now they are rare. Some European countries suffer worse terrorism —and there is very little danger of being involved in such an incident. However, anyone wishing to visit the West Bank should keep abreast of events in order to avoid any local disturbances or trouble spots. It is always a sensible precaution to travel by Arab bus or by local taxi in these areas, rather than in an Israeli-rented car, with its tell-tale yellow license plates. It is worth knowing, too, that most of Israel's own Arab towns and villages are in the Galilee. If you are in any doubt about your itinerary, check with tourist offices (see page 272), hotel staff or Israeli fellow travelers.

Police
In Jerusalem a special unit of the Tourist Police operates from the Kishle Police Station, close to the tourist office just inside the Jaffa Gate of the Old City. These officers speak English, French and German and will deal with all problems concerning tourists, ranging from crime to lost companions. They also use the services of volunteers who speak other languages.There is a similar police unit in Tel Aviv, which shares premises with the tourist office at 46 Herbert Samuel Street on the seafront boulevard.

Embassies and consulates

Israeli embassies abroad
- 3514 International Drive, Washington DC 20008 (tel: 202/364-5500; www.israelemb.org).
- 50 O'Connor Street, No. 1005, Ottawa, Ontario K1P 6L2 (tel: 613/567-6450; www.embassyofisrael.ca).
- 2 Palace Green, London W8 4QB (tel: 0207 957-9500; http://london.mfa.gov.il).

Embassies in Israel
- United Kingdom: 192 Hayarkon Street, 63405 Tel Aviv (tel: 03-7251222); 1 Ben-Yehuda Street, Jerusalem (tel: 02-5100166; www.britemb.org.il).
- United States: 71 Hayarkon Street, 63903 Tel Aviv (tel. 03-5197575); 27 Nablus (or Shechem) Road, Jerusalem (tel: 02-253288; www.usembassy-israel.org.il).
- Canada: 3–5 Nirim Street, Tel Aviv (tel: 03-6363300; www.dfait-maeci.gc.ca).

Emergency phone numbers
Ambulance: 101
Police: 100
Fire: 102

Health

The standard of health care provided in Israel is among the best in the world, and most doctors speak adequate English.
In an emergency, any hospital (Beit holim) will offer treatment. There are hospitals, clinics and duty doctors in almost every community, no matter how small. You should take your passport, insurance documents and money for payment with you. Do not forget to keep your receipts so that you can be reimbursed by your travel insurance.

For out-of-hours treatment or, non-emergency medical attention, look for details in the *Jerusalem Post*. This publication lists duty hospitals and pharmacies. Magen David Adom, the Israeli equivalent of the Red Cross, has first-aid stations in many towns.

Lost property

Always report serious losses to the police, who will supply you with a copy of their report for your insurance claim.

Report all lost passports to your embassy; it is a good idea to carry a photocopy of your passport's data page (separate from your passport) to speed the replacement process in case of loss.

Report stolen or lost credit cards and traveler's cheques to an issuing bank or the issuing company's emergency telephone number.

Soldiers praying at Judaism's holiest site, the Western Wall in Jerusalem

Other information

Camping

There are campsites throughout Israel, offering accommodations in cabins, chalets and caravans as well as tents. Facilities usually include shops and / or restaurants, around-the-clock security, showers and a swimming pool. Some have electrical hook up. Information concerning locations, booking arrangements, and tariffs can be obtained from local tourist offices.

Travelers with disabilities

Israeli attitudes to travelers with disabilities, and facilities provided, are generally good, but fall short of what is expected in some American cities. Ramps, curb cuts on main streets, wheelchair accessible lifts, doorways, hotel rooms, and accessible toilets are common—but not universal. State-owned sites and museums generally have good wheelchair access. Most inconvenient is that buses and taxis are not equipped for passengers with disabilities. Israel Government Tourist Offices provide a fact sheet entitled *Holidays in Israel for the Disabled* (see page 272 for addresses).

Electricity

The power supply in Israel is 220 volts AC. Wall plugs are of the small three-pin type, and a suitable transformer and plug adaptor are necessary for many European and American appliances.

Places of worship

The many places of worship in Israel represent dozens of different religions. All large Israeli towns have synagogues representing the various orthodox and progressive viewpoints, including Masorti (Conservative) synagogues in several towns. The main synagogue in large cities usually follows the Ashkenazi Orthodox rite.

There are numerous mosques in Israel's Islamic neighborhoods.

Most of Israel's Christian population is Greek Orthodox. The Christian Arabs are Maronites. Many other Christian denominations have churches in Israel. Roman Catholics are particularly well represented. Various Protestant denominations

Beautiful menorahs, symbol of the Israeli state and the Jewish faith

Women and a teacher reading and discussing the Koran in the Dome of the Rock in Jerusalem

have churches in the main towns. In Jerusalem, for example, Episcopalians, Baptists, Lutherans and Seventh Day Adventists are represented.

Many houses of worship are also major tourist attractions, and visitors should behave and dress with consideration for worshipers. Modest dress is essential for both sexes: shoulders, arms and legs should be covered, skirts should be at least knee-length and women should not wear trousers when visiting mosques or synagogues. Men should cover their heads in synagogues (paper caps are provided for those with no hat). Women should carry a hat or scarf to cover their heads, if required, in churches and mosques. When visiting mosques take off your shoes before you enter (see panel page 99).

If you arrive during services you may take part if you wish. Do not interfere in any way with the service.

Tourist offices (see page 272) have details of local churches and times of services.

Tipping

Israelis do not normally expect to give or receive tips. Unfortunately, in some places catering to tourists, that is not the case and serving staff will sometimes even inform you that tips are expected. Ten percent of the bill is more than adequate. Where service is already included, no tip is required. It is not necessary to tip taxi drivers, but it is customary to tip hairdressers.

Toilets

Public toilets are rare. Some leave much to be desired and little to the imagination. They are usually marked with the sign "00," plus a male or female symbol. Most restaurants, museums and cinemas have modern, clean toilet facilities, as do some of the bigger shops. Often, the best bet is to use the facilities in the larger hotels' public areas. Attendants do not normally expect a tip.

Student and youth travel
For low-cost youth travel to Israel, check out specialist travel operator STA at www.sta-travel.com. Within Israel, an International Student Identity Card gives 25 percent discounts on the country's minimal rail network, and 10 percent reduction on most town-to-town bus fares. The Israel Youth Hostels Association (tel: 02-2588900; web: www.youth-hostels.org.il) provides over 30 well-managed hostels around the country.

If you want to take part in an archeological dig contact either the Youth Section Promotion Department at the Ministry of Tourism (23 Hillel Street, Jerusalem; tel: 02-6237311) or the Israel Antiquities Authority (PO Box 586, Jerusalem; tel: 02-5602627).

❑ Working as a volunteer on a kibbutz is an inexpensive and interesting way to see something of Israel and learn about its society. However, be forewarned: it is more work than play. Most of Israel's 300 kibbutzim and *moshavim* use volunteers who get full board and pocket money. They generally do menial labor and unskilled tasks, unless they have some qualification that the community can make use of. For all that, most volunteers come away thinking the experience was valuable. For information contact the Jewish Agency, Kibbutz Aliyah Desk, 110 East 59th Street, New York, NY 10022 (tel: 212/318-6130); or Kibbutz Representative, 1A Accommodation Road, London NW11 8ED (tel: 020 8458 9235). ❑

Hitch-hiking
Hitching (called "tremping") is widely practised by all sorts of people, not just tourists. Vast numbers of off-duty soldiers, carrying weapons as they are required to do, hitch around the country (even though they have free bus passes). Getting lifts is quick and easy, as people who stop usually take more than one person. There are known hitchhiking spots on the major road—you can recognize them by the soldiers hitchhiking. They are almost like bus stops, with drivers stopping every couple of minutes to pick people up. To hitch a lift, do not hold up your thumb, instead, simply point your index finger.

Women travelers
Women can travel alone safely in Israel, but they should, of course, maintain the precautions they would usually adopt at home. Lone women may occasionally experience a certain amount of comment from male passersby, especially teenage boys. This is best ignored, as a response might be misunderstood. As everywhere, modest dress and discreet conduct will minimize hassle. In Arab areas, women may receive more persistent and unwanted attention from men. Emulation of the extreme modesty of Arab women can be helpful in these circumstances. Wearing a headscarf, in addition to very modest dress, can alleviate the situation. Locals advise against walking on the

ramparts of Jerusalem's Old City alone, though in fact women visitors often do this. Incidents are extremely rare. Women hitchhiking alone, or with another female companion, should maintain a sense of caution. If women do get inside a car with strange men, it is best to behave and talk with great modesty and reserve.

CONVERSION CHARTS

MEN'S SHOES

UK	7	7.5	8.5	9.5	10.5	11
Rest of Europe	41	42	43	44	45	46
US	8	8.5	9.5	10.5	11.5	12
Israel	41	42	43	44	45	46

WOMEN'S SHOES

UK	4.5	5	5.5	6	6.5	7
Rest of Europe	38	38	39	39	40	41
US	6	6.5	7	7.5	8	8.5
Israel	38	38	39	39	40	41

CONVERSION CHARTS

MEN'S SHIRTS

UK	14	14.5	15	15.5	16	16.5	17
Rest of Europe	36	37	38	39/40	41	42	43
US	14	14.5	15	15.5	16	16.5	17
Israel	36	37	38	39/40	41	42	43

MEN'S SUITS

UK	36	38	40	42	44	46	48
Rest of Europe	46	48	50	52	54	56	58
US	36	38	40	42	44	46	48
Israel	46	48	50	52	54	56	58

DRESS SIZES

UK	8	10	12	14	16	18
France	36	38	40	42	44	46
Italy	38	40	42	44	46	48
Rest of Europe	34	36	38	40	42	44
US	6	8	10	12	14	16
Israel	32	34	36	38	40	42

FROM	TO	MULTIPLY BY
Inches	Centimeters	2.54
Centimeters	Inches	0.3937
Feet	Meters	0.3048
Meters	Feet	3.2810
Yards	Metres	0.9144
Meters	Yards	1.0940
Miles	Kilometers	1.6090
Kilometers	Miles	0.6214
Acres	Hectares	0.4047
Hectares	Acres	2.4710
Gallons	Liters	4.5460
Liters	Gallons	0.2200
Ounces	Grams	28.35
Grams	Ounces	0.0353
Pounds	Grams	453.6
Grams	Pounds	0.0022
Pounds	Kilograms	0.4536
Kilograms	Pounds	2.205
Tons	Tonnes	1.0160
Tonnes	Tons	0.9842

Tourist information

Tourist offices

There are branches of the Israel Government Tourist Office (IGTO) in all the larger towns and places of tourist interest. They display a sign showing the letter "i" in white on a blue background. They can provide a wide variety of information in English about accommodations, excursions, local sights and events. Free town maps are available, as well as a free weekly English-language magazine called *Hello Israel*, which gives news and entertainment listings for the entire country. Offices in major cities also produce their own local listings magazines.

These are the main IGTO offices:

- Jaffa Gate, Jerusalem (tel: 02-620382);
- 2 Geula Street, Tel Aviv (tel: 03-5166188);
- City Hall lobby, 69 Ibn Gavrol Street, Tel Aviv (tel: 03-5218500);
- 48 Ben Gurion Boulevard, Haifa (tel: 04-8535606);
- Arava Highway Corner, Yotam Road, Eilat (tel: 07-6372111).

There is also an office at Ben Gurion Airport. Addresses and telephone numbers for other tourist offices can be obtained at any of the above.

IGTOs overseas

- Israel Government Tourist Office, UK House, 180 Oxford Street, London W1N 9DJ, UK (tel: 0207 299-1100; www.go-israel.org).
- Israel Government Tourist Office, 19th floor 350 Fifth Avenue, New York, NY 10119 (tel: 212/560-0600; www.goisrael.com).
- Israel Government Tourist Office, 6380 Wilshire Boulevard, Los Angeles, CA 90048 (tel: 213/658-7462; www.goisrael.com).
- Israel Government Tourist Office, 180 Bloor Street West, Suite 700, Toronto, Ontario M5S 2V6, Canada (tel: 416/964-3784; fax: 416/964-2420).

Hotels & Restaurants

HOTELS

The Israeli Ministry of Tourism lists over 300 places to stay throughout the country, from pilgrim hostels to luxury hotels. Details can be obtained from IGTO offices anywhere in the world (see page 272). There is no hotel grading system, but most hotels in Israel reach a high standard, and price is generally a reliable guide to a hotel's facilities and level of service. Note that hotel pools shut early by US standards. Arrive back in early afernoon for that refreshing dip or you may be disappointed.

Kibbutzim Most of Israel's 300 kibbutzim have guest accommodations. These vary enormously in style, quality and price. Some only offer a couple of basic guest rooms, while others are comparable to high-class hotels. In the case of the latter, guests are accommodated away from the kibbutz living and working areas. A free tour is always available, giving a glimpse into the day-to-day workings of a textbook utopia.

Some 40 kibbutzim, located in resort areas, are members of the highly professional Kibbutz Hotels Chain, which has its own Tel Aviv head office (see below). These are well placed all over the country and always within a few minutes of beaches, main towns, historic sites or resorts. For many people, their peaceful setting, informality and lack of traffic make them preferable to staying in town hotels. Bookings can be made through travel agents, or direct through the Kibbutz Hotel Chain in Israel (Kibbutz Hotel Reservation Centre, Montefiore 41, Tel Aviv; tel: 03-5608118; www.kibbitz.co.il). There are excellent package deals too, including kibbutz hotels fly-drive and special discounts for ex-kibbutz volunteers.

Apart from these better kibbutz hotels, scores of kibbutzim and *moshavim* (co-operative villages) offer inexpensive guest accommodation on a bed-and-breakfast basis. They must be booked by calling the kibbutz direct. Many are in peaceful, off-the-beaten-track locations, and a car is essential. Tourist offices also have details of other kibbutz accommodations.

Hostels The Israel Youth Hostels Association (www.youth-hostels.org.il) runs high-grade hostels throughout the country offering dormitories and family rooms to guests of all ages. Meals are usually provided, as well as a kitchen for guests' use. To enforce a degree of peace and quiet at night, most hostels close their doors at times varying from around 11pm to 3am—and not even paid-up guests will be allowed back in! Further details can be obtained from the Israel Youth Hostel Association, PO Box 6001, jerusalem 91060 (tel: 02-6558400; email iyha@iyha.org.il).

Christian hospices There are Christian hospices of various denominations near most Christian sights. They offer simple, clean, well-maintained, and very inexpensive accommodations, either with full board or on a lodging-only basis. It is not strictly necessary to be a pilgrim, or even a Christian, to use them. However, it is vital to abide by the rules of the hospice, which often include a curfew and an early start. Advance booking is essential. Full details, including prices and facilities, can be found in the leaflet *Christian Hospices in Israel* published by the Ministry of Tourism, from tourist offices or the Christian Information Centre at Jaffa Gate in Jerusalem (tel: 02-272692).

The big chains The best of Israeli hotels nearly all belong to chains. However, these are not always the familiar international names. While Hilton, Meridien, Sheraton, Hyatt and Holiday Inn exist in Israel, equally high standards are set by Israeli companies. These include the top-of-the-range Dan hotels, with 12 locations (in Israel tel 03-5202552; or toll-free from the UK and Europe on 00-800-326-46835; or toll-free from North American on 800-233-7773-4; www.danhotels.co.il); and Isrotel, with 11 establishments, 8 of them in Eilat (www.isrotel.co.il).

Hotel price grading Hotel rates vary widely according to the week and the season. The price categories given here are an approximate guide, and are per person, per night, sharing a double room, including full Israeli breakfast:

● budget	$	less than $85
● moderate	$$	$85–$175
● expensive	$$$	more than $175

JERUSALEM – OLD CITY

See also page 106.

Within the walls, there are small, very inexpensive hotels, hostels and hospices.

Citadel Youth Hostel ($)
20 St. Marks Road tel: 02-6274375
This good, clean, friendly hostel is in a 700-year-old building with atmospheric, cavernlike interiors. it has great views over the city. In a side street in the Christian Quarter, a few minutes from Jaffa Gate, it has easy access to all the sights and simple rooms at rock-bottom prices. Open 24 hours.

Lutherian Hospice and Guest House ($)
7 St. Marks Road tel: 02-6282120, 02-6285150
A fine-looking small hotel near Jaffa Gate, arranged around a very pretty courtyard, and also a rooftop garden with good views of narrow streets and shops. Decent simple rooms with showers.

New Swedish Hostel ($)
29 David Street tel: 02-6264124
Friendly, inexpensive hostel in the heart of the Old City, with hot showers, kitchens, a laundry, personal lockers to keep your belongings in, and free hot drinks—tea and coffee. Choose between proper bedrooms, or much less expensive dormitory sleeping. Knock the price down even more by asking to sleep on the roof.

JERUSALEM – NEW CITY

East Jerusalem

There is a string of low-budget Arab hotels ($) all the way up Salah ed-Din Street.

American Colony ($$$)
1 Louis Vincent Street, Nablus Road
tel: 02-6279777; www.americancolony.com
This Relais-et-Château hotel in the fairly smart American Colony district north of the Old City is one of the city's best, a grand former pasha's palace. Full of Arabic atmosphere, the beautiful old Oriental building has real charm and style, as well as a good pool, lovely terrace and superb breakfasts and buffets. A favorite with Arab leaders and Western journalists.

Jerusalem Novotel ($$$)
9 St. George Street tel: 02-5320000;
www.novotel.com or www.accor.com
At the meeting point of East and West Jerusalem, this modern, comfortable, well-equipped hotel is very popular for conventions, functions and celebrations. There's an outdoor pool, fitness center, entertainment, and several restaurants with Israeli style and international favorites, plus poolside barbecue.

Olive Tree Royal Plaza ($$$)
23 St. George Street tel: 02-5410410;
www.olivetreehotel.com
By the American Colony neighborhood north of the Old City, this large extremely comfortable modern hotel has a rather grandiose mock-traditional theme in the public areas. Good restaurants, including one in the roof garden. Indoor pool, fitness center and a luxurious spa.

Downtown

Most of the top-class luxury hotels, including members of international chains, are located on King David, Keren Hayesod and King George V streets.

Beit Shmuel ($)
6 Shama Street (entrance at 3 Shama Street)
tel: 02-62 3473; www.beitshmuel.com
Non-Orthodox Jewish hostel and cultural center (open to all) beside the city walls. Comfortable and friendly, with regular evening entertainment (folklore, etc) and an attractive garden.

Dan Panorama ($$$)
39 Keren Hayesod Street tel: 03-5202552;
www.danhotels.com
An immaculate, large, comfortable modern hotel, with elegant rooms, rooftop swimming pool, and numerous facilities. Just 15 minutes' walk from the Old City and the main sights.

David Citadel Hotel ($$$)
7 King David Street tel: 02-6211111;
www.tdchotel.com
A superbly luxurious rival for its neighbor, the King David, this beautiful building has glorious Old City views. Interiors are exceptionally comfortable and tasteful. Heated outdoor pool, health club, spa and four good restaurants, including a sushi bar and a poolside restaurant.

Inbal ($$$)
3 Jabotinsky Street tel: 02-6756666
www.inbalhotel.co.il
Modern, popular luxury hotel overlooking Old City; good value in its class.

Jerusalem Hostel ($)
44 Jaffa Road tel: 02-6236102;
www.jerusalem-hotel.com
This fascinating old building at busy Zion Square is one the best-known budget addresses in the city. A former 2-star hotel in the midst of all the sights, restaurants and entertainment of central Jerusalem, it offers good clean comfort at modest prices, with a choice of private rooms or dorms.

Jerusalem Inn ($)
6 Histadrut Street tel: 02-6251294;
www.jerusaleminn.co.il
Good, clean, low-budget downtown hostel accommodations. Well placed and very well equipped—a bargain.

King David ($$$)
32 King David Street tel: 02-6208888 (toll free from Europe and UK 00-800-326-46835, from US 800-223-773-4); www.danhotels.com
The city's stately and dignified number-one luxury hotel, a legend as well as a piece of Israel's history. The place where you are most likely to see visiting heads of state, stars and tycoons (see page 90 and 106).

Saint Andrew's Scottish Guest House ($)
1 David Remez Street tel: 02-6732401;
www.scotsguesthouse.com
Home from home for Scots, but open to everyone else as well, this agreeable, peaceful hostel enjoys a good view toward the Old City and is also conveniently placed for the city center. Rooms are comfortable, well-equipped and have showers. There's a handy Scot's Coffee Shop next door for snacks, drink and meals.

Sheraton Jerusalem Plaza ($$$)
47 King George Street tel: 02-6298666;
www.sheraton.com
Excellent modern hotel with great views and a superb restaurant.

YMCA (or Three Arches Hotel) ($$)
King David Street tel: 02-6253433
fax: 02-623- 5192 www.ymca3arch.co.il
Standing opposite the great King David Hotel, and arguably just as grand and imposing, the YMCA has basic, small but adequate rooms and a good range of facilities, especially for sports. More expensive than other hostels and hospices.

Farther out

Jerusalem Hotel ($$–$$$)
31 Lehi Street, Mount Scopus
tel: 02-5331234 fax: 02 581 5947;
www.hyattjer.co.il
Dramatic modern building (the six-story atrium has waterfalls and lush vegetation) covering a huge area and overlooking the city from Mount Scopus on the east side. Masses of artwork, luxurious rooms, good restaurants, and superb sport facilities. Relatively inexpensive for its class.

Kibbutz Mitzpe Ramat Rachel Hotel ($$)
D N Tsfon Yehuda, 90900 Jerusalem
tel: 02-6702555 www.ramatrachel.co.il
This excellent, well-equipped hotel (see page 107) is part of the only kibbutz within the city limits (though technically not part of Jerusalem). It makes a green haven after the noise and traffic of Israel's capital. Guests have access to kibbutz facilities, which include a big grassy playground

and a heated (all-year) swimming pool, as well as plenty of hotel amenities and its own pampering Health Centre. Great views of Bethlehem. Easy and frequent access by bus from downtown.

Neve Ilan Hilltop Resort ($$)
tel: 02-5339339 www.neve-ilan.co.il
A 15-minute drive along the main Tel Aviv highway, set in a quiet airy location, this pleasant, modern hotel has large gardens, excellent sports facilities, and a good restaurant.

Park Plaza ($$$)
2 Ze'er Vilnay tel: 02-6582222
fax: 02-6582211
A first-class hotel close to Herzl Boulevard, the Knesset and the major museums.

Yitzhak Rabin Guest House and Hostel ($$)
1 Nahman Avigad Street tel: 02-6780101
fax: 02-6796566; email: rabin@iyha.il
Excellent youth hostel close to the Israel Museum. Neat, comfortable, modern rooms (some with TV), air-conditioning, and there's also a cafeteria and dining room.

TEL AVIV AND THE COAST

See also page 132.

In Tel Aviv, and right up Israel's Mediterranean coast, there are numerous modern, well-equipped hotels ranged along the beachfronts of popular seashore areas.

Tel Aviv

The main beach and city hotel area is Hayarkon Street, between Trumpledor and Ben-Gurion streets. This is where you will find the main high-quality hotels, as well as several catering to those on smaller budgets. Bargain-basement places and hostels are scattered over the whole area west of Dizengoff Street.

Adiv ($$)
5 Mendele Street tel: 03-5229141
fax: 03-5229144; www.adivhotel.com
Near the sea and well placed for the city center restaurants and sights, this is an attractive, comfortable and moderately priced hotel. Some rooms have kitchenettes. There is free parking and some excellent special offers on room rates.

Ami ($–$$)
152 Hayarkon Street tel: 03-5249141
A comfortable and unpretentious mid-range hotel, very well placed for the beach and the city center, the Ami has friendly staff, air-conditioned rooms and a full Israeli buffet breakfast. Other meals are available on request.

Basel ($$)
156 Hayarkon Street tel: 03-5244161
fax: 03 527 0005
Reliable, well-liked, reasonably placed modern hotel, set back just a few paces from the main beach area. Comfortable rooms, cable TV and outdoor pool.

Carlton ($$$)
10 Eliezer Peri Street tel: 03-5201818
fax: 03-5271043 www.carlton.co.il
Set a little north of the main beach, overlooking the yachting marina, this big landmark hotel is in the highest class.

Cinema ($$)
1 Zamenhoff Street tel: 03-5027100
www.atlashotels.co.il
A beautifully restored former cinema in the Bauhaus style, the Hotel Cinema is something really different. Grand and attractive interiors, and cinematic memorabilia that incudes black-and-white movies flickering on a wall at reception. Rooms are comfortable, with air-conditioning, good bathrooms, satellite TV, and some have kitchenetttes. The location at Dizengoff Circle is a bit scruffy, but convenient for shops, restaurants and the beach.

City ($$)
9 Mapu Street tel: 035246253
fax: 03-5246250
An appealing, popular hotel just a couple of minutes' walk from the main beach area; comfortable and reasonably equipped.

Dan Panorama ($$)
10 Kaufmann Street tel: 03-5190190
fax: 03-5171777; www.danhotels.com
A little away from things, facing Clore Park and not near the best part of the beach, this hotel offers luxurious accommodations at lower rates and has a strong bias to children and families. Good food, excellent breakfast buffet. A free shuttle bus runs throughout the day to the Dan Tel Aviv.

Dan Tel Aviv ($$$)
99 Hayarkon Street tel: 03-5202525
fax: 03-5249755; www.danhotels.com
Said to have been the city's first hotel, this is still most people's first choice for comfort, service, and convenience. Large and modern, but surprisingly personal, with excellent facilities and superb sea views (rooms on the street side without the sea view are cheaper).

David Intercontinental Hotel ($$$)
12 Kaufman Street tel: 03-7951111
fax: 03-7951112 www.interconti.com
Very plush, spacious, classy hotel with huge atrium filled with greenery. Facilities include beauty center, gym, an excellent restaurant and an internet café. It's close to the beach but not particularly well placed—on the busy junction facing the mosque, opposite the scruffy Dolphinarium. Reasonable prices though.

Dizengoff Square Hostel ($)
13 Ben Ami Street tel: 03-5225184
fax: 03-5225181
Next to Dizengoff Square, this modern, well-equipped hostel, with accommodations from dorms to private rooms (with bath), could hardly be closer to the heart of Tel Aviv.

Gordon Inn ($)
17 Gordon Street tel: 03-5238239
fax: 03-52374119
Something between a small budget hotel and a better-than-average hostel, the Gordon is well placed on a city center corner just a few minutes' walk from the main beach. Choose between basic dorms and simple private rooms. It's open 24 hours a day, and there's a pleasant little coffee bar where breakfast is served. Good value.

Hilton ($$$)
Independence Park/Hayarkon Street
tel: 03-5202222 fax: 03-5272711
On a seafront ridge overlooking the shore, but well

to the north of the main beachfront area. Not in the best place for either beaches or city. The building has been thoroughly renovated and is a luxury hotel up to the usual Hilton standard.

Isrotel Tower ($$)
78 Hayarkon Street tel: 03-5113636
fax: 03-5113666; www.isrotel.co.il
This well-placed high-rise landmark building close to the seafront combines a comfortable all-suite hotel with unserviced self-catering aparthotel in an unusual concept. Each of the comfortable two-room suites has two TVs with cable, a stereo CD player and two phone lines. There's no restaurant, but a basement bar provides refreshments. Business-class guests get added benefits.

Metropolitan Suites ($$$)
9 Trumpeldor Street tel: 03-5192727
www.hotelmetropolitan.co.il
Really top-quality suites, with home-from-home comforts and tasteful interiors. Mainly geared to business travelers, the suites have a sitting room, kitchenette and simultaneous phone and modem connections. There's a fitness center, outdoor pool, laundry and a good restaurant, as well as 24-hour room service.

Renaissanace ($$–$$$)
121 Hayarkon Street tel: 03-5216666
email: resrv@renaissance-tlv.co.il
A large and comfortable hotel, well-equipped and good value. Rooms have Pay TV. At the northern end of the beach, overlooking the marina, and quite a long walk to the city center and the sights.

Sheraton Moriah ($$$)
115 Hayarkon Street tel: 03-5216666
fax: 03-5271065
A landmark on the Tel Aviv waterfront, a few paces from the beach and within walking distance of downtown. A top-class luxury hotel.

Travellers Hostel ($)
38 and 47 Ben Yehuda Street
tel: 03-5272108
Small but popular, clean and inexpensive hostel with attractive garden. Fully equipped kitchens, luggage room, and reception staffed almost round the clock. Easy walk to the beach and downtown. Also at 122 Allenby Street (tel: 03-5606656).

Yamit Park Plaza ($–$$$)
79 Hayarkon Street tel: 03-5197111
email: yamit@pplaza.co.il
Well situated by the beach and close to the city center, the Park Plaza offers a wide range of good-quality accommodations from standard rooms to executive studios. Outdoor pool, private parking and fitness club and business center.

Akko

Argaman Motel ($)
tel: 04-9916691 fax: 04-9916690
Modern hotel on the beach providing comfortable but basic accommodations, with a good view of Old Akko.

Palm Beach Hotel ($$)
tel: 04-9815815 fax: 04-9910434
Neighbor to Argaman, above, this better hotel is equipped with good sport facilties, including tennis and squash courts, pool, sauna and Jacuzzi, as well as a nightclub.

Caesarea

Dan Caesarea ($$–$$$)
tel: 06-6269111 fax: 06-6269122
In a green parkland setting, this delightfully relaxed and luxurious resort hotel emphasises sport—including golf at Israel's only golf course, nearby.

Kef Yam Resort ($$)
Sdot Yam Kibbutz tel: 06-6364444
fax: 06-6362211 www.kef-yam.co.il
Close to the Caesarea beach, this imaginative and lively kibbutz resort offers a wide range of sports, activities, classes and tours for all age groups. There's a restaurant, and accommodations in family apartments or simpler hostel-style quarters.

Carmel Forest

Carmel Forest Spa Resort ($$$)
P O Box 9000, Haifa 31900
tel: 04-8307888 fax: 04-8323988
Hidden in a tranquil Mediterranean woodland about 2-mile (3km) south of Kibbutz Beit Oren (near Haifa), this luxury spa hotel offers non-stop pampering and pleasure, rather than the usual health cures and Dead Sea mud.

Haifa

High-quality hotels are clustered in the tiny Carmel Center district up the Carmel slope, above the heart of the city. Top-rung places are the **Dan Carmel** ($$$), *HaNasi Avenue (tel: 04-8306306; fax: 04-8387504)* and its near neighbor, the **Dan Panorama** ($$$), *HaNasi Avenue (tel: 04-8352222; fax: 04-8352235).* The top floors have fantastic views. Both have an abundance of facilities.

Shulamit ($)
15 Kiryat Sefer Street tel: 04-8342811
fax: 04-8255206
An excellent hotel a bit farther from downtown.

Herzliya

Dan Accadia ($$$)
Ramat Yam Street tel: 09-597070
fax: 099597090
Magnificent family resort hotel on the beachfront. Popular and lively. Sport and activity oriented, with lots provided for children. Good buffets.

Sharon ($$)
Ramat Yam Street tel: 09-575777
fax: 09-9572448
Good, comfortable modern hotel near the beach.

Nahsholim

Kibbutz Nahsholim Guesthouses ($–$$)
MP Hof Carmel tel: 06-399533
fax: 06-6397614
This kibbutz on the Carmel coast offers accommodations in simply furnished, rather spartan, terraced chalets, right on a spectacular beach. The restaurant is below average.

Netanya

There are almost 50 ministry-approved hotels in this town.

Grand Metropole ($–$$)
17 Gad Mahnes Street tel: 09-624777
fax: 09-8611556
A good-value resort hotel located near the beach.

The Seasons ($$–$$$)
1 Nice Boulevard tel: 09-601511
fax: 09-8623022
One of the friendliest and best hotels in this popular resort.

Shavei Zion
Hotel Hofit Beit Hava ($–$$)
Moshav Shavei Zion tel: 04-9820391
www.hotel-hofit.com
This quiet *moshav* (cooperative village), 2 miles (3km) south of Nahariya, runs a remarkable high-quality modern hotel and restaurant. Immaculate, with good service, attractive grounds and good facilities, including a large swimming pool.

Shefayim
Kibbutz Shefayim Guest House ($–$$)
Shefayim 60990 tel: 09-595595
fax: 09-9595555
This kibbutz outside Herzliya runs a big, busy hotel, restaurant and water park, and is patronized almost exclusively by Israelis. The atmosphere is warm and animated, with functions and events occurring almost every evening. The rooms are well-equipped and comfortable. A good base for much of the coast, including Tel Aviv.

Zichron Yaakov
Carmel Gardens ($$)
1 Etzion Street tel: 06-300111
fax: 06-6397030
On a hilltop close to town, this smart hotel hosts a lot of conferences, has spacious gardens, a high standard of luxury and sweeping green views.

GALILEE AND THE NORTH

Amirim
Amirim guest-houses ($)
near Sefat tel: 06-6989571 or 04-6987594
www.amirim.org.il
Several families offer comfortable guest accommodations at this beautifully located all-vegetarian *moshav* (co-operative village) west of Sefat.

Ayelet Hashahar
Ayelet HaShahar ($–$$)
near Kiryat Shmona tel: 06-6932302
fax: 09-9597091
Excellent kibbutz guest house offering accommodations and a lively, enjoyable resort atmosphere, with plenty of entertainment and activities.

Ginosar
Nof Ginosar Kibbutz Hotel ($$)
tel: 06-6700300
e-mail: ginosar@netvision.net.il
Delightful, high-quality modern kibbutz hotel with comfortable rooms in several blocks set in beautiful grounds on the banks of the Sea of Galilee. Good restaurant. Well placed for sights. The Museum of the Ancient Boat is next door.

HaGoshrim
HaGoshrim Kibbutz Hotel ($$)
tel. 06-6816000 fax: 06-6816002
www.hagoshrim_hotel.co.il
They have good, comfortable, simple rooms in guest accommodations complexes at this prosperous kibbutz, set in pleasant and attractive grounds. Pool and plenty of other facilities. Inner-tubing down the nearby Jordan River is great fun.

Karmiel
Hotel Kalanit ($)
10 Nesiei Israel Boulevard tel: 04-9983878
You may find newly arrived immigrants lodged in the next room at this simple, but modern and adequate, hotel in the heart of town. Well-placed for Galilee touring, and very inexpensive.

Kinar
Kinar Hotel ($$)
tel: 06-6738888 fax: 06-6738811
Attractive, efficient kibbutz hotel with good accommodations. Glorious garden setting on the eastern shore of the Sea of Galilee. Pleasant, spacious public areas and restaurant.

Korazim Junction
Vered Hagalil ($$)
just off Route 90, north of Sea of Galilee
tel: 06-6935785 fax: 06-6934964
e-mail: avril@canaan.co.il
A riding center, meaty restaurant and rustic ranch-style (actually very comfortable) complex of cottages and cabins, with swimming pool in a peaceful country location.

Rosh Pina
Kibbutz Kfar Hanassi ($$)
near Rosh Pina tel: 06-6914870
fax: 06-6914077 e-mail: corrin@canaan.co.il.
A few neat, clean, simple guest rooms with kitchenette, plus breakfast in the kibbutz dining room, and Golan views, make for a peaceful break at this easy-going community.
Mizpe Hayamim Hotel and Spa ($$$)
On the Sefat-Rosh Pina Highway
tel: 04-6884555 Toll-free in Israel 1-800-555-66; www.mizpe-hayamim.com
This strongly health-oriented hotel is a member of the Relais & Château federation and offers the best accommodations in the region. There's a tennis court, a pool, saunas and a very serious spa offering a variety of treatments. The hotel earns its name—which means Sea View—from a splendid vista towards the Sea of Galilee. Rooms are not especially large, but attractively furnished. It has its own organic farm, fruit groves and vegetable gardens, as well as a bakery and vineyard, so the hotel produces most of the ingredients for its two excellent restaurants—one meat, the other vegetarian (and fish).

Sefat
Ron ($)
near Metzuda, Sefat tel: 06-6972590
Decent mid-range hotel with good clean rooms and restaurant, a 10-minute walk from the synagogue.
Howard Johnson's Ruth Rimon Inn ($$)
Artists' Quarter tel: 06-6994666
fax: 06-6920456
Attractive and well placed in a pleasant area. One

of the best hotels in town, housed in lovely restored Ottoman buildings. Very comfortable and equipped with gardens, pool, health club and good restaurant.

Tiberias

Several budget hostels ($) and pilgrim hospices can be found around the town. One of the very best is the **Church of Scotland Sea of Galilee Centre** ($)
tel: 06-6723769
e-mail: scottie@rannet.com
A delightful place with air-conditioned rooms and private bath. Not far from the lake.
Galei Kinneret ($$$)
1 Eliezer Kaplan Street tel: 06-792331
The best, and most civilized place in town, by the lake in a lovely setting.
Kibbutz Lavi Hotel ($$)
Kibbutz Lavi, southwest of Tiberias
tel: 04-6799450; www.lavi.co.il
Gorgeous greenery surrounds the very comfortable, pleasant accommodations of this Orthodox Jewish kibbutz not far from Tiberias. All are welcome but Jewish observance is the rule.
Sheraton Moriah Plaza ($$$)
Habanim Street tel: 06-6792233
fax: 06-6792320
Big, lavishly equipped modern luxury hotel in the Old City.

THE SOUTH

Arad

Margoa ($$) *tel: 07-951222*
and the **Inbar Arad** ($$) *tel: 07-957056*
are conventional, modern mid-range hotels located close to one another on Moav Street, the road out of town on the eastern side. Both have treatment centers for respiratory conditions.

Dead Sea

Dead Sea Gardens ($$$)
Ein Bokek tel: 07-6584351 fax: 07-6584383
Resort and health hotel, with entertainment and sports facilities. Heated indoor pool, filled with water from the Dead Sea.
Kibbutz Ein Gedi ($$)
Ein Gedi tel: 07-6594222 fax: 07-6584328
The kibbutz runs a hotel with basic accommodation in simple terraced blocks scattered around attractive grounds full of flowerbeds. There is a good self-service dining room.
Sheraton Moriah ($$$)
Neve Zohar tel: 07-6591591
fax: 07-6584238
Big, top-flight health-oriented spa hotel on the salty shore in weird, desert location. Full spa in the hotel—pools, mud baths,and more. Lots of facilities, including good restaurants.

Eilat

There are over 60 hotels in Eilat. Most reach a high standard and cater to well-to-do visitors on family holidays. The cream of the selection—the Princess, Dan Eilat, Royal Beach and Herods—are probably among the best holiday hotels in the world.

In addition to the beach hotels, lower-priced modern, comfortable hotels, popular with Israeli families, can be found in the town center away from the beach. Examples include the huge, all-suite **Club Hotel** ($$), Arava Road *tel: 07-6361666*; the fully equipped aparthotel **Nova Hotel** ($$), 6 Hativat Hanegev *tel: 07-6382444*; and **Shalom Plaza** ($$), 2 Hatmarim Ave *tel: 07-6366777.*

Closer to the beach, between the town airport and the lagoon, are popular mid-range quality hotels with pools, restaurants, good facilities and bargain prices, such as **Americana Inn** ($$) (tel: 07-6333777); and **Palmyra** ($–$$) (tel: 07-6366000).

Dalia Hotel ($)
North Beach tel: 07-6334004
Probably the best low-cost hotel, with a good position near the seafront.
Dan Eilat Hotel ($$$)
North Beach tel: 03-6362222;
www.danhotels.com
East of the lagoon. A large, opulent, state-of-the-art hotel with everything, including jazz, sport facilities, pool area, plus amenities for children.

Herods Palace and Herods Vitalis ($$$)
North Shore tel: 07-6380000
fax: 07-6380010; www.sheraton.com
At the eastern end of the resort, set back from the shore. Unabashed luxury on an Ancient Roman theme. Several excellent restaurants. The Vitalis is also a magnificent spa hotel, for total self-indulgence in the name of health. All food is organic.
Hilton Queen of Sheba ($$$)
North Beach tel: 07-6306655
fax: 07-6306644
Well placed beside lagoon and beach, this luxurious, grandiose hotel claims to be based on the Queen of Sheba's palace.
Kibbutz Eilot Apartments ($$)
Kibbutz Eilot, M P Eilot 88805
tel: 07-6358816
Two miles (3km) north of Eilat on the main road, the kibbutz has a small complex of simple apartments in attractive grounds surrounded by desert hills. Breakfast is served in the kibbutz members' dining room. There's a children's zoo and play area and an "Israeli folklore evening" every Saturday. A good spot for birdwatchers in spring and fall. Car essential. Handy for the Jordan crossing.
King Solomon's Palace ($$$)
North Beach tel: 07-6334111
Eilat's refurbished family favorite, a comfortable luxury hotel backing onto the east side of the lagoon. Crowded, informal resort atmosphere, but with many facilities.
Lagoona Hotel ($$)
North Beach tel: 07 636 6666
All-inclusive family-fun hotel built around a large pool and sunbathing terraces. Masses of facilities, including six cafés and restaurants.
Le Meridien ($$$)
North Shore tel: 07-6383333
fax: 07-6383300; www.eilat.lemeridien.com
High standard chain offers all-suite beachside luxury a few minutes down the Taba Road. Lots of

greenery and polished wood, and excellent facilities.

Neptune ($$–$$$)
North Beach tel: 07-6369369
This is a popular luxury resort hotel with superb facilities set beside the North Beach promenade.

Orchid Hotel and Resort ($$$)
Coral Beach tel: 07-6360360
Inspired by Thai architecture and set on a hill overlooking the sea, this attractive chalet complex has footpaths winding through clusters of greenery.

Princess Hotel ($$$)
Taba Beach tel: 07-6365555
Opulent, top price hotel, set amid desert cliffs just a few paces from the narrow beach. Near the Taba crossing, 5 miles (8km) from Eilat. A free shuttle bus operates into town. Huge atrium, marble floors and an amazing wall of glass almost touching a rocky mountainside.

Reef Hotel ($)
Coral Beach tel: 07-6364444
fax: 07-6364488
Unpretentious, attractively equipped sea-facing hotel, popular with Israelis.

Riviera Apartment Hotel ($$)
North Beach tel: 07-6303666
Isrotel's low-rise apartments provide unpretentiously furnished rentals for two, four or five people. The complex is arranged around a large pool with children's pool and playground. Ten minutes' walk to the beach. Cafés and a small supermarket in the building.

Royal Beach ($$$)
North Beach tel: 07-6368888
Sumptuous top-of-the-line hotel near the lagoons. White marble reception area full of light, magnificent atrium with acrobatic sculpture, hallways made of glass with fantastic views. A dozen good restaurants and two large, palm-fringed pools with waterfalls, plus a huge array of other facilities.

Sheraton Moriah Hotel ($$$)
North Beach tel: 07-6361111
Large and luxurious hotel, closest to North Beach promenade. Vast range of facilities, with plenty for children, five restaurants, two pools, a nightclub, and regular entertainment.

Sport Club Hotel ($$)
North Beach tel: 07-6368818
fax: 07 636 8886 e-mail:
cro_asst@isrotel.co.il
Comfortable, quieter-than-average offering all-inclusive hotel accommodations with two pools and many sports facilities.

Youth Hostel ($)
corner of Elot Boulevard and Arava Road
tel: 07-6370088; www.youth-hostels.org.il
An unappealing location, but within easy walking distance of everything (including main bus station). Good, large, modern hostel, with family rooms and an inexpensive dining room.

Mitzpe-Ramon

Ramon Inn ($$)
1 Ein Akev tel: 07-6588822 fax: 07-6588151
Unusual modern apartment-hotel in a desert town beside the breathtaking Ramon crater. Rooms are spacious suites, each with a kitchen/dining room. Excellent value. Bar and restaurant.

RESTAURANTS

Almost all luxury hotels have high-quality restaurants open to the public. There are also numerous "full-service" restaurants around town, some achieving a high standard of cuisine. Even in the best places, the atmosphere is always very friendly and informal—not just in dress, but also in the approach to dining: No-one is fussed if you just want a starter and dessert, or a couple of starters but no main course, for example. Service tends to be helpful but amateurish. For cheap-and-cheerful eating there is little distinction to be made between bars, cafés and restaurants. They can be found with ease in the center of any city or town. Especially characteristic of Israel are small open-fronted eateries, which in some parts of town can be on almost every corner, offering an array of finely chopped salads, pickles and sesame-based hummus and tahina, served with three or four falafel (fried chick-pea balls, or schwarma (slices of grilled pressed meat from a spit) all in a pita (like a flat pocket of bread) or lafa (a larger flat wrap-around bread). if you want a drink to go with it, most likely you'll be offered water, juice or a soft drink. Almost all restaurants, cafés and entertainment venues have security barriers and guards—be prepared to open your bag if asked.

Price and dining guide:

● budget	$	less than $17
● moderate	$$	$17–$50
● expensive	$$$	more than $50

JERUSALEM

The heartland of eating out in Jerusalem is the mostly pedestrianized streets around **Ben Yehuda Street** in the enter of the city. The area lies roughly between Zion Aquare, King George V Street and Hillel Street. Here—but also scattered across the city center—you'll find a vast selection of fast-food restaurants, pizza parlors, dairy bars and cafés, along with better restaurants serving every conceivable type of cuisine from around the world, as well as fine Israeli cooking. They are open until late. Most are kosher, so these will be closed Friday night and until dark on Saturday. By contrast in the Old City and East Jerusalem, there are plenty of snack stalls and budget lunchtime eateries but only a small number of good restaurants. In this part of town, very few are kosher, except in the Jewish Quarter, and most places are closed by 6pm.

3 Arches Restaurant ($)
26 King David Street tel: 02-5692692
Jerusalem's landmark YMCA has risen far above other hostels. Not only is it a good place to stay, but it even has a smart and attractive restaurant with a good range of international dishes—business lunches, even—all at very modest prices.

El Gaucho ($$)
22 Rivlin Street, off Nahalat Shia tel: 02-6242227
On a totally Argentinian theme, the "First South American restaurant in Israel" serves juicy steaks in a busy, popular setting. Kosher, too.

Foccaccia ($$)
4 Rabbi Akiva Street tel: 02-6256428
There's a lovely indoor-outdoor feeling at ths popu-lart bar and restaurant with tables under the stars. Obviously it's supposed to be Italian, but the menu lists a wide range of delicious Mediterranean and Middle Eastern dishes too.

La Guta ($)
18 Rivlin Street tel: 02-6232322
At the end of this narrow pedestrian street off Nahalat Shiva you'll find this peaceful kosher restaurant, offering an eclectic mix of French and British cuisine with dishes like lamb chops.

Primavera ($$$)
Sheraton Plaza Hotel, 47 King George Street tel: 02-6298666
Classic Italian food of a high standard at this hotel restaurant includes peppers with mozzarella, fish specialties, and tasty desserts. Kosher.

Quarter Café ($–$$)
Off Misgav Hadach Road, Jewish Quarter
Climb the steps called Ma'alot Rabbi Yehuda Halevi that come up into the Jewish Quarter from Western Wall Plaza, go through the arch to the Burnt House, and climb some more steps to reach this wonderfully positioned café and snack bar. There's a range of tasty light dishes, cakes and freshly squeezed juice (including pomegranate). Tables on the covered terrace look right across Temple Mount to the Mount of Olives.

Rimon ($$)
Luntz Street tel: 02-6243712
Right in the heart of the crowded Ben Yehuda pedestrian leisure district, a buzzing area in the evenings, this relaxed Glatt Kosher restaurant is (for reasons of Kashrut) divided into two sections. One serves popular steaks, burgers and an array of Jewish American, Italian and East European favorites along the lines of schnitzel and goulash. The other is a coffee house and dairy restaurant open 24 hours a day.

La Rotisserie ($$$)
Notre Dame Guest House, New Gate, Paratroopers Road tel: 02-6279111
A curious gastronomic find, this extremely good French restaurant is attached to a guest house frequented by pilgrims and owned by the Vatican. Located just outside the walls of the Old City, the building itself is over 100 years old, though the restaurant was only established in 1978. Under vaulted ceilings, enjoy coquilles St. Jacques, Châteaubriand, crêpes suzettes, and a fine selec-tion of imported French wines. Open: dinner only Monday to Friday, lunch and dinner Saturday. Closed: Sunday.

Shemesh ($$)
21 Ben Yehuda Street tel: 02-6252418
Middle Eastern food in a buzzing spot in central Jerusalem. Salad starters of eggplant, tomato, pickles, hummus and tahini are followed, if you have room, by hearty grills, kebabs and shishliks (grilled meats).

Spagettim ($$)
8 Rabbi Akiva Street tel: 02-6235547
A convivial and inviting spaghetti house in charming old premises. Sit on the terrace and try any of around 50 different pasta sauces.

TEL AVIV

There are thousands of eating places in Tel Aviv, with constant change on the restaurant scene. Most are small and stylish and offer acceptable cooking in a multitude of different styles—but don't be deceived by the rather meaningless gourmet tag. In the city center, look around Kikkar Dizengoff and Kikkar Yitzhak Rabin, and along Dizengoff, Ben Yehuda, Allenby, and Yehuda Hamaccabi avenues and their side streets. South of the center are districts noted for their inexpensive characterful local eateries—in Old Jaffa and Jaffa port, the Neve Tzedek quarter, the Yemenite quarter and the increasingly trendy Shekunat Florentin area near Jaffa. Just stroll and choose. As well as restaurants, typical Tel Aviv eating places include informal falafel bars, juice bars, cake shops and coffee bars, bagel bakeries and ice-cream parlors.

Ali Oli ($$)
2 Brenner Street tel: 03-5281378
Warm, welcoming and popular, this convivial Spanish bar-restaurant has a range of excellent tapas, and you're free to make a complete meal of them. Alternatively, choose from the menu of well-prepared Spanish dishes and Spanish wines.

Aubergine ($$$)
David Intercontinental, 12 Kaufman Street tel: 03-7951255 fax: 03-7951108
This elegant Italianate restaurant within the huge atrium of a top modern hotel offers a variety of light, fresh, delicious dishes combining Israeli, Provençal and Italian themes—but everything is kosher and all ingredients are sourced locally.

Café London ($$)
On the Tayelet below the Sheraton Hotel
The food's nothing special and the service is friendly but it's rare to see a table wiped. However, this hugely popular diner on the promenade has an immense choice of dishes and drinks, serves huge portions, is open all day every day, and has a beachside position that can't be beaten.

Le Central ($$)
29 Rothschild Boulevard tel: 03-5667822 fax: 03-7951108
Everyone is packed in at the wooden tables of this vivacious café-restaurant near the southern end of Rothschild. It has a big, generous menu and is open till 1am every night.

Gilly's ($$$)
Tel Aviv Port tel: 03-6057777
For decades a fixture on the Jerusalem scene, Gilly's meat-and-salads eatery has moved to Tel Aviv's revitalized port area. Warm, vibrant and popular, the premises are bigger, with a warehouse feel, unpretentious and with a view of the sea. The specialty of the house is best beef done is several ways. On the menu, there are other ambitious, delicious meat preparations, plus

a range of dishes reflecting the seafront setting, including fish soup, pan-fried sea bream with tomato sauce and grilled shrimps. The spinach and cheese pastry is good too. Portions are generous.

Helena ($$)
4A Tarsat, Jacob Gardens tel: 03-5289289
Set up by the founder of the former Apropo—once a famed Tel Aviv café—this bright and cheerful restaurant bar adjacent to the Helen Rubinstein Art Pavilion and the Habima Theater appeals to a cultured crowd. Light, elegant snacks are accompanied by a range of cocktails and fine liquors. A DJ plays jazz, and sometimes there's live music.

Houmous Ashkara ($)
45 Yirmiyahu Street tel: 03-5464547
An institution among hummus houses, and useful to remember as it's open 24 hours a day except Shabbat (Friday evening to Saturday evening). It's hummus with everything, from broad beans to pine nuts and, of course, pita, pickles and salad.

Maganda ($$)
26 Rabbi Ma'ir Street, Yemeni Quarter tel: 03-5161895
The proprietor's huge, imposing gray beard is as famous here in the heart of the Yemenite Quarter as his popular meat restaurant close to Carmel Market. Service is helpful, and the menu includes meze starters, stuffed vegetables and savory filled pastries as well as classic meat dishes. Wooden tables and greenery make it attractive inside.

Manta Ray ($$)
Alma Beach tel: 03-5174773
Head along the beach in the Jaffa direction until you're past the Yemenite Quarter to find this excellent informal restaurant. A friendly atmosphere and a wide range of tasty East Mediterranean meals and snacks, including Greek- and Cypriot-style meze, makes this one of the most enjoyable restaurants in town. Try the delicious rosemary flavored foccaccio. For main courses, fish and seafood are the specialties.

Matzada Café ($$)
Kikkar London tel: 03-5103353
Kikkar London is a little "park" of terraces across the road from the beach, close to the main hotels. Here you'll find a modern, attractive and funkily stylish place, with a big menu of snacks and meals, just perfect for breakfast, lunch, dinner, or anything in between. Relax, nosh, enjoy the view.

Max Brenner Chocolate Bar ($$–$$$)
45 Rothschild Boulevard tel: 03-5604570
Everything's coming up chocolate at this choco-crazy chocolaterie, where there are three kinds of hot chocolate and unbelievably scrummy chocolate pastries, cakes and snacks. Surprisingly, perhaps, there are lots of other dishes too, and you can have a complete meal in this very attractive building at the popular southern end of Rothschild.

Mika ($$$)
27 Montefiore tel: 03-5283255
One of the top names in Israel's haute "world cuisine" brings together, for example, a delicious tuna tartare with tempura goat cheese and salad.

Moul Yam ($$$)
Tel Aviv Port tel: 03-5469920
One of the new Israeli greats, this excellent seashore restaurant has a Mediterranean focus with seafood specialties such as coquilles St. Jacques with morel mushrooms, or black pasta and *fruits de mer*. Coffee ice-cream with espresso sauce makes a good finish.

Providence ($$)
66 Hayarkon Street tel: 03-5105969
A block back from the beach, this pleasant little kosher restaurant has simply, but attractively laid tables and serves a selection of fish dishes.

Shaul's Inn ($$)
11 Elyashiv Street, Yemenite Quarter tel: 03-5177619/3303
Two-level restaurant, with two levels of prices, at this extremely popular Yemenite eating house. Set up in the 1970s, it's a veteran of the Tel Aviv restaurant world and is now something of a tourist trap, but the food—typically succulent offal meat and sauce served with a selection of Oriental dips and salads—is delicious and authentic.

Shipudei Hatikva ($)
37 Ezel Street tel: 03-6878014
Part of a popular chain, this is a simple restaurant in the less frequented south of Tel Aviv but which the locals know is the place to get outstanding salads, kebabs, shwarma (doner kabob), and falafel. Immediate service, with no frills. If this place is full, fear not, the street is teeming with similar choices —several of them run by the same people.

Spaghettim ($)
18 Yavne Street tel: 03-5664479
www.spagetim.co.il
Businesslike by day, bohemian by night, this bright, modern restaurant serves no fewer than 50 variations of pasta and sauce—so the customers keep coming back to try the next one on the menu.

Yotvata–Kibbutz in the City ($$)
80 Herbert Samuel Boulevard tel: 03-5104667
The name is written in Hebrew only—Yotvata b'Ir. it's the one with a sign of two palm trees, and a long line waiting for a table at this big, bright and cheerful yogurt ice-cream parlor and fish restaurant facing the beach. You may have to remain patient, too, even after you're seated. But when the food does come, portions are vast and the specialty smoothies and fresh fruit shakes are made using milk from the Yotvata Kibbutz dairy in the Negev. When lines are *very* long, waitresses sometimes come out and give free samples!

Zion ($$)
28 Peduyim Street tel: 03-5178714
In the Yemenite quarter, this much-liked eating place specializes in the classic Jewish Yemenite fare—offal meats, tasty sauces and a spread of delicious dips and salads. The lavish decor has a touch of the exotic, with Oriental arches, fabrics, and lamps. It's open all day and until late at night.

Haifa

Jacko ($)
12 Hadkalim Street tel: 04-8664109
This thriving Middle Eastern canteen, in the heart of Haifa's Turkish market, lures diners from Tel Aviv, such is its reputation. Traditional Middle Eastern *mezze* begin the meal (try the ikra—fish eggs), followed by whatever happens to be fresh that day—shrimp, sea bass, squid, or perhaps sole. Fast service, and friendly to children.

Yotvata in Town ($$)
Bat Galim Promenade, by cable-car station tel: 04-8526853
A bright and cheerful Kibbutz Yotvata diner by the sea, serving its usual generous portions of salads, fish, and excellent dairy dishes.

GALILEE

Amirim
Amirim Restaurant ($)
Amirim tel: 06-6989349
Light modern dishes skillfully prepared can be enjoyed at this convivial, relaxed eating place in the vegetarian *moshav* high in the hills near Sefat.

Hananya
Ein Kamonim ($$)
Off Route 85 near Hananya tel: 06-6989680
On a hillside with fantastic views, this must be one of the only restaurants in the world where they don't cook. Instead, eat delicious sheep and goat cheeses (*kamonim* means goats) with salads. The set price also includes as much bread, wine, and coffee as you want, and a dessert.

Korazim Junction
Vered Hagalil ($$)
Just off Route 90 tel: 06-6935785
Guests sit at wooden tables for good meat and salads at this amiable ranch-style restaurant in the countryside. The restaurant forms part of a popular riding center, and you can visit the stables before or after your meal.

Rosh Pina
Auberge Shulamit ($$)
David Shuv Street tel: 04-6931485; www.shulamit.co.il
Ambitious, accomplished and imaginative French-style cooking is served in the restaurant of a romantic little guest house, maked of solid stone and decorated with rustic elegance. Try, for example, chicken livers in orange sauce. Service is attentive and the food excellent.
Indigo ($$)
30 Hachaluzim Street tel: 06-6935333
Appealing tables outdoors hold huge portions of delicious vegetarian and fish dishes at this low-key café-restaurant complete with mellow music.

Sefat
Almost all Sefat's eating places are arranged along central Rehov Yerushalayim (Jerusalem Street). There's a selection of shwarma and falafel diners, bars and other restaurants. Among the best are **HaMifgash** (tel: 06 692 0510) for meat dishes and **Café Bagdad** (no phone) for meat-free cooking.

Tiberias
Though not noted for fine food, Tiberias at least offers an attractive lakeside setting. Cheap diners and fish restaurants can be found on or near the waterside promenade, while for better quality, book a table at one of the restaurants of the big hotels in town.

The Pagoda ($$)
Lido Beach tel: 06-6725513
Decently acceptable dishes, but the Thai and Oriental cuisine served here has the advantage of being right beside the waters of the Sea of Galilee.

Dan and Upper Galilee
Dag al HaDan ($$)
Kibbutz Hagoshrim tel: 06 6959 008
A charming cabin-style fish restaurant poised right over the pool from which you select your dinner. Trout with nuts and garlic is a specialty.

THE SOUTH

Eilat
Eilat's more expensive beach hotels nearly all have at least one restaurant open to the public. In opulent settings, but often with poor service, these generally have acceptable cooking. There are many cheap-and-cheerful eateries in the scruffy New Tourist Center in town.

Au Bistro ($$$)
Eilot Street tel: 07 6374333
Romantics head here for good French food. Small, secluded and friendly; seafood and meat specials.
The Dolphin Reef Pub ($)
Dolphin Reef tel: 07 374293
Tree stumps to sit on, cushioned booths to curl up in, and a menu ranging from seafood—such as shrimps in garlic and white wine—to meat meals. It is also perfect for hummus and salads. Open late (except December and January), with some live music—the dolphins apparently love it.
El Gaucho ($$)
Ha'arava Street tel: 07 6331549
The "grill man" is flown in from Argentina to perform his wonderful ways with beefsteak. You can skip the main course and just have a meal of Argentinian starters—such as *empanadas* filled with cheese and beef, or spicy sausages. Serving a young and noisy crowd, the waiters act the part in embroidered vests and dashing red sashes.
The Last Refuge ($$$)
Coral Beach tel: 07-6373627).
This the first place a seafood lover should come to. Rustic and comfortable, it is hung with fishing nets and oil lamps and serves top-quality food.
Red Sea Star ($$$)
Southern Square (opposite Le Meridien Hotel) tel: 07-6347777
This is an amazing place in the water. You arrive at a café with great views across the gulf, while on an upper deck there's an informal "pub." Then go down to reach the underwater bar and restaurant, with windows looking straight out onto the magical world beneath the waves—it's thought to be the world's largest underwater observatory. Seafood and meat dishes.
Tricolore ($$$)
Meridien Hotel tel: 07 638 3333
Rated one of Israel's best, this imaginative kosher restaurant brings together international flavors. The emphasis is on fish, but also with such dishes as goat cheese salad on rösti, and fish and mushroom ravioli in a sushi cone.

Principal references are given in **bold.**

Acknowledgements

The Automobile Association would like to thank El Al Israel Airlines, car hire specialists Holiday Autos, and the Israeli hotel chain Dan Hotels for their help in researching this book.

The Automobile Association would like to thank the following photographers, companies and picture libraries for their assistance in the preparation of this book.

Abbreviations for picture credits are as follows – (t) top; (c) centre; (l) left; (r) right; (AA) AA World Travel Library).

Alamy 141t (Popperfoto), 146b (Israel Images), 158t (yoel harel); **Jon Arnold Photography** 11, 21,26, 28t, 60c, 80, 81, 83, 90, 97c, 99t, 125b, 128, 130b, 136t, 136b, 147, 153, 160, 172t, 185, 197, 205b, 208, 213t, 225t, 226, 228b, 229r, 229b, 237b, 239, 242t, 246, 247, 249b, 251, 263b; **Bridgeman Art Library** 36; **Mary Evans Picture Library** 14/5, 30, 33, 39, 40c, 41t, 41b, 42l, 43, 122c, 141c, 175, 216t; **Getty Images** 22, 27 (AFP), 42b, 44b, 122b, 210/1 (AFP), 249c; **Israel Government Tourist Office** 124b, 131c, 145b, 214t; **The Israel Museum, Jerusalem** 222l, 223c; **Israel Railways** 261b; **Magnum Photos** 13l; **Paul Murphy** 32/3, 82r, 118t, 126/7, 170, 232, 242b, 250; **Nature Photographers Ltd** 230t, 244/5, 248t, 248b; **Pictures Colour Library** 28b; **Rex Features** 23, 123, 210, 211t, 211b; **Spectrum Colour Library** 137, 236b;

All remaining pictures are held in the Association's own library (AA World Travel Library) and were taken by Pat Aithie with the exception of the following pages:
Charles Aithie 195; Terry Harris 16/7; Cameron Lees 99b, 148t; Julian Loader 8t, 48, 62b, 78, 215; Simon McBride 30/1; Dario Mitidieri 34t; Jonathan Smith 31; Tony Souter 5t, 5c, 9r, 10b, 16, 17l, 20/1, 20, 24, 29l, 34b, 38/9, 42/3, 44t, 46, 50t, 53r, 54b, 55r, 59l. 68, 72, 73t, 73b, 75, 84, 85b, 87, 88t, 88l, 89b, 91b, 94b, 95, 97b, 98, 100l, 100r, 101t, 101b, 104, 106b, 108, 110, 111t, 122t, 229t, 242/3, 267, 269t, 270, 271; Wyn Voysey 74t.

Every effort has been made to trace the copyright holders, and we apologise for any accidental errors. We would be happy to apply the corrections in the following edition of this publication.

Contributors
Revision edit and design: Bookwork Creative Associates Ltd. Original copy editor: Christopher Catling
Revision verifier: Andrew Sanger